Lecture Notes in Computer Science 13949

Founding Editors

Gerhard Goos
Juris Hartmanis

The series Lecture Notes in Computer Science (LNCS), including its subseries Lecture Notes in Artificial Intelligence (LNAI) and Lecture Notes in Bioinformatics (LNBI), has established itself as a medium for the publication of new developments in computer science and information technology research, teaching, and education.

LNCS enjoys close cooperation with the computer science R & D community, the series counts many renowned academics among its volume editors and paper authors, and collaborates with prestigious societies. Its mission is to serve this international community by providing an invaluable service, mainly focused on the publication of conference and workshop proceedings and postproceedings. LNCS commenced publication in 1973.

Georgios Goumas · Sven Tomforde ·
Jürgen Brehm · Stefan Wildermann ·
Thilo Pionteck
Editors

Architecture of Computing Systems

36th International Conference, ARCS 2023
Athens, Greece, June 13–15, 2023
Proceedings

Springer

Editors
Georgios Goumas (iD)
National Technical University of Athens
Athens, Greece

Sven Tomforde (iD)
Kiel University
Kiel, Germany

Jürgen Brehm (iD)
Gottfried Wilhelm Leibniz Universität
Hannover
Hannover, Germany

Stefan Wildermann (iD)
Friedrich-Alexander-Universität
Erlangen-Nürnberg (FAU)
Erlangen, Germany

Thilo Pionteck (iD)
Otto-von-Guericke University Magdeburg
Magdeburg, Germany

ISSN 0302-9743   ISSN 1611-3349 (electronic)
Lecture Notes in Computer Science
ISBN 978-3-031-42784-8   ISBN 978-3-031-42785-5 (eBook)
https://doi.org/10.1007/978-3-031-42785-5

Preface

The 36th International Conference on Architecture of Computing Systems (ARCS 2023) was hosted at the Museum of Cycladic Art in Athens, Greece, June 13–15, 2023 in cooperation with the National Technical University of Athens. It was organized by the special interest group on "Architecture of Computing Systems" of the GI (Gesellschaft für Informatik e.V.) and ITG (Informationstechnische Gesellschaft im VDE).

Following a successful restart in Heilbronn, Germany in 2022, ARCS23 was the second conference after the break caused by the Corona epidemic. We were very pleased to be able to hold a physical meeting again this year. Despite all the manifold options of virtual conferences, we believe that nothing beats face-to-face meetings and exchanges of ideas. Besides the discussion in the sessions, we see the personal exchange during the social events as essential for the scientific discourse.

The ARCS conferences series has 36 years of tradition reporting leading edge research in computer architecture, operating systems, and other related low-level system software, and a wide range of software techniques and tools required to exploit and build new hardware systems efficiently. ARCS addresses the complete spectrum from fully integrated, self-powered embedded systems up to plant-powered high-performance systems and provides a platform covering new emerging and cross-cutting topics, such as autonomous and ubiquitous systems, reconfigurable computing and acceleration, neural networks, and artificial intelligence. ARCS was the basis for the founding of the Organic Computing (OC) Initiative and has been one of the driving forces ever since, so that self-adaptation, learning capability and distributed control through self-organisation in technical systems have been part of the focus for two decades. Recently, further related topics such as Quantum Computing and next-generation memory technologies have become part of the scope of ARCS, reflecting the dynamic nature of the field of computing architectures.

ARCS 2023 attracted 29 submissions from authors in 10 countries, including Brazil, Canada, France, Greece, Iceland, Sweden, Thailand, the UK, and the USA. Each submission was reviewed by a diverse and dedicated Program Committee. Almost all papers received four qualified reviews. The reviews summed up to a total of 103 reviews from which 91 were provided by the members of the program committee while 12 originated from external reviewers. The Program Committee selected 21 submissions to be presented at ARCS and published in the proceedings, which corresponds to a 72% paper acceptance rate.

The conference included three basic tracks: Architecture of Computing Systems (ARCS), Organic Computing (OC), and Dependability and Fault Tolerance (VERFE). While ARCS accepted 10 papers, OC accepted 9, and VERFE 2. The accepted papers formed eight entertaining sessions with 25-minute slots per presentation: Accelerating Neural Networks (2 papers), Organic Computing Methodology (3 papers), Dependability and Fault Tolerance (2 papers), Computer Architecture Co-Design (2 papers), Computer Architectures and Operating Systems (3 papers), Organic Computing Applications 1 (3 papers) and Organic Computing Applications 2 (3 papers), as well as a session on Hardware Acceleration (3 papers).

There is no successful conference without keynote talks. At ARCS 2023, we were delighted to host two very interesting keynotes, on "Reconfigurable Technologies in HPC and Data-centers", by Dionisios Pnevmatikatos, and on "Optimizing the Memory Access Path Across the Computing Stack", by Vasileios Karakostas.

We further thank all authors for submitting their work to ARCS and presenting accepted papers. The special track on Organic Computing was co-organized and coordinated by Anthony Stein. VERFE was organised by Bernhard Fechner, Peter Sobe, and Karl-Erwin Großpietsch. Thanks to all these individuals and all the many other people who helped in the organization of ARCS 2023. Finally, we thank Springer for sponsoring this year's conference.

June 2023

Georgios Goumas
Sven Tomforde
Jürgen Brehm
Stefan Wildermann

Organization

General Chairs

Sven Tomforde — Kiel University, Germany
Georgios Goumas — National Technical University of Athens, Greece

Program Chairs

Jürgen Brehm — Gottfried Wilhelm Leibniz Universität Hannover, Germany
Stefan Wildermann — Friedrich-Alexander-Universität Erlangen-Nürnberg, Germany

Proceeding Chair

Thilo Pionteck — Otto von Guericke University Magdeburg, Germany

Publicity and Web Chair

Lars Bauer — Karlsruhe Institute of Technology, Germany

Program Committee

Lars Bauer — Karlsruhe Institute of Technology, Germany
Andreas Becher — Technische Universität Ilmenau, Germany
Mladen Berekovic — Universität zu Lübeck, Germany
Andre Brinkmann — Johannes Gutenberg-Universität Mainz, Germany
Uwe Brinkschulte — Goethe-Universität Frankfurt am Main, Germany
Joao Cardoso — Universidade do Porto, Portugal
Thomas Carle — Institut de Recherche en Informatique de Toulouse, France
Ahmed El-Mahdy — Egypt-Japan University of Science and Technology, Egypt

Special Track on Dependability and Fault Tolerance

Program Chairs

Bernhard Fechner   University of Hagen, Germany
Peter Sobe   HTW Dresden, Germany
Karl-Erwin Großpietsch   St. Augustin, Germany

Program Committee

Fevzi Belli   University of Paderborn, Germany
Rainer Buchty   Technische Universität Braunschweig, Germany
Klaus Echtle   University of Duisburg-Essen, Germany
Wolfgang Ehrenberger   University of Fulda, Germany
Rolf Ernst   Technische Universität Braunschweig, Germany
Michael Gössel   University of Potsdam, Germany
Jörg Keller   FernUniversität in Hagen, Germany
Hans-Dieter Kochs   University of Duisburg-Essen, Germany
Miroslaw Malek   USI-Lugano, Switzerland
Erik Maehle   Universität zu Lübeck, Germany
Dimitris Nikolos   University of Patras, Greece
Francesca Saglietti   Friedrich-Alexander-Universität
                            Erlangen-Nürnberg, Germany
Martin Schulz   Technical University of Munich, Germany
Janusz Sosnowski   University of Warsaw, Poland
Carsten Trinitis   Technical University of Munich, Germany
Peter Tröger   Technische Universität Chemnitz, Germany
Norbert Wehn   Technische Universität Kaiserslautern, Germany
Josef Weidendorfer   Technical University of Munich, Germany
Sebastian Zug   Technische Universität Bergakademie Freiberg,
                            Germany

Special Track on Organic Computing

Program Chairs

Anthony Stein   University of Hohenheim, Germany
Sven Tomforde   Kiel University, Germany
Stefan Wildermann   University of Erlangen-Nuremberg, Germany

Program Committee

Thomas Becker	Karlsruhe Institute of Technology, Germany
Uwe Brinkschulte	University of Frankfurt, Germany
Ada Diaconescu	Télécom Paris, CNRS LTCI, France
Jörg Hähner	Universität Augsburg, Germany
Martin Hoffmann	Bielefeld University of Applied Sciences, Germany
Christian Krupitzer	University of Hohenheim, Germany
Erik Maehle	Universität zu Lübeck, Germany
Gero Mühl	University of Rostock, Germany
Mathias Pacher	University of Frankfurt, Germany
Marc Reichenbach	Friedrich-Alexander-Universität Erlangen-Nürnberg, Germany
Wolfgang Reif	University of Augsburg, Germany
Hartmut Schmeck	Karlsruhe Institute of Technology, Germany
Gregor Schiele	University of Duisburg-Essen, Germany
Jürgen Teich	Friedrich-Alexander-Universität Erlangen-Nürnberg, Germany
Sebastian von Mammen	University of Würzburg, Germany
Torben Weis	University of Duisburg-Essen, Germany

Keynote Talks

Reconfigurable Technologies in HPC and Data-Centers. Challenges and Opportunities

Dionisios Pnevmatikatos

National Technical University of Athens, Greece

Abstract. Reconfigurable technology has been successfully showcased in several computationally intensive applications that exploit the underlying adaptability to extract performance. When applying this technology to more general environments (HPC and or data-centers), the necessary tradeoffs and performance tuning are more challenging. In this talk I will describe the current state of play in the field and our activities and progress towards the two settings. For the HPC environment we are building a set of open-source libraries for typical HPC kernels, starting from basic ones (BLAS L1), and gradually moving towards the more involved, interesting and difficult ones: (e.g. BLAS L2 & L2, SpMv, Jacobi, LU decomposition). For deploying accelerators at the data center we are building a substrate able to flexibly support multi-tenancy while ensuring isolation of the data accessed by the accelerators. Scalability in the number of accelerators and support of high-performance memory systems (with multiple channels) is supported via a properly dimensioned NoC.

Optimizing the Memory Access Path Across the Computing Stack

Vasileios Karakostas

National and Kapodistrian University of Athens, Greece

Abstract. The performance gap between accessing data and processing them has been a long-standing problem. Accessing data consists of two steps: (i) performing address translation to identify where the data lives, and (ii) retrieving the data itself. However, two critical trends in modern computing systems prevent closing or even widen this performance gap even further. First, the memory resources become larger to satisfy the immense demand of modern applications for processing increasingly large datasets, stressing address translation. Second, the introduction of persistent memory allows data retrieval much faster compared to traditional devices, revealing new sources of overheads. In this talk, we will discuss the challenges and opportunities that these trends introduce, and will present some concepts and approaches for improving memory accesses across the computing stack.

Contents

Accelerating Neural Networks

Energy Efficient LSTM Accelerators for Embedded FPGAs Through Parameterised Architecture Design

Chao Qian[✉][iD], Tianheng Ling[iD], and Gregor Schiele[iD]

Embedded Systems Lab, University of Duisburg, Essen, Duisburg, Germany
{chao.qian,tianheng.ling,gregor.schiele}@uni-due.de

Abstract. Long Short-term Memory Networks (LSTMs) are a vital *Deep Learning* technique suitable for performing on-device time series analysis on local sensor data streams of embedded devices. In this paper, we propose a new hardware accelerator design for LSTMs specially optimised for resource-scarce embedded Field Programmable Gate Arrays (FPGAs). Our design improves the execution speed and reduces energy consumption compared to related work. Moreover, it can be adapted to different situations using a number of optimisation parameters, such as the usage of DSPs or the implementation of activation functions. We present our key design decisions and evaluate the performance. Our accelerator achieves an energy efficiency of 11.89 GOP/s/W during a real-time inference with 32873 samples/s.

Keywords: LSTM · Energy Efficiency · Embedded FPGAs

1 Introduction

Recent studies have shown the superiority of *Deep Learning* algorithms over traditional methods for time series analysis [11,12]. Among these algorithms, Long Short-term Memory Networks (LSTMs) have been extensively studied for their ability to model and predict nonlinear time-varying systems [13]. Running LSTMs at the edge, especially on embedded sensor devices, is preferable for tasks with data privacy and security requirements, such as data collection at public locations [9]. In addition, on-device inference with low latency is critical for many applications, like human voice analysis with wearable devices [6]. However, deploying LSTMs on devices faces challenges due to limited local computational resources and energy. Microcontrollers are often not fast enough, while GPUs consume too much energy. One promising approach is to design LSTM accelerators for Field-Programmable Gate Arrays (FPGAs), which offer fast computation and reconfigurability while being typically more energy-efficient [5]. This paper proposes a novel LSTM accelerator architecture for embedded FPGAs. We use an Xilinx *Spartan-7 XC7S15* FPGA. Our main contributions are as follows:

G. Goumas et al. (Eds.): ARCS 2023, LNCS 13949, pp. 3–17, 2023.
https://doi.org/10.1007/978-3-031-42785-5_1

- Our LSTM accelerator architecture achieves superior resource utilisation compared to state-of-the-art approaches. We accomplish this by using more efficient activation functions and quantising to 8 bits. We achieve an average reduction of 29.62% in LUT utilisation and 33.33% in LUTRAM utilisation.
- Our design offers the option of not using DSPs for arithmetic logic to overcome the limitations of prior work that heavily relies on DSPs. This way, we can support LSTM models with up to 5 LSTM layers, each of which can have a maximum hidden size of 60.
- We significantly reduce the logic and net delay in the LSTM accelerator by optimising the activation function and Arithmetic-Logic Unit (ALU) implementation. The accelerator's maximum clock frequency increases to 204 MHz, leading to nearly a 2× increase in throughput.
- We validate our proposed architecture by implementing it in Vivado and real hardware. Our results demonstrate a reduced power consumption of up to 18.57% and an improved energy efficiency per inference of 59.19%.

In the remainder of this paper, we first discuss related research in Sect. 2. Then, Sect. 3 provides background information on LSTMs. Our design is described in Sect. 4, while Sect. 5 presents implementation details. An evaluation of our work is conducted in Sect. 6. Section 7 concludes the paper and outlines future research plans.

2   Related Work

Numerous studies have investigated the design of LSTM accelerators for FPGAs, but most research has concentrated on either server-grade FPGAs installed in the Cloud [1] or mid-range FPGAs in Edge servers [3,16,18]. To our knowledge, only a few papers have discussed the design of LSTM accelerators for embedded FPGAs. Due to their low cost, compact size, and low power consumption, such FPGAs can provide flexible hardware acceleration for embedded devices, e.g., in the Internet of Things. However, they have far fewer resources (in terms of LUTs, DSPs, RAM, etc.) than bigger FPGAs, requiring compact accelerator designs. In addition, such accelerators must be optimised for energy efficiency to not limit the lifetime of battery-operated devices. To achieve the required performance while adhering to size and power limits, careful study and hardware resource optimisation are necessary to design LSTM accelerators on embedded FPGAs.

According to a study by Hasib-Al-Rashid et al. [14], the static power consumption of the *Artix 7 XC7A100T* FPGA has a significant negative impact on the overall energy efficiency of their LSTM accelerators. One possible solution to mitigate this issue is to use FPGAs with negligible static power consumption. For instance, Chen et al. [4] implemented their LSTM accelerator on the *iCE40* UltraPlus *UP5K* FPGA, which has a static power consumption at the μA level, resulting in an energy efficiency reported to be 7.6× better than that of [14]. However, the low maximum clock frequency (17 MHz) of the chosen FPGA limited the maximum throughput of the accelerator to 0.067 GOP/s, which could pose challenges in supporting real-time inference applications. Furthermore, their accelerator implemented an LSTM model with a single LSTM cell but already occupies 75% of DSPs, 100% of SPRAM, 73.3% EBR-RAM and 94.5% of LUTs. This makes scaling up to bigger LSTM models impossible.

In 2022, Qian et al. [15] proposed an approach to reduce the proportion of static power in the overall power consumption of the *Spartan-7 XC7S15* FPGA. They achieved this by increasing the dynamic power consumption through parallelism in the LSTM cell, resulting in a throughput of 0.363 GOP/s at 100 MHz. This throughput is 5.4× faster than the maximum throughput achieved by the approach proposed by Chen et al. [4]. In addition to the higher throughput, Qian et al. achieved 1.37× better energy efficiency with 5.33 GOP/J compared to Chen et al.'s approach.

While previous studies have shown promising results in accelerating LSTM models, there are still limitations concerning the scalability of the FPGA and its maximum usable clock frequency. For example, the FPGAs from the *Spartan-7* family can implement fixed-point arithmetic at frequencies up to 239 MHz [2], which presents an opportunity for optimising the accelerator for higher operating frequencies and better energy efficiency. Therefore, further research is necessary to identify and develop optimisations for more scalable and energy-efficient LSTM accelerators for embedded FPGAs.

3 LSTM Background

This section presents the fundamental concepts of LSTMs necessary to understand our proposed architecture design. For simplicity, we use a basic LSTM model specifically developed for single-step ahead time series prediction. The model comprises an LSTM layer with one LSTM cell, followed by a dense layer, as detailed in [7]. We assume that the input sequence $X = \{x_{t-N+1}, \ldots, x_{t-1}, x_t\}$ has length N and each element is of M dimensions, where $M \geq 1$ to support both univariate and multivariate time series. The input sequence X is iteratively processed through an LSTM cell within the LSTM layer.

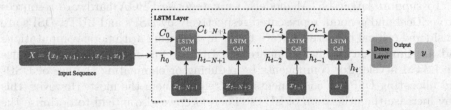

Fig. 1. Unfolding the LSTM Model Architecture in the Time Dimension

To better describe the iteration process, we unfold it in the time dimension (see Fig. 1). Taking time step $t - 1$ as an example, the LSTM cell takes the previous hidden state h_{t-2} and cell state C_{t-2}, as well as the current input x_{t-1}

as input, and produces the current hidden state h_{t-1} and cell state C_{t-1}. These states are then propagated to the next time step, allowing the model to retain contextual information. The initial values for h and C are typically set to 0 and denoted as h_0 and C_0.

The LSTM cell contains three gates: input gate i_t, output gate o_t, and forget gate f_t, to regulate which information to keep or discard. The intermediate result g_t is used to update C_t. Equations 1 to 6 represent the computations within the LSTM cell and are explained in more detail in [8]. The $*$ denotes the *Hadamard* product, $[\cdot, \cdot]$ represents vector concatenation, and W denotes the weight matrices of each gate [15].

$$i_t = \text{Sigmoid} \left(W_i[h_{t-1}, x_t] + b_i \right) \tag{1}$$

$$f_t = \text{Sigmoid} \left(W_f[h_{t-1}, x_t] + b_f \right) \tag{2}$$

$$g_t = \text{Tanh} \left(W_g[h_{t-1}, x_t] + b_g \right) \tag{3}$$

$$C_t = f_t * C_{t-1} + i_t * g_t \tag{4}$$

$$h_t = o_t * \text{Tanh} \left(C_t \right) \tag{5}$$

$$o_t = \text{Sigmoid} \left(W_o[h_{t-1}, x_t] + b_o \right) \tag{6}$$

The LSTM layer outputs its newest hidden states h_t of length K when all elements in the input sequence are processed. Subsequently, the dense layer processes this output to generate the final output y with P dimensions. The specific task that the model needs to solve determines the exact meaning of y.

4 Solution Design

Our overall goal is to create a template-based *register-transfer level* (RTL) design for FPGAs that is (a) able to support larger LSTM models with multiple cells and layers as well as large hidden size, and (b) is optimised for energy efficiency by maximising throughput. In addition, we aim to provide a flexible design that can be tailored to different usage contexts.

To support larger LSTM models, we categorise FPGA hardware resources into critical and general, represented respectively by DSPs and LUTs. DSPs are considered critical because they are faster in executing arithmetic computations and are limited in number compared to LUTs. Our design aims to optimise the LSTM accelerator components by reducing or eliminating the use of DSPs and allocating DSPs to components that require them the most. However, this may increase the utilisation of LUTs. Therefore, we also intend to optimise the components to utilise fewer general resources, minimising the overall system resource utilisation.

$$Energy\ Efficiency\ [GOP/s/W] = \frac{Throughput[GOP/s]}{Power[W]} \tag{7}$$

In addition, energy efficiency is an essential metric for embedded applications. We employ performance per watt to measure it. As demonstrated in Eq. 7, *throughput*, normalised by 10^9, refers to the number of equivalent operations executed per second, and *power* is the power consumption of the FPGA while running. We believe that the energy efficiency of an accelerator can be improved by increasing the throughput while consuming less power.

4.1 8-Bit Fixed-Point Quantisation

In FPGA designs, applying fixed-point data is a common approach to balance the trade-off between precision and resource efficiency. In this work, we use the notation (a, b) to represent fixed-point data, where a represents the number of fractional bits (i.e. bits representing numbers smaller than 1) and b represents the total width in bits. When we refer to 8-bit quantisation or 8-bit fixed-point data in the following context, we mean that b is set to 8.

We observed that when using fixed-point data less than or equal to 8-bit, implementing a fixed-point multiplier with LUTs can reach a speed comparable to DSPs, which is in line with our idea of reducing or avoiding the use of DSPs. At the same time, studies have shown that 8-bit fixed-point quantisation can conserve more resources while maintaining an acceptable model precision [10,17]. Hence, although we support larger bit widths, our design uses 8-bit fixed-point quantisation as its standard. Note that although our design also supports lower bit widths, ternarisation and binarisation quantisation are difficult to use for LSTMs and have mostly been used for partially quantised LSTM models, which do not meet our needs.

4.2 Activation Function Optimisation

As described in Sect. 3, the calculation of the LSTM cell necessitates the use of Tanh and Sigmoid activation functions. However, since these functions involve exponential computations, their arithmetic implementation on the FPGA can be resource inefficient and slow. One solution for this is to implement Tanh and Sigmoid with lookup tables. This avoids using DSPs and works without iterative computation. However, as demonstrated by Qian et al. [15], a large lookup table with 256 entries is required to provide an acceptable precision. This can again be resource-inefficient and adds delay due to the increased logic complexity.

As an alternative, we can replace Tanh and Sigmoid with HardTanh[1] (shown in Eq. 8) and HardSigmoid[2] functions (shown in Eq. 9). They have piecewise-linear characteristics, which typically take no more than two iterations for computation, requiring fewer hardware resources. Although they behave differently from Tanh and Sigmoid functions, the performance of a model using them as alternative activation functions is comparable after training [14]. Hence, we opt to implement the HardTanh and HardSigmoid functions instead of the Tanh and Sigmoid functions.

---

[1] https://pytorch.org/docs/stable/generated/torch.nn.Hardtanh.html.
[2] https://pytorch.org/docs/stable/generated/torch.nn.Hardsigmoid.html.

$$\text{HardTanh(x)} = \begin{cases} \text{max\_val} & \text{if x} > \text{max\_val} \\ \text{min\_val} & \text{if x} < \text{min\_val} \\ \text{x} & \text{otherwise} \end{cases} \quad (8)$$

$$\text{HardSigmoid(x)} = \begin{cases} 0 & \text{if x} \leq \text{-3} \\ 1 & \text{if x} \geq 3 \\ x/6 + 1/2 & \text{otherwise} \end{cases} \quad (9)$$

The HardSigmoid function in the PyTorch framework has a slope of $1/6$ for its linear interval $(-3, 3)$. Hasib-Al-Rashid et al. [14] demonstrated that setting the slope to $1/5$ in their LSTM accelerator design yields good results. However, both $1/6$ and $1/5$ are not supported by 8-bit fixed-point data. We implement a customised HardSigmoid function with a configurable slope. To distinguish it from the HardSigmoid function in the PyTorch framework, we refer to our customised implementation as HardSigmoid*, where its slope must be supported by the fixed-point configuration in our architecture. The slope of the HardSigmoid function is approximately 0.167. For our standard fixed-point configuration of $(4,8)$, numbers close to 0.167 are 0.125 and 0.1875. Since 0.125 equals $1/8$, we can use bit-shifting to perform the division. Thus, in our experiments, we set the slope of the HardSigmoid* function to 0.125.

4.3   ALU Optimisation

Equations 1 to 6 illustrate that most computations in an LSTM cell are vector inner product calculations. Fixed-point Multiply-Accumulation (MAC) operations (see Algorithm 1) can be used to perform such calculations. Thus, optimising MAC operations with respect to speed and resource consumption is crucial.

Qian et al. [15] proposed an ALU that integrates lines 3–6 in Algorithm 1 into a single operation. This allows the LSTM cell to perform one MAC iteration in a single clock cycle. However, this limits them to a maximum operating clock frequency of 100 MHz, which cannot be increased without failing the timing requirement. Additionally, all their ALUs require the use of DSPs. One LSTM cell needs 7 of the 20 DSPs available on the *XC7S15* FPGA, restricting their accelerator to support a maximum of 2 LSTM cells.

A possible solution is to employ parallel ALUs to speed up the vector inner product calculations. For instance, if two ALUs are used for one vector inner product calculation, the time required for this calculation can be reduced by half, improving throughput. However, using more ALUs leads to additional resource consumption, further limiting the potential model size.

A more efficient approach that does not require more ALUs is to construct a pipeline where each stage completes a single line in Algorithm 1. The stage with the highest latency determines the maximum clock frequency. Line 4 has the highest latency, given that multiplication is the most complex operation in the loop. Although this approach may add development overhead, it is still worth considering for embedded applications that require extreme energy efficiency.

Algorithm 1. MAC implementation for fixed-point vectors inner product

---

Input: W, x, each of them is N element vector
1: Initialisation: $sum \leftarrow 0$, $i \leftarrow 0$
2: **repeat**
3:     Load $W[i]$ and $x[i]$
4:     $mul_{16} \leftarrow W[i] * x[i]$ {mul_{16} is a fixed-point data in (8,16)}
5:     $mul_8 \leftarrow f_{round}(mul_{16})$ {mul_8 is a fixed-point data in (4,8) }
6:     $sum \leftarrow sum + mul_8$
7:     $i \leftarrow i + 1$
8: **until** $i = N$
Output: sum

---

5   Implementation

In this section, we present our implementation-level optimisations and design decisions. Firstly, we outline how we implemented the chosen activation functions and characterise the resulting performance and resource consumption. We then present the details of our pipelined ALU implementation, which substantially improves the maximum operating clock frequency. Finally, we present the overall resulting accelerator architecture and describe supported meta-parameters.

5.1   Activation Function Implementation

Based on our decision in Sect. 4 to replace the original activation functions, we describe the implementation details of HardTanh and HardSigmoid*. Implementing the HardTanh function on the FPGA is straight-forward. Only two fixed-point comparators are required because the slope of its linear interval is 1 (see Eq. 9). This slope value enables the implementation to maintain the same precision as the PyTorch framework, as long as the selected val_max and val_min are supported by our fixed-point configuration. We synthesised the HardTanh function in Vivado and found that it consumes only 5 LUTs.

The implementation of the HardSigmoid* function is more complex, and the best choice depends on the optimisation goal and the used quantisation. We experimented with three methods. The first method is referred to as HardSigmoid*-arithmetic (abbreviated as arithmetic). If the input is below -3 or above 3, it simply returns 0 or 1, respectively. Otherwise, the output is generated by performing a right arithmetic shift on the input and then adding a fixed-point value of 0.5. These two steps must be executed sequentially, increasing delay. The two remaining methods for implementing HardSigmoid* are based on lookup tables. Both produce the same behaviour as the arithmetic method. They are referred to as HardSigmoid*-1to1 (abbreviated as 1to1) and HardSigmoid*-step (abbreviated as step). The lookup table in the 1to1 method enumerates all input-output pairs of HardSigmoid*. For a fixed-point configuration (4,8), this results in 96 entries. The step method merges entries in the lookup table that have the same output. The output of HardSigmoid* is in $[0, 1]$. With a fixed-point configuration (4,8), only 16 output values can be represented in this range. Thus, some entries have the same output. To merge these entries, we take advantage of the monotonically increasing nature of HardSigmoid* and merge adjacent entries with the same output. After performing the merge operation on all entries, we obtain a step function with 14 entries.

Table 1. Comparing Methods for Implementing the HardSigmoid* Activation Function

Fixed-point Configuration	Metrics	arithmetic	1to1	step
(4,8)	Logic Delay [ns]	3.765	3.778	**3.660**
	LUTs utilisation	6	8	**3**
(6,8)	Logic Delay [ns]	5.897	**3.908**	4.175
	LUTs utilisation	36	**27**	28
(8,10)	Logic Delay [ns]	10.883	**4.872**	6.360
	LUTs utilisation	**46**	117	1793

We compared the performance of the three methods using measures obtained from the Vivado synthesis report. The results are summarised in Table 1. For the fixed-point configuration (4,8), we observed that the step method outperforms the others regarding resource utilisation and logic delay. This is consistent with the fact that the step method has far fewer entries than the 1to1 method. However, it is worth noting that decreasing the number of entries by 85.43% only saves 62.5% of LUTs because merging entries creates additional overhead for building more complex comparators.

Interestingly, for higher fractional bit widths, the situation changes. When using six fractional bits, the 1to1 method outperforms the others. The step method involves too much additional overhead. This becomes even more prominent for larger fixed-point representations. For (8,10) fixed-point configuration, the step method uses the most LUTs. The 1to1 method is the fastest. However, while being the slowest of the three methods, the arithmetic method now uses the least LUTs. As a result of these measurements, we decided to offer all three methods and let the user select one as needed.

5.2   Pipeline-Based ALU Implementation

We constructed a pipeline-based ALU with a 5-stage depth for fixed-point MAC operation. Taking the vector length of eight as an example, as depicted in Fig. 2, the first stage (S_1) involves initialisation, identical to line 1 in Algorithm 1. In the subsequent stage (S_2) (see line 3), two numbers from the corresponding vectors are loaded. In stage S_3 (i.e. line 4), they are multiplied, and the result is stored as 16-bit fixed-point data and propagated to the next stage. At stage S_4 (see line 6), the intermediate result is added to the accumulation sum. After the final iteration, in the last stage (S_5), the accumulation sum is rounded to 8 bits and output. Note that in contrast to Algorithm 1, this rounding is not done after each multiplication but only at the end.

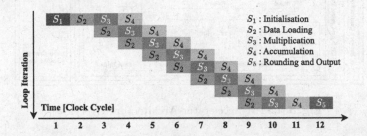

Fig. 2. Pipelined Loop with Five Stages and Eight Iterations

As shown in Fig. 2, from the 4th to the 9th clock cycle, our pipeline executes 3 lines of Algorithm 1 in parallel, potentially providing 3× higher throughput. Nevertheless, in the beginning (from 1st to 3rd clock cycle) and the end (from 10th to 12th clock cycle), the pipeline performs lower throughput. The longer the vector is, the higher the average throughput can be obtained with our pipeline-based ALU approach. For instance, suppose we need to calculate the dot product of 20-length vectors. In such cases, our pipeline approach can offer up to a 2.5× increase in throughput. However, since the multiplication stage is slower than the others, the essential throughput gain is below 2.5× in practice.

5.3 Parameterised Architecture

The overall architecture of our LSTM accelerator is shown in Fig. 3. The presented LSTM model consists of (1) a single LSTM layer with a single LSTM cell and (2) a single dense layer afterwards. This model is also used for our experiments in Sect. 6. The architecture contains two parallel instances of our pipelined ALU implementation, one for x_t and h_{t-1}, the second one for C_{t-1}, the two activation functions, and all weights and biases. No additional off-chip memory is needed. We provide a number of meta-parameters for our design (see Table 2), that can be used to adapt it to different usage contexts. Some are used to specify the functional structure of a cell or layer. As an example, *hidden_size* specifies the number of hidden units in the internal state of the LSTM cell. Others can be used to configure the implementation of the resulting accelerator. For example, *ALU_resource_type* specifies if an ALU implementation in a LSTM cell should use DSPs or LUTs. This way, the designer can choose to save DSPs for other cells or layers in a more complex model.

Note that due to the limited number of DSPs available on the FPGA, the system prioritises allocating DSPs to ALUs on the critical path to increase the system clock frequency. This strategy is employed to make the most out of the available DSP resources. Furthermore, when selecting the *weight_resource_type*

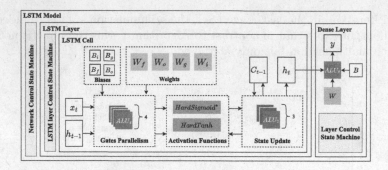

Fig. 3. LSTM Accelerator Architecture Overview

parameter, if weights such as W_f are assigned to BRAM-type resources, a multiple of 18 Kbit BRAM-type resources will be utilised.

Table 2. Meta-Parameters of LSTM Accelerator Architecture

Meta-Parameter	Description
hidden_size (integer)	number of the hidden units in [1, 200]
input_size (integer)	dimension of input sample in [1, 10]
ALU_resource_type (string)	type of utilised resource of an ALU in [DSP, LUT]
weight_resource_type (string)	type of utilised resource of a weights matrix in [LUTRAM, BRAM, AUTO]
HardSigmoid*_method (string)	method of implementation of HardSigmoid* in [arithmetic, 1to1, step]
HardTanh_threshold (fixed-point)	threshold for the HardTanh implementation
in_features (integer)	size of each input sample
out_features (integer)	size of each output sample

6   Evaluation

To discuss our evaluation, we first describe the experimental settings. Then we present our evaluation results focusing on FPGA resource utilisation and throughput. Finally, we compare our power consumption and energy efficiency to related approaches.

6.1   Experimental Settings

To make our results comparable, we based our experiments on the study presented in [15]. Like them, we used the **PeMS-4W**[3] dataset to predict single-step ahead traffic speed. We also adopted the LSTM model used in their study. It

---

[3] https://doi.org/10.5281/zenodo.3939793.

comprises an LSTM layer with one LSTM cell having a hidden size of 20 and a dense layer with 20 neurons. However, our design uses our replacement activation functions HardTanh (max_val=1, min_val=-1) and HardSigmoid*, respectively. We also changed the quantisation, moving from (8,16) to (4,8) fixed-point configuration. We implemented and trained the modified LSTM model using the *ElasticAI-Creator*[4] tool. We followed the same general training settings but employed Quantisation-Aware Training instead of Post-Training Quantisation. Despite our additional optimisations, our model outperforms theirs, achieving an MSE of 0.040, which is 78% lower than in [15].

6.2 Resource Utilisation

We conducted a series of experiments assessing resource utilisation to identify how complex LSTM models can be supported by our LSTM accelerator design on *XC7S15* FPGA. Both Figs. 4 and 5 show that as the hidden size of the LSTM cell increased from 20 to 200, the utilisation of BRAM, represented by the blue dotted line, changed the most significantly, which suggests that BRAM is the most critical resource to support a larger hidden size. BRAM utilisation reached a maximum of 100% at a hidden size of 130 and remained so until the hidden size reached 180. Beyond this point, BRAM utilisation decreased, and the utilisation of LUTs increased significantly. This is because when BRAM was exhausted, Vivado switched to using LUTRAM (included in LUT Slices utilisation in Figs. 4 and 5) to implement some of the weights. Storing weights in the BRAM is preferred because it has fast access latency. Therefore, for an LSTM model with only one LSTM layer, the maximum hidden size of the LSTM cell should be 180 to ensure optimal speed on the *XC7S15* FPGA.

In addition, Figs. 4 and 5 were obtained under different settings of the metaparameter *ALU_resource_type*. In Fig. 4, all ALUs were set to use "LUT" as their resource type, resulting in a constant value of 0 for the utilised DSPs. On the other hand, in Fig. 5, all ALUs were set to use "DSP" as their resource type, resulting in a constant value of 40% for the utilised DSPs, as the LSTM and dense layers occupy 8 out of the 20 available DSPs.

As we mentioned before, not utilising DSPs will inevitably increase the overhead of LUTs to realise ALUs. Comparing these two figures, we can see that the utilisation of LUTs shows a consistent difference. Before the BRAM is exhausted, the difference in LUT utilisation is between 4.375 and 6.03%. This indicates that the LUTs consumed by implementing an 8-bit fixed-point multiplier account for at most 0.74% of all LUTs in the *XC7S15* FPGA, which is equivalent to about 60 LUTS. Based on this, we can estimate that up to five LSTM layers can be instantiated simultaneously on this FPGA when the hidden size of each cell is 60. This is especially beneficial for complex LSTM models, such as Bi-LSTM and Auto-encoders, which often require multiple LSTM layers and large hidden size. By contrast, [15] relied on DSPs to perform arithmetic logic in their approach,

---

[4] https://github.com/es-ude/elastic-ai.creator.

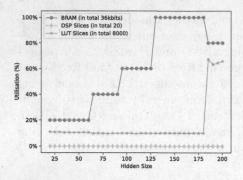
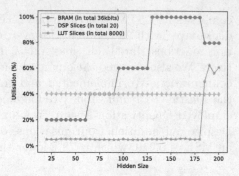

Fig. 4. Utilisation without DSPs   **Fig. 5.** Utilisation with DSPs

which limited their ability to implement more than two LSTM layers on this FPGA, as each layer consumes 7 of 20 available DSPs.

6.3 Throughput

The aim of this set of experiments is to assess the effect of different implementations of our LSTM accelerator architecture on throughput. To determine the throughput of the accelerator, we first need to obtain its maximum operating frequency by conducting timing analysis in Vivado.

Table 3. Frequency and Throughput for Different Optimisation Options

	[15]	this work†			Pipelined ALU & step
		HardSigmoid* without Pipelined ALU			
		arithmetic	1to1	step	
Maximal Clock[MHz]	100	104	109	115	**204**
Latency[μs]	57.25	55.05	53.09	49.75	**28.07**
Throughput[GOP/s]	0.363	0.378	0.399	0.417	**0.740**
Improvement	1×	1.04×	1.09×	1.15×	**2.04×**

† All implementations used the HardTanh

Table 3 indicates that replacing the Tanh and Sigmoid functions with the HardTanh and HardSigmoid (Columns 2 through 4) functions resulted in a slight improvement in maximum clock frequency and accelerator performance, as compared to the work by Qian et al. [15] (Column 1). This is because the ALU implementation without pipeline constraint the maximum clock frequency. The step method led to the highest increase in throughput among the three methods, at 1.15×, while the arithmetic method resulted in the lowest increase, at 1.04×. When combined with pipelined ALUs implementation (Column 5), the step method further increased the maximum clock frequency and resulted in a nearly twofold increase in throughput of 2.04×, along with a 50.97% reduction in latency. It is important to note that the maximum improvement in throughput being less than 2.5× is not surprising, as multiplication takes more time than the other stages.

6.4 Power Consumption and Energy Efficiency

We estimated the power consumption of the accelerator at its maximum operating frequency of 204 MHz using the Xilinx Power Estimator[5] software. This allows us to determine the energy efficiency of the accelerator and compare it with the state-of-the-art. Table 4 shows that our work achieved higher energy efficiency (Column 4) compared to the recently published work by Qian et al. [15] (Column 3), with a 2.33× improvement. Our proposed optimisation method achieved this, which reduced latency by 2.04× and power consumption by 1.22×.

Table 4. Comparison with State-of-the-Art

		[14]	[4]	[15]	this work	
FPGA Model		XC7A100T	UP5K	XC7S15		
Utilised DSPs		4	6	8	**8**	**0**
Maximal Clock[MHz]		52.6	17	100	**204**	**204**
Power[mW]	Static	$92^{\dagger}$	0	$32^{\dagger}$	$32^{\dagger}$	$32^{\dagger}$
	Dynamic	$17^{\dagger}$	17	$38^{\dagger}$	$\mathbf{25}^{\dagger}$	$31^{\dagger}$
	Total	$109^{\dagger}$	17	$70^{\dagger}$	$\mathbf{57}^{\dagger}$	$63^{\dagger}$
Latency[μs]		incomparable		53.32	**28.07**	**28.07**
Energy[μJ]		incomparable		3.70	**1.51**	1.67
Throughput [GOP/s]		0.055	0.067	0.390	**0.740**	**0.740**
Energy Efficiency [GOP/s/W]		0.50	3.90	5.57	**12.98**	11.75

† Measurements come from Xilinx Power Estimator

Interestingly, the implementation of the ALU without DSPs (Column 5) exhibits higher dynamic power than the implementation with DSPs (Column 4), resulting in 9.47% lower energy efficiency. Nevertheless, this approach has the advantage of not being limited by DSP resources, allowing it to support more complex LSTM models. In contrast, implementing ALUs with DSPs can be a practical choice for power efficiency applications. Moreover, we observed that using DSPs to implement all the ALUs does not lead to further increases in the maximum operating clock frequency. This is likely since using DSPs introduces net delay, as DSPs are only available in a restricted area. Consequently, the reduced logic delay achieved by using DSPs is offset by the increased net delay.

---

[5] https://www.xilinx.com/products/technology/power/xpe.html.

To ensure the correctness of our values, we also measured on real hardware. The results are similar to the ones obtained by the Estimator. The average power consumption during inference when using DSPs for all ALUs is 57.4mW. Not using DSPs consumes 65.7mW. In addition, the processing time per inference for both accelerators is 2.35 μs slower than the estimated time. Our approach achieved 11.89 GOP/s/W energy efficiency on real hardware, confirming its effectiveness.

7   Conclusion and Future Work

Our LSTM accelerator architecture for embedded FPGAs shows that by combining 8-bit quantisation with an accompanying activation function implementation as well as with optimisations to support higher clock frequencies, we can achieve superior resource utilisation and energy efficiency compared to state-of-the-art approaches. We can reduce utilised LUTs by 29.62% and LUTRAM by 33.33%. Our design supports LSTM models with up to 5 layers, each with a maximum hidden size of 60, on small embedded FPGAs and allows designers to tailor accelerators to their specific needs, e.g. by choosing to get by without DSPs if needed. We can achieve a nearly 2× increase in throughput with a maximum clock frequency of 204 MHz. Power consumption is reduced by up to 18.57% and energy efficiency per inference 59.19%.

In future work, we plan to verify the effectiveness of our optimised LSTM accelerator architecture in more challenging applications with bigger models. Furthermore, we plan to integrate our design into the *ElasticAI-Creator* tool to enable users to generate optimised LSTM accelerators for their applications more easily. Finally, we plan to extend our work to automatically select the best parameterisation for a given context, leading to end-to-end optimisations of complex *Deep Learning* models.

Acknowledgements. The authors acknowledge the financial support provided by the Federal Ministry of Economic Affairs and Climate Protection of Germany in the RIWWER project (01MD22007C).

References

1. Boutros, A., et al.: Beyond peak performance: comparing the real performance of ai-optimized FPGAS and GPUs. In: 2020 International Conference on Field-Programmable Technology (ICFPT), pp. 10–19. IEEE (2020)
2. Burger, A., Urban, P., Boubin, J., Schiele, G.: An architecture for solving the eigenvalue problem on embedded FPGAS. In: Brinkmann, A., Karl, W., Lankes, S., Tomforde, S., Pionteck, T., Trinitis, C. (eds.) ARCS 2020. LNCS, vol. 12155, pp. 32–43. Springer, Cham (2020). https://doi.org/10.1007/978-3-030-52794-5_3
3. Cao, S., et al.: Efficient and effective sparse LSTM on FPGA with bank-balanced sparsity. In: Proceedings of the 2019 ACM/SIGDA International Symposium on Field-Programmable Gate Arrays, pp. 63–72 (2019)

4. Chen, J., Hong, S., He, W., Moon, J., Jun, S.W.: Eciton: very low-power LSTM neural network accelerator for predictive maintenance at the edge. In: 2021 31st International Conference on Field-Programmable Logic and Applications (FPL), pp. 1–8. IEEE (2021)
5. Chen, J., Ran, X.: Deep learning with edge computing: a review. Proc. IEEE **107**(8), 1655–1674 (2019)
6. Conti, F., Cavigelli, L., Paulin, G., Susmelj, I., Benini, L.: Chipmunk: a systolically scalable 0.9 mm 2, 3.08 gop/s/mw@ 1.2 mw accelerator for near-sensor recurrent neural network inference. In: 2018 IEEE Custom Integrated Circuits Conference (CICC), pp. 1–4. IEEE (2018)
7. Fu, R., Zhang, Z., Li, L.: Using LSTM and GRU neural network methods for traffic flow prediction. In: 2016 31st Youth Academic Annual Conference of Chinese Association of Automation (YAC), pp. 324–328. IEEE (2016)
8. Hochreiter, S., Schmidhuber, J.: Long short-term memory. Neural Comput. **9**(8), 1735–1780 (1997)
9. Huang, C.J., Kuo, P.H.: A deep CNN-LSTM model for particulate matter ($PM_{2.5}$) forecasting in smart cities. Sensors **18**(7), 2220 (2018)
10. Krishnamoorthi, R.: Quantizing deep convolutional networks for efficient inference: a whitepaper. arXiv preprint arXiv:1806.08342 (2018)
11. Lara-Benítez, P., Carranza-García, M., Riquelme, J.C.: An experimental review on deep learning architectures for time series forecasting. Int. J. Neural Syst. **31**(03), 2130001 (2021)
12. Lim, B., Zohren, S.: Time-series forecasting with deep learning: a survey. Phil. Trans. R. Soc. A **379**(2194), 20200209 (2021)
13. Lindemann, B., Müller, T., Vietz, H., Jazdi, N., Weyrich, M.: A survey on long short-term memory networks for time series prediction. Proc. CIRP **99**, 650–655 (2021)
14. Manjunath, N.K., Paneliya, H., Hosseini, M., Hairston, W.D., Mohsenin, T., et al.: A Low-power LSTM processor for multi-channel brain EEG artifact detection. In: 2020 21st International Symposium on Quality Electronic Design (ISQED), pp. 105–110. IEEE (2020)
15. Qian, C., Ling, T., Schiele, G.: Enhancing energy-efficiency by solving the throughput bottleneck of LSTM cells for embedded FPGAS. In: Koprinska, I., et al. Machine Learning and Principles and Practice of Knowledge Discovery in Databases. ECML PKDD 2022. Communications in Computer and Information Science, vol. 1752, pp. 594–605. Springer, Cham (2023). https://doi.org/10.1007/978-3-031-23618-1_40
16. Varadharajan, S.K., Nallasamy, V.: P-SCADA-a novel area and energy efficient FPGA architectures for LSTM prediction of heart arrthymias in BIoT applications. Expert. Syst. **39**(3), e12687 (2022)
17. Yang, Y., Deng, L., Wu, S., Yan, T., Xie, Y., Li, G.: Training high-performance and large-scale deep neural networks with full 8-bit integers. Neural Netw. **125**, 70–82 (2020)
18. Zhang, Y., et al.: A power-efficient accelerator based on FPGAs for LSTM network. In: 2017 IEEE International Conference on Cluster Computing (CLUSTER), pp. 629–630. IEEE (2017)

A Comparative Study of Neural Network Compilers on ARMv8 Architecture

Theologos Anthimopulos[1]([✉]), Georgios Keramidas[1,2], Vasilios Kelefouras[3], and Iakovos Stamoulis[2]

[1] School of Informatics, Aristotle University of Thessaloniki, Thessaloniki, Greece
{tanthimop,gkeramidas}@csd.auth.gr
[2] Think Silicon, S.A. An Applied Materials Company, Patras, Greece
i.stamoulis@think-silicon.com
[3] School of Engineering, Computing and Mathematics, University of Plymouth, Plymouth, UK
vasilios.kelefouras@plymouth.ac.uk

Abstract. The deployment of Deep Neural Network (DNN) models in far edge devices is a challenging task, because these devices are characterized by scarce resources. To address these challenges various deep learning toolkits and model compression techniques have been developed both from industry and academia. The available DNN toolchains can perform optimizations at different levels e.g., graph level, Intermediate Representation (IR) or machine-dependent optimizations, while they operate in an Ahead-of-Time (AOT) or Just-in-Time (JIT) manner. Although the area of DNN toolchains is an active research area, there is no available study that analyses the performance benefits achieved by the different optimization levels e.g., the performance boost reported by the graph-level vs. the machine-dependent optimizations. This work performs a comprehensive study of three popular neural network (NN) compiler frameworks that target (mainly) far edge devices: TensorFlow Lite for MCUs, GLOW, and IREE. For a fair comparison, our performance analysis targets to reveal the performance benefits offered by the different optimization levels for the three studied frameworks as well as the strength of specific graph-level optimizations e.g., in quantizing the input NN models. Our evaluation is based on various NN models with different computational/memory resources and the experiments are performed in a state-of-the-art high-performance embedded platform by Nvidia.

Keywords: Deep Neural Networks · Neural Network Compilers · Network Optimization · Network Compression · Quantization

1 Introduction

Deep Neural Networks have demonstrated significant advances in various application domains including (but limited to) image processing, audio translation, and speed recognition. Embedded platforms, such as smartphones and smartwatches, frequently rely on DNN models to provide digital smart assistants to the end-users. As a result, the efficient deployment of DNN models in resource-constrained devices is an active research area

© The Author(s), under exclusive license to Springer Nature Switzerland AG 2023
G. Goumas et al. (Eds.): ARCS 2023, LNCS 13949, pp. 18–33, 2023.
https://doi.org/10.1007/978-3-031-42785-5_2

in both industry and academia. DNN models consist of a series of matrix multiplication functions along with other complex kernel functions that cannot be efficiently optimized by modern compilers. Therefore, in the recent years various graph or deep learning (DL) compilers have been developed, such as GLOW [10], IREE [45], and TFLM [7]. The main goal of a DL compiler is to take as input a high-level, (typically graph-based) description of a DNN (e.g., extracted from TensorFlow [43] or PyTorch [35]) and transform it into executable code that can run on a target hardware platform, such as a CPU, a GPU, or a specialized accelerator. The compilation process typically involves a series of optimizations and model transformations that reduce the arithmetic operations and the memory utilization of the input DNN models.

This paper presents an evaluation study of three widely used Neural Network (NN) compilers (GLOW, IREE, and TFLM) on ARMv8 architectures by focusing on the performance boost offered by the frontend, backend, and various IR level optimizations of the studied compilers. To the best of our knowledge, three other papers provide a survey of DL compilers [27, 29, 39]. However, the latter papers exhibit specific limitations. For example, the work in [39] studies DNN models trained only with the MNIST dataset (which is a small dataset, not representative of state-of-the-art datasets [26]). The evaluation in [29] is performed only using the floating-point representations of the DNN models. Finally, none of the previous papers include an analysis about the recently announced IREE compiler and/or offer a performance evaluation on edge platforms based on the ARMv8 architecture.

Table 1. Related papers and positioning of this work

	Studied frameworks	int8 optimized kernels	Graph-level optimizations	Machine-dependent optimizations	Number/ datatype of tested models
[39] *(2021)*	GLOW, TFLM, TVM, OpenVINO [34], ONNC [28]	×	×		1 / FP32, INT8
[29] *(2020)*	TFLM, Caffe2 [3], Pytorch mobile [37]	×	×	×	6 / FP32
[27] *(2020)*	TVM, XLA [24], nGraph [16], GLOW	×	×	×	19 / INT8
This work	GLOW, IREE, TFLM	✓	✓	✓	12 / INT8

Table 1 summarizes the contributions of this work with respect to [27, 29, 39]. It is important to mention that when the analyses of [27, 29, 39] were performed, the support (and the associated maturity level) for the efficient execution of the quantized DNN models (e.g., in int8) was limited. For example, in [39] is mentioned that the floating-point versions of the DNN models are faster to the corresponding quantized versions. Obviously, the latter issue is due to the fact that the previous evaluations were done using unoptimized quantized DNN kernels. Generally speaking, this is an expected behavior in a fastmoving area: the majority of the DL compilers are in a continuous development phase and new features are being regularly added. Moreover, as noted, there is no available paper that studies the impact of the graph level vs. machine-dependent level optimizations on the final execution time (inference time) of the DNN models.

As an additional contribution of this work and in order to end-up with a fair evaluation among the three studied DL compilers, the well-known CMSIS-NN [22] library is ported and integrated in GLOW (open-source repository [11]). The latter enabled us not only to compare the reported performance of TFLM and GLOW using the same backend library (i.e., the CMSIS-NN), but also to study the impact of graph-level optimizations when an optimized backend engine is used.

The Remainder of this Paper is Organized as Follows Section. 2 outlines the commonly used DNN optimization techniques. The main features of the studied compiler frameworks are presented in Sect. 3. Section 4 describe the evaluation methodology and provide the details of the edge platform and the DNN models that used throughout this work. Section 5 offers our experimental results and Sect. 6 concludes this paper.

2 Background

The NN optimizations can be categorized as follows: model compression techniques, graph-level optimizations, and machine-dependent optimizations. The various model compression techniques (e.g., pruning, low-rank factorization) can be also deemed as graph level optimizations. However, as part of this work, we will consider as graph-level optimization only the techniques that are part of the available NN compiler toolchains.

2.1 The Three Categories of NN Optimizations

Model compression techniques are typically used to reduce the number of arithmetic operations of input NN models and/or the memory required to store the model parameters. Popular NN compression techniques include quantization, pruning, and low-rank factorization. A good survey of these techniques can be found in [5]. By applying these optimizations, NN compilers can significantly improve the performance-power efficiency of NN models making them more practical to be deployed on wide range of hardware platforms, e.g., in far-edge devices.

A graph-based representation is a widely-used way to depict the architecture of a NN model. The graph-based approach is actually a high-level intermediate representation (IR) of a NN model i.e., each node in the graph corresponds to specific layer of the input model. MLIR [23] and Relay [38] are, among others, two well-known IRs for NN models that formulate the basis for the various proposed graph-level optimizations (a.k.a. high-level optimizations). In general, high-level IRs provide a modular and extensible way to represent and optimize graphs. Graph optimizations are machine-independent optimizations applied in the graph of a NN model targeting to identify and eliminate redundant computations, simplify the graph structure, and improve the memory usage of the model [12].

Table 2. NN compilers based on hand-optimized kernels

	IR	Optimizations			Backend	
	High-level IR	Kernels	Compression tec	High-low level opt	Compilation method	Supported devices
TVM	Relay	CMSIS, NNAPI [31], OneDNN	Quant.	Target ind./ specific level opt	JIT/AOT	CPUs, GPUs, FPGAs, Accel.
ONNC	Own high-level IR	CMSIS, OneDNN	Quant.	Target ind./ specific opt	AOT	CPUs, GPUs, Accel.
TFLM	x	Own kernels, CMSIS, NNAPI,	Quant.	x	AOT	CPUs
PyTorch Mobile	x	Own kernels, NNAPI	Quant.	x	AOT	Mobile, CPUs GPUs, Accel.
nGraph	nGraph IR [30]	Own kernels, OneDNN	Quant., Pruning, etc. [30]	Target independent opt.	JIT	CPUs, GPUs, Accel.
XLA	HLO [14]	OneDN, cuDNN [6]	x	Target ind.	JIT/AOT	CPUs, GPUs, Accel.

Well-known graph optimizations are node fusion, constant folding, and dead code elimination (DCE) [9]. Node fusion combines multiple nodes into a single node (i.e., convolution with reshape) [53]. Constant folding computes (during compilation) parts of the graph that rely only on constant initializers [44]. DCE removes nodes that are not used by the model (i.e., dropout). General purpose compiler frameworks typically contain the said optimizations, but is preferable to include a separate compilation step when targeting NNs. Moreover, additional domain-specific specialized optimizations (tailored to specific models and/or devices) have been proposed. For example, in [38] is proposed to fuse multiple 2D convolutions that share the same input. The goal of this pass is to produce a larger kernel and it is particularly efficient for GPU architectures, as the kernel launch on a GPU exhibits a significant overhead. This approach is showcased in the Inception model [40], as this model contains blocks of convolutions that share the same input.

Going one step deeper, state-of-the-art NN compilers leverage the well-known compiler optimizations to produce efficient NN microkernels [4, 54]. Microkernels are optimized kernels (i.e., computationally intensive functions) that use vectorization techniques (typically in the form of intrinsics) along with other compiler optimizations techniques (e.g., loop tiling and register blocking [8]). During the compilation process the latter kernels can be autogenerated based on the MLIR representation, they can be optimized at run-time via auto-tuning techniques [48], or they rely on hand-optimized code templates. For example, CMSIS-NN is a library that contains hand-optimized, highly-efficient NN microkernels for Arm Cortex-M CPUs. As noted, in the context of this work the CMSIS-NN is ported in the GLOW compiler and its correct integration has been verified.

Table 3. NN compilers based on auto-tuning

	IR		Optimizations			Backend
	High-level IR	Low-level IR	Compression tec	High-low level opt	Compilation method	Supported devices
TVM	Relay	Halide [13]	Quant	Target independent/ specific level opt	JIT/AOT	CPUs, GPUs, FPGAs, Accel
TC [42]	Own high-level IR	Polyhedra [47]	✗	Target independent opt	JIT	Nvidia GPUs, CPUs
TensorRT [44]	Own high-level IR	✗	Quant	Target independent opt	JIT	Nvidia GPUs
MNM [17]	Own high-level IR	✗	Quant	Target independent opt	AOT	CPUs, GPUs, Accel

2.2 The NN Compilers Landscape

The NN compilers are used to employ the various optimizations. Typically, multiple optimization passes are followed in a pipelined fashion until the actual executable code is generated. Table 2 illustrates the main features of the compilers that rely on hand-optimized kernels. In this case, the code from hand-optimized libraries, like OneDNN [32] and CMSIS, are injected to the IR/code of the input NN model during the compilation process. As we can see, graph level optimizations can be acquired by the frond-end part of the toolchain using high-level IR. The latter method is straightforward, but it exhibits specific limitations. For example, when the target device consists of multiple processing elements and complex memory hierarchies (e.g., in GPUs), full utilization of the hardware resources is difficult to be achieved. On the contrary, the NN compilers that rely on auto-tuning take as input specific hardware details, such as cache sizes, number of threads, size of vectorization lanes (e.g., AVX-512) as well as run-time measurements, and follow various iterative steps until a desired micro-kernel is found. The main features of the compilers that rely on auto-tuning can be seen in Table 3. As show in Table 3, specific compilers, like TVM and ONNC, can be configured (by the user) to operate in more than one compilation mode.

Table 4. Basic features of the widely-used NN compilers

	IR		Optimizations		Backend	
	High-level IR	Low-level IR	Compression tec	High-low level opt	Compilation meth	Supported devices
TVM	Relay	Halide	Quant	Target independent/ specific level opt	JIT/AOT	CPUs, GPUs, FPGAs, Accel
GLOW	Own high-level IR	Own low-level IR	Quant	Target independent/ specific opt	JIT/AOT	CPUs, GPUs, Accel
XLA	HLO	HLO	×	Target independent/ specific opt	JIT/AOT	CPUs, GPUs, Accel
ONNC	Own high-level IR	Own low-level IR	Quant	Target independent/ specific opt	AOT	CPUs, GPUs, Accel
IREE	MLIR	MLIR	×	Target independent/ specific level opt	JIT/AOT	CPUs, GPUs, Accel
nGraph	nGraph IR	nGraph IR	Quant., Pruning, etc	Target independent/ specific level opt	JIT	CPUs, GPUs, Accel

It is important to note that low-level IR optimizations (as depicted in Table 3 and 4) include various machine independent techniques. For example, if we create a specialized function by declaring all parameters as constants, then the runtime checks will be eliminated and the control flow will be simplified, leading to a performance increase. Finally, with respect to AOT (Ahead-of-Time) vs. JIT (Just-in-Time) compilation approaches, this is typically not a design option when the deployment targets edge devices. Edge devices are resource-constrained devices, thus the "in-field" invocation of the compiler cannot be done in a reasonable time, especially when the NN models are part of latency-critical applications (which is usually the case [50]). The basic features of the widely-used NN compilers are presented in Table 4. TensorRT, TC, and MNM are the only frameworks that have not been included in an evaluation study. Such analysis is left for future work.

3   Basic Features of the Selected Toolchains

As mentioned, this work presents an evaluation study of three widely used NN compilers (GLOW, IREE, and TFLM) on ARMv8 architectures by focusing on the performance boost offered by the frontend, backend, and various IR level optimization parts of the studied NN compilers. Figure 1 depicts the main compilation steps followed by modern NN compilers until the NN model is transformed into machine code. Initially, the NN model is taken as input in a NN format (e.g., ONNX [33]) and it is transformed in an IR format. The latter IR goes through multiple passes until an optimized graph/IR is generated. At this point, the compiler injects the kernels/microkernels in the optimized IR and performs various target-specific compiler optimizations.

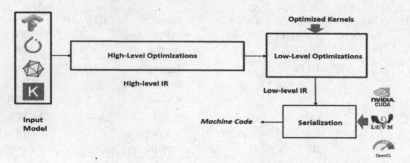

Fig. 1. Typical flow of a NN compiler

The NN compilers typically support different back-ends tailored to the unique architectural characteristics of the target devices. The back-end part of the NN compiler is invoked to generate the final executable code (the latter process is called serialization). Among the three studied framework, TFLM is the only framework that does not support high-level or low-level IR optimizations.

TFLM (TensorFlow Lite for Microcontrollers) is a kernel-based framework designed to run NN models on edge devices and/or bare metal systems. TFLM encodes the NN model into a flat buffer, which is a compact binary format that can be loaded in MCUs. Prior to this conversation, the model can be further optimized by reducing the precision of the weights/activations using a suitable quantization scheme provided by TensorFlow lite. Once the model is quantized, it can be dispatched to an MCU. TFLM provides a set of NN kernels specifically developed for MCU systems. At runtime, TFLM offers an APIs for handling the input/output data and memory allocation policies.

GLOW (Graph Lowering Compiler Techniques for Neural Networks) is based on a proprietary IR. It contains tools for training, quantizing, and model partitioning (for devices with heterogeneous processing elements). When a NN model is imported to GLOW, each layer of the model is mapped to a specific node-based graph representation (high-level IR). The latter graph is optimized to improve its performance using a variety of transformations such as constant folding, DCE, and function inlining. The next step is to transform the high-level IR into a set of linear algebra operations (low-level IR). As a next step, the operator nodes are translated into one or more instructions. In this step, the low-level IR is converted into instructions that can be executed on the target hardware. These instructions are optimized kernels in the form of bytecode (LLVM IR). The latter translation is accompanied by a set of low-level memory optimizations, e.g., register allocation and instruction scheduling. The final step is to invoke LLVM to serialize the generated functions and output the optimized binary code taking into account the unique features of the target hardware. To run the model, GLOW offers an executable bundle, a self-contained compiled network that can be used to execute the model in a standalone mode. The bundle API can handle the model input and output, allocate memory, and finally to execute the model.

IREE (Integrated Runtime for Edge Execution) is an MLIR-based NN compiler and the associated runtime system specifically designed to execute the inference phase of a model on edge devices. The initial MLIR representation (high-level IR) goes through a series of high-, mid-, and low-level optimizations. High-level and mid-level optimizations are graph optimizations like node fusion, redundant operation removal, DCE etc. IREE also contain domain-specific specialized optimizations. Low-level optimizations include code transformations, like loop tilling, loop unrolling, register blocking, vectorization etc. The IR is optimized using a set of passes that apply transformations to the graph to improve performance, reduce memory usage, and support new operators. Once the final (low-level) IR is built, IREE invokes LLVM (CPU backend) to generate efficient code for the target hardware platform. LLVM and MLIR are strongly coupled and each MLIR instruction can be serialized using LLVM. By using the notion of HAL, IREE provides a runtime that handles device-specific details, such as memory allocation, data transfers, and multi-threading execution.

4 Evaluation Methodology

As noted, the premise of this work is to perform a thorough comparison among three different NN toolchains. To the best of our knowledge, this is the first work that reveals the performance benefits offered by the optimizations of the different parts (high-level, low-level, and backend) of NN compilers. However, extracting the latter performance breakdowns is not a straightforward process. In order to end up with a fair comparison, a step-by-step approach is followed (explained in Sect. 5).

To continue, the evaluation of the three studied compilers is based on multiple datasets and 11 CNN models that can be considered as representative models for low-end and mobile devices. Ending-up with the specific set of models was a challenging process, because not all NN compilers support all the model layers. Table 5 depicts the characteristics (number of parameters and FLOPs, number and type of layers, and corresponding dataset) of the selected CNN models. FLOPs were calculated using Keras-FLOPS tool [18]. Three of the CNN models (EfficientNet lite [41], MobileNetV1, MobileNetV2 [15]) are relatively complex models, while the remaining CNNs are considered as more lightweight networks. Among them, Person Detection, Keyword Spotting, Image Classification (Resnet), and Anomaly Detection are part of the TinyML suite [46].

Finally, the reported execution times are measured in a high-performance ARM V8.2, 64-bit, 1.9 GHz CPU equipped with a 4MB L2-cache and 8MB L3-cache. In order to have accurate timing measurements, each inference phase of each model is executed for 20 times; among the 20 measurements, the one with the smallest time is selected. The setup time that each framework requires to load the model is not included in our execution time results.

Table 5. Characteristics of the 11 CNN studied models

Models	Param	FLOPs	Number and Type of Layers	Dataset
Lenet5 [25]	62K	859.5K	3 Conv., 3 F.C	Mnist [26]
Person Dect	377K	15.70	14 Conv., 14 DW_conv2d, 3 F.C	V.W.W. [1]
Clock	960K	127.5	10Conv., 6F.C., 2Add, 2Mul	self-created
AlexNet [2]	21.6M	84.7M	9 Conv., 3F.C	CHIFAR-10 [49]
Mobilenet_v1	4.25M	1.15G	15 Conv., 13 DW_conv2d	ImageNet [21]
Mobilenet_v2	3.504M	615M	36 Conv., 17 DW_conv2d	ImageNet
Efficientnet lite	4.652	385M	33Conv., 16 DW_conv2d, 10 Add, 1 F.C	ImageNet
K.W.S	25K	900K	5Conv., 4 DW_conv2d + 1 F.C	Speech Commands [51]
A.D	267K	538K	12 F.C	ToyADMOS [19] [20] [36]
Resnet	78.5K	25.3M	9Conv., 1 F.C., 3 Add	CIFAR-10
Lenet300 [25]	268K	536K	3 F.C	Mnist

5   Evaluation Results

This section is organized in five main parts. The first four parts focus on analyzing particular features of the three studied NN frameworks. In the last part, a performance evaluation of the three frameworks (assuming the best performing configuration in each case) and for the 11 models is presented. As noted, for a fair comparison, as part of this work the CMSIS-NN library is ported and integrated in GLOW.

Alternative Quantization Schemes AOT compilation and quantization support are two first-class features that must be included in an NN compiler targeting edge use cases. Among the studied toolchains, GLOW is the only toolchain that includes quantization support (via a tool called model-tuner). In contrast to Tensorflow Lite, model-tuner includes a variety of quantization schemes (asymmetric, symmetric, int8 symmetric, symmetric with power of two) offering different precision levels (int8, int16, int32) and dequantization strategies (e.g., quantization of weight and/or biases) [10]. The latter is an important feature, since far-edge devices are typically custom devices employing alternative quantization schemes.

Figure 2 shows the accuracy validation results when four of the studied models are fed to model-tuner (quantization via the model-tuner is a very time-consuming process, thus we only report results for four out of the 11 models that we consider in this work). The input to the model-tuner are pre-trained models and the validation accuracy of the (initial) floating-point (FP32) model is shown in the graph legend. The vertical axis in Fig. 2 depicts the reported increase in validation accuracy with respect to the initial validation accuracy. At the bottom of the horizontal axis, the selected quantization scheme is shown. The data type above the quantization schemes refers to the precision of the weights, while the data type juxtaposed the x-axis corresponds to the precision of the biases. To the best of our knowledge, GLOW and PyTorch Mobile are the only NN frameworks that support the quantization of biases to int8 format.

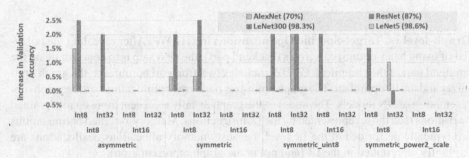

Fig. 2. Quantization aware training using the model-tuner tool of GLOW

As Fig. 2 indicates, model-tuner manages to offer significant improvements in the validation accuracy for the two out of the four models (in LeNet300 and LeNet5 the room for further improving the accuracy is meager, since in these models the initial validation accuracy is already > 98%). For AlexNet and ResNet, an accuracy increase of up to 2.5% is reported also when the precision of the weights and the biases is equal to int8.

Performance Improvements by Hand-Optimized NN Kernels The aim of this part of the evaluation section is to reveal the performance benefits of hand-optimized NN kernels. The CMSIS-NN library is a collection of efficient NN kernels developed to maximize the performance and minimize the memory footprint of NNs on ARM Cortex-M cores. Figure 3 shows the speedups of the TFLM toolchain for the 11 studied models when the CMSIS-NN is activated (CMSIS_On)/deactivated (CMSIS_Off). In the latter case, the vanilla (unoptimized) TFLM kernels are used. There are four bars in each case corresponding to the different LLVM optimization levels: O0, O1, O2, and O3, respectively. The statistics in Fig. 3 are normalized to the leftmost bar (CMSIS_Off/O0) of the two groups of bars that are attached to each model.

It is important to note that TFLM does not include graph- or low-level optimizations. Therefore, the results presented in Fig. 3 can be considered as the potential representative speedups that can be achieved by hand-optimized kernels. This is also evident from the fact that almost no improvements can be observed when the different LLVM optimization levels are employed. The reason for this is the following: TFLM invokes the NN kernels associated to an input model during the initialization phase of the execution leaving no room to LLVM to perform (backend) optimizations.

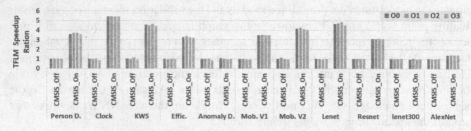

Fig. 3. TFLM speedups based on CMSIS-NN library

Graph-level vs. Target-Specific Optimizations in GLOW After revealing the potential of using hand-optimized kernels (backend part), the next step is to concentrate on the frontend part of the compilers. GLOW includes two frontend optimizers: the graph optimizer and the IR optimizer. The graph optimizer performs optimizations on the graph representation of NN models. The nodes of the graph usually represent more coarse-grained operations than those represented by the IR instructions. Memory-oriented optimizations are typically performed at the IR level, because memory allocations/deallocations are explicitly represented in the IR (and not in the graph representation).

GLOW frontend IR optimizer supports a set of graph-level optimizations and only eight of them can be enabled/disabled/configured [9]. Delving into more details about these optimizations is out of the scope of this paper. However, it is important to note that the various optimizations have different (and in some cases conflicting) objectives and of course specific optimizations can be more effective in GPU or CPU architectures. Moreover, the architecture of the NN model (e.g., shapes of layers) must also be taken into account when these optimizations are devised. Unfortunately, no specific guidelines are provided by GLOW on how the various optimizations must be configured. Creating suitable configuration recipes (in an automatic or semi-automatic way) for a given architecture/model requires a multiparametric analysis and it is part of our on-going work.

Figure 4 depicts the speedups reported by GLOW. The GLOW API exposes only an ON/OFF knob (shown juxtaposed the x-axis in Fig. 4) that enables/disables all the frontend optimizations altogether, respectively. The results in Fig. 4 are extracted using the original NN kernels of GLOW (the results from CMSIS-NN are presented later in this section). As in Fig. 3, there are four bars in each case in Fig. 4 corresponding to the different LLVM optimization levels. Again, the results are normalized to the leftmost bar of the two groups of bars attached to each model. During the serialization phase, LLVM is invoked to perform optimized code generation. The original GLOW kernels are written in a way to facilitate the LLVM auto-vectorization process. More specifically, the outer loop of NN kernels is unrolled (using a constant factor equal to 8 for 256-bits vectorized lanes), so as the inner loop can be vectorized.

As shown in Fig. 4, the different LLVM optimizations levels (O1, O2, O3) manage to ramp-up the performance up to 6.42x and by 3.58x on average. This is an expected result, since during code generation a single IR file with the whole model is fed to LLVM. However, if we concentrate on the improvements offered by the frontend part of GLOW, the results exhibit a non-intuitive behavior. Although in many cases, there are noticeable improvements (e.g., 32.1% in Person Detection Model/O1 case), there are a few cases in which a slowdown can be seen. It is evidence that this specific graph level optimization pass of GLOW does not offer significant benefits in the majority of the studied models. Part of our current work is to further analyze this issue.

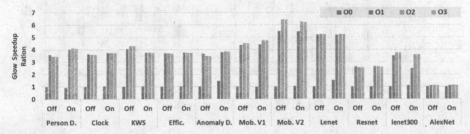

Fig. 4. Speedups offered by GLOW high-level graph and IR optimizers for various LLVM optimization levels

Graph-level vs. Target-specific Optimizations in IREE Fig. 5 shows the gathered speedups when the IREE toolchain is used. As we show later, IREE offers significant performance improvements compared to the two other frameworks. However, in Fig. 5 our focus is to evaluate the impact of: i) IREE graph levels optimizers and ii) LLVM optimization levels. As in the previous graphs, the labels juxtaposed the x-axis indicate if the graph-level optimizations are enabled (ON) or disabled (OFF). However, a different approach is used to extract the execution time in the ON case.

IREE contains six domain-specific optimizations and four high-level graph optimizations [45]. All optimizations are exposed as command-line arguments. As in the GLOW case, formulating a suitable combination (and configuration) of these optimizations is a challenging and multi-objective task. For a safe comparison, we revert to a brute-force approach: each model is run for all possible (2^{10}) configurations of these parameters and in Fig. 5 the configuration with the lowest execution time is presented. In addition, although IREE contains native support to enable thread level parallelism, GLOW and TFLM do not (for CPU implementations). Therefore, IREE is configured to extract single-thread executables.

In addition, as noted, IREE is based on MLIR representation and due to this, the well-refined MLIR optimizers are able to generate very efficient IR instructions leaving almost no room for improvement in the LLVM code generation part. By checking the disassembly code, it was noticed that IREE produced efficient vectorized code. Indeed, as Fig. 5 depicts, the different LLVM optimization levels (O1, O2, O3) exhibit almost similar performance in all cases. In most cases, the "opt-const-eval" and "opt-strip-assertions" passes offer speedups, at least for a subset of the studied models. The former pass calculates parts of global initializations (initializations only depend on constant values) at compile-time. The second pass strips-out all "std.assert" ops in the input program. Assertions provide useful user-visible error messages, but can prevent critical optimizations to take place. Finally, also in this case, the graph-level optimizations do not manage to offer any noticeable speedups. To sum-up, in IREE, the performance improvements stem from the multiple, highly-optimized MLIR passes.

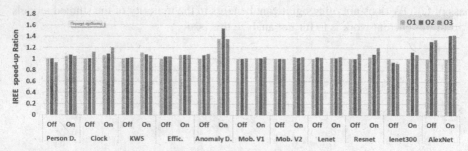

Fig. 5. Speedups offered by IREE

Overall Comparison Fig. 6 shows our full range of results for all studied frameworks. For every model (shown in x-axis in Fig. 6), the following cases (bars) are depicted (from left to right): TFLM, GLOW, IREE, TFLM with CMSIS-NN, and GLOW with CMSIS-NN. All results are normalized to the TFLM case. Also, in all cases the best combination of LLVM optimization levels and graph-level optimizations are used. In the MobileNet V1 and V2 models, the execution times of GLOW/CMSIS-NN are not reported because the original CMSIS-NN library does not include quantized kernels with a common scale factor across all channels.

As Fig. 6 illustrates, among IREE (third bar) and GLOW (without CMSIS-NN) (second bar), IREE is clearly the best performing mechanism (2.22x on average and up to 5.2x). However, when GLOW is equipped with the CMSIS-NN (rightmost bar), the situation is not clear. IREE is superior in four cases (K.W.S., EfficientNet, A.D., LeNet300), while GLOW/CMSIS-NN is better in six cases. Identifying the culprit of this behavior required to delve into each case and manually inspect the code at the assembly level. However, even in this way, our investigation revealed that these performance variations are the result of different effects or combination of effects in each model. A more thorough analysis on this is left for future work.

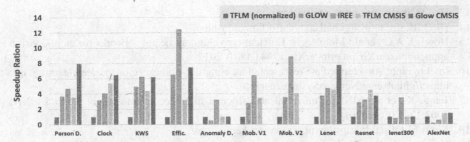

Fig. 6. Overall comparison of TFLM and GLOW (with and without the CMSIS-NN library), and IREE

6 Conclusions

In this paper, we presented a comparison between three widely-used NN compilers. Our analysis concentrated on the performance achieved by the different parts of the NN compilers. Our experimental findings revealed that the high-level (target-agnostic) optimizations offer meager performance improvements in both GLOW and IREE. On the contrary, remarkable speedups are reported when the machine-dependent (backend) optimizations are activated and appropriately configured. Part of our future work include to extend our analysis by including more CPU architectures as well as devices equipped with GPU and AI accelerators.

Acknowledgements. This research has been supported by a sponsored research agreement between Applied Materials, Inc. And Aristotle University of Thessaloniki, Greece.

References

1. Aakanksha, C., Warden, P., Shlens, J., Howard, A., Rhodes, R.: Visual wake words dataset. arXiv preprint arXiv:1906.05721 (2019)
2. AlexNet. url: https://cvml.ista.ac.at/courses/DLWT_W17/material/AlexNet.pdf
3. Cafee2 framework. url: https://caffe2.ai/
4. Chen, T., et al.: An automated end-to-end optimizing compiler for deep learning. arXiv preprint arXiv:1802.04799 (2018)
5. Cheng, Y., Wang, D., Zhou, P., Zhang, T.: A survey of model compression and acceleration for deep neural networks. arXiv preprint arXiv:1710.09282 (2017)
6. CuDNN. url: https://developer.nvidia.com/cudnn
7. David, R., et al.: TensorFlow Lite Micro: Embedded machine learning on TinyML systems. arXiv preprint arXiv:2010.08678 (2020)
8. Diniz, P.C., Cardoso, J.M.P., Coutinho, J.G.F.: Embedded computing for high performance (2017)
9. GLOW graph-level optimization. url: https://github.com/pytorch/glow/blob/master/docs/Optimizations.md
10. GLOW. url: https://github.com/pytorch/glow
11. GLOW with CMSIS support. url: https://github.com/Theoo1997/glow
12. Graph Optimizations url: https://onnxruntime.ai/docs/performance/model-optimizations/graph-optimizations.html#graph-optimization-levels

13. Halide library. url: https://halide-lang.org/
14. HLO IR. url: https://github.com/tensorflow/mlir-hlo
15. Howard, A.G., et al.: Mobilenets: Efficient convolutional neural networks for mobile vision applications. arXiv preprint arXiv:1704.04861, 2017
16. Intel ngraph: An intermediate representation, compiler, and executor for deep learning. url: https://github.com/NervanaSystems/ngraph
17. Jiang, X., et al.: MNN: a universal and efficient inference engine. arXiv preprint arXiv: 2002.12418v1 (2020)
18. Keras FLOPs. url: https://pypi.org/project/keras-flops/
19. Koizumi, Y., et al.: Unsupervised anomalous sound detection for machine condition monitoring. arXiv:2006.05822 (2020)
20. Koizumi, Y., Saito, S., Harada, N Uematsu, H., Imoto, K.: ToyADMOS: A dataset of miniature-machine operating sounds for anomalous sound detection. Workshop on Applications of Signal Processing to Audio and Acoustics (2019)
21. Krizhevsky, A., Sutskever, I., Hinton, G.E.: Imagenet classification with deep convolutional neural networks. Commun. ACM **60**, 84–90 (2017)
22. Lai, L., Suda, N., Chandra, V.: CMSIS-NN: efficient neural network kernels for Arm Cortex-M CPUs. arXiv preprint arXiv:1801.06601, 2018
23. Lattner, C., et al.: MLIR: A compiler infrastructure for the end of moore's law. arXiv preprint arxiv:2002.11054 (2020)
24. Leary, C., Wang, T.: XLA: TensorFlow (2017)
25. LeCun, Y., Bottou, L., Bengio, Y., Haffner, P.: Gradient-based learning applied to document recognition. Proc. IEEE **86**, 2278–2324 (1998)
26. LeCun, Y., Cortes, C., Burges, J.C.: The MNIST database of handwritten digits. Microsoft Res. 1998
27. M. Li, et al.: The deep learning compiler: a comprehensive survey. arXiv preprint arXiv: 2002.03794 (2020)
28. Lin, W.F., et al.: ONNC: a compilation framework connecting ONNX to proprietary deep learning accelerators. In: 2019 IEEE International Conference on Artificial Intelligence Circuits and Systems (AICAS) (2019)
29. Luo, C., He, X., Zhan, J., Wang, L., Gao, W., Dai, J.: Comparison and benchmarking of AI models and frameworks on mobile devices. arXiv preprint arXiv: 2005.05085 (2020)
30. nGraph IR. url: https://docs.openvino.ai/2020.2/_docs_IE_DG_nGraph_Flow.html
31. NNAPI. url: https://developer.android.com/ndk/guides/neuralnetworks
32. oneAPI. url: https://github.com/oneapi-src/oneDNN
33. ONNX. url: https://onnx.ai/
34. OpenVino toolkit: Neural network compression framework (NNCF). url: https://docs.openvino.ai/2022.1/docs_nncf_introduction.html
35. Paszke, A., et al.: PyTorch: An imperative style, high-performance deep learning library. arXiv preprint arXiv: 1912.01703 (2019)
36. Purohit, H., et al.: MIMII dataset: sound dataset for malfunctioning industrial machine investigation and inspection. In: Workshop on Detection & Classification of Acoustic Scenes and Events (2019)
37. PyTorch Mobile. url: https://pytorch.org/mobile/home/
38. Roesch, J., et al.: Relay: a high-level compiler for deep learning. arXiv preprint arXiv:1904.08368 (2019)
39. M. Sponner, B. Waschneck, and A. Kumar. Compiler toolchains for deep learning workloads on embedded platforms. arXiv preprint arXiv:2104.04576, 2021
40. Szegedy, C., et al.: Going deeper with convolutions. In: Proceedings of the IEEE Conference on Computer Vision and Pattern Recognition (CVPR) (2015)

41. Tan, M., Le, Q.V.: EfficientNet: rethinking model scaling for convolutional neural networks. arXiv preprint arXiv:1905.11946arXiv: 1905.11946, 2019
42. Tensor comprehensions. url: https://github.com/facebookresearch/TensorComprehensions
43. TensorFlow. url: https://www.tensorflow.org
44. TensorRT constant folding example. url: https://www.ccoderun.ca/programming/doxygen/tensorrt/md_TensorRT_tools_onnx-graphsurgeon_examples_05_folding_constants_REA DME.html
45. TinyIREE. url: https://openxla.github.io/iree/
46. TinyML Benchmarks. url: https://github.com/mlcommons/tiny
47. Grosser, T., Größlinger, A., Lengauer, C.: Polly - performing polyhedral optimizations on a low-level intermediate representation. Parallel Processing Letters (2012)
48. Tollenaere, N., et al.: Autotuning convolutions is easier than you think. ACM Trans. Archit. Code Optimizations **20**, 1–24 (2023)
49. The CIFAR-10 dataset. url: http://www.cs.toronto.edu/~kriz/cifar.html
50. Wade, A.W., Kulkarni, P.A., Jantz, M.R.: AOT vs. JIT: Impact of profile data on code quality, In: Proceedings of the 18th ACM SIGPLAN/SIGBED Conference on Languages, Compilers, and Tools for Embedded Systems (2017)
51. Warden, P.: Speech commands: a dataset for limited-vocabulary speech recognition. arXiv preprint arXiv:1804.03209, 2018
52. Xia, X., et al.: TRT-ViT: TensorRT-oriented vision transformer. arXiv preprint arXiv: 2205.09579 (2022)
53. Yi, X., et al.: Optimizing DNN compilation for distributed training with joint OP and tensor fusion. arXiv preprint arXiv:2209.12769 (2022)
54. L. Zheng, et al.: Ansor: generating high-performance tensor programs for deep learning. In: 14th USENIX symposium on operating systems design and implementation (OSDI 20) (2020)

Organic Computing Methodology (OC)

A Decision-Theoretic Approach
for Prioritizing Maintenance Activities
in Organic Computing Systems

Markus Görlich-Bucher(✉), Michael Heider, Tobias Ciemala, and Jörg Hähner

Organic Computing Group, University of Augsburg, Augsburg, Germany
{markus.goerlich-bucher,michael.heider,tobias.ciemala,
joerg.haehner}@uni-a.de
https://www.uni-augsburg.de/en/fakultaet/fai/informatik/prof/oc/

Abstract. Organic Computing systems intended to solve real-world problems are usually equipped with various kinds of sensors and actuators in order to be able to interact with their surrounding environment. As any kind of physical hardware component, such sensors and actuators will fail after a usually unknown amount of time. Besides the obvious task of identifying or predicting hardware failures, an Organic Computing system will furthermore be responsible to assess if it is still able to function after a component breaks, as well as to plan maintenance or repair actions, which will most likely involve human repair workers. Within this work, three different approaches on how to prioritize such maintenance actions within the scope of an Organic Computing system are presented and evaluated.

Keywords: Organic Computing · Predictive Maintenance · Decision Theory

1 Introduction

The interdisciplinary research domain of *Organic Computing* (OC) [8] is concerned with solving the increasing complexity in information- and communication technology by allowing systems to freely adapt and organize themselves. In order to interact with their surrounding environment, OC-based systems are expected to include various kinds of *sensors* and *actuators*. Accordingly, a significant amount of OC research conducted over the past two decades focused on building systems and architectures that are inherently focused on dealing with various real-world scenarios. [9] Hereby, a prominent aspect of OC systems is their ability to remain *robust* with respect to various kinds of *disturbances* that may happen within the scope of the OC system. In terms of OC, the idea of robustness is to remain functioning at a desired level of system performance while a disturbance occurs. Strongly related is the concept of *self-healing*, which describes a systems capability of *healing* itself from disturbances or system failures in an abstract manner [9]. As for now, most OC research concerned with

G. Goumas et al. (Eds.): ARCS 2023, LNCS 13949, pp. 37–47, 2023.
https://doi.org/10.1007/978-3-031-42785-5_3

robustness and self-healing focuses on dealing with software-sided disturbances, as discussed in [4]. Although quite relevant due to the real-world focus, a rarely discussed aspect in OC research is robustness against hardware-related disturbances, such as component failures or breakdowns. Besides the quite obvious challenges of identifying or predicting hardware-related disturbances, a notable problem lies in actually *solving* such a disturbance: As for now, one can expect that sensors and actuators (or summarized: *components*) of an OC system settled in a real-world context need to be repaired or maintained by some sort of human repair worker. Furthermore, until the human repair worker is able to maintain or replace a broken component, the overall robustness of the system may be endangered: In contrast to software-sided disturbances, which may be compensated by e.g. starting another instance of a software module, a hardware-related persists until being repaired. If the overall system configuration does not provide some sort of hardware redundancy, the system may not be able to remain robust. Accordingly, it is of interest to both *assess* how the system will be perform in the future considering known (that is: current) or potential (that is: predicted) broken components, as well as to *plan* or *prioritize* certain repair or maintenance actions involving said human repair workers. Within the scope of this paper, we present a brief example on how to plan such maintenance actions. We evaluate our approach using an example of an *organic production line* as well as a datacenter.

The remainder of this paper is structured as follows. In Sect. 2, we give a brief overview on existing work on the topic from the field of OC, as well as relevant work from other research domains. Afterwards, we describe some assumptions and prerequisites as well as the overall system model for our concept in Sect. 3. We describe our methodology in detail in Sect. 4 before providing evaluating and discussing our approach in Sect. 5. We conclude with a brief outlook on possible future work in Sect. 6.

2   Related Work

A brief introduction of the original concept of robustness, as it is considered in OC can be found in [8]. A more contemporary approach focusing on actually measuring robustness is given in [13]. As already outlined in the introduction, existing OC research on self-healing mostly focuses on software-sided disturbances (cf. [11,12]). The few work concerned with self-healing of hardware-related disturbances mostly focuses on compensating breakdowns rather than repairing or maintaining them, as for example [7]. A more detailed introduction on the general problem of hardware-sided disturbances in OC can be found in [3] as well as [4].

A research domain concerned with quite similar problems as those discussed in this work is the broader field of *Predictive Maintenance* (PdM). PdM focuses both on aspects of predicting breakdowns in various kinds of machinery, usually using some sort of machine learning algorithm or statistical methods, as well as the aspect of planning actual maintenance tasks. A brief introduction on the general topic can be found in [2]. Some notable work on planning maintenance actions can be found in [6,14] as well as [5].

A quite relevant aspect of maintenance planning work from the PdM domain is that PdM usually focuses on long-term planning of maintenance actions, as comes clear when considering e.g. [5]. This does not come to much of a surprise, as plenty existing PdM work is motivated by various subdomains of mechanical engineering. Shutting down whole production plants with static manufacturing processes and complex machinery, as for example in the automotive sector, may require a significant amount of planning in advance. OC systems, as we expect on the other hand, are affiliated with a more agile and flexible mode of operation. Accordingly, it is more of interest to provide a more short-hand and flexible way of planning maintenance actions.

3   Prerequisites

In the following section, various prerequisites necessary for the remainder of this paper are discussed. First of all, we give a brief overview on the overall system model based on the existing *Multi Level Observer Controller*-architecture. Afterwards, the actual problem statement of this paper is discussed thoroughly.

We assume an Organic Computing system S based on the *Multi-Level Observer Controller*-architecture (MLOC) [8]. In brief words, a *System under Observation and Control* (SuOC), which kind of acts as a representation for the real world aspect of S, is equipped with a *Control Mechanism* (CM) incorporating various *Observers* as well as a *Controllers* situated in several *Layers*. Layer 0 refers to the productive part, accordingly, to the SuOC. Layer 1 can be summarized as the reactive part of the whole architecture and is responsible for taking immediate action depending on the current system state. Layer 2 is responsible for gaining new knowledge (e.g. on previously unknown system states), probably by utilizing a simulation of the SuOC. Finally, Layer 3 consists various kinds of collaboration mechanisms, such as communication with other MLOC instances as well is responsible providing monitoring or goal management capabilities for external users. We refer to [9] for a broader introduction on the overall topic.

In a more formal way, the OC system S is affiliated with a *state space* of possible system states Z. For each observed state $z(t)$ at timestep t, S reacts with an (preferably suitable) action a. A disturbance θ at timestep t is defined as a change of a system state $z(t)$ to some other state $\theta(z(t))$. Taking the quantification methodology from [13] into account, each z is furthermore associated with a utility measure U, which can be used to asses the overall performance of S. If a disturbance θ is able to change U below some predefined threshold, U_{acc}, S performs no longer in an acceptable manner. If the system is not able to recover from this drop in utility, it cannot be considered as robust.

Considering the actual composition of S, we assume that the SuOC consists of several *components* $c \in C$. Each component is associated with an unknown degree of wear, therefore, will presumably *fail* some time in the future. We assume that S is able to both identify currently broken components (e.g. by some sort of health signal) as well as to, affiliated with some uncertainty, predict future breakdowns of components (e.g. by using some sort of prediction algorithm trained on previous sensor readings from failing components). Accordingly, each $c \in C$ is associated with a specific measurement of its current wear state, that is, if it is functioning or broken. We call this measurement *integrity*. In a more formal way, the integrity measure for a component c_j can be defined as $c_j^i \rightarrow \{0, 1\}$ with 1 determining a functional and 0 determining a broken component. The uncertain prediction of a components functionality in a discrete, known time horizon can be defined as $c_j^p \rightarrow \{0, 1\}$ with 0 determining a predicted breakdown and 1 determining a predicted functional component. This prediction is furthermore associated with a *confidence* measure $c_j^c \rightarrow [0, 1]$ determining how reliable the prediction is. In order to reflect the physical state of the system in the state space of S, we define $Z_C \subset Z$ as a state space containing limited system state descriptions only concerned with describing the integrity measures of all $c \in C$, that is, information on identified or predicted breakdowns. We furthermore assume that S entirely knows the cost function $Z_C \rightarrow U$, meaning that S is able to evaluate how its overall utility is affected by the integrity of its components.

From an architectural point of view, the methodology for identifying and predicting breakdowns would be found in the layer 1 observer, while the algorithms for prioritizing maintenance actions would be executed within the layer 1 controller. The component for calculating the cost function for evaluating the influence of a broken component on the system utility, however, would be located in the layer 2 controller, as one can expect that it makes use of the corresponding simulation component in order to learn the cost function. Taking these known measurements into account, it is of interest to plan necessary maintenance actions such that the overall system performance in terms of utility is ensured. Three suitable approaches are presented in the following section.

4   Methodology

At each discrete timestep, S is expected to assign a *priority* ω to each $c \in |C|$, taking the current system state as well as predictions of future breakdowns into consideration. As mentioned earlier, it is expected that S has access to a perfect cost function, allowing it to assess how the system will perform in case of a breakdown, presumably by utilization of a simulation on MLOC layer 2. The approach presented in this paper focuses on prioritizing maintenance activities for a horizon of one discrete timestep. However, the concept should be applicable to more extensive time horizons as well.

Two of the three algorithms presented in this work are based on concepts from the broader field of decision theory. In brief words, the general idea of decision theory is to formalize the problem of making decisions under uncertainty. In order to do so, decision theory-based methodologies assess potential outcomes based on their probability, combined with a utility function, in order to calculate an expected utility for a discrete timestep. We refer to [10] for a broader introduction on the topic. Taking the formalization of the previous chapter into account, the *expected utility* $E_U(z)$ for a system state z is calculated as follows:

$$E_U(z) = \sum_{i=0}^{|Z_C|} p(z_i) * U(z_i) \tag{1}$$

Here, a (physical) system state z_i consists of the integrity measures of all $c \in C$. Accordingly, the expected utility for a given state is calculated using the current occurrence probabilities of all possible system states as well as their corresponding system utilities. The occurrence probabilities are calculated using the breakdown predictions as well as the confidence scores for all components as follows:

$$p(z_i) = \prod^{c \in C} \begin{cases} c_j^c & \text{if } c_j^i = 0 \\ 1 - c_j^c & \text{if } c_j^i = 1 \end{cases} \tag{2}$$

In simple words, the expected utility describes the expectation value for the system utility under consideration of all possible system states. The probability of a single system state is therefore calculated using the prediction confidences under assuming the specific integrity values taken from this very system state. From a practical point of view, calculating $E_U(z)$ would allow S to assess how its utility would presumably develop under consideration of its current state, as well as its current predictions. However, in general, calculating $E_U(z)$ is quite expensive due to the combinatorial complexity of taking all conceivable system states into account.

The *priority* ω of performing a maintenance action a_j on component c_j can be regarded as directly proportional to improvement of the expected utility after performing said maintenance action. More formally, ω can be defined as follows:

$$\omega(a_j) \propto \Delta E_U(a_j) \tag{3}$$

Two decision theory-based methods implementing ΔE_U are discussed in the following. The simple stochastic planing algorithm, as explained in the next section, focuses on a simplified approach by reducing the complexity coming from taking all possible system states into account. The complex stochastic planing algorithm, which is explained afterwards, actually utilizes $E_U(z)$ for planing maintenance operations.

4.1   Simple Stochastic Planing

Within the simple stochastic planing algorithm, ΔE_U is calculated using a *simplified* expected utility function. This function does not take all possible system states and their probabilities into account, but focuses only on the prediction confidence associated with the component c_j. The function can be defined as follows:

$$E_U'(z, c_j) = U(z|c_j^i = 0) * c_j^c + U(z|c_j^i = 1) * (1 - c_j^c) \tag{4}$$

Using E'_U, ΔE_U can be calculated as follows:

$$\Delta E_U(a_j) = E'_U(z, c_j | a_j) - E'_U(z, c_j) \qquad (5)$$

Hereby, $E'_U(z, c_j | a_j)$ refers to the simplified expected utility function under the assumption that a maintenance action was performed on c_j just as E'_U is calculated. In these cases, it is assumed that $c^c_j = 0$, therefore, that probability of c_j failing equals 0. Briefly, the calculation of ω for a component c_j is based on the difference between expected utility if c_j is maintained and the expected utility if it is not maintained.

4.2   Complex Stochastic Planing

The complex stochastic planing algorithm works quite similar to the simple stochastic planing algorithm. The major difference is that the both the simplified expected utility, as well as the actual expected utility are utilized for the calculation of the priorities:

$$\Delta E_U(a_j) = E'_U(z, c_j | c^i_j = 1) - E_U(z) \qquad (6)$$

In simple words, using the original expected utility instead of the simplified version makes sure that the calculation considers interactions between components. Accordingly, other possible breakdowns and their probabilities are taken into account. As mentioned before, the calculation of $E_U(z)$ may be quite expensive, depending on $|C|$.

At this point, one could argue that it is unnecessary to calculate $E_U(z)$, as it is subtracted in each priority calculation. Accordingly, the sequence of the priorities remains the same, when it is left out of the equation. This is indeed correct, however, as it may be of interest to assess if the acceptance or survival boundaries of the system might be violated, the calculation might be necessary, depending on the actual application scenario.

4.3   Naive Planing

In order to provide some sort of most simple ground truth, a naive, greedy planing algorithm is implemented. The naive algorithm is defined as follows:

$$\omega(a_j) = p(z_i) \qquad (7)$$

Accordingly, following Eq. 2, a component currently broken is prioritized with 1 (as a maximum priority), while functioning components are prioritized based on their predictions and prediction confidences.

5   Evaluation

We evaluate our approach using two scenarios of different complexity. In the following, both scenarios are described briefly. Afterwards, the results of the evaluation are shown and discussed.

5.1   Datacenter Scenario

The idea of the datacenter scenario is to simulate the behaviour of hard drives in RAID-arrays, more specifically, RAID5. Accordingly, the components in this scenario are hard drives. Each RAID-array consists of three hard drives. The utility of a single RAID-array is the reading speed of the combined hard drives. Accordingly, if one drive fails, the reading speed decreases. If two drives fail, the RAID is no longer functional, therefore, its reading speed decreases to 0. In order to simulate a realistic behaviour, the runtimes and breakdowns of the hard drives are calculated based on datasets from the hosting company backblaze[1]. There exists work on predicting hard drive failures using the S.M.A.R.T. logging data provided by a hard drive's controller (e.g. [1,16]).

The hard drives within the datacenter are used as components within this scenario, therefore, additional components like RAID-controllers are not considered. The scenario consists of 200 RAID-arrays with a runtime of 365 discrete timesteps. Here, one timestep equals one day.

5.2   Organic Production Line Scenario

In order to emphasize the inherent real world aspect of OC, our Organic Production Line (OPC) scenario is inspired by a pulley factory layout as shown in [15]. The overall layout of the production line is shown in Fig. 1 and briefly described in the following. An *Entry* describes the entry point for raw material necessary for the production line. As can be seen, three different types of raw material are induced into the OPC. A *Buffer* describes some sort of buffering appliance where semi-processed work pieces or, later on, fully processed products are stored until their further processing. Various buffers are used for *splitting* the production line—for example, when two redundant machines work in parallel—as well as for *combining* processing lines—accordingly, when two machines in parallel produce the same work piece. A single *Exit* describes the end of the production line, therefore, the final execution step where processed units leave the OPC. Finally, various kinds of *Processing Machinery* (shown by the rectangles) are involved in processing the work pieces from step to step.

From an OC point of view, the processing machinery can be regarded as all components existing in C. For the scope of our evaluation, we assume that the buffers, entries and exits, as well as other equipment not shown in the layout (e.g. conveyor belts) do not feature sensors/actuators or do not belong to the scope of S. U can be regarded as the number of assembled units per time leaving the exit, while the maximum number of produced units per discrete timestep is $U_{max} = 100$. Intuitively, the minimal number of produced units is $U_{min} = 0$. The scenario consists of 25 equal OPCs and 500 discrete timesteps. Here, one discrete timestep equals one hour, therefore, the overall simulation covers about

---

[1] https://www.backblaze.com/b2/hard-drive-test-data.html.

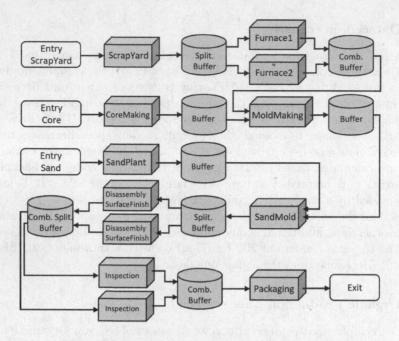

Fig. 1. Layout of the OPC scenario based on [15]

three weeks. Runtimes and breakdown behaviour of the machines in the scenario is based on the Azure AI Predictive Maintenance Dataset[2].

5.3   Results

As mentioned before, a perfect cost function is assumed for both scenarios. Besides, for predicting upcoming disturbances, we assume a maximum prediction horizon of three discrete timesteps. In order to simulate uncertainty, the predictions for the longest horizon are correct with a chance of 50%, while those with the shortest prediction horizon (that is: next discrete timestep) are correct with a chance of 90%. Additionally, the probabilities are altered using a normally distributed spread of 10%. 30 runs with different random seeds were conducted for each experiment. For now, no survival space boundary was incorporated.

The cumulated total utility per repetition as well as the average utility per timestep for the datacenter scenario are shown in Table 1. In order to check the results on significance, one-sided t-Tests with $\alpha = 0.05$ were performed on each pair of algorithms. A previously performed Shapiro-Wilk-Test showed that the assumption of a normal distribution cannot be rejected for all data. In total, the complex stochastic algorithm performed significantly superior to all other algorithms with $p = 9.48 * 10^{-15}$ for the naive algorithm as well as $p = 1.02 * 10^{-17}$ for the simple stochastic algorithm.

---

[2] https://www.kaggle.com/datasets/arnabbiswas1/microsoft-azure-predictive-maintenance.

Table 1. Cumulated utility per repetition and average utility per timestep for the datacenter scenario

Algorithm	Cumulated utility	Average utility
Simple stochastic	6877133.33 ± 104284.60	94.21 ± 1.43
Complex stochastic	6879315.56 ± 103708.81	94.24 ± 1.42
Naive	6810626.67 ± 129186.03	93.29 ± 1.77

The cumulated total utility per repetition as well as the average utility per timestep for the OPC scenario are shown in Table 2. Again, a previously performed Shapiro-Wilk-Test showed that the assumption of a normal distribution cannot be rejected for all data. Therefore, this scenario was also tested using one-sided t-Tests with $\alpha = 0.05$. Hereby, the complex stochastic algorithm also performed significantly superior to the other algorithms with $p = 1.66 * 10^{-18}$ for the naive algorithm and $p = 2.36e * 10^{-5}$ for the simple stochastic algorithm.

Table 2. Cumulated utility per repetition and average utility per timestep for the OPC scenario

Algorithm	Cumulated utility	Average utility
Simple stochastic	914905.52 ± 26934.46	73.19 ± 2.15
Complex stochastic	930305.83 ± 27585.01	74.42 ± 2.21
Naive	869469.17 ± 26718.52	69.56 ± 2.14

5.4   Discussion

For both scenarios, the decision theory-based algorithms show a significantly better performance compared to the naive approach.

While the results for the datacenter scenario appear quite similar, the production line scenario shows a quite notable difference between the three algorithms. This might be due to the fact that the production line scenario incorporates more interdependencies between the various components: For the datacenter, only three components, that is, hard drives per raid show direct dependencies, while one production line consists of twelve dependent components. Accordingly, one single breakdown in a production line has a bigger influence on the whole utility as it would have in the datacenter scenario. This results in slightly worse prioritizations—as, for example, the naive algorithm deciding greedily based on the breakdown probability—having a bigger impact on the overall utility. This aspect could also explain the noticeably better performance of the complex stochastic method (when compared to the simple stochastic method), as it takes the potential influences of other broken components into account. Accordingly, consideration of all possible futures system states within the complex stochastic method appears to be beneficial for systems with a higher degree of dependencies.

6   Conclusion and Outlook

In this work, two decision-theoretic approaches on prioritizing maintenance actions in organic computing systems were presented and evaluated alongside a naive method. It was shown that the decision-theoretic approach is indeed able to perform significantly better than the naive approach. Also, it was shown that the presented complex variant may yield better results in scenarios with a higher amount of dependencies between components.

In general, the presented methodologies base on rather simplified assumptions on how a real-world scenario may look like. There are various aspects not considered yet, such as parallel maintenance actions or different maintenance costs. Another relevant aspect, especially considering the OPC scenario, would be the explicit consideration of breakdowns affecting the utility in a delayed manner. Finally, within the scope of this work, a perfect utility function as well as rather simplified assumptions on the behaviour of the overall system were assumed, although is questionable if these assumptions could made for more complex OC scenarios in real world settings. This could incorporate the necessity to actually learn a suitable (probably imperfect) utility function, as well as to deal with unknown system states, changing probabilities for their occurrence, as well as imperfect or inaccurate predictions.

References

1. Aussel, N., Jaulin, S., Gandon, G., Petetin, Y., Fazli, E., Chabridon, S.: Predictive models of hard drive failures based on operational data. In: 2017 16th IEEE International Conference on Machine Learning and Applications (ICMLA), pp. 619–625. IEEE (2017)
2. Carvalho, T.P., Soares, F.A., Vita, R., Francisco, R.D.P., Basto, J.P., Alcalá, S.G.: A systematic literature review of machine learning methods applied to predictive maintenance. Comput. Ind. Eng. **137**, 106024 (2019)
3. Görlich, M., Stein, A., Hähner, J.: Towards physical disturbance robustness in organic computing systems using MOMDPs. In: ARCS Workshop 2019; 32nd International Conference on Architecture of Computing Systems, pp. 1–4. VDE (2019)
4. Görlich-Bucher, M.: Dealing with hardware-related disturbances in organic computing systems. In: INFORMATIK 2019: 50 Jahre Gesellschaft für Informatik-Informatik für Gesellschaft (Workshop-Beiträge). Gesellschaft für Informatik eV (2019)
5. Hardt, F., Kotyrba, M., Volna, E., Jarusek, R.: Innovative approach to preventive maintenance of production equipment based on a modified TPM methodology for industry 4.0. Appl. Sci. **11**(15), 6953 (2021)
6. Ji, B., et al.: A component selection method for prioritized predictive maintenance. In: Lödding, H., Riedel, R., Thoben, K.-D., von Cieminski, G., Kiritsis, D. (eds.) APMS 2017. IAICT, vol. 513, pp. 433–440. Springer, Cham (2017). https://doi.org/10.1007/978-3-319-66923-6_51

7. Maehle, E., et al.: Application of the organic robot control architecture ORCA to the six-legged walking robot OSCAR. In: Müller-Schloer, C., Schmeck, H., Ungerer, T. (eds.) Organic Computing-A Paradigm Shift for Complex Systems, pp. 517–530. Springer, Basel (2011). https://doi.org/10.1007/978-3-0348-0130-0_34

8. Müller-Schloer, C., Schmeck, H., Ungerer, T.: Organic Computing-A Paradigm Shift for Complex Systems. Springer, Basel (2011). https://doi.org/10.1007/978-3-0348-0130-0

9. Müller-Schloer, C., Tomforde, S.: Organic Computing – Technical Systems for Survival in the Real World. AS. Springer, Cham (2017). https://doi.org/10.1007/978-3-319-68477-2

10. Pratt, J.W., Raiffa, H., Schlaifer, R., et al.: Introduction to Statistical Decision Theory. MIT Press, Cambridge (1995)

11. Satzger, B., Pietzowski, A., Trumler, W., Ungerer, T.: Variations and evaluations of an adaptive accrual failure detector to enable self-healing properties in distributed systems. In: Lukowicz, P., Thiele, L., Tröster, G. (eds.) ARCS 2007. LNCS, vol. 4415, pp. 171–184. Springer, Heidelberg (2007). https://doi.org/10.1007/978-3-540-71270-1_13

12. Schmitt, J., Roth, M., Kiefhaber, R., Kluge, F., Ungerer, T.: Using an automated planner to control an organic middleware. In: 2011 IEEE Fifth International Conference on Self-Adaptive and Self-Organizing Systems, pp. 71–78. IEEE (2011)

13. Tomforde, S., Kantert, J., Müller-Schloer, C., Bödelt, S., Sick, B.: Comparing the effects of disturbances in self-adaptive systems - a generalised approach for the quantification of robustness. In: Nguyen, N.T., Kowalczyk, R., van den Herik, J., Rocha, A.P., Filipe, J. (eds.) Transactions on Computational Collective Intelligence XXVIII. LNCS, vol. 10780, pp. 193–220. Springer, Cham (2018). https://doi.org/10.1007/978-3-319-78301-7_9

14. van Horenbeek, A., Pintelon, L.: A dynamic predictive maintenance policy for complex multi-component systems. Reliab. Eng. Syst. Saf. **120**, 39–50 (2013). https://doi.org/10.1016/j.ress.2013.02.029

15. Watanapa, A., Kajondecha, P., Duangpitakwong, P., Wiyaratn, W.: Analysis plant layout design for effective production. In: Proceeding of the International Multi Conference of Engineers and Computer Scientists, vol. 2, pp. 543–559 (2011)

16. Zhu, Y., Wu, P.H.J., Liu, F., Kanagavelu, R.: Disk failure prediction for Software-Defined Data Centre (SDDC). In: 2021 IEEE International Conference on Dependable, Autonomic and Secure Computing, International Conference on Pervasive Intelligence and Computing, International Conference on Cloud and Big Data Computing, International Conference on Cyber Science and Technology Congress (DASC/PiCom/CBDCom/CyberSciTech), pp. 264–268. IEEE (2021)

Predicting Physical Disturbances in Organic Computing Systems Using Automated Machine Learning

Markus Görlich-Bucher[✉], Michael Heider, and Jörg Hähner

Organic Computing Group, University of Augsburg, Augsburg, Germany
{markus.goerlich-bucher,michael.heider,joerg.haehner}@uni-a.de
https://www.uni-augsburg.de/en/fakultaet/fai/informatik/prof/oc/

Abstract. Robustness against internal or external disturbances is a key competence of Organic Computing Systems. Hereby, a rarely discussed aspect are physical disturbances, therefore, failures or breakdowns that affect a systems physical components. Before experiencing such a disturbance, physical components may show various measurable signs of deterioration that might be assessed through sensor data. If interpreted correctly, it would be possible to predict future physical disturbances and act appropriately in order to prevent them from possibly harming the overall system. As the actual structure of such data as well as the behaviour that disturbances produce might not be known a priori, it is of interest to equip Organic Computing Systems with the ability to learn to predict them autonomously. We utilize the Automated Machine Learning Framework TPOT for an online-learning-inspired methodology for learning to predict physical disturbances in an iterative manner. We evaluate our approach using a freely available dataset from the broader domain of Predictive Maintenance research and show that our approach is able to build predictors with reasonable prediction quality autonomously.

Keywords: Organic Computing · Automated Machine Learning · Predictive Maintenance

1 Introduction

Organic Computing (OC) [9] is intended to solve the increasing complexity in information- and communication technology by allowing systems to freely adapt and organize themselves. OC-based systems are expected to involve various kinds of *sensors* and *actuators* and are explicitly designed to cope with plenty different types of real-world scenarios and use-cases. A notable focus in OC research over the last years lies on investigating how OC systems can be built to be *robust*, therefore, to remain functioning within a desired range of performance even though various kinds of internal or external *disturbances* may appear [14] Hereby, most of the existing research focuses on software-sided disturbances.

G. Goumas et al. (Eds.): ARCS 2023, LNCS 13949, pp. 48–62, 2023.
https://doi.org/10.1007/978-3-031-42785-5_4

Only few works on how to deal with hardware-sided disturbances, termed *physical disturbances* throughout this work, exist, although being a serious, yet unresolved problem in OC, as outlined in [6]: A damaged actuator, for example, remains damaged until it is repaired or exchanged and may affect the overall performance of the entire system. Although human repair works may be necessary to replace broken hardware, it may indeed be possible and useful to reduce the amount of human participation to an absolute minimum. In order to do so, it is necessary to be able to *predict* when future physical disturbances will happen. This could allow the OC system to estimate how long it will be able to function in a desired way, therefore, to assess how long it will be robust. In order to be able to predict upcoming physical disturbances, it is both necessary to collect a suitable amount of training data as well as to choose a suitable *Machine Learning* (ML) algorithm depending on the overall structure and type of the collected data. As OC systems are intended to move design-time decisions to runtime, it is not possible to choose an appropriate algorithm a priori. We suggest the utilization of an *Automated Machine Learning* (AutoML) framework for overcoming this issue. AutoML-approaches are intended to automatically choose and parametrize an appropriate ML algorithm based on the given input data, as well as to incorporate necessary data preprocessing steps. In this work, we present an AutoML-based approach for predicting upcoming physical disturbances using the *Tree-based Pipeline Optimization Toolkit* (TPOT) [10]. We present an iterative process that gathers measurements from the OC systems' hardware components and utilizes TPOT to continuously learn and optimize until a desired prediction quality is reached.

The remainder of this paper is structured as follows. In Sect. 2, we give a brief overview on existing related research from the field of OC as well as the related field of *Predictive Maintenance*. Furthermore, we refer to various existing AutoML frameworks. Afterwards, we provide a more detailed motivation of the underlying problem of this work and provide a brief introduction to TPOT in Sect. 3. We thoroughly explain our approach in Sect. 4 before evaluating it using a simple smart factory scenario in Sect. 5. We conclude with a short outlook on possible future work in Sect. 6.

2 Related Work

There are several aspects in OC research that are relevant to our work. First of all, the concept of robustness, as already mentioned in the introduction, is related to the occurrence of disturbances. A contemporary approach on measuring robustness can be found in [14]. The latter work also gives a good introduction on this topic in general. Quite similar is the self-x property *self-healing*, therefore, the ability of an OC system to resolve disturbances by taking appropriate countermeasures. However, existing research on self-healing mostly focuses on healing software-sided disturbances, e.g. in [12]. Finally, various ML approaches have been utilized in OC research so far. Hereby, the XCS classifier system (XCS) [3] as well as some of its derivates have gained plenty of attention in the

OC community. However, they are mostly utilized to learn appropriate control strategies based on the current situation in the underlying System. We refer to [13] for a broader introduction to the usage of XCS in OC, as well as for an overview of other ML techniques used in OC so far.

Predictive Maintenance (PdM), sometimes also termed as *Condition-based Maintenance* is a quite active area of research in various other scientific disciplines. Especially over course of the last years, ML techniques have gained an important role in PdM research. We refer to [4] for a more detailed introduction and broader overview on current research in this topic. A notable difference between our proposed approach and PdM concepts lies in the inherent design-time to runtime idea of OC: ML methodologies are usually developed with a notable amount of domain knowledge, their applicability can be tested and evaluated thoroughly. Contrary, utilizing ML for predicting hardware failures in OC necessitates methodologies that do not rely on such optimal conditions.

AutoML has become a quite active domain of research over the course of the last years, too. Various state-of-the-art frameworks make use of *Bayesian Optimization* in order to optimize both chosen algorithms and preprocessing steps as well as their hyperparameters. A contemporary survey on various AutoML frameworks is given in [17].

3   Prerequisites

The overall system model can be briefly described as follows: We assume a *System under Observation and Control* (SuOC) controlled by a *Control Mechanism* (CM), for example an instance of the *Multi-Layer Observer Controller*-architecture [15]. The SuOC is associated with a set of various *components C*. Here, a component refers to possible *sensors and actuators* an OC system may be associated with in order to interact with its surrounding environment. However, the term *sensors and actuators* does not necessarily refer to sensors *or* actuators, but could also be taken as a description for more sophisticated components or machinery involving both of them, i.e. soft-sensing mechanisms.

We assume that the CM is able to assess individual health states for each single component $c \in C$ at each discrete timestep t. This means that the CM is able to decide wether a component is *functioning* or *defective* (therefore disturbed) at timestep t. This can happen, for example by a component shutting down after an error, meaning that the CM can no longer gather data from it, or by an utility metric measuring the system performance that suddenly decreases.

We assume that a component is able to return some sort of status information or *internal* sensor readings somehow reflecting the internal state of a component. The term internal sensor readings should not be confused with sensors an OC system is equipped with for interacting with its environment: The former refers to measuring, as explained, the internal state of a component, the latter refers to a designated component that is used to assess the environment. Under the assumption that the gathered measurements reflect the actual physical state of the component, this information appears useful to predict future physical disturbances: If an upcoming physical disturbance is known a priori, the CM might be able to proactively take countermeasures to ensure a robust system state. The OC approach of moving design-time decisions to runtime can yield various problems at this point: It is not known in advance how the gathered data may look like. There exist scenarios where one has to expect quite simple, structured data (e.g. vibration and temperature sensor measurements in a simple mechanical machinery). On the other hand, there may exist scenarios where the gathered information is quite complex (e.g. images of produce taken by a camera installed for quality assurance purposes). Also, the data can be enriched with information actually useless for predicting physical disturbances. This can necessitate different types of machine learning algorithms as well as various possible preprocessing steps depending on structure and type of the incoming data. Finally, it is also necessary to determine suitable hyperparameters for the used algorithms - a non-trivial task requiring an appropriate amount of data for training and testing purposes. Accordingly, traditional OC-related learning paradigms such as XCS appear inappropriate for this kind of learning problem, as they are not necessarily applicable to e.g. unprocessed, high-dimensional or unstructured data. More precise, XCS is a single learning paradigm, whereas the described learning problem may necessitate multiple different suitable learning algorithms, depending on the actual data available within specific scenario. We therefore focus on methods from the broader field of AutoML in order to tackle previously motivated problem. Within the scope of this work, we use the TPOT framework as an AutoML framework, as it is based on *Genetic Algorithms*—a class of optimization heuristics that are commonly used in OC.

The overall idea of TPOT is to utilize *Genetic Programming* (GP) [1] for building and optimizing ML pipelines. TPOT is able to use various preprocessing and decomposition algorithms, feature selectors as well as actual ML models as *operators*. The operators are combined in tree-based structures. Both the structure of these trees as well as the parameters of the chosen operators are evolved by means of GP: In the very beginning, a population of such tree-based individuals is generated randomly. Each individual is trained and tested using an appropriate train/test-split of the given training data. Using a suitable selection scheme, some of the individuals are chosen for breeding or applying genetic operators, such as crossover, for the next generation of the population. From generation to generation, TPOT is able to iteratively generate and optimize ML pipelines for the given data. As a broader introduction would be beyond the scope of this work, we refer to [10] for a more detailed explanation of the individual parts of TPOT, as well as for an evaluation of the approach on several datasets from the UCI machine learning repository.

4   Methodology

Our overall approach is divided in three phases: Right after setting up the OC system, the *BOOTSTRAP*-phase takes place. It is used to collect an initial amount of training data that is (presumably) sufficient enough to train a first pipeline. As this goal is reached, the system changes to the *OPTIMIZATION*-phase. In this phase, pipelines are trained in an iterative manner at certain discrete timesteps until the system reaches a desired prediction quality. Afterwards, the system switches to the *PRODUCTION*-phase, where the actual predictions of the trained pipeline should be used by the CM in order to cope with upcoming disturbances.

In order to simplify the following explanations, we assume that all components in C are of the same type (in order to allow the CM to use gathered data from all components for training one ML pipeline that is used to predict disturbances in all components). Of course, OC systems presumably feature various different kinds of components. Accordingly, in an actual real-world scenario, the CM would conduct the following process individually for each type of component existing in its SuOC.

4.1   Data Collection and Labeling

At each discrete timestep t, the CM gathers a row of sensor readings for each component $c_i \in C$ and saves them for later use. Additionally, the CM examines the current physical state of each component $c_i \in C$.

If the CM identifies a component c_i as broken, it recalls all sensor measurements gathered for c_i since the component's last breakdown (or since the installation of the overall system, if no breakdown for the corresponding component happened before), resulting in a set of chronologically ordered *rows* for c_i. Afterwards, all rows that are younger than a certain threshold Θ_{pred} are *labeled* as *positive*, all other rows are labeled as *negative*. Θ_{pred} can be described as the desired *prediction horizon* for predicting upcoming breakdowns: If the trained learner is able to make perfect predictions, an upcoming disturbance would be predicted Θ_{pred} timesteps in advance. The choice of a suitable Θ_{pred} is not a trivial task and may depend on various aspects that might not be known a priori. For now, we assume that Θ_{pred} is given in advance (e.g. during setting up the corresponding system). After the data is collected and labeled, c_i is reported to the CM, e.g. for repair or maintenance operations. This overall functionality is refered to as LABELANDREPAIR() in the algorithms later on.

At the end of a timestep, all collected sets of data rows are merged. Afterwards, a *train/test-split* is applied to the merged data: The major amount of collected data is added to the *training dataset* $\mathcal{D}_{train}$. The minor amount is added to the *test holdout dataset* $\mathcal{D}_{test}$. The split is done proportional to the positive/negative labels (that is, the proportion of positives and negatives among the data added to the training set is the same as for those added to the test holdout set). The intuition behind these sets is as follows: $\mathcal{D}_{train}$ is used as data for training actual AutoML pipelines. $\mathcal{D}_{test}$, on the other hand, is used as previously unseen data to *validate* the results of the trained pipelines after they are optimized. Both sets are extended with novel training (respectively testing) data each time a component breaks. We refer to this functionality as CONSOLIDATE-DATA() in the algorithms later on.

4.2   Bootstrap Phase

The goal of the Bootstrap Phase is to gather enough data for training a first pipeline for predicting future disturbances. Here, the term *enough data* should be taken as a rough estimate rather than an explicit boundary: Deciding if enough data for training a machine learning algorithm exists is not a trivial task and of subordinate importance for our overall approach. The idea of the bootstrap phase is just to avoid too early trainings that can lead to irritating results: For example, we found that training a pipeline with very few examples can lead to unrealistic good results during the first training episodes in our evaluation. The trained pipeline apparently overfits on the training data. As both the training data as well as the test data holdout are sampled from very few components in the beginning, the test holdout dataset did not indicate an overfitting—leading to very good results which later on declined iteratively, as more and more data is added to both datasets.

Accordingly, nothing except the previously explained data collection and labeling takes place during the bootstrap phase. Whenever a component fails, its collected measurements are labeled and, at the end of a timestep, split and added to $\mathcal{D}_{train}$ and $\mathcal{D}_{test}$ respectively. We furthermore assume that the component is repaired afterwards, allowing the CM to collect data from this component again. At the end of each timestep, it is assessed if enough training data was collected as shown in Algorithm 1.

Algorithm 1. IsBootstrapDone()

1: **function** IsBootstrapDone()
2:     **if** $|\mathcal{D}_{train+}| * \Theta_{sr} / \mathrm{Fib}(fp) >= d$ **and** $|\mathcal{D}_{train-}| * \Theta_{sr} / \mathrm{Fib}(fp) >= d$ **then**
3:         **return** true
4:     **else**
5:         **return** false

Here, $|\mathcal{D}_{train+}|$ and $|\mathcal{D}_{train-}|$ refer to the number of positive (or negative) training data rows available. Θ_{sr} determines the *sample ratio* and is a fixed multiplier set in advance. Fib(i) is a function returning the ith element from a list of Fibonacci numbers. The purpose of the variable fp (Fibonacci pointer) and the corresponding list of Fibonacci numbers is explained in the next subsection. Finally, d refers to the dimensionality of the used input data. The idea of the IsBootstrapDone() is as follows: It is checked if both the amount of positive labeled training data as well as negative labeled training data lies above a certain threshold. This threshold is calculated using a simple heuristic based on a fixed, predefined sample ratio, a variable Fibonacci number as well as dimensionality of the used data. The Bootstrap phase ends once these conditions hold by executing the first training and starting the optimization phase.

4.3   Optimization Phase

The optimization phase is meant to iteratively train ML pipelines using TPOT and continuously assess their performance, until the latter reaches an acceptable level for beeing used productively. The corresponding algorithm is shown in Algorithm 2.

Algorithm 2. Optimization phase

```
 1: function OPTIMIZATION()
 2:     for c in C do
 3:         if isBroken(c) then
 4:             labelAndRepair(c)
 5:             evaluateMachine(c)
 6:     consolidateData()
 7:     if nextTrainingNecessary() then
 8:         training()
 9:     if isOptimizationDone() then
10:         production()
```

The overall procedure is as follows: Upon entering the optimization phase, the method TRAIN() is called in order to train a first usable pipeline, as shown in Algorithm 2 in the previous subsection. It should be denoted that the training happens *during* the current discrete timestep, accordingly, ending the Bootstrap phase, entering the Optimization phase and training the first pipeline happens at the end of the same timestep. Afterwards, the system still continues to gather labeled data similar to the Bootstrap phase. The method EVALUATEMACHINE() is used to evaluate the performance of the current trained TPOT instance on the (labeled) data of the newly broken component, therefore, to assess how good the performance of the instance would have been in an (actual) productive scenario. The calculated score is saved internally. Furthermore, if enough data was gathered, the method calculates the moving average for the last $\Theta_{OptWindow}$ scores that have been recorded. The moving average is appended to the list `movingAverageScores`, which then acts as a rolling window to assess how the overall performance changes over time. At the end of each timestep, measurements from newly broken components are added to the corresponding data sets. Besides, it is checked if another retraining is necessary using NEXTTRAIN-INGNECESSARY(). If this is the case, TRAINING() is called again. Finally, ISOP-TIMIZATIONDONE() is called in order to assess if the Optimization phase can come to an end. The individual functions are explained in the following.

Algorithm 3 shows the TRAIN()-method. First of all, in line 2, the existing training data in $\mathcal{D}_{train}$ is divided into k *stratified folds* or *splits* used internally in TPOT for training and testing. Actually, TPOT would be able to split the training data for cross-validation (CV) purposes internally. The reason why this is done in advance follows in line 3 and line 4: Due to the high class imbalance,

Algorithm 3. TRAIN()

```
 1: function TRAIN()
 2:     splits := StratifiedKFold(𝒟_train)
 3:     for trainSplit in splits do
 4:         SMOTEENN(trainSplit)
 5:     newLearner := fitTpot(splits)
 6:     if currentLearner is not null then
 7:         newPrediction := newLearner.predict(𝒟_test)
 8:         currentPrediction := currentLearner.predict(𝒟_test)
 9:         if score(newPrediction) > score(currentPrediction) then
10:             currentLearner := newLearner
11:             fp := fp - 1
12:         else
13:             fp := fp + 1
14:     else
15:         currentLearner := newLearner
16:         fp := fp - 1
```

TPOT tends to overfit on the majority class, as we found out in some preliminary test runs. In order to cope with this issue, we integrated suitable over- and undersampling methods. We used the SMOTEENN-algorithm, a combination of SMOTE and Edited Nearest Neigbours (ENN) [2]. Applying SMOTEENN on the whole training data and letting TPOT create the CV-folds by itself would lead to synthetical data within the (internal) test splits. The internal test splits need to be as imbalanced as the (expected) data the pipeline is confronted with afterwards in order to avoid biasing the chosen scoring function. Accordingly, only those splits that are used as training data afterwards are altered. After the data augmentation is done, a new TPOT instance is created and fitted using the splits in Line 5. The pipeline created by the new TPOT instance is now used to create predictions for the existing test holdout set $\mathcal{D}_{test}$. Additionally, the *last* TPOT instance (that is: the TPOT instance that was created in the previous training run) is also used to create predictions for $\mathcal{D}_{test}$. Afterwards, a scoring function is applied to both predictions in order to determine if the last instance or the newly trained one performs better on the test holdout dataset. If the newly trained instance performs better, it is saved and the previous instance is discarded. Additionally, the Fibonacci pointer fp is decremented. If the older instance performs better than the newly trained one, the latter is discarded and fp is incremented. This also happens when no previously trained instance exists.

The idea of incrementing/decrementing the Fibonacci pointer followed our first preliminary experiments, where we found that rather short training intervals do not show any notable change in performance. Moreover, it could happen that a newly trained pipeline performs worse than the previous one. The idea of the Fibonacci pointer is to introduce some sort of adaptive threshold for deciding if a retraining is necessary: Increasing the pointer leads to a longer interval until the next retraining, reflecting the case that no increased performance was reached in the current training. Decreasing it leads to a shorter interval, as obviously the size of the previous interval was sufficient to increase the prediction performance. In general, the overall method would also work with fixed intervals, as a new training does not depend on the previous training. However, as the trainings are quite time expensive, it is of interest to reduce the overall number of trainings. Fibonacci numbers as multiplicator for the intervals show favourable characteristics. Their slope is larger compared to linear functions, which avoids smaller training intervals and thus expensive training cycles. Furthermore, its slope is smaller than a quadratic functions which would grow too quick. The influence of the Fibonacci pointer can be seen in the NEXTTRAININGNECESSARY() method, shown in Algorithm 4.

Algorithm 4. NEXTTRAININGNECESSARY()

1: **function** NEXTTRAININGNECESSARY()
2:     **if** $(|\mathcal{D}_{train+}| - |\mathcal{D}_{train+}^{-1}|) \cdot \Theta_{sr}/Fib(fp) >= d$ **and** $(|\mathcal{D}_{train-}| - |\mathcal{D}_{train-}^{-1}|) \cdot \Theta_{sr}/Fib(fp) >= d$ **then**
3:         **return** true
4:     **else**
5:         **return** false

The algorithm is quite similar to Algorithm 1 that is used to decide if the bootstrap phase shall end. The only difference here is the usage of $|\mathcal{D}_{training+}^{-1}|$ and $|\mathcal{D}_{training-}^{-1}|$, referring to the amount of positive (and negative) training samples that were available during the *last* training. Therefore, it is investigated if the amount of training data gathered since the last training exceeds a certain threshold, again determined by the fixed sample ratio Θ_{sr} and the a Fibonacci number gathered through the previously explained Fibonacci pointer.

Finally, Algorithm 5 shows the algorithm that is used to decide if the optimization phase has come to an end.

Algorithm 5. ISOPTIMIZATIONDONE

1: **function** ISOPTIMIZATIONDONE()
2:     **for** i=1 to $\Theta_{OptWindow}$ **do**
3:         **if** movingAverageScores[-i] $< \Theta_{OptThreshold}$ **then**
4:             **return** false
5:     **return** true

The method uses the moving average score list that is extended each time a physical disturbance occurs, as previously explained. If the last $\Theta_{OptWindow}$ scores lie above a predefined threshold $\Theta_{OptThreshold}$, the optimization phase ends, as TPOT is now able to provide predictions that are considered good enough for the CM to be used for assessing the SuOC's future state. At the end of the corresponding timestep, the production phase starts.

4.4 Production Phase

The overall goal of the production phase is to use TPOT to predict upcoming physical disturbances, report those to the CM and to continuously assess if TPOTs performance is still acceptable. The procedure executed after each timestep is shown in Algorithm 6.

Algorithm 6. Production Phase

```
 1: function PRODUCTION()
 2:     for c in C do
 3:         if isBroken(c) then
 4:             labelAndRepair(c)
 5:             evaluateMachine(c)
 6:         else if c.mode == EXPLOIT then
 7:             prediction := currentTpot.predict(c)
 8:             if prediction := true then
 9:                 reportPrediction(c)
10:         consolidateData()
11:         if nextTrainingNecessary() then
12:             training()
13:             resampleExploreExploit()
```

The algorithm is quite similar to the optimization phase. The major difference is that each component in C is associated with a *mode* that can be either *EXPLOIT* or *EXPLORE*. If a component is set to *EXPLOIT*, TPOT is used to predict whether the component c is expected to break or not, as can be seen in Line 6. If so, the CM is informed by calling REPORTPREDICTION(). It is now up to the CM to decide on proper countermeasures, e.g. by repairing or changing c in advance. Components set to *EXPLORE* are not considered in the predictions: Their purpose is to run until being hit by a physical disturbance. This makes it possible to continuously assess if the TPOT instance still makes acceptable predictions. The same obviously holds for components set to *EXPLOIT* that break without the disturbance being predicted properly. For now, NEXTTRAININGNECESSARY() and TRAINING() in Line 11 and 12 follow the functionality they have in the optimization phase: Data is gathered, another training run is started, and if the prediction performance of the current TPOT instance declines, it is replaced by a newly trained one. However, it is also conceivable to, for example, return to the optimization phase if the performance drops below a certain threshold. Another possible option would be to adapt the ratio between *EXPLOIT* and *EXPLORE* towards more machines set to *EXPLORE* in order to speeden up the learning process, if necessary. Finally, the method RESAMPLEEXPLOREEXPLOIT() is called to resample the distribution of *EXPLORE*, respectively *EXPLOIT*-modes among all components in C. The ratio between the two modes is set in advance. A rather small number of *EXPLORE* components appears suitable in order to allow the overall system to benefit from the predictions made for the *EXPLOIT* components.

5   Evaluation

The overall evaluation scenario is structured as follows. The SuOC consists of 5 components in form of identical *production machines*. In general, any other number of components would be applicable too - with lesser components, the overall process would take longer, with more components, is would be faster. We assume that the CM is able to assess if a machine is working properly or is broken. In the given scenario, this could be the case by assessing the number of work-pieces a machine produces in a discrete timestep. Furthermore, each machine delivers various internal measurements that can be used to assess its internal state. Additionally, no configuration changes or other disturbances except actual machine breakdowns will take place, resulting in a quite simple evaluation scenario. The Azure AI Predictive Maintenance Dataset[1] was used for simulating the measurements from the individual machines. The dataset consists of 4 different machine types in total, type number 1 was used throughout this evaluation. The CSV-files in the dataset were preprocessed such that a single CSV-file exists for each machine in the dataset (containing measurements from installation until breakdown in chronologial order). Incomplete traces (that is, machines without breakdowns and machines that were repaired although no breakdown happened) were removed. Furthermore, the *error* column was removed, therefore, the only measurements available are *volt, rotate, pressure* and *vibration*. This results in a total of 672 machines. The 5 components of the SuOC are equipped with 5 uniformly chosen machine CSV-files. A component is regarded as broken when the corresponding CSV-file reaches its last row. The component is then repaired in the next timestep by replacing the CSV-file by a newly sampled one.

5.1   Implementation and Parametrisation

We implemented our approach using Python as well as the original TPOT implementation [10]. Scikit-learn [11] was used for the stratified cross validation as well as for the scoring functions. Furthermore, the SMOTEENN-implementation from the *imblearn* library [8] was used. If not stated otherwise, the default parametrizations for the algorithms were used.

We used the *balanced accuracy* as a scoring function both internally in TPOT as well as afterwards for scoring in our own implementation due to the imbalanced nature of the available data: As the balanced accuracy is defined as the mean between sensitivity and specificity, it is less vulnerable to false predictions of the minority class, at least compared to the non-balanced accuracy metric. TPOT was configured with 10 generations, a population size of 25 and an early stopping of 2. This results in TPOT stopping the optimization process if no progress was made after 2 generations. At this point, it should be mentioned that TPOT features a *warmstart*-function. This allows TPOT to use the last population as a start population for a new run, however, we found that this

---

[1] https://www.kaggle.com/datasets/arnabbiswas1/microsoft-azure-predictive-maintenance.

leads to a notably worse performance compared to starting with a complete new population each time, therefore, we did not use it.

The fixed sample ratio Θ_{sr} was set to 0.025. The optimization threshold $\Theta_{optThreshold}$ as well as the optimization sliding window size $\Theta_{optWindow}$ were set to 0.9 and 20, respectively. The Fibonacci pointer fp was set to 5 for the bootstrap phase, resulting in the number 8. Additionally, we limited the fp to 6 to make sure the variable amount of the retraining interval does not get too large. The split between $\mathcal{D}_{train}$ and $\mathcal{D}_{test}$ was set to 0.9/0.1.

We evaluated 20 repetitions with different, fixed random seeds. Each repetition was limited to 80000 timesteps. The production phase was limited to 5000 timesteps, therefore, once the algorithm reaches production, it continues to run for another 5000 timesteps.

As a simple baseline, we used a naive Random Forest Classifier (RF) with sklearn-default parameters. The rest of the algorithm remains the same, therefore instead of TPOT, RF instances were trained.

5.2 Results

In order to give an idea how the overall procedure behaves over time, a single repetition is depicted in Fig. 1. The graph shows the behaviour of TPOT over the course of the execution. *Single Component* refers to the scoring that is done after a component broke, smoothed over 50 steps. *Current TPOT* and *Newly Trained TPOT* show the scores for the predictions on $\mathcal{D}_{test}$ in Line 7 and Line 8 from Algorithm 3. Figure 2 shows a similar experiment using RF classifiers.

We evaluated the balanced accuracy for all components broke during the production phase. As explained earlier, the idea of the balanced accuracy is to compensate the class imbalance in the dataset: In a worst-case scenario, the simple, non-balanced accuracy score can show quite good results when the ML algorithm simply classifies all incoming samples as the majority class, as the (wrong predictions) for the minority class simply have a unsignificant influence on the result. If the production phase was not reached, the last 5000 timesteps of the optimization phase were used. A mean balanced accuracy of 0.865 ± 0.047 was reached by the TPOT-based approach, the RF runs achieved values of 0.816 ± 0.027. The optimization phase of the former takes an average of 44829 timesteps, while the latter takes an average of 67741 timesteps. As the data appears to be not normally distributed according to a performed Shapiro-Wilk-test, both evaluated measurements were tested on significance using a Wilcoxon-rank-sum-test. It showed that the TPOT-based approach was able to reach a significantly better performance than the RF (with a p-value of 0.00043). Furthermore, it took significantly less timesteps to reach the production phase (with a p-value smaller than 0.00001).

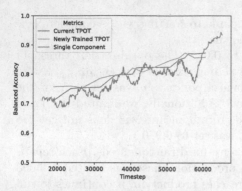

Fig. 1. A single TPOT-based run   **Fig. 2.** A single RF-based run

5.3   Discussion

The results show that our approach is indeed able to achieve an acceptable prediction quality in a comparable amount of time. However, as the naive RF-classifier also reaches quite comparable results, one cannot necessarily state that the utilization of an AutoML framework intuitively leads to a superior performance. Rather, one can suspect that the chosen dataset is of quite simple structure, therefore, the RF-classifier is able to learn it without sophisticated preprocessing steps.

The Azure AI Predictive Maintenance Dataset is used in various other ML-related research work on PdM. In order to give an idea what performances are possible with manually optimized ML pipelines in general, a brief overview on suitable references is given in the following. Gęca [5] investigated several ML algorithms on the dataset. Various preprocessing (such as calculating statistical measures and including them in the data, as well as normalizing the whole dataset) was conducted. The labeling was done similar to our approach, a prediction window of 24 h was used. Most of the algorithm evaluated were able to reach an accuracy of over 0.99, with a Gradient boosting machine reaching 0.9993. Similar results were achieved by Hrnjica et. al. [7]. An accuracy of 0.948 was reached by their approach for the first machine type, also using 24 h as a prediction window and a gradient boosting manchine. However, a direct comparison of these results to our approach must be taken with caution: First of all, there is a quite obvious methodological difference between iterative online learning and an offline learning setting, when taking the amount of data a learner can use into account. Besides, both papers use a different prediction horizon. Furthermore, they do not use the balanced accuracy, which we do in order to compensate the class imbalance in the dataset. However, they provide solid precision and recall values, which at least allows the assumption that their approaches are able to deal with the class imbalance properly.

6   Conclusion and Outlook

In this paper, we presented a novel approach on learning to predict disturbances of physical nature in Organic Computing systems, or, to be more precise, in the SuOC controlled by an OC-based CM. We motivated the advantages of AutoML-methodologies for such an use-case over ML-approaches used in existing OC-research so far. We introduced and explained our TPOT-based approach and evaluated it with a simple Smart Factory-simulation scenario. We showed that our approach is indeed able to learn to predict physical disturbances in an automated manner, with suitable prediction quality and better than a simple random forest-based approach. However, taking existing research work using the Azure PdM dataset into account, it can be suspected that a significantly better prediction quality could be possible–at least under the assumption, that a balanced accuracy score for both works shows a similar performance. A In order to investigate if the results from these papers are indeed as good as they appear, it is necessary to manually build and optimize a suitable ML pipeline using the balanced accuracy as a scorer. By doing so, it would be possible to assess how well the AutoML-based methodology performance compared to what is generally possible for the dataset.

As a next step, we plan to evaluate the overall concept using other AutoML-frameworks as well as Neural Architecture Search–based frameworks like AutoKeras. Furthermore, it is of interest to evaluate our approach using other datasets from the broader domain of PdM. Especially more complex dataset than the one used in the evaluation provided here will be necessary to investigate if the overall methodology can benefit from AutoML-based approaches. Hereby, a notable focus could lie on noise or wrong sensor readings. Besides, we plan to investigate how the parameters of our own methodology as well as the parametrisation of TPOT (or any other AutoML-framework we employ in the future) affects the overall prediction quality. Another interesting question is how the approach deals with an upcoming concept drift [16]: Intuitively, the continuous assessment in the production phase would lead to more frequent trainings if the existing pipelines increasingly fail on novel, drifted data. This would be a quite interesting aspect, as it can be expected that OC-related real world scenarios, due to their approach to adapt to changes, would involve some sort of drift. Another interesting aspect would be a further investigation of the actual pipelines generated by TPOT in terms analyzing if e.g. common patterns or algorithms are evolved. Finally, the evaluation in this work relates to a quite optimistic real-world setting: The (internal) sensor data from components in a SuOC might not always be reliable. Accordingly, additional methodologies for validating the information gathered for the AutoML-algorithms might be necessary. This would include mechanisms to actually identify already disturbed components in a reliable manner, in order to provide a correct labeling for the learning process.

References

1. Banzhaf, W., Nordin, P., Keller, R.E., Francone, F.D.: Genetic Programming: An Introduction: on the Automatic Evolution of Computer Programs and its Applications. Morgan Kaufmann Publishers Inc., Burlington (1998)

2. Batista, G.E., Prati, R.C., Monard, M.C.: A study of the behavior of several methods for balancing machine learning training data. ACM SIGKDD Explor. Newsl **6**(1), 20–29 (2004)
3. Butz, M.V., Wilson, S.W.: An algorithmic description of XCS. Soft. Comput. **6**(3), 144–153 (2002)
4. Carvalho, T.P., Soares, F.A., Vita, R., Francisco, R.D.P., Basto, J.P., Alcalá, S.G.: A systematic literature review of machine learning methods applied to predictive maintenance. Comput. Ind. Eng. **137**, 106024 (2019)
5. Gęca, J.: Performance comparison of machine learning algotihms for predictive maintenance. Informatyka, Automatyka, Pomiary w Gospodarce i Ochronie Środowiska 10 (2020)
6. Görlich-Bucher, M.: Dealing with hardware-related disturbances in organic computing systems. In: INFORMATIK 2019. Gesellschaft für Informatik eV (2019)
7. Hrnjica, B., Softic, S.: Explainable AI in manufacturing: a predictive maintenance case study. In: Lalic, B., Majstorovic, V., Marjanovic, U., von Cieminski, G., Romero, D. (eds.) APMS 2020. IAICT, vol. 592, pp. 66–73. Springer, Cham (2020). https://doi.org/10.1007/978-3-030-57997-5_8
8. Lemaître, G., Nogueira, F., Aridas, C.K.: Imbalanced-learn: a python toolbox to tackle the curse of imbalanced datasets in machine learning. J. Mach. Learn. Res. **18**(17), 1–5 (2017). http://jmlr.org/papers/v18/16-365
9. Müller-Schloer, C., Tomforde, S.: Organic Computing-Technical Systems for Survival in the Real World. Springer, Cham (2017)
10. Olson, R.S., Bartley, N., Urbanowicz, R.J., Moore, J.H.: Evaluation of a tree-based pipeline optimization tool for automating data science. In: Proceedings of the Genetic and Evolutionary Computation Conference 2016, pp. 485–492. GECCO 2016, ACM, New York, NY, USA (2016)
11. Pedregosa, F., et al.: Scikit-learn: machine learning in Python. J. Mach. Learn. Res. **12**, 2825–2830 (2011)
12. Schmitt, J., Roth, M., Kiefhaber, R., Kluge, F., Ungerer, T.: Using an automated planner to control an organic middleware. In: 2011 IEEE Fifth International Conference on Self-Adaptive and Self-Organizing Systems, pp. 71–78. IEEE (2011)
13. Stein, A.: Reaction learning. In: Organic Computing - Technical Systems for Survival in the Real World, pp. 287–328. Springer (2017)
14. Tomforde, S., Kantert, J., Müller-Schloer, C., Bödelt, S., Sick, B.: Comparing the effects of disturbances in self-adaptive systems - a generalised approach for the quantification of robustness. In: Nguyen, N.T., Kowalczyk, R., van den Herik, J., Rocha, A.P., Filipe, J. (eds.) Transactions on Computational Collective Intelligence XXVIII. LNCS, vol. 10780, pp. 193–220. Springer, Cham (2018). https://doi.org/10.1007/978-3-319-78301-7_9
15. Tomforde, S., et al.: Observation and control of organic systems. In: Müller-Schloer, C., Schmeck, H., Ungerer, T. (eds.) Organic Computing-A Paradigm Shift for Complex Systems, vol. 1, pp. 325–338. Springer, Basel (2011). https://doi.org/10.1007/978-3-0348-0130-0_21
16. Wang, S., Schlobach, S., Klein, M.: What is concept drift and how to measure it? In: Cimiano, P., Pinto, H.S. (eds.) EKAW 2010. LNCS (LNAI), vol. 6317, pp. 241–256. Springer, Heidelberg (2010). https://doi.org/10.1007/978-3-642-16438-5_17
17. Zöller, M.A., Huber, M.F.: Benchmark and survey of automated machine learning frameworks. J. Artif. Intell. Res. **70**, 409–472 (2021)

Self-adaptive Diagnosis
and Reconfiguration in ADNA-Based
Organic Computing

Utkarsh Raj[1]([✉]), Simon Meckel[1], Aleksey Koschowoj[2], Mathias Pacher[2],
Roman Obermaisser[1], and Uwe Brinkschulte[2]

[1] University of Siegen, Siegen, Germany
utkarsh.raj@uni-siegen.de
[2] Goethe University of Frankfurt a.M., Frankfurt a.M., Germany

Abstract. The increasing openness and dynamism in embedded systems necessitate the continuous advancement of diagnostic methodologies, particularly in contexts where safety is paramount and system operability must persist despite faults or failures. The implementation of Organic Computing offers substantial benefits to these intricate, dynamic systems, such as decreased development effort, enhanced adaptability, and resilience. Nonetheless, safety-critical systems that must preserve functionality amid failure by maintaining a fail-operational status require additional characteristics. This paper presents approaches such as adaptive diagnostics employing neural networks for fault detection and localization, adaptive probing for fault identification, and strategies for degraded performance states and system reconfiguration to circumvent complete service disruption when computational resources are insufficient.

Keywords: Organic computing · artificial DNA · adaptive diagnosis

1 Introduction

To manage the growing complexity in distributed systems, bioinspired techniques like self-organization and self-healing have been introduced through the research focus of organic computing [13]. This approach offers significant benefits such as reduced development efforts and increased adaptability and robustness. However, for safety-critical systems, it is essential to maintain their ability to function in situations where faults or failures may arise. To ensure the preservation of these systems' core functionalities, supplementary features are needed to safeguard system performance even when confronted with the failure of non-redundant system resources. This paper introduces the architecture and components for combining application diagnosis with ADNA-based Organic Computing [3].

The ADNA of an application contains the entire blueprint of the target system on each processing element. Based on this blueprint, the system builds itself at runtime and adapts autonomously to changes in the computation environment.

G. Goumas et al. (Eds.): ARCS 2023, LNCS 13949, pp. 63–77, 2023.
https://doi.org/10.1007/978-3-031-42785-5_5

Task distribution and management in distributed computational systems require dynamic control to allow runtime fault tolerance. ADNA-based organic computing relies on Artificial Hormone System (AHS) to distribute and configure tasks on different processing elements in the distributed system [4]. This paper develops the components used for diagnosis, including state variables for tasks and processing elements; adaptive diagnosis using neural networks for fault detection and fault localization on application and hardware layer; adaptive probing as a second layer of diagnosis for fault identification; degraded application state to avoid total service failure when not enough compute resource is available; reconfiguration to allow activation of backup ADNA with a different logical model to ensure service when the computational resource is severely limited.

Section 3 describes the diagnosis architecture used for fault tolerance in ADNA-based organic computing. It consists of (1) *LocDiag* – handles local PE faults and (2) *SysDiag* – handles preventive fault tolerance of PEs and complex faults arising from interdependencies of tasks. Section 4 introduces the components of adaptive diagnosis for detecting and localizing faults in the application running atop organic computing middleware, and active probing for fault identification; this saves communication and computational resources compared to pre-planned probing. Active probing allows *SysDiag* to select probes to collect further relevant information about faults in tasks and PEs with a high confidence score (as calculated by the neural networks). Section 5 introduces the metric Quality of Service (QoS) for a generalized application, which involves maximizing service availability and minimizing critical failures in the application. Section 6 introduces reconfiguration when insufficient compute resource is available. Section 7 presents the use case of Explorer Robot to demonstrate degraded service and reconfiguration, which are not inherently handled by Organic Computing.

2 Related Work

In the state of the art, numerous active fault-diagnosis techniques exist. Moreover, some methods for automatic generation of diagnostic mechanisms have been described recently. [11] summarizes the intelligent fault diagnosis methods and presents the roadmap for end-to-end diagnosis. [16] utilizes deep reinforcement learning algorithms to train agents for maintenance in Internet of Things (IoT) networks.

[9] provides an introduction to fault-diagnosis systems, including classification and inference methods. Classification methods consist of techniques such as pattern recognition, statistical classification, and artificial intelligence-based approaches, such as neural network classifiers. These approaches are designed to distinguish and categorize faults based on their unique characteristics. Inference methods, on the other hand, involve drawing conclusions about the underlying causes of the faults. These methods may involve the use of binary and approximate reasoning, as well as more advanced techniques that leverage predicate logic or fuzzy logic. By combining the insights provided by classification and inference methods, a system diagnosis can more effectively identify and address faults in complex systems [10].

3   Diagnosis Architecture

In most embedded applications, tasks only interact via messages. The message-based communication consists of sending and requesting data from other tasks in the application. Thus, any runtime application diagnosis must rely only on the exchange of messages. Figure 1 shows the diagnosis architecture where *SysDiag* runs only on one of the PEs in the system, unlike *LocDiag* and AHS that run on every PE. Other components required for application diagnosis include PE logs, task logs, alarms for critical state changes, probes, and global states for critical system-variables.

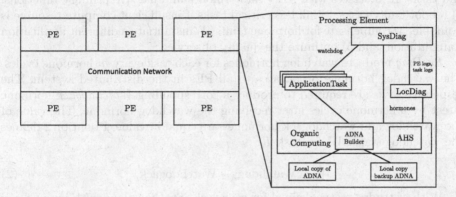

Fig. 1. Diagnosis architecture for ADNA-based organic computing

3.1   Local Diagnosis

LocDiag is a lightweight program that runs along with the AHS on each PE in the distributed system. *LocDiag* extends the current AHS to handle hormone-level faults and allows for more robust fault handling. At runtime, *LocDiag* monitors variables that affect the performance of the PE and that can predict imminent failures (e.g., local temperature, radiation level, and memory errors). In response to these monitored variables, *LocDiag* produces corresponding hormones to ensure tasks migrate away from faulty PEs. Equation 1 shows the relationship between the produced suppressor and the variable of interest, which is T_t. When the variable is higher than the threshold (T_{Th}), the suppressor produced follows a PID relationship, or otherwise, it exponentially decays to zero.

$$Sp_T(t) = \begin{cases} K \cdot (T_t - T_{Th}) + S \cdot (T_t - T_{Th})^2 \\ \quad +P \cdot Sp_T(t-1), \text{ if } T_t \geq T_{Th} \\ a \cdot e^{-r} \cdot Sp_T(t-1), \text{ otherwise} \end{cases} \quad (1)$$

In addition, *LocDiag* performs rule-based checks and threshold checks to contain hormone faults and to limit error propagation to other PEs. It ensures that the values of suppressors, accelerators, and modified eager values for tasks are correct before being transmitted. *LocDiag* acts like a communication guardian responsible for checking hormone values received and sent by the PE. It is further responsible for generating a local log file consisting of local runtime variables associated with the PE and the locally running tasks; this log is periodically sent to the *SysDiag*.

3.2   System Diagnosis

SysDiag handles complex faults arising from inter-dependencies between PEs and tasks. It interfaces with AHS via hormones and has five primary functions: 1) reboot faulty tasks, 2) kill less critical tasks if insufficient compute resource is available, 3) compensate for hormone faults, 4) instantiate a different application configuration, and 5) optimize the quality of service.

SysDiag produces watchdog hormones for each task every m hormone cycles. The watchdog hormone propagates to all PEs in the distributed system. The respective tasks are required to produce a corresponding *Watchdogack* hormone latest by p hormone cycles after receiving the watchdog hormone. The value of the watchdog and watchdogack hormones are equal in value. Equation 2 defines the watchdog status W_i for task T_i.

$$W_i = \text{Watchdog}_i - \text{Watchdogack}_i \tag{2}$$

With watchdog status defined for each task, *SysDiag* along with instances of *LocDiag* monitor the status of the task TS_i for the task T_i, defined by Eq. 3.

$$TS_i = \begin{cases} 1, & \text{if } W_i = 0 \text{ after } p \text{ hormone cycles} \\ 0, & \text{else.} \end{cases} \tag{3}$$

TS_i equal to 1 translates to the task T_i being operational. When $TS_i = 0$, the task is supposed to be non-responsive, and therefore, the respective negator hormone is produced by *SysDiag* to reboot the task.

3.3   Alarms

Specific alarms are required to detect the causality of events in case of multiple faults in the system. *LocDiag* generates alarms local to a PE, and *SysDiag* generates system-level alarms. The alarms are associated with state changes necessary for diagnosis by event correlation. The alarms emitted by *LocDiag* do not propagate to other PEs. The global alarms generated by *SysDiag* disseminate and allow all tasks to be aware of global faults in the systems, which allows the application to implement fault-tolerant mechanisms.

Alarms generated by *LocDiag* include:

- PE temperature or radiation crosses threshold values
- Input buffer overflow for a local running task

- Mean current and mean voltage cross threshold values
- Peripherals unreachable or non-responsive
- Missing suppressor hormones
- Abnormal monitor hormone values

Alarms generated by *SysDiag* include:

- PE flagged to be faulty
- Task flagged to be faulty
- Not enough compute resources available to run all critical tasks
- Instantiating different configurations for the application
- Alarms generated by Probes.

3.4   Probes

A probe functions as a diagnostic tool, consisting of a test transaction designed
to assess the performance of specific components within a system. By selecting
suitable probes and analyzing their outcomes, diagnosis tasks can effectively
detect issues and provide insights into the system's overall functionality. For
example, the *traceroute* and *ping* commands are two of the most popular probing
tools used in Linux for network availability [1].

Adaptive probing presented in [15] is used by *SysDiag* as the second layer
of diagnosis. To achieve fault localization, it is required to have a set of probes
that the *SysDiag* can deploy to assess various faults in the distributed system.
The probing can be done on 1) application level, 2) task cluster level, 3) task
level, 4) PE level.

Application-level probing involves sending a request at the application level
and monitoring the outputs as the request flows through the logical model
from one task to another. The data collected during application-level probing
involves measuring the variables of interest involving individual tasks and PEs.
Application-level probing is costly as it involves the required time dedicated to
diagnosis where it might not be possible to provide the requisite service. Thus,
an application-level probe must be deployed when low-cost probes are insufficient to collect the desired information for fault localization. Task cluster-level
probing involves probing a set of tasks that provide a sub-service. Thus, during
the diagnostic probing of the cluster, the sub-service is unavailable. Task level
and PE level probes are the cheapest as they form the smallest unit for fault
localization. Furthermore, these probes can be designed with a predefined set
of inputs, and their outputs can be monitored along with the associated state
variables.

4   Adaptive Diagnosis

In most embedded applications, tasks only interact via messages. The message-
based communication consists of sending and requesting data from other tasks

and communicating with *SysDiag*. A processing element in the distributed system is assumed to be a fault containment region. Each task and PE is considered the unit of fault, i.e., a task or a PE is deemed faulty as a whole. Task dependency can lead to error propagation, and thus the logical model has to be considered for the detection of faulty tasks; in contrast, a hardware fault in a PE is assumed to be independent of faults in other PEs.

4.1 Processing Element Diagnosis

A state vector of a PE X_i in the distributed system is given by the vector P_i defined by Eq. 4

$$P_i = \left[T, M_{\text{cpu}}, V_{\text{cpu}}, M_{\text{vol}}, V_{\text{vol}}, M_{\text{cur}}, V_{\text{cur}}, S_{\text{p1}}, S_{\text{p2}}\right]^T, \tag{4}$$

where T is the mean temperature, M_{cpu} is the mean CPU usage, V_{cpu} is the variance in CPU usage, M_{vol} is the mean voltage, V_{vol} is the variance in voltage, M_{cur} is the mean current, V_{cur} is the variance in current, S_{p1} is the status of the first peripheral, and S_{p2} is the status of the second peripheral. The peripherals can be, for example, a GPU or a flash storage device. The state of a peripheral N (S_{pN}) is mapped to a number from the set $\{-1, [0,1]\}$. $S_{pN} \in [0,1]$ reflects the peripheral's utilization and its diagnostic signals, whereas if $S_{pN} = -1$, then either the peripheral is missing on a PE or is not to be considered for fault classification.

The state vector of a processing element is generated using the local PE data collected by the *LocDiag*, which is periodically sent to *SysDiag* as logs. Given the state vector of the processing elements, the problem reduces to training a binary classifier to identify faulty processing elements. A deep neural network [5] with sigmoid activation for the output layer and cross-entropy for the loss function serves as the classifier. In a heterogeneous system, the required number of binary classifiers equals the number of different types of PEs (in the system).

The output of the deep neural network (Confidence Score) lies in the range $[0,1]$, which is used by *SysDiag* to produce suppressor hormones proportional to the network's output; this ensures that processing elements likely to be faulty take up fewer tasks or offer taken tasks to other PEs in the distributed system.

4.2 Task Diagnosis

Faults in processing elements are assumed to be independent of each other, however, the same is not valid for tasks in the application. Here, the interdependencies of tasks need to be considered by the diagnosis model for which a Long Short-term Memory (LSTM) [6] network is suitable. The state of a task (T_j) is defined by Eq. 5

$$S_j = \left[M_{\text{TS}}, V_{\text{TS}}, I_{\text{AT}}, I_{\text{B}}, O_j\right]^T, \tag{5}$$

where M_{TS} is the mean time to service, V_{TS} is the variance in time to service, I_{AT} is the input inter-arrival time, I_{B} is input-buffer free size, and O_j is the feature vector associated with output of task T_j. The tasks running on a PE forward the necessary information to the local instance of the *LocDiag*, which forwards the collected information in a log to *SysDiag*. This reduces the diagnosis communication load on the shared network between the PEs, as each task on a PE does not directly communicate with the *SysDiag*.

LSTM neural networks are suited for processing sequences of data, and the logical model of the application defines such a sequence. Since a task down the logical model is affected by an upstream task, using the LSTM network traditionally used to process language-related problems like machine translation and speech recognition is desirable [17]. The LSTM network takes as input the state vector $(S_t(T_j))$ of the tasks arranged sequentially as represented in the logical model. The LSTM network produces a confidence score for each task in the range $[0, 1]$, highlighting the probability of the task being faulty. The training data required to train the network depends on the logical model and the specific application. For each application, data needs to be generated using fault injection and simulation, and once the network is trained, the inference can be made during the run time. *SysDiag* produces suppressor hormones for the tasks depending on the confidence score produced by the LSTM network for the respective tasks. Thereafter, tasks with high confidence scores can be further investigated using probes in the second stage of diagnosis.

4.3 Probing Based Diagnosis

Probes are end-to-end test transactions that collect information about the performance of various devices in the distributed system. In organic computing, a probe is a program initiated by the *SysDiag*. The PEs and tasks with high confidence scores (outputs of neural networks) are selected for probing. The choice of probes can vary depending on the device/task being probed. For example, a probe to confirm a faulty sensor might differ from a probe to confirm a faulty PE. Further, a heterogeneous distributed system consists of different types of PEs, for example, PEs with general digital processing cores, analog cores, or memory cores. Probes are only run-on demand rather than periodically. Thus, it allows designing probes to collect all necessary device/task information to detect the type of fault and reaffirm that components are indeed faulty.

SysDiag uses multi-level probing [15], where the first level of probes are lightweight programs to collect basic information. *SysDiag* uses the data collected by the first-level probes to send more specialized probes to gather more details about the nature and type of the fault. Figure 2 exemplifies the above multi-level probing.

5 Quality of Service

An application running on the distributed system might have a variable of interest that represents the application's quality of service. We define the quality of service of an application as the availability of critical tasks. Thus, the goal is to

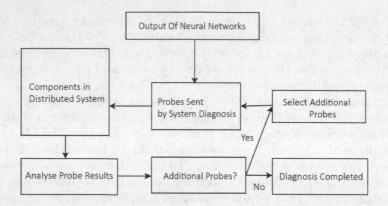

Fig. 2. Control flow for probe-based diagnosis.

maximize the availability of the set of critical tasks necessary for providing core system functionality and to avoid critical system failures, especially when insufficient compute resource is available to run all application tasks. [7] presents the extension of AHS where it is possible to assign each task a priority. [8] uses the priority extension of AHS to allow service degradation by stopping low-priority tasks when insufficient computation power is available for all application tasks.

Consider a logical model of the application to be composed of a n tasks, S_A is defined as the set of all application tasks,

$$S_A = \{T_1, T_2, T_3, T_4, ..., T_n\}. \tag{6}$$

The subset of S_A, CT_A denotes the set of critical tasks crucial to the application such that any of these tasks being non-responsive is equivalent to a critical failure. For example, consider the below set of tasks to be in the set CT_A

$$CT_A = \{T_2, T_5, T_6, T_8, ..., T_m\}. \tag{7}$$

Each task T_i has an associated criticality score given as CS_i. The parent tasks have at least the same or higher criticality score as the maximum of CS_i amongst all children tasks. The tasks in the set CT_A have the highest CS_i. With this, the quality of service is defined as minimizing the Service Parameter SP given by Eq. 8

$$SP = \sum_{i=1}^{i=n} m \cdot CS_i + m_{cf} \cdot P_{cf}, \tag{8}$$

herein m is the number of hormone cycles task T_i not available, P_{cf} is the hyperparameter associated with critical failure, m_{cf} is the number of hormone cycles the system is in critical failure mode, and n is the number of tasks in the set S_A.

The subset of tasks in the set S_A might be various runtime services the application provides, each sub-service being of varying criticality. For example, in a car, one sub-service might be associated with the entertainment system, while other critical sub-services might be associated with the anti-lock braking system. Thus, in events where enough PEs have failed in the system such that not all sub-services can run, it is desirable to deallocate the compute resources dedicated to the less critical sub-services and allocate them to tasks providing the critical sub-service. [14] details application in a dynamic environment with sub-services where ADNA can merge at runtime to form a new system.

6   Application Reconfiguration

Application reconfiguration is required when insufficient compute resource is available to run all critical tasks. Different application configurations are defined by different sets of ADNAs stored in each PE in the distributed system. The logical model described in the ADNA for a given configuration might differ and require higher/lower compute resource requirements. When the compute resource falls below a threshold such that the currently active configuration no longer provides the desired service, a different configuration (i.e., ADNA) consisting of a lighter version of the application needs to be instantiated. This application configuration might consist of bare-bones implementation of the service to avoid catastrophic failures or to provide the best service possible with the remaining compute resources. For each configuration, the set of critical tasks CT_A should always be available even in situations where not enough computing resource is available to run all tasks S_A in the given configuration.

6.1   Compute Resource Unit

Compute Resource Unit (CRU) is the unit to measure the compute resource available on the PEs and that required by the application tasks. Each PE's available compute resource is defined at design time and is an integer multiple of CRU. In a heterogeneous system, different PEs might differ in their available compute resources. Thus, defining compute resource as an integer multiple of CRU helps map requirements of tasks to be the set of available PEs.

SysDiag monitors the available compute resource (CA_i) for each task in CT_A for a given configuration which is defined by Eq. 9,

$$CA_i = a + \sum_{l=1}^{i=t} \lfloor C_l / K_i \rfloor \tag{9}$$

where $a = 1$, if the task T_i is running, otherwise 0. t is the number of PEs suited to run the task T_i; C_l is the compute resource, not dedicated to any task in the set CT_A on PE_l, measured as a multiple of CRU; K_i is the compute resource required to run task T_i measured as a multiple of CRU. In the above equation, the floor function ensures that when none of the PEs have enough free compute resources to instantiate the task T_i, the summation results in zero. Thus, when a task belonging to set CT_A is not running ($a = 0$), and none of the PEs have free compute resources (either unallocated or running a task, not in the set CT_A) then CA_i for the task T_i evaluates to zero.

$SysDiag$ decides to perform reconfiguration when CA_i evaluates to zero for any task T_i in CT_A. To avoid reconfiguration in the case of transient failures, $SysDiag$ waits for a predefined number of hormone cycles before instantiating reconfiguration. Since each application configuration might have a different set of critical tasks with varying compute resource requirements, each set of ADNA stores the associated compute resource required to run its set of critical tasks.

7   Use Case - Explorer Robot

The use case for quality-of-service optimization and reconfiguration in situations where not enough compute resource is available is demonstrated via a use case of an Explorer Robot set in an office environment, where the robot's objective is to explore the environment while avoiding stationary and moving obstacles. The environment and robot are modeled in Coppelia Simulation distributed by Coppelia Robotics, Ltd. [12].

7.1   Physical Model

The robot has sixteen proximity sensors spread all around the robot, with two sensors on either side, six proximity sensors in the front, and six on the back. In addition, the robot has a differential drive, i.e., two motors drive each wheel independently. The differential drive allows the rotational speed of each wheel to be independently controlled, allowing for a range of motion, including in-place rotation.

Figure 3 shows the physical hardware model of the Explorer Robot with four general-purpose processing elements connected to proximity sensors and drive motors via the System Bus. The PE Bus connects the four processing elements allowing for inter-processor communication. In addition, the system bus enables each PE to access every sensor and to set the rotational speed of the left and right wheel motors.

PEs are identical and have a computational resource of 2 CRU each. The available CRU decides the viability of the ADNA configuration to run as intended. Therefore, at any point in time, the total available CRU must be higher or equal to the CRU required to run all tasks in a configuration to avoid degraded performance or outright service failure. $SysDiag$ monitors available CRU and performs reconfiguration when this falls below the threshold required to run all critical tasks in the current configuration.

7.2   Logical Model

The application involves three following significant steps. The first involves processing proximity sensor data to detect obstacles and the distance of the detected obstacle from the robot. The second step involves planning the direction and

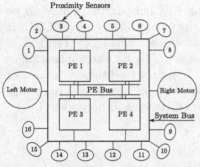

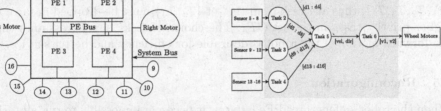

Fig. 3. Physical model of Explorer Robot

Fig. 4. Logical model of Explorer Robot

velocity of the robot based on the sixteen sensors' data. The third step is to set the rotational speeds of the wheel motors to achieve the desired robot motion as planned in step 2. Figure 4 shows the logical model of the robot. Each task in the set $\{T_1, T_2, T_3, T_4\}$ interfaces with sensor hardware, calculates the distance of detected obstacles, and forwards the array of distances to task 5, which is responsible for path planning. Task 5 decides the robot's direction and speed, and sends the velocity and direction data to task 6, which controls the motors connected to the two wheels, enabling the Explorer Robot to explore the environment.

7.3   Initial Configuration

The primary ADNA of the application consists of six tasks. A copy of the primary ADNA is stored on each processing element and is used by the AHS to perform the initial configuration. AHS distributes six tasks to four processing elements. Each PE is equally suited to run any of the six tasks, as there are no constraints on the task suitability to a PE.

The computational resource requirement of each task in the primary ADNA is 1 CRU each; thus, each PE can run at most two tasks. Therefore, the system has a redundancy of one PE allowing organic computing to handle up to one PE failure without adversely affecting the application's quality of service. For example, after one initial configuration, PE-2 and PE-4 take one task each, and thus they have 1 free CRU available, which can be used to redistribute tasks in case of failure of either PE-1 or PE-3, each of which runs two tasks.

7.4   Degraded Performance

The Explorer Robot can tolerate a permanent failure of one PE without impacting the performance and quality of service since organic computing inherently redistributes tasks in case of PE failures via the hormone loop that runs in the local instance of AHS on each PE.

In a failure situation, when two out of four PEs fail, six tasks have to be redistributed to the two operational PEs, but since one PE has only 2 CRU, it can only run a maximum of any two tasks from the set $\{T_1, T_2, T_3, T_4, T_5, T_6\}$. Thus, critical tasks need to be prioritized. The set CT_A for the application is $\{T_1, T_2, T_5, T_6\}$; thus any task from the set $\{T_3, T_4\}$ must be dropped in favor of higher priority tasks in the set CT_A. The choice of tasks in CT_A assumes that the forward motion of the robot is desirable for efficiency and better service.

7.5   Reconfiguration

When the robot suffers three PEs failures, it becomes impossible to run all tasks in the set CT_A. Therefore, it is required to trigger a reconfiguration, initiating operational PEs to load the backup ADNA with a logical model that provides the minimum service level and requires computation resources less than or equal to what is available. Figure 5 shows such a logical model of backup ADNA for the Explorer Robot. It consists of two tasks. Task 1B is responsible for processing the six frontal sensors (sensors 2–7) to detect obstacles and calculate the distance of detected obstacles from the robot. In addition, task 1B forwards the distance value of detected obstacles to task 2B, which uses the Braitenberg algorithm [2] to calculate the velocity of the wheels. This configuration is not as sophisticated as the one denoted by the logical model in Fig. 4. Yet, it allows the robot to operate with one PE, which is desirable when fail-operational is required.

The robot's motion is limited in this configuration as it cannot move backward because of no visibility of obstacles behind it. Furthermore, the left and right turns are constrained due to a lack of side visibility. The total CRU needed to run all tasks in this configuration is equal to the CRU capacity of one PE. Thus, the backup ADNA allows the robot to stay operational with only one functioning PE.

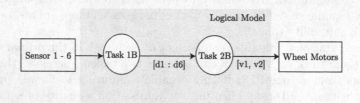

Fig. 5. Logical model of backup ADNA

7.6   Results and Evaluation

Simulation is performed for fifteen minutes in each configuration to evaluate the robot's objective function to maximize exploration and minimize collision. Figure 6 presents a scatter plot of the robot's position during the simulation.

The robot's movement is limited within the area bounded by the x-coordinate $[-2.2, 2.2]$ and y-coordinate $[-2.2, 2.2]$. In the primary configuration, the robot uses a randomized turning angle in either direction to cover the maximum area. It successfully avoids most obstacles and suffers collisions at the rate of 1.2 collisions/min. The major causes of such collisions are moving objects colliding with the robot's side where insufficient space is available to perform speedy maneuvers. As shown in Fig. 6, Explorer Robot covers most of the area not blocked by obstacles (corresponding to the white gaps in the scatter plot).

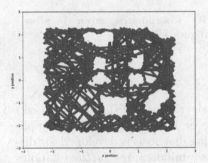 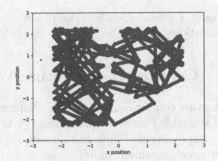

Fig. 6. Coordinates covered in primary configuration

Fig. 7. Coordinates covered in degraded configuration

When two PEs fail, the system has to enter degraded performance mode, where only the front eight sensors are used to plan the robot's motion, thus reducing the rate of exploration. Figure 7 shows the area covered by the Explorer Robot in degraded performance mode during the ten minutes of simulation. It is observed that the area covered is significantly less than in Fig. 6. The observation is explained by limited randomness in the robot's motion due to limited visibility. The collision rate also increases to 2.1 collisions/min, as shown in Fig. 8.

When three processing elements fail, the backup ADNA configuration is initialized, and the Explorer Robot uses only six frontal sensors to plan its motion. The robot uses the Braintenberg algorithm for collision avoidance. Figure 9 shows the area covered by the robot in this configuration, which is severely limited compared to the primary configuration. The collision rate increases from 1.2 collisions/min in the primary configuration to 2.9 collisions/min. This configuration's service quality is limited, but it avoids service availability failure as would have happened if the classical organic computing principles were not extended with degraded performance and reconfiguration.

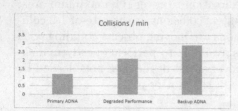

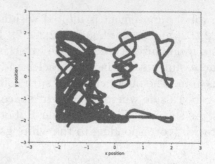

Fig. 8. Collisions/min in different configurations

Fig. 9. Coordinates covered after reconfiguration

8   Conclusion and Future Work

Organic computing handles PEs failures and task crashes by redistributing tasks to available PEs in the distributed system. However, it does not provide the application diagnosis. Thus, in this paper self-adapting diagnosis is developed for distributed systems running organic computing as a middleware. *SysDiag* handles faults and failures on the application and global levels. In addition, *LocDiag* is responsible for diagnosing faults in local PE and cooperating with *SysDiag* via sending diagnosis data and locally monitored variables in terms of periodic logs. The Explorer Robot use case demonstrates that self-adapting application diagnosis improves the reliability of the application running on organic computing middleware.

Future work comprises the development and implementation of the diagnostic models and algorithms based on the semantic description of the application and using the semantics to trigger reconfiguration without explicitly storing backup ADNA.

Acknowledgment. This work was supported by the DFG research grants BR 2024/25-1 and OB 384/11-1.

References

1. Linux User's Manual (2022). Accessed 28 Feb 2023
2. Braitenberg, V.: Vehicles: Experiments in Synthetic Psychology. MIT press, Cambridge (1986)
3. Brinkschulte, U.: An artificial DNA for self-descripting and self-building embedded real-time systems. In: Proceedings of the 2014 IEEE 17th International Symposium on Object/Component-Oriented Real-Time Distributed Computing, pp. 326–333. ISORC 2014, IEEE Computer Society, USA (2014)
4. Brinkschulte, U., Pacher, M., Renteln, A.: An artificial hormone system for self-organizing real-time task allocation in organic middleware. In: Organic Computing. UCS, pp. 261–283. Springer, Heidelberg (2009). https://doi.org/10.1007/978-3-540-77657-4_12

5. Goodfellow, I.J., Bengio, Y., Courville, A.: Deep Learning. MIT Press, Cambridge (2016)
6. Hochreiter, S., Schmidhuber, J.: Long short-term memory. Neural Comput. **9**, 1735–1780 (1997)
7. Hutter, E., Brinkschulte, U.: Towards a priority-based task distribution strategy for an artificial hormone system. In: Brinkmann, A., Karl, W., Lankes, S., Tomforde, S., Pionteck, T., Trinitis, C. (eds.) ARCS 2020. LNCS, vol. 12155, pp. 69–81. Springer, Cham (2020). https://doi.org/10.1007/978-3-030-52794-5_6
8. Hutter, E., Brinkschulte, U.: Handling assignment priorities to degrade systems in self-organizing task distribution. In: 2021 IEEE 24th International Symposium on Real-Time Distributed Computing (ISORC), pp. 132–140 (2021)
9. Isermann, R.: Fault-Diagnosis Systems: An Introduction from Fault Detection to Fault Tolerance. Springer, Heidelberg (2006)
10. Isermann, R.: Fault-Diagnosis Applications: Model-Based Condition Monitoring: Actuators, Drives, Machinery, Plants, Sensors, and Fault-tolerant Systems. Springer, Heidelberg (2011)
11. Lei, Y., Yang, B., Jiang, X., Jia, F., Li, N., Nandi, A.K.: Applications of machine learning to machine fault diagnosis: a review and roadmap. Mech. Syst. Signal Process. **138**, 106587 (2020)
12. Ltd., C.R.: Coppeliasim user manual (2022). https://www.coppeliarobotics.com/helpFiles/index.html. Accessed 20 Feb 2023
13. Müller-Schloer, C., Schmeck, H., Ungerer, T.: Organic Computing - A Paradigm Shift for Complex Systems, Autonomic Systems, vol. 1. Springer, Basel (2011)
14. Pacher, M., Brinkschulte, U.: Monitoring of an artificial DNA in dynamic environments. In: Wehrmeister, M.A., Kreutz, M., Götz, M., Henkler, S., Pimentel, A.D., Rettberg, A. (eds.) Analysis, Estimations, and Applications of Embedded Systems. IESS 2019. IFIP Advances in Information and Communication Technology, vol. 576, pp. 167–178. Springer, Cham (2023)
15. Rish, I., et al.: Adaptive diagnosis in distributed systems. IEEE Trans. Neural Netw. **16**, 1088–1109 (2005)
16. Stamatakis, G., Pappas, N., Fragkiadakis, A., Traganitis, A.: Autonomous maintenance in IoT networks via AOI-driven deep reinforcement learning. In: IEEE Conference on Computer Communications Workshops, pp. 1–7 (2021)
17. Yao, L., Guan, Y.: An improved LSTM structure for natural language processing. In: IEEE International Conference of Safety Produce Informatization (IICSPI), pp. 565–569 (2018)

Dependability and Fault Tolerance
(VERFE)

Error Codes in and for Network Steganography

Jörg Keller$^{(\boxtimes)}$ ⓘ and Saskia Langsdorf ⓘ

FernUniversität in Hagen, Hagen, Germany
joerg.keller@fernuni-hagen.de
https://www.fernuni-hagen.de/pv

Abstract. We illustrate the inter-relationship between network steganography and error coding through examples where error codes (correction or erasure codes) are used in steganographic channels and examples where steganographic channels are established in data on which error codes are applied. In particular, we experimentally investigate an existing approach of a steganographic channel in a transmission with error correction code with respect to bandwidth, robustness and detectability, and expand this construction to provide another example of multi-level steganography, i.e., a steganographic channel within a steganographic channel.

Keywords: Error Correcting Block Codes · Erasure Codes · Network Steganography · Covert Channels

1 Introduction

Error codes and steganography both use redundancy in transmitted or stored messages or data to embed additional information, albeit with different purpose. Error codes, under which term we subsume correction and erasure codes, add some redundant bits to a message to enable reconstruction of the original data in the case of modified or lost message bits [4]. In contrast, steganography uses the transmitted data as a cover and exploits redundancy to embed a secret message without destroying the original data [16]. Due to the commonalities, both fields partly use similar techniques, and sometimes even appear in conjunction. This can come in two flavors. Robustness of the secret message, which is affected by loss or modification of bits in the same way as the cover message, can be achieved by error codes. Redundancy provided by error codes for the cover message can be abused to also transmit secret data. However, both fields are researched by largely different communities, so that the intersection of these fields has only received limited interest so far. The combination can also lead to examples of the otherwise rare multi-level steganography [6]: a steganographic message within an error code needs to be protected by another error code, into which a second steganographic message can be embedded.

G. Goumas et al. (Eds.): ARCS 2023, LNCS 13949, pp. 81–93, 2023.
https://doi.org/10.1007/978-3-031-42785-5_6

In the present work, we therefore present a caleidoscope of the use of error codes (both erasure codes and correction codes) in steganography, and the use of steganography in both forms of error codes for cover messages. While part of this work is kind of a survey, yet without claim of completeness or systematic treatment (hence the term caleidoscope), we investigate one idea in more detail and provide experimental results both with respect to steganographic bandwidth, robustness and detectability of the steganographic method. Especially the latter is often neglected, but seems especially necessary as steganographic channels are frequently used for criminal purpose, e.g., in the communication of botnet computers with their command and control server, to avoid detection.

In particular, we make the following contributions:

- Examples of constructions for steganographic channels in error correction codes and erasure codes, and examples of the use of error correction codes and erasure codes in steganographic channels are given.
- A construction from literature [17] of a steganographic channel within a transmission with error correction code is experimentally investigated with respect to steganographic bandwidth, robustness and detectability.
- This construction is expanded to provide another example of multi-level steganography.

The remainder of this paper is organized as follows: Section 2 presents background on error codes and steganography, and discusses related work. Section 3 explains the different approaches how to combine error codes and steganographic channels in different ways. Experimental results on a steganographic channel within error correction codes are presented in Sect. 4. Section 5 concludes and suggests future work.

2   Background

2.1   Error Codes

Forward error correction serves to protect transmission over a noisy channel without necessity of re-transmission or a back channel for acknowledgements. The field of error codes is very large, hence we will focus on block codes for error correction and rateless erasure codes. A good overview of the field is given in [13] on which this subsection is based.

When a data word $w \in \Sigma^k$ over symbol alphabet Σ of size q is transmitted over a noisy channel, some symbols might be modified. Hence, prior to transmission the data word is extended into a codeword $C(w) \in \Sigma^n$ with the help of a block code $C : \Sigma^k \to \Sigma^n$, where $n > k$. Let d be the minimum Hamming distance between any two codewords. Then, as long as fewer than $d/2$ symbol modifications occur during transmission, the received word c' can be successfully corrected into the unique codeword c with minimum Hamming distance to c', and the data word w can be reconstructed by $w = C^{-1}(c)$. The so-called error correction codes (ECC) normally can be arranged such that $C(w) = w, w'$ with

$w' \in \Sigma^{n-k}$. The former part of the codeword is then called data part, the latter is often called parity part. Codes are commonly denoted by a tuple $(n, k, d)_q$, or (n, k) if d is maximum or not known. n/k is called the rate of the code. For $q = 2$, codes are called binary. Examples of popular binary block codes are Hamming codes, Reed-Muller codes and BCH codes.

Erasure codes (over a symbol alphabet Σ of size q) extend the data word of k symbols into an n-symbol code word and allow the reconstruction of the data word as long as a sufficient number of the n symbols are received. Optimal erasure codes only need k of n symbols to reconstruct the data word, while fountain codes, which are near-optimal, can generate an infinite sequence of code symbols and need $(1 + \varepsilon)k$ received symbols to reconstruct the data word with very high probability. For example, for each code symbol to be transmitted, a Luby-Transform (LT) code [15] randomly chooses a degree d, where $1 \leq d \leq k$ according to a given distribution. Then it chooses d (of k) data symbols randomly with equi-distribution, and combines these d data symbols into one code symbol.

Typically, data symbols are bit strings of fixed length, and the combination is bitwise exclusive or. The code symbol is transmitted together with some encoding of the subset that describes which data symbols have been combined, e.g. a k-bit vector.

2.2 Network Steganography

A steganographic transmission hides the transmission of a secret message (also called covert message) within the transmission of an innocent looking message (also called overt or cover message or carrier). Thus, while an encrypted transmission would keep the content of the covert message secret, the steganographic transmission tries to hide the existance of the secret communication [16].

Embedding of a secret message can either be done by modifying temporal behaviour of the carrier (timing channel) or by modifying the content of the carrier (storage channel). As network transmission usually contains some redundancy such as unused or reserved header fields in IP packets, the embedding often can take place without disturbing the overt communication. Alternatively, also random values can be replaced by random-looking parts of the secret message, e.g., by encrypting the secret message prior to transmission. Finally, also part of the overt communication can be overwritten by the secret message, which may however lead to speedy detection. A complete set of hiding patterns has been published in [22]. The established steganographic channel is also called covert channel, a term introduced by Lampson [11] to describe communication via means that have never been intended for communication.

Characteristic parameters of a steganographic transmission, which are interdependent via the so-called magic triangle, are steganographic bandwidth, robustness, and stealthyness [16].

As steganographic transmission can be used for good and bad (human rights activists leaking information from autocratic regimes, or botnet computers communicating secretly with their command-and-control server), new approaches for secret transmission as well as approaches for detection, limitation and preventation of steganographic transmission must be researched. However, the latter is often neglected.

Robustness of the steganographic transmission is often assumed as a property of the carrier, however this is not always the case as the next section will show. Robustness of the secret message can be achieved by forward error correction within the steganographic transmission, or with the help of micro-protocols [20], which however typically require the use of a steganographic back channel that is often not available.

2.3 Related Work

A steganographic method using error correction codes was introduced in [17]. Medvedeva et al. used BCH correction codes and analyzed the impact of channel noise on hidden messages. However, no second level of hidden information was provided and an in-depth analysis on detectability is missing.

Liu et al. [14] investigate error correction codes in image steganography. They use different error syndromes to embed different symbols of secret message, however the relation between the error correction code and its use in encoding the image is not detailed.

Munuera [19] investigates the systematic construction of algorithms to embed secret messages in images with the help of error correction codes. The codes are chosen such that as few pixels as possible must be modified. This line of research has been followed in a string of articles up to [12].

Keller and Magauer [8] investigate robustness of watermarks or secret messages in jpeg images under re-encoding of those images with lower quality. They design an error code which is able to correctly retrieve the secret message from the re-encoded image in a majority of cases.

3 Combining Error Codes and Steganography

3.1 Error Correction Codes in Covert Channels

A steganographic message embedded into network packets may be subject to modifications, e.g., if it is placed in a packet header field of which some bits may also be modified by a router on the way due to rules of the network protocol. In this case, the steganographic message should be protected by an error correction code. The choice of the particular code depends on the type of modification, i.e., are there only single bit errors possible or also multi-bit errors.

However, error correction codes have also found less straightforward uses. In [23], the authors present a steganographic scheme where a secret message is partitioned into h-bit blocks, and covert sender and receiver both monitor the same stream of network packets that serves as carrier. Each time when the h-bit hash value of a packet matches the contents of the next block, the covert sender signals the covert receiver via a different channel, thus reducing the bandwidth requirements by factor h, and avoiding the need to modify the network packets themselves. When investigating steganographic bandwidth and detectability, the authors propose to also use partial matches, where up to t bits of the hash value may be wrong. To be able to correctly decode the secret message, they partition the message into blocks of length $h - c$ bits and append a BCH error correction code of length c that is able to correct up to t bit errors.

3.2 Covert Channels in Error Correction Codes

So far error correction codes were introduced as redundancy to achieve robustness of a secret message. However, the redundancy of error correction codes used in a carrier can also be abused to create a covert channel itself. Transmission errors commonly happen, but the ratio of errors to redundancy often allows for a lot more errors to happen until a message content is lost. For example, if up to two bit errors in a word can be corrected, but commonly only single bit errors happen, then a specific bit can be flipped by the covert sender as a signal. Hence, additional information can be injected as errors in data transmission. A receiver unaware of secret information will perceive this additional information as further transmission errors, while a covert receiver knowing of the hidden message can extract the secret data by decoding the manipulated errors in the received data. Please note that we assume two transmission errors in one block to be sufficiently seldom to be ignored. Otherwise, a Hamming code would not be suitable to protect the cover message.

In order to extract the secret information correctly, covert sender and receiver must align where to insert or extract the information from, respectively. In its simplest form, they can agree to use each t-th block. To distribute the manipulated errors in a pattern observed as random by an observer, a pseudo random number generator (PRNG) can be used [10], which outputs values from 0 to $t - 1$ with similar frequency. The covert sender will only use a block to embed secret information if the generator outputs a 0. Pseudo random number generators follow a deterministic algorithm, allowing covert sender and receiver to use the same number sequence if they agree beforehand on the seed value.

To embed bit values 0 and 1 into a carrier medium, i.e. error correction encoded data, a bit error is only injected into the content if a 1 is to be transmitted. For a 0, no error will be injected in the respective code block. This idea is borrowed from [17], yet transferred from BCH to Hamming codes and put into a new setting where e.g. blocks to insert errors are chosen pseudo-randomly.

The steganographic bandwidth of such a covert channel strongly depends on the error correction code of the medium, in which the secret information will be embedded in. For example, a (7, 4)-Hamming code can transmit one error in a block of seven bits, while in a (63, 57)-Hamming code one bit can only be carried by 63 bits in the encoded carrier since all Hamming codes have minimum distance $d = 3$ and, thus, only one error can be corrected within one encoded block. For a given carrier transmission of length l, which is Hamming encoded with block length n, the maximum capacity $C_{\max}$ for secret information is $\lceil l/(tn) \rceil$.

The robustness of such a covert channel is impacted by transmission errors in the physical transmission channel. If a 0 is transmitted, a transmission error gets it decoded as a 1. If a 1 is transmitted, a transmission error will mostly lead to a second faulty bit, and, thus, to still decoding a 1 for the secret message, but wrong decoding of the block of carrier message. If the inserted error bit is flipped back by the transmission error, then the received carrier block is error-free and a 0 is decoded for the secret message. This indicates that the secret message should be protected by an error correction code as well. Figure 1 depicts three example situations to illustrate the above scheme.

Sender	add ECC	add ECC	add ECC
	0000 000	0000 000	0000 000
Covert Sender	insert **1**: flip lsb	insert **0**: do not flip lsb	insert **1**: flip lsb
	0001 000	0000 000	**0001** 000
Transmission	no bit error	bit error in parity	bit error in lsb
	0001 000	0000 0**1**0	000**0** 000
Covert Receiver	notify bit error in lsb	notify bit error not in lsb	notify no bit error
	extract **1**	extract **0**	extract **0** wrong!
Receiver	correct 1 bit error	correct 1 bit error	no error
	000**0** 000	0000 000	0000 000

Fig. 1. Example situations when transmitting data 0000 with (7,3) Hamming code: (a) secret bit 1 is inserted into a block by flipping the least significant bit prior to transmission. (b) secret bit 0 is inserted by not flipping any bit, but a transmission error occurs. (c) secret bit 1 is inserted by flipping the least significant bit prior to transmission, but a transmission error occurs on that bit.

The scheme above can be varied by differentiating between injecting the error on the data bits and the redundant parity bits. A bit value 1 of the secret message can be sent as an error in data bits and accordingly a 0 will be transmitted by injecting an error in parity bits. For inefficient error correction codes, i.e., large ratio n/k, the probability of an error appearing in a parity bit is close to the probability of errors in data bits. Thus, this differentiation is less obvious to an observer than choosing two specific bit positions. Robustness issues remain as before. For example, a transmission error that results in a flipped data bit, while a bit value 0 from the secret message has been injected as a bit error in a parity bit, makes unique decoding impossible.

Multi-level Approach. Inserting secret information through error correction codes offers the opportunity to hide further data in that secret information, i.e., enables multi-level steganography. The first obvious possibility opens because the secret information itself is encoded using an error correction code and, thus, applying the previously explained approach is possible again on the encoded secret information.

Another approach can be made through the positioning of injected errors as described above. By using the bit position to embed secret data, either the secret symbol alphabet can be extended to improve the steganographic bandwidth of the first secret message, or a second message not correlated to the primary hidden message can be transmitted. While the latter approach does not have the advantage of an improved bandwidth for the first secret message, it might hide the amount of secret information that is transmitted. It is unlikely that an observer of the secret transmission, who already deciphered one message is looking for the existence of a secondary hidden message.

Deployment Scenario. Error-correction codes are used both in transport protocols [2,21] and in cellular networks [1]. They have also been considered for protocols such as QUIC [18]. Hence, the proposed covert channels can be deployed similarly to other scenarios where the value modulation pattern is applied in transport or higher layer protocols. Examples of such deployment are given in [22].

3.3   Erasure Codes and Covert Channels

In [7], the author demonstrates that within a fountain code, which is a rateless erasure code without the need for a backwards channel to signal message loss [3], a random subset index in a cover message protected by such code against message loss can be replaced by the quasi-random looking encrypted part of a secret message of appropriate size. The challenge here was that the index range is not a power of 2 as there are $\binom{k}{d}$ possible subsets of size d from the set of k carrier symbols to be transmitted. At the same time, the secret message must be protected against message loss due to loss of a cover message, yet without having a channel back to the covert sender. Thus, a fountain code is also applied here, which opens the door for a second level covert channel, which however has a much smaller steganographic bandwidth. Even a third level channel could be implemented [9].

4   Experimental Results

The covert channel presented in Sect. 3.2 has been implemented and analyzed. To encode two secret messages, an overt message was encoded with a Hamming code. For robustness purposes, each hidden message was encoded with an error correction code, too. A PRNG was used to determine a code block in the cover message for bit manipulation. Then the next bit of the primary secret message was embedded. If that bit was a 0, no error was injected. If the message bit was a 1, the next symbol of the secondary message, that is the message encoded in the bit position of the manipulated error, was checked to determine the bit position of the manipulated error. A 1 was injected in a data bit, while a 0 was induced through parity bit manipulation.

The error manipulated cover message was then sent through a simulated physical channel. Additive white Gaussian noise (AWGN) was used to simulate the channel quality. Hereby, the standard deviation correlates to the probability of a bit being correctly transmitted or not. While AWGN might not exactly fit every physical link model (see e.g. [5]), it is still widely used and thus also applied in our study.

The noise value added to a transmitted bit is being calculated randomly across a standard normal distribution. If the resulting bit value is above 0.5, the receiver will read the message bit 1, while a value below 0.5 will be read as 0. Hence, a minimum of 0.5 must be added or subtracted from the bit value to produce a transmission error. For a standard deviation of 0.1 for example, the probability of a bit error is being further away from the mean of the normal distribution than the 5σ-area and, therefore, is approximately 0.000000287. Having this channel quality, in one million bit transmissions the mean errors happening are 0.287. A standard deviation of 0.2 has already a significantly increased probability of 0.006209666, i.e. 6209.666 errors in one million transmitted bits.

Without any transmission errors, the proposed covert channel successfully delivers secret messages on both described levels, that is by manipulating error existence and by manipulating the error position. To investigate the robustness of the covert channel, simulations varying the channel noise, i.e. the standard deviation of the AWGN, the chosen Hamming code and the occupancy rate, that is the ratio of actually hidden information to maximal possible steganographic bandwidth, have been conducted.

Figure 2 shows the influence of channel noise and chosen error correction code based on different Hamming code length on the transmitted data. The occupancy rate of primary and secondary message were set to 10% and 100%, respectively. As the secondary message theoretically does not have any impact on the error characteristics, the difference of occupancy rate between primary and secondary message can be neglected. The calculated percentage of the error ratio is the ratio of transmitted data to wrongly transmitted data. Specifically, for bit errors during transmission, that is the ratio of occurring transmission bit errors to total amount of transmitted bits. By visible errors in the cover message, we denote the ratio of wrongly decoded symbols to total number of transmitted symbols. Equivalently, errors in primary and secondary message are also calculated from the ratio of wrongly decoded symbols to total amount of transmitted symbols.

In Fig. 2a the standard deviation correlates to the standard deviation of the AWGN used to simulate a data transmission. All error correction encoding, i.e. for cover message, primary and secondary message, was done using the (7, 4)-Hamming code. It can be seen that the secret message encoding using the existence of errors (referred to as the primary message) is more robust to channel noise than the encoding using the error positioning (referred to as the secondary message).

The chosen Hamming code length has a significant impact on the robustness of the primary hidden message, as shown in Fig. 2b. The channel quality was set constant using $\sigma = 0.2$. While the bit errors do not increase, several bit errors are more likely to be observed within the same error code block with increasing code block length and, thus, are more likely to result in more errors in the cover message as well as the primary message. For the secondary message, a worsening of the message errors can also be observed. Since the message modification is already over 80% at (7, 4)-Hamming code due to the standard deviation of $\sigma = 0.2$, the overall increase is not as drastic as for the primary message.

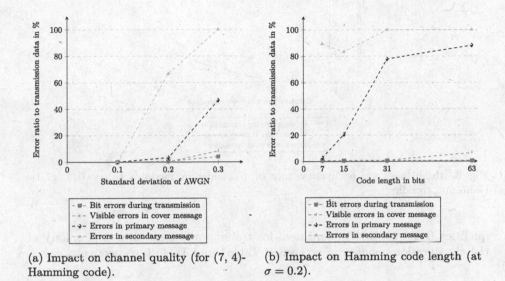

(a) Impact on channel quality (for (7, 4)-Hamming code).

(b) Impact on Hamming code length (at $\sigma = 0.2$).

Fig. 2. Robustness of data transmission.

In Fig. 3, the influence of the occupancy rate is shown. Since the secondary message does not have any impact on the error characteristics or steganographic bandwidth of the first message, the secondary message is missing in this graph. It can be seen that the impact of occupancy rate up to 10% of the steganographic bandwidth is rather small. Only the errors in the primary secret message increase continuously. At 100% occupancy rate, the impact on the robustness is clearly visible. The bit errors do not increase since they are not linked to the occupancy rate, as manipulated bit errors are not included in that value. At 100% occupancy rate every channel error on a block carrying a hidden 1 directly results in an error that cannot be corrected using the Hamming code, because each code block is already occupied by a manipulated error. Thus, the amount of visible errors in the cover message increases. For the primary message, not every channel error disturbs the error encoded message since two channel errors in two blocks are necessary to result in a not-correctable error. Thus, the impact is less severe on the primary message compared to the cover message.

Various messages, that possibly serve as carriers for covert communication, were classified by a trained Naive Bayes classifier to investigate the detectability of secret messages based on the scheme proposed in Sect. 3.2. Two runs were performed: One, in which the channel quality had AWGN with a standard deviation in the range of $\sigma = 0.1...0.2$, and a second one, in which only specific channel

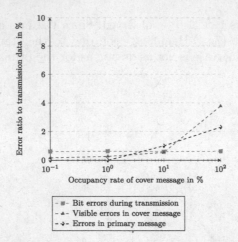

Fig. 3. Robustness vs. occupancy rate of transmission medium ($\sigma = 0,2$, (7,4)-Hamming encoding).

qualities (e.g. $\sigma = 0.175$) were used for training and test data. A summary of the classification results can be seen in Table 1 and Table 2, respectively.

Table 1. Classification for unknown channel noise ($\sigma = 0.1, 0.125, 0.15, 0.175, 0.2$).

contains message:	classified as:		
	Yes	No	$\sum$
Yes	14	6	20
No	3	17	20
$\sum$	17	23	40

Both classification scenarios show a statistically significant accuracy above 75% using only error rate and error position ratio for classification characteristics. Specifically, the Naive Bayes classifier for unknown channel noise has an accuracy of 77.5% and a precision of 82.4%. The sensitivity can be calculated to 70% resulting in a F-measure of 0.5768.

The Naive Bayes classifier for known channel noises has a slightly better accuracy of 80% and an improved precision of 92.9%. However, the sensitivity has decreased to 65%. The resulting F-measure exceeds the case of unknown channel noise with 0.7649. It can be assumed that for further adjustments in regards to the steganographic method, an improvement of classification quality can be achieved.

In Tab. 3 the wrong prediction in contrast to the channel quality during transmission can be seen. For the first classification case, i.e. unknown channel quality (σ), the number of messages classified as *not containing a secret message*

Table 2. Classification for known channel noise ($\sigma = 0.1, 0.125, 0.15, 0.175, 0.2$).

contains message:	classified as:		
	Yes	No	$\sum$
Yes	13	7	20
No	1	19	20
$\sum$	14	26	40

for high channel quality can be observed. A very low channel quality results in the opposite false-positive prediction.

In contrast to the first classification case, the second classification case, i.e. classification only within one specific standard deviation σ of the AWGN, wrong predictions are only visible for low channel qualities. No wrong classification appears for $\sigma = 0.1$ and $\sigma = 0.125$. For $\sigma = 0.2$, the incorrect classification changed from false-positive to false-negative, resulting from the change of average errors in the cover message.

Table 3. Wrongly classified messages.

σ	σ unknown		σ known	
	Prediction no	Prediction yes	Prediction no	Prediction yes
0.1	1	0	0	0
0.125	2	0	0	0
0.15	1	0	1	0
0.175	2	0	2	1
0.2	0	3	4	0

Based on the results on steganographic bandwidth, robustness and detectability, it can be assumed that an optimum of transmission channel quality exists for the proposed covert channel using error correction codes. With decreasing channel quality the errors in cover message and secret message increase, while the detectability — especially in the case of known channel quality — decreases. If the channel quality drops too low, neither cover message nor secret messages can be read. Having few transmission errors, the message is likely to be detected. Hence, the optimum is somewhere in between.

5   Conclusions

We have pointed out the relationships between steganographic transmission channels and transmissions with error correction and erasure codes. We did so with the help of examples where both appear in different combinations. Furthermore, we have extended the proposal from [17] from BCH codes to Hamming codes, added the capability for multi-level steganography, and experimentally investigated detectability, which was not done in the original paper. The results obtained from the investigation suggest an optimum of transmission quality for covert channels in error correction codes.

Future work will comprise a systematic survey of the intersection between those fields and a categorization of the possible forms of interaction between steganographic channels and error coding, thereby possibly deriving new forms of steganographic channels. Furthermore, detection by other means such as monitoring error patterns with time series analysis will be investigated.

References

1. Alexiou, A., Bouras, C., Papazois, A.: Adopting forward error correction for multicasting over cellular networks. In: 2010 European Wireless Conference (EW), pp. 361–368 (2010). https://doi.org/10.1109/EW.2010.5483446
2. Barakat, C., Altman, E.: Bandwidth tradeoff between TCP and link-level FEC. Comput. Netw. **39**(2), 133–150 (2002). https://doi.org/10.1016/S1389-1286(01)00305-X
3. Byers, J.W., Luby, M., Mitzenmacher, M., Rege, A.: A digital fountain approach to reliable distribution of bulk data. In: Proceedings of the ACM SIGCOMM 1998 Conference on Applications, Technologies, Architectures, and Protocols for Computer Communication (SIGCOMM 1998), Vancouver, B.C., Canada, pp. 56–67. ACM (1998). https://doi.org/10.1145/285243.285258
4. Clarke, G.C., Jr., Cain, J.B.: Error-Correction Coding for Digital Communication. Springer, New York (1981)
5. Cunningham, D., Dawe, P.: Review of the 10Gigabit Ethernet link model. White Paper AV02-2485EN, Avago Technologies (2010). https://docs.broadcom.com/doc/AV02-2485EN
6. Fraczek, W., Mazurczyk, W., Szczypiorski, K.: Multilevel steganography: improving hidden communication in networks. J. Univ. Comput. Sci. **18**(14), 1967–1986 (2012). https://doi.org/10.3217/jucs-018-14-1967
7. Keller, J.: Multilevel network steganography in fountain codes. In: Jaatun, M.G., Køien, G.M., Kulyk, O. (eds.) EICC 2021: European Interdisciplinary Cybersecurity Conference, Virtual Event, Romania, November 10–11, 2021, pp. 72–76. ACM (2021). https://doi.org/10.1145/3487405.3487420
8. Keller, J., Magauer, J.: Error-correcting codes in steganography. In: Karl, W., Becker, J., Großpietsch, K., Hochberger, C., Maehle, E. (eds.) ARCS 2006–19th International Conference on Architecture of Computing Systems, Workshops Proceedings, March 16, 2006, Frankfurt am Main, Germany. LNI, vol. P-81, pp. 52–55. GI (2006). https://dl.gi.de/items/928b33e5-ed16-4746-bc83-979877a4a28f
9. Keller, J., Marciniszyn, E.: Improved concept and implementation of a fountain code covert channel. J. Wireless Mob. Netw. Ubiquit. Comput. Dependable Appl. **13**(3), 25–36 (2022). https://doi.org/10.22667/JOWUA.2022.09.30.025
10. Kneusel, R.T.: Random Numbers and Computers. Springer, Cham (2018). https://doi.org/10.1007/978-3-319-77697-2
11. Lampson, B.W.: A note on the confinement problem. Commun. ACM **16**(10), 613–615 (1973). https://doi.org/10.1145/362375.362389

12. Li, W., Zhang, W., Li, L., Zhou, H., Yu, N.: Designing near-optimal steganographic codes in practice based on polar codes. IEEE Trans. Commun. **68**(7), 3948–3962 (2020). https://doi.org/10.1109/TCOMM.2020.2982624

13. Lin, S., Costello, D.J.: Error Control Coding, Fundamentals and applications. 2nd edn Prentice Hall, Upper Saddle River NJ (2004)

14. Liu, C.Q., Ping, X.J., Zhang, T., Zhou, L.N., Wang, Y.H.: A research on steganography method based on error-correcting codes. In: 2006 International Conference on Intelligent Information Hiding and Multimedia, pp. 377–380. IEEE (2006). https://doi.org/10.1109/IIH-MSP.2006.265021

15. Luby, M.: LT codes. In: Proceedings of the 43rd Annual IEEE Symposium on Foundations of Computer Science (FOCS 2002), Vancouver, BC, Canada, pp. 271–280. IEEE (2002). https://doi.org/10.1109/SFCS.2002.1181950

16. Mazurczyk, W., Wendzel, S., Zander, S., Houmansadr, A., Szczypiorski, K.: Information Hiding in Communication Networks: Fundamentals, Mechanisms, and Applications. Wiley, IEEE Series on Information and Communication Networks Security (2016)

17. Medvedeva, E., Trubin, I., Blinov, E.: Steganography method in error-correcting codes. In: 24th International Conference on Digital Signal Processing and its Applications (DSPA), pp. 1–4. IEEE (2022). https://doi.org/10.1109/DSPA53304.2022.9790782

18. Michel, F., De Coninck, Q., Bonaventure, O.: QUIC-FEC: bringing the benefits of forward erasure correction to QUIC. In: 2019 IFIP Networking Conference (IFIP Networking), pp. 1–9 (2019). https://doi.org/10.23919/IFIPNetworking.2019.8816838

19. Munuera, C.: Steganography and error-correcting codes. Signal Process. **87**(6), 1528–1533 (2007). https://doi.org/10.1016/j.sigpro.2006.12.008

20. Naumann, M., Wendzel, S., Mazurczyk, W., Keller, J.: Micro protocol engineering for unstructured carriers: on the embedding of steganographic control protocols into audio transmissions. Secur. Commun. Networks **9**(15), 2972–2985 (2016). https://doi.org/10.1002/sec.1500

21. Pristupa, P.V., Mikheev, P.A., Suschenko, S.P.: Performance of forward error correction in transport protocol at intrasegment level. In: Vishnevskiy, V.M., Samouylov, K.E., Kozyrev, D.V. (eds.) DCCN 2020. CCIS, vol. 1337, pp. 546–556. Springer, Cham (2020). https://doi.org/10.1007/978-3-030-66242-4_43

22. Wendzel, S., et al.: A revised taxonomy of steganography embedding patterns. In: Reinhardt, D., Müller, T. (eds.) ARES 2021: The 16th International Conference on Availability, Reliability and Security, Vienna, Austria, August 17–20, 2021, pp. 67:1–67:12. ACM (2021). https://doi.org/10.1145/3465481.3470069

23. Wendzel, S., Schmidbauer, T., Zillien, S., Keller, J.: Did you see that? a covert channel exploiting recent legitimate traffic. arXiv 2212.11850 (2022). https://doi.org/10.48550/arXiv.2212.11850

Modified Cross Parity Codes for Adjacent Double Error Correction

Georg Duchrau[✉] and Michael Gössel

Universität Potsdam, Institut für Informatik und Computational Science, Potsdam, Germany

duchrau@uni-potsdam.de

Abstract. The cross parity code is a well known single error correcting and a double error detecting (SEC-DED) code with fast decoding. Databits are abstractly arranged in a rectangular array. Checkbits are determined as parities along rows and columns. In this paper we propose to divide the data bit array into four quadrants Q_1, Q_2, Q_3 and Q_4. For every quadrant a parity bit is determined. Compared to a non-modified Cross-Parity Code the number of checkbits is increased by 3.

All single bit errors as well as all 2-bit errors with a first error in Q_1 and a second error in Q_3 or with a first error in Q_2 and a second error in Q_4 can be corrected. Incorrectable 2-bit errors are detected.

By placing bits which are for instance stored in adjacent memory elements into appropriate quadrants Q_1 and Q_3 or Q_2 and Q_4, adjacent 2-bit errors can be corrected. Up to 2-bit check bit errors are detected as well as all burst errors shorter than the side length of the data array. Correct check bits can be recomputed from the corrected data bits. The correction is as fast as for an unmodified cross-parity code.

Keywords: error correction · adjacent errors · cross parity code · DED

1 Introduction

Cross Parity Codes (CPC) are known for 1-bit error correction, two-bit error detection and burst error detection. The data bits are arranged in a rectangular (usually quadratic) array. A row parity for every row, a column-parity for every column and an overall parity of all the data bits are determined. Figure 1a displays the data array, row and column parities as well as the overall parity for the side length 4 and 16 data bits. The parities are determined as modulo 2 sums of bits in a row (r_i) or column (c_i) or of all bits (p).

In some applications adjacent two bit errors occur more often than other double bit errors. With smaller memory sizes errors can spread along two neighbouring cells, causing adjacent errors. We propose a method for modifying well known CPCs, to be able to correct certain double bit errors, like adjacent ones.

This is achieved by dividing the CPC array (Fig. 1a) into 4 quadrants (Fig. 1b) and determining the block parity p_i for each quadrant, replacing the overall parity. This increases the number of checkbits by 3.

G. Goumas et al. (Eds.): ARCS 2023, LNCS 13949, pp. 94–102, 2023.
https://doi.org/10.1007/978-3-031-42785-5_7

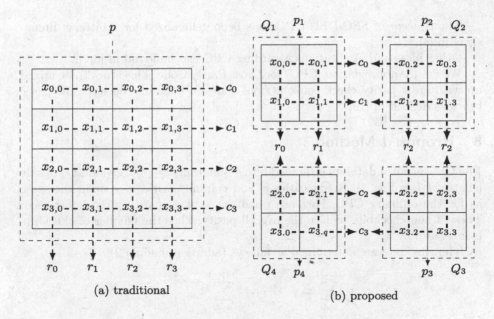

(a) traditional

(b) proposed

Fig. 1. Cross parity arrangement of databits, the array is divided into 4 quadrants the overall parity p is split into 4 Block parities $p_1 \ldots p_4$.

2   Related Work

A common method for SEC-DED is the well known Hsiao Code [1]. For k data bits $\log k + 1$ check bits are required in comparison to $2\sqrt{k} + 1$ for CPC. The latter comes with an advantage in correction speed and burst error detection. The modification at hand, enabling roughly 25% of 2-bit error correction, is adding another advantage at the cost of 3 additional checkbits.

CPCs for higher error correction were first investigated by Wieder in [2]. He shows the existence of CPCs for correcting 3 errors and detecting 4 by using 4 types of lines (compared to 2 types for SEC-DED). The general approach is to prove the uniqueness of syndromes.

The correction of two-bit errors is considered for instance in [2,5] and [9]. Besides the row parities and the column parities also diagonal parities are needed and the number of checkbits is increased by the side length.

Argyrides et al. use matrix codes, with 2 or more checkbits per row/column to be able to correct adjacent errors in the array [8].

In [3] Pflanz, Vierhaus et al. apply a 3 line scheme to detect a large number of errors in a register array. The authors propose a correction method for errors restricted to a single row or a single column and a syndrome based correction method for other errors.

The correction of higher errors can be difficult in CPC like Codes. Some methods have been proposed in [5] and [9].

The concept of SEC-DED CPCs has been generalized for arbitrary dimensions in [4].

Other ideas and applications regarding CPC can be found in [6,7].

We use the abbreviation "CPC" for Cross Parity Code. This is not to be mixed up with cross parity check convolutional codes, a class of Codes for magnetic tapes as defined in [10].

3   Proposed Method

The CPC array of databits is divided into 4 quadrants Q_1, Q_2, Q_3 and Q_4 of side length M (see Fig. 2). Row parities r_i and column parities c_i remain the same as for the ordinary CPC. For each quadrant a block parity p_i is determined. These 4 new checkbits replace the overall parity. Thus the number of checkbits is increased by 3.

The checkbits are determined as follows (addition modulo 2):

$$r_i = \sum_{j=0}^{2M-1} x_{i,j} \qquad c_i = \sum_{j=0}^{2M-1} x_{j,i}$$

$$p_1 = \sum_{i,j<M} x_{i,j} \qquad p_2 = \sum_{i<M,j\geq M} x_{i,j}$$

$$p_3 = \sum_{i,j\geq M} x_{i,j} \qquad p_4 = \sum_{i\geq M,j<M} x_{i,j} \quad .$$

A two bit error with a first error in Q_1 and a second error in Q_3 can be corrected, as well as a first error in Q_2 and a second error in Q_4.

If adjacent bits, e.g. bits stored in neighbouring memory elements, are mapped to the appropriate quadrants, they can be corrected. This will be explained in more detail below.

Up to the length $2M - 1$ any burst in the databits can be detected (see Sect. 4).

3.1   Decoding

For decoding the following rules apply:

1. If there is exactly one inverted column parity, row parity and block parity in a quadrant, an error can be corrected via $\Delta x_{i,j}$.
2. If there are at least two inverted checkbits regarding a single quadrant and the correcting conditions (rule 1) are not fulfilled in any quadrant, an incorrectable error is detected.

The correction value for the bit $x_{i,j}$ is defined as

$$\Delta x_{i,j} = \Delta r_i \cdot \Delta c_j \cdot \Delta p_q, \quad q : \text{quadrant index.} \tag{1}$$

(The point operation denotes the logical AND operation.) For burst error detection (see Sect. 4) the following third rule comes into effect:

3. Two inverted column bits in any quadrant always cause detection of an incorrectable error.

At first we describe the correction of data bits. Check bit errors are considered in Sect. 3.2.

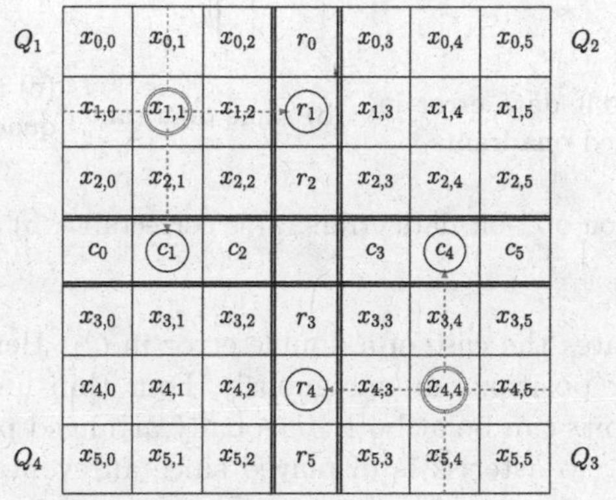

Fig. 2. Modified array with quadrant length $M = 3$, 2-bit error in encircled bits $x_{1,1}$ and $x_{4,4}$. Such errors can be corrected. To distinguish this error pattern from an error in $x_{1,4}$ ad $x_{4,1}$ one uses the block parities p_i.

As an example we consider a 2-bit error in the data bits $x_{1,1}$ and $x_{4,4}$ as illustrated in Fig. 2. The set of inverted checkbits is $\{r_1, r_4, c_1, c_4, p_1, p_3\}$. In Q_1 there is exactly one inverted row, column and block parity ($\{c_1, r_1, p_1\}$). Likewise in Q_3, here the inverted set of parities is $\{c_4, r_4, p_3\}$. According to rule 1 and Eq. 1 the bits $x_{1,1}$ and $x_{4,4}$ will be corrected. The block parities p_i are necessary to distinguish this error from a double error in $x_{1,4}$ and $x_{4,1}$.

We illustrate different cases with diagrams. In these diagrams an inverted row or column parity corresponds to a line in the data array, on which an error is located. The four quadrants are separated by thick lines. The thin lines express inverted row and column parities. Asterisks express inverted block parities.

The example above is illustrated in Fig. 3a. The first erroneous bit is located in Q_1 at the intersection of 2 thin lines. Since also the block parity is inverted the quadrant is marked by an asterisk. According to rule 1) the bit in Q_1 located at the intersection is corrected. Both neighbouring quadrants (Q_2 and Q_4) also contain an intersection of thin lines but no inverted block parity (no asterisks). No bit of these quadrants is corrected. In the remaining quadrant (Q_3, lower right) is a crossing point of to thin lines and a inverted block parity. According to rule 1) the bit at the intersection is corrected. After this both erroneous bits are correct.

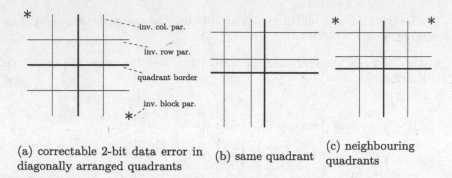

(a) correctable 2-bit data error in diagonally arranged quadrants

(b) same quadrant

(c) neighbouring quadrants

Fig. 3. Illustration of 2-bit data errors; a) is correctable, b) and c) are not.

Figure 3b illustrates the case of a double error in Q_1. Here it is not possible to localize the error positions unambiguously. Four thin lines intersect in Q_1. The two erroneous bits can be at both diagonally arranged positions marked by the crossing points. No asterisk is displayed since an even number of errors is not visible modulo 2.

Also in scenarios represented by Fig. 3c it is not possible to locate the error positions unambiguously. Here the two errors are located in neighbouring quadrants, marked by asterisks (change in block parity). Both errors invert a column and a row check bit, hence the 4 thin lines. The errors can either be located at the top or bottom intersection of the marked quadrants. Due to rule 2) an incorrectable error is detected in the two latter cases.

If both errors are located on the same row/column the according checkbit will not be inverted. A localization of the errors is not possible and due to rule 2) an incorrectable error will be detected.

By mapping the data bits (y_i in Fig. 4) to the bits in the abstract arrangement ($x_{i,j}$) one can choose, to a certain point, which errors are actually corrected.

If one desires to correct adjacent bits, two bits that succeed each other have to be mapped to diagonally arranged quadrants. We refer to this as *adjacent mapping*. This can be achieved by mapping the first bit to Q_1, the second bit to Q_3 the third bit to Q_1 etc. until Q_1 and Q_3 are filled. Thereby the quadrants are filled in reading direction (from left to right). After this the two remaining quadrants (Q_2 and Q_4) are filled similarly. By doing so an adjacent error becomes correctable with one exception—the adjacent error between the last bit of Q_3 and the first bit of Q_2. If one desires to correct this error as well, an additional check bit can be added.

3.2   Checkbit Errors

Since two-bit errors are considered only the following cases are possible:

– A single check bit error,

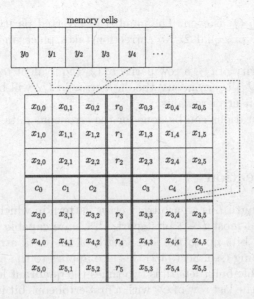

Fig. 4. Mapping of adjacent memory cells to bits in diagonally arranged quadrants. This way 2-bit errors in adjacent memory cells can be corrected.

- a double check bit error

  or
- a single check bit error and a single data bit error.

In case of a single check bit error either a row parity, a column parity or a block parity is inverted. In none of the quadrants more than 1 check bit will be inverted, and according to rule 1 no correction is possible. Also rule 2) does not apply. This is because the data remains correct here. If correct checkbits are of interest, they can be redetermined from the correct data bits. We refer to this as a correctable checkbit error.

In the case of a double bit error in the check bits at most two check bits are inverted in a quadrant. According to rule 1 no correction is possible. According to rule 2 an incorrectable error will be detected if two checkbits are inverted in the same quadrant. If at most one checkbit is inverted in every quadrant, the data bits are error-free and a correctable check bit error remains.

In the case of a single check bit error together with a single data bit error we assume without loss of generality that the erroneous data bit is located in Q_1.

If additional to the data bit error a row, column or the block parity in Q_1 is erroneous, the number of inverted check bits in $Q1$ is even and the number of inverted check bits in the quadrants Q_2, Q_3 and Q_4 is less or equal 2 and no correction can take place. Due to rule 2 an incorrectable error is detected.

If the block parity in one of the quadrants Q_2, Q_3 or Q_4 is erroneous, the data bit in Q_1 will be corrected and an correctable checkbit error remains.

An erroneous row parity in Q_2 or a column parity in Q_4 is equivalent to a erroneous row/column parity in Q_1. Here, as mentioned above, the number of inverted parities in Q_1 is even. The number of inverted parity bits in the other quadrants is lower or equal 2. No correction takes place and an incorrectable error is detected.

If a column parity of Q_2, a row parity of Q_4 (equivalent to a row parity or a column parity of Q_3) is erroneous, the data error in Q_1 will be corrected and a correctable checkbit error remains.

Similar considerations can be done for the erroneous data bit located in Q_2, Q_3 or Q_4.

4   Burst Detection

A burst error of length L is an arbitrary error pattern in which the first and last erroneous bit are at most $L-1$ bits apart. CPCs are capable of detecting burst errors in the data bits up to the side length of the data array ([5]). Without the adjacent mapping (see. Sect. 3.2) this also applies to the modification of the CPC. The detectable burst length is two times the quadrant length ($2M$). 2-Bit Bursts starting in the last row of Q_2 with a first erroneous bit in Q_2 and a second erroneous bit in Q_4 become correctable.

In the following we consider burst detection with the adjacent mapping.

As described above, adjacent bits in a memory cell are alternatingly placed in Q_1 and Q_3 for the first half, and in Q_2 and Q_4 for the second half of the data bits. The quadrants are filled in reading direction (from left to right).

Each erroneous bit in a burst of length $2M$ restricted to the first or second half will invert a unique column check bit. Thus the length of detected bursts here is $2M$ (see positions a to f in Fig. 5a).

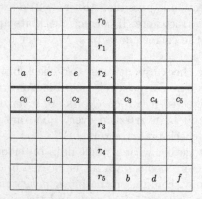 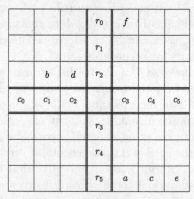

(a) unique column for every bit in a burst of length M restricted to one half of the data bits

(b) Error pattern $\{a, f, c\}$ yields single bit syndrome. Detectable burst length is reduced by one.

Fig. 5. Possible burst positions for length $2M$, restricted to one half (a) and spread across two halves (b)

Only if the burst starts in the last M bits of Q_3 (see. Fig. 5b) the detection length is reduced by one. This is because the $2M$th bit occurs in the same column as the 1st one. This reduces the detectable burst length by one, unless one starts the mapping in Q_4 for the second half.

5   Conclusion

This paper shows how a cross parity code can be modified to correct a large number of 2-Bit errors and detect all incorrectable 2-bit errors including 2-bit errors in the check bits. The data array was divided into four quadrants Q_1, Q_2, Q_3 and Q_4 of data bits. An additional parity bit for every quadrant is required. The general parity of the data bits of an unmodified cross-parity- code was replaced by these four block parities, increasing the number of check bits by 3. It was shown how 2-bit errors with their first erroneous data bit in block Q1 and their second erroneous data bit in Q3 (or in Q2 and Q4) can be corrected. If the bits stored in neighboring memory cells are alternatingly placed in the blocks Q1 and Q3 (or Q2 and Q4), adjacent two-bit errors in the memory are correctable. It was explained how all burst errors up to two times the side length of the quadrants can be detected and that corrected check bits can be recomputed from the corrected data bits. Compared to an unmodified cross parity code no additional delay for correction is needed.

References

1. Hsiao, M.Y.: A class of optimal minimum odd-weight-column SEC-DED codes. IBM J. Res. Dev. **14**, 395–401 (1970)
2. Wieder Jr, E.J.: "N-Dimensional Codes for Detecting Four Errors and Correcting Three", Master Thesis, University of Pennsylvania, Mai (1961)
3. Pflanz, M., Walther, K., Galke, C., Vierhaus, H.T.: On-line techniques for error detection and correction in processor registers with cross-parity check. J. Electron. Test. Theory Appl. **19**, 501–510 (2003)
4. Wong, T.F., Shea, J.M.: Multi-dimensional parity-check codes for bursty channels. In: Proceedings of 2001 IEEE International Symposium on Information Theory (IEEE Cat. No. 01CH37252). IEEE (2001)
5. Hosp, S: Modifizierte Cross-Parity Codes zur schnellen Mehrbit-Fehlerkorrektur, Dissertation, Universität Potsdam (2014)
6. Anne, N.B., Thirunavukkarasu, U., Latifi, S.: Three and four-dimensional parity-check codes for correction and detection of multiple errors. In: International Conference on Information Technology: Coding and Computing, 2004. Proceedings. ITCC 2004. vol. 2. IEEE (2004)
7. Poolakkaparambil, M., et al.: Low complexity cross parity codes for multiple and random bit error correction. In: Thirteenth International Symposium on Quality Electronic Design (ISQED). IEEE (2012)
8. Argyrides, C.A., et al.: Matrix-based codes for adjacent error correction. IEEE Trans. Nucl. Sci. **57**(4), 2106–2111 (2010)

9. Duchrau, G., Gössel, M.: A new decoding method for double error correcting cross parity codes. In: 2022 IEEE 28th International Symposium on On-Line Testing and Robust System Design (IOLTS). IEEE (2022)

10. Fuja, T., Heegard, C., Blaum, M.: Cross parity check convolutional codes. IEEE Trans. Inf. Theory **35**(6), 1264–1276 (1989)

Computer Architecture Co-Design

COMPESCE: A Co-design Approach for Memory Subsystem Performance Analysis in HPC Many-Cores

Antoni Portero[1][(✉)], Carlos Falquez[1], Nam Ho[1], Polydoros Petrakis[2],
Stepan Nassyr[1], Manolis Marazakis[2], Romain Dolbeau[3],
Jorge Alejandro Nocua Cifuentes[4], Luis Bertran Alvarez[4], Dirk Pleiter[5],
and Estela Suarez[1]

[1] Jülich Supercomputing Centre, Novel System Architectures Design,
Forschungszentrum Jülich GmbH, Jülich, Germany
{a.portero,c.falquez,n.ho,s.nassyr,e.suarez}@fz-juelich.de
[2] Institute of Computer Science, Foundation for Research and Technology - Hellas
(FORTH), Heraklion, Greece
{ppetrak,maraz}@ics.forth.gr
[3] SiPearl, Rennes, France
romain.dolbeau@sipearl.com
[4] ATOS, Les Clayes-sous-Bois, France
{alejandro.nocua,luis.bertranalvarez}@atos.net
[5] KTH, Royal Institute of Technology, Stockholm, Sweden
pleiter@kth.se

Abstract. This paper explores the memory subsystem design through gem5 simulations of a non-uniform memory access (NUMA) architecture with ARM cores equipped with vector engines. And connected to a Network-on-Chip (NoC) following the Coherent Hub Interface (CHI) protocol. The study quantifies the benefits of vectorization, prefetching, and multichannel NoC configurations using a benchmark for generating memory patterns and indexed accesses. The outcomes provide insights into improving bus utilization and bandwidth and reducing stalls in the system. The paper proposes hardware/software (HW/SW) advancements to reach and use the HBM device with a higher percentage than 80% at the memory controllers in the simulated manycore system.

Keywords: Co-design · HPC · Network on Chip · gem5

1 Introduction

ARM-based high-performance processors have lately joined the High-performance computing (HPC) sector, appearing on the Top500 list and proving that ARM-based systems can deliver significantly high computing performance [1]. An example of a relatively recent successful deployment of ARM-based systems is the Fugaku supercomputer at Riken. Being ranked #1 on

G. Goumas et al. (Eds.): ARCS 2023, LNCS 13949, pp. 105–119, 2023.
https://doi.org/10.1007/978-3-031-42785-5_8

the Top500 list in 2020 [2], the Fugaku supercomputer outperformed all competitors by using the Fujitsu A64FX processor, one of the most potent ARM-based processors available today [3,4]. Key innovations that led to the success of the Fugaku design are the Scalable Vector Extension (SVE) – a SIMD extension introduced by ARM [5,6].

This paper explores a path for accurately simulating an HPC chiplet-based processor [7]. To do this, we simulate the system before building the silicon and perform co-design exploration to determine the optimal hardware parameters for executing applications and kernels of interest. Such kernels, which are abstractions of the most characteristic HPC codes, represent the most computationally and memory intensive parts of the software that runs on a supercomputer.

The primary focus or this paper is the memory system, which offers more potential for improvement than the Central Processing Unit (CPU). Processors in the market implementing the AArch64 architecture already include the SVE.

Besides, the memory system design must be large enough to handle applications, libraries and codes with high bandwidth demands, rather than linear algebra programs such as GEneral Matrix to matrix MultiplicationS (i.e. HPL [8], GEMMS) architectures [9].

The HW/SW co-design approach relies on a reliable and accurate hardware simulation via the gem5 simulator [33]. The gem5 simulator is a modular, open-source, computer-system architecture research platform containing system-level architecture and processor microarchitecture features. The simulation setup description follows the AMBA-CHI protocol implemented in gem5 Ruby for the network. Furthermore, it provides a cycle-accurate model of the CPU [10].

The benchmark selected for our study is Spatter [11], which provides a tunable and configurable framework to test a variety of indexed access patterns, including variations of the Gather/Scatter patterns that are observed in HPC applications.

Our setup depicts a part of the chiplet with all its components. It is a set of RISC CPUs supporting the Scalable Vector Extension (SVE). These CPU cores are connected with a two-dimensional mesh Network-on-Chip (2D MESH NoC). The simulated setup has similar hardware components as encountered in current state-of-the-art hardware designs as A64FX [12], Graviton2 [13] or Graviton3 [14]. The paper explores the most critical knobs for optimising the memory subsystem. The results show a configuration that can benefit from external memory modules of High Bandwidth Memory (HBM2 [29])). A rational explanation about the specific architecture decisions are described further in the paper (see Sect. 4 Fig. 1a presents a diagram of the architecture, and the specific values for the simulations are in Table 1, first column).

The contributions of the paper can be divided into two categories:

- The paper presents a HW/SW co-design methodology that can help to create a manycore processor for an HPC system in which the memory system is composed of a NoC AMBA-CHI configuration where the memory controller utilisation is higher than 80%. In terms of bandwidth, the System Cache Group (SCG) (which corresponds to a quadrant of the chiplet) achieves more

than 250 GB/s; if the chiplet is composed of four quadrants and each quadrant has one HBM2 [18] module, the chiplet would reach a bandwidth higher than 1 TB/s.
- The paper describes the main components involved and how to employ them to get such bandwidth performance. Our records show that few manycore processor chips can deal deftly with HBM [16], and in manycore systems, the NoC or memory wall could be the bottleneck of all system [15].

The rest of the paper can be divided into seven sections. Section 2 presents the background and motivation. Section 3 explains the related work. Section 4 depicts the proposed HPC architecture; Sect. 5 describes the design space exploration methodology. Section 6 presents the case studies. Finally, the last section has the conclusions and future work.

2   Background and Motivation

The research objective is to reproduce a methodology via simulations of the proper architecture that ultimately benefits from the external HBM memories where the sustainable bandwidth (BW) at the CPUs is 80% or higher.

Existing, many-core designs benefit from HBM modules [16], but without the correct co-design for new designs, the NoC can become a bottleneck [15].

The Fujitsu A64FX [19] CPU has a sustainable bandwidth of 62% when running the Stream benchmark (triad) [20]; unless *zfill* compile flag is specified, which eliminates unnecessary memory accesses, then the bandwidth achieved is 80%—allowing a high usage of the external HBM devices.

Although the research question can be broader, the technical challenge is if achieving one terabyte per second in a manycore chiplet with 64 ARM cores armed with SVE 2×256bits, and which network-on-chip design would allow such performance?

The significance of the research is related to uncovering architectures that attenuate the memory wall, which implies solving the processor/memory performance gap. The memory wall limits many current HPC computation applications [21]. Therefore, memory-bound codes profit from the highest sustainable bandwidth at the core level. This research manuscript's significance and relevance are finding strategies to achieve the correct usage of the HBMs and which are the leading software and hardware features that bring an optimal design.

The paper innovations are about the Design Space Exploration (DSE) methodology to encounter optimal design, where the complex problem of the optimal memory system splits into more tractable subproblems with uni-direction constraints propagation. The quantitative assessment for the optimal architecture features, how the benchmarks are utilised to stress the memory system and observe stalls, how to detect them, and offer solutions. Many experiments use the Spatter [11] benchmark. The microbenchmark Spatter is used to assess the impact of indexed access patterns of Gather and Scatter (G/S) operations, which are widely used in many modern HPC applications. The design of Spatter is composed of Gather and Scatter kernels that enable users to benchmark different access patterns to understand the implications of memory prefetching and compiler development.

3   Related Work

Our effort goes toward co-designing the memory subsystem for an HPC architecture based on RISC CPUs technology. Similar previous works are Qureshi, Yasir Mahmood at al. [22] with gem5-X an infrastructure to simulate an Out-of-Order cluster with 3D high-performance memory (HBM2). But our effort, rather than embedded systems, emphasises HPC architectures, adding Vector Engines to the CPUs and networks with high bandwidth and low latencies. Our simulation choice was gem5 [33] because it is a full-system (FS) architectural simulator widely used in academia and industry, as it supports multiple Instruction Set Architectures (ISAs), such as x86, ARMv8, RISCV, and others. In addition to various ISAs, it supports different CPU models for these ISAs, such as atomic, in-order, and out-of-order (OoO) CPU models, as well as multiple caching protocols and coherences. On the memory side, it supports many traditional and emerging memories. Further, gem5 supports FS simulations via several Linux-based operating systems, enabling applications to execute as they would on a real platform. Although gem5 is cycle-accurate and detailed in statistics created during execution, the turnaround is a long simulation time.

Other simulators for co-design of HPC systems are based on SystemC-TLM [34] plus QEMU; however, such a description can miss details on the out-of-order paths or trace base [35], where traces must come from a very similar architecture and hence not effective for detailed and heterogenous design exploration. Other simulators have their niche [36–38] for specific ISAs, but gem5 is more publicly proven.

4   HPC Architecture

The architecture selected for the simulation is in several parameters similar to the Graviton3 (G3). The G3 comprises 64 Neoverse-V1 [39] cores, and each tile of the NoC or CPU has two cores with two SVE of 256 bits. Here, we describe the main differences between our setup defined as *Open Processor for Inception Systems* OPIS (see Table 1 parameters details), the G3 architecture, and A64FX. The simulated designs [10] setup is not outside the parameters ARM offers for their architectures. Moreover, we employ it to explore the memory system. For this study, when there is slack, we always take the larger size of the memories, but we design the decision to keep the two cores per tile as G3. In the case of G3, there is only one NUMA domain for the complete chiplet, while our setup has 4 NUMA domains of 16 cores each, also called System Cache Groups (SCGs). The design is for the SCG2 quadrant: the NUMA domain on the top-left of the chiplet (see Fig. 1a). Another difference is that G3 is connected to four external Double Data Rate (DDR5) memories with eight channels for 64 cores, while we are simulating a configuration with four HBM2 modules with 32 memory channels in total. We only simulate one SCG, with one HBM2 module and eight channels, with 35.82 GiB/s per channel. G3 can exhaust the bandwidth with a few cores executing a memory-bound application like *STREAM*. The ARM CMN-700 [40] for G3 setup seems to follow an LVS1 strategy, meaning one channel per Virtual Network (VNET).

At the same time, we are exploring a higher number of VNETs (i.e. LVS2) to benefit from the higher bandwidth available from the HBM2.

Table 1. Details of fixed and **explored** parameters setup for one OPIS SCG architecture

OPIS SCG (gem5)	Architectural parameters
Clocks	System: 1.6 GHz; CPU: 2.4 GHz; NoC: 2.0 Ghz
CPU	#Cores: 16; Adjusted A76; Branch Pred.: BiMode;
	Vector Unit: 2xSVE; None, SVE length:{256}
L1	Line size: 64B; Size: 64~KiB; Associativity: 4-way;
	Inclusion policy: strict inclusive; TBEs: 256;
	Hit latency: 2-cycles (L1-D), 1-cycles (L1-I);
L2	Unified cache; Line size: 64B; Size: 1 MiB;
	Associativity: 8-way; Hit latency: 4-cycles;
	Inclusion policy: strict inclusive; TBEs: 256;
SLC	Shared SLC cache; #Slices: 16; Line size: 64B;
	Associativity: 16-way; Hit latency: 20-cycles;
	Inclusion policy: Exclusive; TBEs: 256 per slice;
	Size per slice: 4 MiB;
NoC	Interconnect: CMN-650, Model: Garnet 3.0; Protocol: AMBA-CHI;
	Flit width: 64B; Router latency: 1-cycle;
	Link latency: 1-cycle; #VNETs: {lvs1:4, lvs2:7}; Routing XY
	Topology: Mesh: 4 × 4;
	Link configuration: {lvs1, lvs2}
Memory Model	HBM2; #Channel: 8; Size: 2 × 8 GiB
	Bandwidth per channel: 35.82 GiB/s
Prefetcher	**off, on**

The main differences between G3 and A64FX [24] are that the A64FX can deal with external HBM memories (see Fugaku arch [12,25]). The A64FX chip includes four NUMA domains named Core Memory Group (CMG). Each CMG contains 12 cores for application execution. Each core has an SVE of 2×512 bits instead of the 2×256 like in G3. In addition, the A64FX Tofu network interconnection is a double-ring buffer [23] instead of the 2D MESH from G3 and OPIS.

Prefetcher: Our simulation gem5-based setup supports different prefetching schemes. In this paper, we focus on the next-line scheme [26], configured at the L2 cache. For every memory access to the L2 cache, the prefetcher immediately triggers sequential cache accesses (up to 32 cache lines) and stores prefetch candidates in the prefetch queue. Before sending prefetch requests to the memory, the prefetcher needs to search (snoop) in the cache and drops the prefetch request if there is duplicate data. The prefetcher and the gather scatter hardware mechanisms are black boxes in G3, while for A64FX, documentation of the mechanisms is available [24].

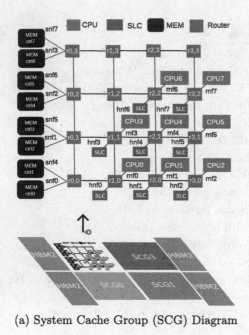

(a) System Cache Group (SCG) Diagram

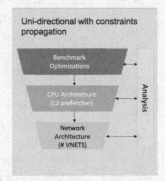

(b) Co-design Methodology: Unidirectional with constraints propagation for memory subsystem study.

Fig. 1. a) Chiplet with SCG Diagram, b) Unidirectional Methodology

The Fig. 1a) presents a chiplet with 4 NUMA regions in the down part. Each NUMA region is named *SCG0-3* (System Cache Group). Each *SCG* has an external HBM2 device connected. Our simulations focus on the *SCG2* that is up-left. In the upper part of Fig. 1a, a 2D MESH network is depicted, and routers are connected in the crosspoints of the SLC/L3 memories and the CPU. The CPU is composed of 1, 2 or 4 cores with 2×256 SVE vector engines. Each CPU has a private per core L1 and shared L2 per cluster. The Subordinate Nodes SN belongs to CHI protocol fundamentals [17]; SNFs nodes connect to memory devices that back the coherent memory space. Eight SNFs nodes connect the number of channels of the HBM2 device [18]. The CPUs work as Coherent Home Nodes (HN-Fs) to compose all requests to coherent memory and issue snoops to Request Nodes (RN-Fs).

5   Design Space Exploration Methodology

Architecture Virtualisation is fundamental for achieving rapid Design Space Exploration (DSE) of HPC microprocessors. The HPC systems design space is vast, with many dimensions to explore. It is the task of the design architects and co-design developers to evaluate and prioritise the most relevant knobs to get the most optimal design.

For this paper, our methodology approach follows the near-optimal design space exploration [27]. In the mentioned DSE, in contrast to existent DSE methods, the partition between the steps is selected so that they can be connected through unidirectional constraint propagation instead of bidirectional constraints. This route achieves a near-optimal result because constraints are not overlooked, which happens when the steps are considered partially independent. Moreover, it divides intractable problems into manageable subproblems.

The DSE methodology is applied to evaluate the memory sub-system. The projected DSE framework pursues step-wise with the division of all the available design space options into cases that correspond to these sub-problems, where the top-down division principle rigorously applies to top-down splits, which are connected through unidirectional constraint propagation.

The architecture exploration considers the SCG, which encloses a set of cores connected in a mesh NoC. The NoC protocol is CHI [28] and the memory model that represents a High Bandwidth Memory (HBM2 [29]) (see Fig. 1b).

5.1   Co-design Exploration: Memory Sub-system

The first split divides the entire design space exploration DSE into two sub-spaces: On one side, the dimensions that belong to the SW optimisations; on the other, the dimensions that belong to the HW ones. From the SW side, we are not experimenting with the different compilers or manual code optimisations. Instead, vectorisation is a crucial dimension affecting the code's performance; for this study, we use auto-vectorisation. Since the developers must adapt the code to the platform, e.g. via loop reordering and specific flags for the compiler, typically, the first step is to vectorise the code to enhance the vector engine utilisation and hence, its influence on the performance (Table 2).

Table 2. Neoverse V1 knobs fixed for the exploration (in bold)

Neoverse V1	Possible knobs value	Chosen Value
Num cores per tile	1, 2, 4	**2**
SVE size	2 × 256	**2 × 256**
L2 size	512 KiB OR 1 MiB (4 banks)	**1 MiB**
SLC size	2 MiB to 4 MiB, 16-way set associative	**4 MiB**

Regarding the HW size, this sub-space can be divided again between CPU knobs and NoC knobs. Regarding the CPU knobs, we set them to a specific value: Although the CPU can have 1, 2 or 4 ARM V1 cores, we selected the two cores' organisation per tile (or in each router) with a total of 16 cores per SCG (see Fig. 1a). One characteristic parameter is the vector size. We specified 2×-width vector units similar to the ARM-V1 architecture [30], with a width of 256 bits. Although there is also flexibility in the L2 and SLC/L3 sizes, we always opted for the larger cache sizes. L2 size can be 512 KiB or 1 MiB (4 banks). For the System-level cache (SLC), we have 1 Bank per core duplex and a size of 2 MiB to 4 MiB, 16-way set associative. Finally, for the memory system and the CPU, the hardware prefetcher in the L2 is a knob that enhances the performance.

The other subspace or subproblem related to the network knobs for this article is the network topology and the routing algorithm. We selected the 2D Mesh, XY algorithm, again similar to architectures like Graviton3 [31]. The external memory device is a High Bandwidth Memory (HBM2) [18,22].

Another knob we changed is the number of NoC physical links per VNET in the routers, intending to find the setup that most benefits from the external memory devices. Link-VNET-Support-1 (LVS1) is defined as one link per VNET, where the 4 VNETS defined in AMBA-CHI Cache Coherence (CC) protocol are: 0-request, 1-snoop, 2-response and 3-data (REQ, SNP, RSP and DATA). The second possibility (LVS2) uses two physical links per VNET. In the case of the snoop VNET (SNP), we still use one link, as there is little traffic in the examples under study. Hence, the LVS2 NoC configuration uses seven links in total.

5.2   Model Validation

To increase the confidence of the presented results, we have executed kernels in real machines prototype and compared them with a corresponding gem5 model. For instance, if the machine is the N1SDP [32] prototype board with two sockets, each containing 2 ARM-N1 cores. We developed the gem5 version of the platform using the board's datasheet. In addition, we considered the Performance Monitoring Unit (PMU) counters and compared the results. Finally, we apply a multi-level consistency validation [10] for reference applications and kernels.

6   Case Studies

The section describes the design exploration of the memory sub-system through the unidirectional with constraints propagation. The subsection defines the Spatter Uniform Stride (US) behaviour in the CPU data path. It simplifies the compiler generation of Gather/Scatter instructions. Each thread performs some portion of the iteration. In addition, each thread's block gathers into a local destination buffer to ensure high performance. The effect avoids false sharing.

The Uniform Stride index buffer in Spatter is specified with UNIFORM: N:STRIDE. It generates an index buffer of size N with STRIDE. For example, the index buffer generated by UNIFORM:8:2 is [0,2,4,8,10,12,14,16] or UNIFORM:8:8 is [0,8,16,24,32,40,48,56]. This manuscript's Spatter Uniform Stride is similar to the Stream benchmark [20]. The added value offers extra information about the pattern's index of common HPC applications too large for cycle-accurate simulation.

6.1 Unidirectional Approach

The Unidirectional approach with constraints propagation method begins in the dimension with a higher impact on the outcomes. Then, when the space exploration dimension is optimised, we continue with the following one with the constraints from the previous one. Hence, no loops or iterations are needed. For example, starting from the previous methodology, we observed and analysed the impact of vectorisation; we then took the vectorised code and used it for the prefetching effect afterwards for the increase of links, the LVS1 vs LVS2 study. The expectation is to find an architecture where the external memory controllers' usage is 80% or higher. After continuing with the following dimensions, for the reasons analysed further below.

The dimension under study are a) vectorisation, b) enhancements due to prefetcher, and c) enhancing the number of links from LVS1 to LVS2. Table 3 presents the improvements due to code vectorisation, which ranges from 23% to 97%. Then we observed the impact of the prefetcher on the bandwidth (see Sub. Fig. 2a), showing improvements of $x2$. The Fig. 2b) shows a saturation in the NoC due LVS1 configuration.

Table 3. Spatter Uniform Stride: Bandwidth increase due to vectorisation

	Spatter Uniform Stride: BW increase due to vectorisation				
Configuration	8:1	8:2	8:4	8:8	8:16
Performance Improvement(%)	60.3	93.9	96.8	29.3	23

Bandwidth in the SCG with LVS1: We experimented with the OPIS SCG with LVS1, where we increased the number of cores per CPU. Instead of using the default SCG with 16 cores, we increased it to 4 and 8 CPUs per router, having an SCG of 32 cores and 64 cores, respectively, all the cores with the prefetcher enabled. The objective is to maximise the bus utilisation in the memory controllers. In addition, we want to observe the optimal use of the HBM2 memory devices. As the number of cores increases, the number of data requests to the memories increases. We want to observe the Miss Status Holding Register (MSHR) since it is the buffer to track outstanding requests.

The results are depicted in Fig. 2b, showing the differences between the bandwidth observable in the memory controllers as a percentage of the bus utilisation versus the bandwidth reported by the Spatter application. While Spatter reports a lower bandwidth when the stride increases (as it measures effective

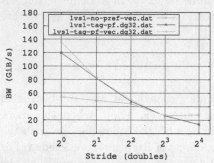

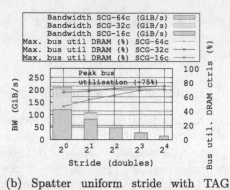

(a) Impact of the prefetcher on the band-width

(b) Spatter uniform stride with TAG prefetcher degree 32 executed in OPIS-SCG (LVS1)

Fig. 2. a) Bandwidth utilisation improvements due to data prefetching, b) HMB2 Bandwidth saturation due to LVS1-NoC.

bandwidth only), the bus utilisation increases to 75%, which means that from the 286.56 GiB that can provide the HBM2 module, only 75% (215 GiB/s) is achieved. Bus bandwidth utilisations start to saturate at *stride-8* and *16*, even when using many more cores and increasing the outstanding requests by 4×.

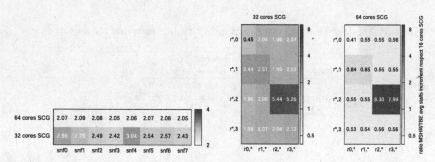

(a) Memory controllers (snf) stalls in-crement from baseline (16 cores SCG) for 32 and 64 cores SCG

(b) SLC (hnf) stalls increment from baseline (16 cores SCG) for 32 and 64 cores SCG

Fig. 3. a) Stalls in memory controllers, b) stalls in the SLCs memories

Therefore, even when the number of MSHR requests increases since more cores (i.e. SCG 32 and 64 cores) request data from the memory controllers, the bandwidth at the memory controllers saturates when it achieves 75% of the peak HBM2 bandwidth. The LVS1 configuration can only partially benefit from the HBM2 bandwidth available. To understand the reason, we observe the situation of the TBE_avg (similar to MSHR but named differently in the gem5 simulator) in the routers for the point 2^4, which is our point of interest. This means there is saturation in LVS1, and the HBM device provides 3/4 of its bandwidth capacity. The architects decide if this limitation is economically viable or if using cheaper devices with lower bandwidth (i.e. DDR5) but larger capacity is a better option.

Increasing stride will downsize the requirements for resource allocation in the micro-architecture (e.g. register file allocation) and thus could reduce stalls. Therefore, with a higher stride, the CPU can stress the memory system by sending more in-flight requests. To observe the saturated point of bus bandwidth utilisation at the memory controller, we ran experiments via a variant stride from 1 to 16. A *stride-16* will advise us of the maximum bus bandwidth utilisation.

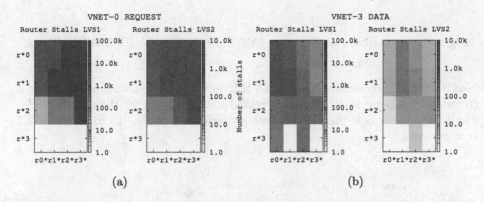

Fig. 4. Heatmap with router stalls (LVS1 vs LVS2). (a) REQUEST (b) DATA VNETs.

Heatmaps of the NoC and Memory Controllers for LVS1 Configuration. Figure 3a, presents the increment of stalls from the baseline architecture (i.e. 16-core SCG) to the architectures with 32- and 64-core SCG in the memory controllers. The increment in cores produces more outstanding requests to the memory controllers. Nevertheless, there are a pair of bottlenecks, a factor of ×3 in stalls in *snf0* and *snf4* (see Fig. 3a), and also a bottleneck in the tiles see Fig. 3b in the routers far away from the memory controllers (i.e. *r22*, *r32*), with increments higher than 5 and 8 times for 32 and 64 cores configuration, respectively.

NoC VNET Stalls LVS1 vs LVS2. Previous experiments provide enough insights to suggest that there are better configurations than LVS1 to optimise the usage of the HBM2 devices. Hence, we experimented with the baseline SCG but with the LVS2 configuration to observe the stalls in the routers.

Figure 4 presents another heatmap comparing the number of stalls for all the VNETS; there is no figure for the SNOOP VNET because the packet traffic is meagre in this study, and the RESPOND channel is similar the to REQUEST. Again, we can observe that the decrease in stalls in LVS2 is a factor of ×10 with respect LVS1.

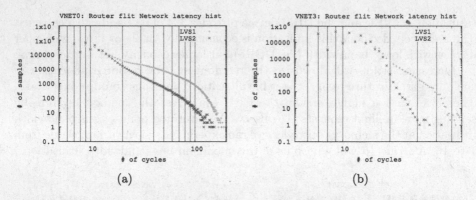

Fig. 5. Latencies histogram (LVS1 vs LVS2). (a) REQUEST; (b) DATA VNETS.

NoC VNET Latencies LVS1 vs LVS2. In the same experiment, we checked the router flit network latency and created the histogram for the main VNETs. Figure 5 presents how the network latency reduces from the LVS1 to the LVS2 configuration.

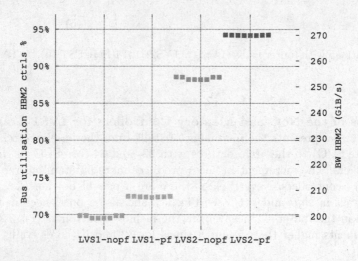

Fig. 6. Bus utilisation for spatter uniform stride, *stride-16* in several OPIS configurations: LVS1 without and with prefetcher(nopf, pf), LVS2 without and with prefetcher (nopf, pf)

Bus Utilisation in MEM Controllers. Figure 6 exhibits the simulation outcomes for uniform *stride-16*. The memory controllers have a utilisation higher than 88% (achieving 252,17 GiB) for LVS2 with the prefetcher disabled and 93% when the prefetcher is enabled. Hence, compared with the LVS1 configuration,

LVS2 decreases the stalls in the system and increases the bus utilisation. Therefore, it is recommended to use LVS2 if the external memory is an HBM module and we are interested in its optimal use. Figure 6 presents the bus utilisation of each of the eight memory controller configurations with and without enabled prefetcher. The best configuration is achieved for LVS2 with prefetcher active (*LVS2-pf*).

Insight: Conversely, to the intuition adding more links (i.e. LVS1 to LVS2) without other improvements in the design does not produce better performance. It is when the combination of several design features like vectorisation and aggressiveness of the prefetcher and extra links in the NoC produces a high usage of the memory device.

7   Conclusions and Future Work

The paper presents a methodology to explore the memory subsystem in a many-core system for HPC connected to HBM devices using the Spatter benchmark. The methodology permits finding bottlenecks in the system. For example, it was able to detect that a NoC configuration with only one link per VNET (defined as LVS1) can only use 75% of the bandwidth of the HBM2 device. Nevertheless, the additional analysis allowed us to observe that a configuration with two links per VNET (i.e. LVS2), with vectorised code and enough aggressiveness of the prefetcher, increases resource utilisation above 90% (observation at the memory controller).

In the future, using novel 3D stacked memory chiplets (i.e. HBM3), we would like to model new network topologies and routing algorithms other than 2D MESH to analyse if there are designs that bring benefit (i.e. reducing stalls and latencies). Another dimension not described in the paper is the power envelope; it would be relevant to estimate the overheads due to, for example, the aggressiveness of the prefetching or due to more oversized packet routing buses. Finally, it is still an open question whether our designs can keep the pace of future characteristics' external memories and use them efficiently.

Acknowledgment. This work has been performed in the context of the European Processor Initiative (EPI) project, which has received funding from the European Union's Horizon 2020 research and innovation program under Grant Agreement №101036168 (EPI-SGA2).

References

1. Sato, M., et al.: Co-design and system for the supercomputer "fugaku". IEEE Micro. **42**(2), 26–34 (2022)
2. Monroe, D.: Fugaku takes the lead. Commun. ACM **64**(1), 16–18 (2021)
3. Yamamura, S., et al.: A64FX: 52-core processor designed for the 442petaflops supercomputer fugaku. In: ISSCC, San Francisco, CA, USA, 20–26 February 2022, pp. 352–354. IEEE (2022)

4. Sato, M.: The supercomputer "fugaku" and ARM-SVE enabled A64FX processor for energy-efficiency and sustained application performance. In: ISPDC 2020, pp. 1–5 (2020)
5. Stephens, N., et al.: The ARM scalable vector extension. CoRR, abs/1803.06185 (2018)
6. Lee, J., et al.: Extending OpenMP SIMD support for target specific code and application to ARM SVE. In: Scaling OpenMP for Exascale Performance and Portability - 13th IWOMP (2017)
7. Reed, D., et al.: Reinventing high performance computing: Challenges and opportunities (2022)
8. Petitet, A., et al.: HPL - a portable implementation of the high-performance LINPACK benchmark for distributed-memory computers, December 2018
9. Wu, D., Li, J., Yin, R., Hsiao, H., Kim, Y., Miguel, J.S.: UGEMM: unary computing architecture for GEMM applications. In: ISCA, pp. 377–390 (2020)
10. Zaourar, L., et al.: Multilevel simulation-based co-design of next generation HPC microprocessors (PMBS), St. Louis, MO, USA, pp. 18–29 (2021)
11. Lavin, P., Riedy, E.J., Vuduc, R., Young, J.S.: Spatter: a benchmark suite for evaluating sparse access patterns. CoRR, abs/1811.03743 (2018)
12. Sato, M., et al.: Co-design for A64FX manycore processor and "Fugaku". In: SC20: International Conference For High Performance Computing, Networking, Storage and Analysis, pp. 1–15 (2020)
13. Mathá, R., Kimovski, D., Zabrovskiy, A., Timmerer, C., Prodan, R.: Where to encode: a performance analysis of ×86 and ARM-based Amazon EC2 instances. In: eScience, pp. 118–127 (2021)
14. ARM: ARM® Neoverse™ V1- Amazon's graviton3 server chip. https://www.nextplatform.com/2022/05/24/the-value-proposition-for-amazons-graviton3-server-chip/
15. ECP: Milestone M1 Report: HBM2/3 Evaluation on Many-core CPU WBS 2.4, Milestone ECP-MT-1000. Exascale Computing Project, June 2018
16. Biswas, A.: Sapphire Rapids. In: 2021 IEEE Hot Chips 33 Symposium (HCS), Palo Alto, CA, USA, pp. 1–22 (2021). https://doi.org/10.1109/HCS52781.2021.9566865
17. ARM: Learn the architecture - Introducing AMBA CHI, Non-Confidential. Issue 01, 102407_0100_01_e
18. High bandwidth memory (HBM) dram. JEDEC (2020)
19. Brank, B., Nassyr, S., Pouyan, F., Pleiter, D.: Porting applications to ARM-based processors. In: 2020 IEEE International Conference on Cluster Computing (CLUSTER), pp. 559–566 (2020)
20. McCalpin, J.: Memory bandwidth and machine balance in current high performance computers. (TCCA) Newsletter **2**, 19–25 (1995)
21. McKee, S.A.: Reflections on the memory wall. In: Proceedings of the First Conference on Computing Frontiers, 2004, Ischia, Italy, 14–16 April 2004
22. Qureshi, Y., et al.: Gem5-X: a many-core heterogeneous simulation platform for architectural exploration and optimization. ACM Trans. Archit. Code Optim. **18**, 1–27 (2021)
23. Okazaki, R., et al.: Supercomputer Fugaku CPU A64FX Realizing High Performance, High-Density Packaging, and Low Power Consumption. Fujitsu Technical ReviewNo.32020 (2020)
24. Hondou, M.: A64fx microarchitecture manual v1.8 released (2019). https://github.com/fujitsu/A64FX
25. Nakamura, Y., et al.: Fugaku codesign report. Technical report, FLAGSHIP 2020 Project, RIKEN Center for Computational Science (R-CCS), RIKEN (2022)

26. Smith, A.J.: Sequential program prefetching in memory hierarchies. Computer **11**, 7–21 (1978)
27. Kritikakou, A., Catthoor, F., Goutis, C.: Scalable and Near-Optimal Design Space Exploration for Embedded Systems. Springer, Cham (2014). https://doi.org/10.1007/978-3-319-04942-7
28. ARM: AMBA® 5 CHI architecture specification. https://developer.arm.com/documentation/ihi0050/ea/ (2020)
29. JEDEC: High bandwidth memory (HBM) dram. Standards JESD235D, Joint Electron Device Engineering Council, March 2021
30. ARM: Developer, ARM® neoverse™ v1 core, rev:r1p1. Technical reference manual. Technical report, ARM- Advanced RISC Machines (2021)
31. '/' Inside amazon's graviton3 ARM server processor. https://www.nextplatform.com/2022/01/04/inside-amazons-graviton3-arm-server-processor. Accessed 17 Oct 2022
32. ARM: ARM® Neoverse™ N1 core - technical reference manual. https://developer.arm.com/documentation/100616/0401/?lang=en (2020)
33. Binkert, N., et al.: The gem5 simulator. ACM SIGARCH Comput. Archit. News. **39**, 1–7 (2011)
34. Ventroux, N., et al.: SESAM: An MPSoC simulation environment for dynamic application processing. In: 2010 10th IEEE CIT, pp. 1880–1886 (2010)
35. Gómez, C., et al.: Design space exploration of next-generation HPC machines. IPDPS **2019**, 54–65 (2019)
36. Hardavellas, N., et al.: SimFlex: a fast, accurate, flexible full-system simulation framework for performance evaluation of server architecture. SIGMETRICS Perform. Eval. Rev. **31**, 31–34 (2004)
37. Magnusson, P.S., et al.: Simics: a full system simulation platform. Computer **35**, 50–58 (2002)
38. Carlson, et al. Sniper: exploring the level of abstraction for scalable and accurate parallel multi-core simulation. In: SC 2011, pp. 1–12 (2011)
39. Microarchitecture description ARM v1. ARM report (2022)
40. ARM: ARM® Neoverse™ CMN-700 Coherent Mesh Network, Technical Reference Manual, 102308_0300_05_en (2022)

Post-Silicon Customization Using Deep Neural Networks

Kevin Weston[1]([✉]), Vahid Janfaza[1], Abhishek Taur[1], Dhara Mungra[2], Arnav Kansal[2], Mohamed Zahran[2], and Abdullah Muzahid[1]

[1] Texas A&M University, College Station, TX, USA
kevin.weston@tamu.edu
[2] New York University, New York, NY, USA

Abstract. Dynamically customizing processor architecture after fabrication, also known as Post-Silicon Customization (PSC) is effective in balancing the conflicting demands of power and performance for various applications. Existing approaches either use application-specific profiles or some adhoc heuristics or simpler machine learning models. These techniques often do not unleash the full potential of PSC as they fail to explore and exploit PSC opportunities to a larger extent. Towards that end, we propose the *first* deep neural network (DNN) based PSC technique, called FORECASTER. FORECASTER exploits several intuitive observations to cope with the long inference latency of a DNN model and boost customization impact. FORECASTER works in two phases. In Phase 1, FORECASTER builds a dataset and then, selects and trains a suitable DNN model offline. In Phase 2, FORECASTER periodically collects hardware telemetry and uses the trained model to customize hardware resources. We provide a detailed design and implementation of FORECASTER and compare its performance against a prior state-of-the-art approach. Our experimental results indicate that on average, FORECASTER provides 2.5X more power efficiency gain over the best static configuration setup while sacrificing less than 1.0% of overall performance and less than 3.5% extra system power. Compared to the prior scheme, FORECASTER increases the power efficiency gain up to 1.5X while reducing the performance degradation by 44%.

Keywords: Deep neural network · FPGA · post-silicon customization

1 Introduction

Dynamically customizing processor architecture after fabrication, also known as Post-Silicon Customization (PSC) is an effective technique to satisfy the conflicting demands of power and performance for a diverse set of applications [24]. There are three general approaches to implement PSC - profiling, heuristic, and learning-based. Profiling-based approaches profile a particular application on specific hardware or platform and use the profiling information to customize the hardware or software [11,12,15]. This line of work requires each program to be instrumented and profiled first. However, the profiled information is useful for

G. Goumas et al. (Eds.): ARCS 2023, LNCS 13949, pp. 120–136, 2023.
https://doi.org/10.1007/978-3-031-42785-5_9

only that application. Heuristic-based approaches are built around some heuristics which are often proposed by the architects or programmers based on their experience or intuition [7,20] on a limited number of hardware or applications. Heuristics often work best for a certain class of applications while other classes may suffer from poor results. Learning-based approaches try to overcome the limitations of profiling and heuristic-based approaches. At the heart of these approaches are some machine learning models that predict application behavior, processor performance, power consumption, or a combination of these factors. Customization is done based on prediction [8,22,24]. Existing learning-based approaches achieve some remarkable results. However, they rely on simple and shallow machine learning models which often fail to unleash the full potential of learning-based approaches. This paper aims to change that by using a deep neural network (DNN) for PSC.

We pinpoint two reasons why existing approaches did not rely on DNN models. *First,* most of the existing works were proposed before the advancement of deep learning techniques [3,6,8,13]. The recent explosion of DNN models and their super-human ability in certain domains, coupled with the availability of hardware accelerators for such models [4,5] makes DNNs the perfect and timely choice to investigate whether they can improve PSC. *Second,* most of the existing works aim to customize hardware frequently (once in every 100K or less instructions) [22,24]. Therefore, DNNs with thousands of cycles per inference operation (Table 6) may not be suitable.

To investigate the feasibility of DNNs for PSC, we make two observations. *First,* applications show repetitive execution phases (Sect. 2). Although phases, when defined at a fine-grained level, might change very frequently, PSC done at such a high frequency does not yield many benefits due to the high customization overhead. Therefore, we have to focus on coarse-grained phases and such phases do not change frequently. *Second, hardware resources that can be customized in the background (without affecting ongoing operations) can boost the customization impact.* Based on these observations, we propose a DNN-based PSC technique, called FORECASTER. FORECASTER relies on hardware telemetry (a set of hardware performance counters) to approximate how an application behaves and targets four hardware resources for customization - L2 and L3 caches, Branch Target Buffer (BTB), and Prefetcher. We target these structures because they consume significant power [14] and can be customized in the background. FORECASTER works in two phases. In Phase 1, it builds a predictive model offline to learn application behavior and the corresponding level of hardware resources to maximize the power efficiency. We use $Instruction\ Per\ Second\ (IPS)^3/Power$ as the metric to calculate power efficiency. This is similar to prior work [8]. FORECASTER builds a training dataset based on the data collected from all possible configurations of the selected hardware resources. This dataset is used to train and determine the best DNN model for PSC. In Phase 2, FORECASTER initializes a DNN hardware with the model selected from Phase 1. During a program's execution, FORECASTER collects hardware telemetry at regular intervals and uses the DNN model to predict the best configuration of hardware resources. FORECASTER customizes those resources accordingly to maximize the power efficiency. In summary, we make the following contributions:

1. We propose FORECASTER, the *first* PSC technique to use a DNN model. We used a DNN model with over 9 billion parameters.
2. We propose to use a longer customization interval and choose hardware resources carefully to cope up with the long inference delay of a DNN model and boost the customization impact.
3. We provide a detailed design and implementation of FORECASTER using Multi2Sim [25] simulator. Our experimental results using PARSEC 3.0 benchmarks show that on average, FORECASTER provides 2.5X more power efficiency over the best static configuration while sacrificing less than 1.0% of overall performance. Compared to a prior learning scheme [8], FORECASTER increases the power efficiency gain up to 1.5X while reducing the performance degradation by 44%.

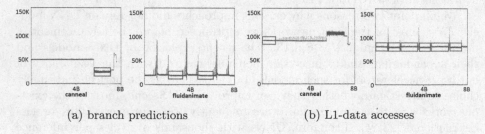

(a) branch predictions   (b) L1-data accesses

Fig. 1. Number of branch predictions and L1-data accesses over time (x-axis unit is number of instructions). Similarities are highlighted in colored boxes.

2 Intuition

FORECASTER is grounded on two simple hypotheses - *(i) there are significant similarities in execution phases across applications, and (ii) each execution phase requires a specific hardware configuration to maximize the power efficiency without hurting performance.*

To support the first hypothesis, we analyze two applications - *canneal* and *fluidanimate* from Parsec. Figure 1a & 1b show the number of branch predictions and L1-data accesses over execution time. The red-colored boxes in Fig. 1a show that one execution phase of *canneal* is similar to two execution phases of *fluidanimate* where the number of branch predictions is steady at around 20K. Thus, the control flow structure of these execution phases between two different applications is similar. If we consider L1-data accesses, Fig. 1b shows that one execution phase of *canneal* is similar to 6 other execution phases of *fluidanimate*. Therefore, the data access patterns of these phases of the applications should be similar too. In other words, despite being two completely different applications with different functionalities, *canneal* and *fluidanimate* share a lot of similarities in their execution phases. In addition to this, we notice in both figures that each execution phase usually contains a significant number of instructions (more than a few millions). Therefore, we do not need frequent customization of L1 and BTB structures.

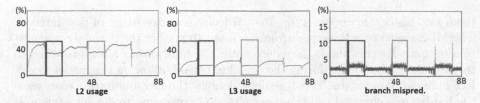

Fig. 2. Time-series data of branch misprediction rate, L2 and L3 usage of *fluidanimate* during execution.

Figure 2 shows the detailed time-series characteristics of L2 and L3 usage as well as branch mispredictions of *fluidanimate*. It shows that the first execution phase (shown in green boxes) has different L2, L3 access, and branch characteristics than the second phase (shown in red boxes). Therefore, the hardware configuration that provides the optimal trade-off between power efficiency and performance for the first phase is different than that of the second phase. For example, since the first phase uses about 45% of L2 and 25% of L3, an optimal cache configuration of the first phase consists of 60% of L2 and 40% of L3. Similarly, the optimal configuration for the second phase is a combination of 40% of L2 and 20% of L3. This clearly demonstrates that every distinct phase requires a different hardware configuration to maximize the power efficiency while maintaining performance. Note that the fourth phase (in yellow box) is quite similar to the second phase and therefore, require the same hardware configuration as the second phase.

3 Background and Related Work

There is a considerable amount of prior work on reconfigurable architecture [2,3, 6–8,11–13,15,20,22,24], which can be grouped into three categories: profiling [11, 12,15], heuristic [2,6,7,20], and learning-based [3,8,13,22,24].

Heuristic-Based Techniques: Choi and Yeung [6] perform microarchitectural resources distribution in an SMT processor using hill-climbing algorithm. Petrica et al. [20] present Flicker, a general-purpose multicore architecture that dynamically adapts to varying limits on allocated power. A Flicker core has reconfigurable lanes through the pipeline that allows tailoring an individual core to the running application with lower overhead.

Profiling-Based Techniques: Hubert et al. [11] propose MEMTRACE, a profiling tool that analyzes memory accesses and runtime performance of applications, enabling a variety of optimization opportunities. Ripple [15] introduces a profiling technique that minimizes the instruction cache miss rate. First, the program is profiled offline to get the basic blocks and reconstruct the oracle replacement behavior. Next, Ripple forcefully evicts those basic blocks that is likely to be evicted under the oracle policy by modifying the program binary code.

Learning-Based Techniques: Dubach et al. [8] use Maximum Likelihood Estimation (MLE) to dynamically reconfigure the processor's components. At runtime, whenever the program encounters a new phase, the system enters a profiling period. During this time, The system collects performance counters and converts them into histograms representing the hardware resource usage of that interval. The MLE model uses these histograms as input to predict the optimal configuration to apply for this phase. To reduce noise, the hardware is always reverted to the default configuration during the profiling period, allowing the model to collect unbiased input data. This technique doubles the reconfiguration cost, since the hardware is changed two times per phase: (1) reverting to default configuration for profiling and (2) reconfiguring to the model's prediction. Additionally, the conversion from runtime counters to histograms may produce extra computational latency and hardware support. On the contrary, FORECASTER can work with simple performance counters and does not need a dedicated profiling period, minimizing runtime overheads. Bitirgen et al. [3] combine performance prediction model of multiple applications to get an aggregate performance prediction of the overall resource distribution. Ravi et al. [22] propose CHARSTAR, a clock tree aware resource optimizing mechanism. CHARSTAR incorporates a shallow multi-layer perceptron with one hidden layer to predict the optimal configuration in each execution phase. The model's performance is then tested on single-threaded programs. Tarsa et al. [24] propose a lightweight ML framework that can be distributed through firmware updates to the microcontroller for post-silicon CPUs. The ML model is first trained offline with a collection of applications to avoid statistical blind spots. During execution, the CPU dynamically sets the issue width of a clustered hardware component while clock-gating unused resources.

There is also a well-established line of work that tries to achieve an energy-performance trade-off without any hardware structural adaptation. Prominent works that fall in this category use dynamic voltage-frequency scaling (DVFS) [7, 10,19]. However, applying this technique in real-world systems can be tricky because reduced frequency means longer execution time.

4   Main Idea: FORECASTER

FORECASTER works in two phases - (i) building a model that predicts the best configuration of hardware resources for maximizing the power efficiency (i.e., $IPS^3/Power$) and (ii) changing the hardware resources accordingly. Figure 3 shows the overall workflow. FORECASTER works in the first phase only once using a set of applications whereas the second phase happens at runtime repeatedly during the execution. Both phases use hardware telemetry collected during the execution of an application. The telemetry consists of various hardware event counters that implicitly capture the behavior of the application. The first phase uses telemetry to build a dataset which is used to train a DNN model. The second phase uses the trained DNN model to customize hardware resources.

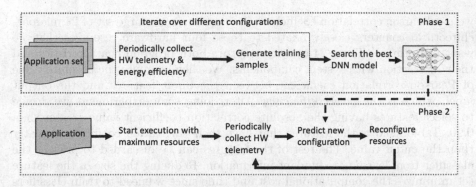

Fig. 3. Overall workflow of FORECASTER.

4.1   Phase 1: Building a Predictive Model

FORECASTER builds a predictive model by first collecting hardware telemetry on a set of benchmarks for different configurations of hardware resources and then, training a DNN model on the dataset.

Table 1. List of reconfigurable hardware. **Table 2.** Pearson correlation coefficients Initial configuration is in bold-face. of counters.

Tunable Resource	Configuration
BTB Size	0.5K, 1K, 2K, and **4K** Entries
Prefetcher	**On**, Off
L2 (private) cache	256K, 512K, 768K, and **1024K** Bytes
L3 (shared LLC) cache	4M, 8M, 12M, and **16M** Bytes

Features	Correlation Coefficient
L2 most usage	0.633786
normalized commit float	0.615692
normalized commit mem	0.505695
normalized commit int	0.450328
L1 data access	0.443464
normalized commit ctrl	0.436718
L2 avg eviction rate	0.337137
L2 most hit rate	0.295210
L3 usage	0.264086
branch mispred rate	0.242080

Selecting Hardware Resources. As reconfigurable hardware resources, we choose L2 and L3 caches, Branch Target Buffer (BTB) and Prefetcher. We choose caches because they are the most power-hungry resources in a modern chip [14]. We choose the other resources because they can be easily clock-gated without making intrusive changes to the pipeline (Sect. 4.2). Moreover, as shown in prior work [8], these structures can be customized in the background with minimal impact on performance. Table 1 shows the reconfigurable resources and possible configurations.

Selecting Hardware Telemetry. Modern processors provide hundreds of hardware event counters as the telemetry. Not all of them are relevant in deciding how to reconfigure various resources. Therefore, to select the most relevant ones, we use Pearson correlation coefficient. We first extract a large set of 24 microarchitectural counters closely related to those four hardware resources that we want to optimize. These 24 counters capture both program characteristics and their interaction with system components. We then compute the absolute value of Pearson correlation coefficient between the input features and the output label, which is the *power efficiency*. After doing some experiments we decide to select features having the absolute correlation coefficient value greater than 0.20. Table 2 shows the features that have their correlation coefficients greater than the cutoff value. The rest of the features can be discarded to prevent the classifier from learning redundant information. Reducing the size of the feature set minimizes the computational cost and time since we need to train classifiers on large dataset. Those counters, combined with the last interval configuration which are consolidated into 4 inputs, form the final set of 14 input features of our DNN model.

Building Dataset. With 4 reconfigurable resources, there are $N = 4*2*4*4 = 128$ possible configurations. Each application is executed and profiled under each of these configurations. During the execution of an application, FORECASTER collects hardware telemetry, calculates the power efficiency periodically after every $\mathbb{I}$ instructions and records them in a profiling file. Let us call every $\mathbb{I}$ instruction an *Interval*. Let us denote the telemetry as $\mathbb{T} = \{t_i\}_{i=1}^{n}$, where each t_i is an individual hardware counter and the power efficiency as $\mathbb{E}$. Thus, the profiling file contains a set of records of $< \mathbb{T}, \mathbb{E} >$, one record for each interval. FORECASTER keeps the input fixed for an application during profiling. Still, there could be slight perturbation during some execution due to the difference in hardware configurations and thread scheduling (in the case of a multithreaded

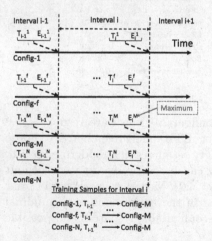

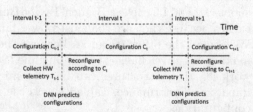

Fig. 4. How training samples are formed from profiles.

Fig. 5. Timing of various steps of FORECASTER.

application). Therefore, we choose $\mathbb{I}$ to be large enough so that the number of intervals remains the same in every profiling file of an application. As a result, each corresponding interval in different profiling files represents (roughly) the same code region of the application. Whatever little difference that could exist among the code regions of similar intervals, adds noise to the training dataset. Such noise works in favor of DNN models to improve their generality.

Let us consider an interval i. The profiling record for i is $< \mathbb{T}_i^f, \mathbb{E}_i^f >$ in the profiling file for $Config - f$ ($Config - f$ could be any of the $\mathbb{N}$ configurations i.e., $1 \leq f \leq \mathbb{N}$). FORECASTER finds the maximum among $\mathbb{E}_i^1$ to $\mathbb{E}_i^\mathbb{N}$. The configuration corresponding to the maximum, say $Config - \mathbb{M}$, provides the highest power efficiency. Therefore, at runtime, when FORECASTER tries to predict the best configuration at the beginning of interval i, it should predict $Config - \mathbb{M}$ as the output of the DNN model. That is why phase 1 forms a training sample by using $\mathbb{T}_{i-1}^f$ as the input and $Config - \mathbb{M}$ as the output. Note that FORE-CASTER uses $\mathbb{T}_{i-1}^f$ instead of $\mathbb{T}_i^f$ as the input because the telemetry collected at the beginning of interval i is the telemetry corresponding to interval $i - 1$. Thus, DNN should be trained to predict $Config - \mathbb{M}$ (the best configuration for interval i) by using the telemetry collected at the beginning of interval i. Figure 4 shows the telemetry and power efficiency of different intervals across different configurations. Last but not least, in addition to $\mathbb{T}_{i-1}^f$, the corresponding configuration i.e., $Config - f$ is provided as part of the input in the training sample. In other words, the training sample is formed by using $< Config - f, \mathbb{T}_{i-1}^f >$ as the input and $Config - \mathbb{M}$ as the output. So, there are $\mathbb{N}$ training samples for interval i.

Selecting a Predictive Model. The dataset built previously is used to train a machine learning model. We initially experiment with simple models such as logistic regression or MLE. Our experiments reveal that such simple models are not able to substantially improve the power efficiency of the system (Sect. 7). We then use more sophisticated models including LSTM, Reinforcement Learning, DNN and see that the fully connected DNN model strikes a good balance between performance and implementation cost. Therefore, we finalize our design with a fully connected DNN model. To find the best model architecture, FORECASTER searches all possible network configurations (e.g., topology, learning rate, activation functions, etc.) within a constrained search space (e.g., all topologies up to the maximum of H hidden layers and L neurons per layer) and picks the one with the highest accuracy. We use cross-validation for model training and tuning to avoid overfitting. The training strategy for both single-program and multi-program scenarios is discussed in Sect. 6. The final DNN architecture and its hardware implementation cost is discussed in Sect. 7.

4.2 Phase 2: Prediction-Based Hardware Reconfiguration

During this phase, FORECASTER loads the trained DNN model in a DNN hardware and uses it to predict the configuration of hardware resources for maximizing the power efficiency. When an application starts execution, FORECASTER starts with maximum resources. This prevents any initial slowdown due to insufficient resources. FORECASTER collects hardware telemetry after every interval of $\mathbb{I}$ instructions. Suppose the telemetry after interval t is $\mathbb{T}_t$ and the resource configuration is C_t. FORECASTER uses the DNN hardware with $< C_t, \mathbb{T}_t >$ as the input to infer the new configuration C_{t+1}. Figure 5 shows the timing of the inference step. After DNN hardware calculates the predicted configuration, C_{t+1}, FORECASTER customizes the hardware resources according to C_{t+1}. Now, we describe how each resource is customized.

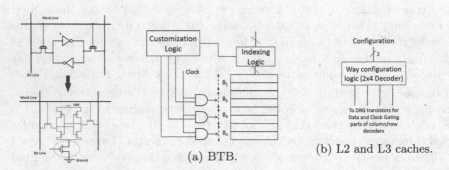

(a) BTB.   (b) L2 and L3 caches.

Fig. 6. SRAM Cell Design (6T-MC) with the gated-Vdd shown on the bottom. **Fig. 7.** Logic for customizing hardware components.

L2 and L3 Caches. Caches, mainly designed in SRAM (we are not considering eDRAM in this paper) are sources of both static and dynamic power consumption. Dynamic power is consumed in row-decoder, column-decoder, pre-charge circuit and some parts of the core cell and depends on the access pattern. Static power, mainly leakage, is dissipated in every cell of the SRAM cache. With the continuous reduction in transistor sizes and, consequently, the switching threshold voltage of the transistor, static power becomes the major source of power dissipation in caches [26]. Therefore, when we turn off parts of the cache, we want to ensure that we target leakage current. For that, we use gated-ground [1,18,21].

There are several ways of implementing SRAM cells. The one most widely used, due to its relatively high noise immunity, is the 6-transistors Memory Cell (6T-MC), shown in Fig. 6. The left part of the figure shows the gate level of a single SRAM cell. The right part shows the circuit level. There is an extra transistor, shown circled, that is used to reduce leakage current that constitutes the major part of the static power dissipation in caches. In our design of cache resizing, we turn-off individual blocks and never a full-set. Therefore, we can use a single transistor per block. That is, one extra transistor per 64 cells for a 64-byte block. This design does not use more than 4% of extra area with around 5%

increase in cache latency [1]. The increased access latency has been taken into consideration in our simulation. When a block is turned-off, that extra transistor is also turned off causing a *stacking effect* that reduces leakage current by orders of magnitude [1].

The next step is to control which blocks will be gated (for static power) and control which parts will be clock-gated to avoid accessing the blocks that are turned-off. From Table 1, we can see that we have four configurations for the cache. We need two bits to represent those configurations. A 2×4 decoder is enough, as shown in Fig. 7b. The output of the decoder that is set to one, is used to turn off the corresponding transistors in the data lines. We turn off blocks starting from the last way in each set. For example, in LLC cache, if we want to go from 16 MB to 12 MB in a 16-way, we turn-off ways 15, 14, 13, and 12. In the current design, FORECASTER only turns off invalid ways, thus incurring no extra data writeback cost. The output of the decoder is also used to clock-gate parts of the column and row decoders to avoid accessing the parts of the cache that are turned off. The customization of the cache does not happen in the critical path of the execution. Therefore, it does not have any effect on performance, except the negligible area and latency increase stated above.

Branch Target Buffer (BTB). BTB has 4 possible configurations (Table 1). Therefore, we can partition BTB into 4 sections - $B1$, $B2$, $B3$, and $B4$ (Fig. 7a). For the first configuration (i.e., 0.5K entries), sections ($B2$, $B3$, $B4$) are clock-gated. Similarly, for the second and third configurations, sections ($B3$, $B4$) and ($B4$) are clock-gated respectively. The last configuration does not clock-gate any section at all. On the other hand, Section $B1$ is never clock-gated because at least those entries in BTB are used in all configurations. We add a customization logic that creates the appropriate clock-gating signal to enable the appropriate sections. Moreover, for each configuration, the indexing logic needs to customize the indexing bits accordingly. The extra logic circuits add negligible latency and require less than 200 cycles for customization [8]. The majority of those cycles are hidden in the background. In a multicore processor with one BTB per core, FORECASTER customizes all BTBs to the same configuration. This is done is to simplify the prediction and customization logic in FORECASTER.

Prefetcher. Prefetcher is used either completely or not at all. Therefore, the prefetcher is clock-gated entirely or not at all. So, the customization logic simply generates a single clock-gating signal for the entire prefetcher. Customization is completely done in the background.

5 Implementation

In this section, we outline the implementation of DNN in FORECASTER. We implement a simple DNN accelerator in FPGA and add a CPU-side DNN Driver Module to control the operation of the accelerator. The module forms inputs, collects outputs from the accelerator, and sends control signals to the FPGA.

There are many DNN accelerator designs in the literature [5,9,23]. We use one similar to the one proposed by Yuanfang Li [17]. Figure 8 shows the overview of our design. The accelerator is constructed as a systolic array of Processing Elements (PEs). The systolic array supports the fast broadcast of inputs and partial sum generation using row and column buses. Each PE contains 2 memories for storing activations and weights, 2 Multiplier, 1 Adder, 2 output buffers for sending results to the row and column buses, 2 input buffers for loading data from the row and column buses, and 4 multiplexers for handling reduction operation during the forward propagation. We consider an extra module for calculating the Softmax function. We distribute the weights of all layers among PEs and stream the inputs.

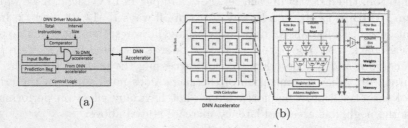

(a)

(b)

Fig. 8. Detailed design of the DNN module.

The DNN driver module has an input buffer, a prediction register, and a control logic. The input buffer is responsible to generate inputs that are provided to the DNN accelerator to infer the predictions. An input consists of various hardware counters and current configuration. Each core collects the counters and current configuration of resources independently and sends them to the driver module after every n (e.g., say $n = 10,000$) instructions. When the module receives counters of at least a total of $\mathbb{I}$ (e.g., $\mathbb{I} =$ interval size) instructions, FORECASTER assumes the start of a new interval. The module aggregates the counters and normalizes each counter with respect to the total instructions of the interval that just finished. The driver module then sends the formed input to the DNN accelerator and receives the predicted configuration. The predicted configuration is stored in the prediction register. The control logic sends the new configuration to the cores and cache controllers to initiate the reconfiguration.

6   Experimental Setup

Interval Size: Determining the right interval size is crucial to strike the optimal balance between performance gain and system overhead. Figure 9 shows the efficiency of different interval sizes across applications, both single and multiprogram scenarios. On average, an interval size of 0.5M instructions is the optimal setting, outperforming the second-best by 1.4%.

Simulators and Benchmarks: We use Multi2Sim [25] and McPAT [16] to evaluate FORECASTER and its power consumption. We implement the DNN in the

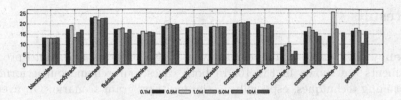

Fig. 9. Efficiency vs. baseline (%) comparison between different interval sizes.

Xilinx FPGA to calculate the latency and overhead. This latency is then used in Multi2Sim. Table 3 shows the hardware parameters for the experiments. We use 8 Parsec 3.0 benchmarks (*blackscholes, bodytrack, canneal, facesim, fluidanimate, freqmine, streamcluster, swaptions*) with small inputs. All benchmarks are run to completion or 1.0 B instructions. The interval size $\mathbb{I}$ is set to 0.5M instructions.

Table 3. Parameters of the simulated hardware.

Parameter	Value
CPU	8-core @ 2.4 Ghz, SMT off
Private L1 cache (I/D)	32 KB, 64 B line, 8-way
Private L2 Cache	1 MB, 64 B line, 16-way
Shared L3 Cache	16 MB, 64 B line, 16-way
Coherence Protocol	Directory-based MOESI

DNN Training and Tuning: For the single-program scenario, we use leave-one-out cross-validation for model training and tuning. This approach ensures the DNN model is not trained with the application it is optimizing. For the multi-program scenario, we randomly select 5 combinations of programs, each containing 4 different programs. The other 4 that are not chosen are used for training. Two instances of each program are launched during the execution of that combination.

Comparison Work: We compare FORECASTER with 5 other schemes. First, we implement the Maximum Likelihood Estimation (MLE) model from [8]. We call this *MLE-histogram*. Second, we implement a version of FORECASTER using an MLE model (*MLE-vanilla*) instead of a DNN model. This is to compare the performance of the DNN model to the simpler MLE model. Third, to verify the potential of the dynamic optimization scheme, we profile all applications and make two configurations: *best-static* and *oracle*. For *best-static*, we select the best overall static setting for all applications, assuming no dynamic reconfiguration. For the *oracle*, we dynamically apply the optimal setting for all hardware components for each execution phase. This serves as the upper bound for this study. Finally, we also compared our scheme with the DVFS algorithm from [19].

7   Results

Efficiency Evaluation: The efficiency of single-program and multi-program experiments are shown in Fig. 10. In both cases, our scheme outperforms all other tuning techniques, especially in the multi-program scenario. On average, FORECASTER improve the system efficiency by 18.1% compared to the baseline in single-program workloads and 15.8% in multi-program workloads. These improvements account for 80% of the highest achievable efficiency, represented by the oracle configuration.

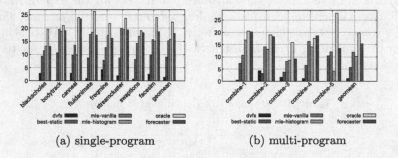

(a) single-program   (b) multi-program

Fig. 10. Normalized efficiency gain vs. baseline (%) of FORECASTER.

Compared to the best static configuration, our technique provides almost 2X more efficiency gain in single-program and 3X more efficiency gain in multi-program scenario. Compared to the MLE-histogram model in [8], FORECASTER provides 15.3% and 49.3% more efficiency in the single and multi-program scenario, respectively. One of the things that separate our work from [8] is that they do not consider the performance of their prediction model in multi-core, multi-program mode, which is a more realistic scenario. The 1.5X performance upgrade in multi-program experiment justifies the use of a more complex DNN model in FORECASTER over the simple MLE technique. The DVFS algorithm we are using puts priority on preserving performance rather than saving power, which is why it has the lowest performance loss, but also the least efficiency gain.

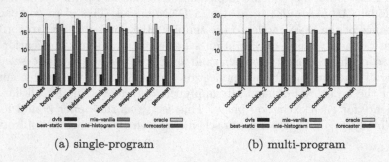

(a) single-program   (b) multi-program

Fig. 11. Normalized power savings vs. baseline (%) of FORECASTER.

This result is achieved thanks to the capability of FORECASTER to accurately predict the hardware demand of applications in each phase to save the most possible amount of power, as shown in Fig. 11. In general, FORECASTER manages to save 16% and 15.3% in power compared to the baseline in the single and multi-program scenarios, respectively. For multi-program workload, FORECASTER outperforms all other techniques.

Table 4. Average percentage saving in cache static power of *swaptions* (single-program) and *combine-5* (multi-program).

Cache Module	swaptions	combine-5
L2-0	0.67	0.64
L2-1	0.67	0.62
L2-2	0.67	0.65
L2-3	0.67	0.64
L2-4	0.67	0.62
L2-5	0.67	0.65
L2-6	0.67	0.65
L2-7	0.67	0.65
L3 (last level cache)	0.61	0.67

Detailed Analysis: Figures 12 and 13 show how FORECASTER manages the hardware resources during program execution in single (*swaptions*) and multi-program (*combination-5*) scenarios. FORECASTER accurately estimates the demand of *swaptions*, then turns off excessive resources, saving a lot of power while maintaining the same performance. Sometimes FORECASTER decision cannot be fully satisfied as shown in Fig. 13(a). In some intervals, only around 65% to 70% amount of L2 cache is disabled even though the prediction is 75%. This is because those cache blocks are valid. To preserve performance, we do not forcefully turn off resources that are being used. Table 4 shows the break down in cache static power savings of FORECASTER. For the single-program scenario, the amount of power saved is identical between L2 private caches. In multi-program scenario, this number is different because it depends on the application running on the core. In general, using gated-ground technique [1,18,21] to turn off cache blocks, we manage to save approximately 90% of static power of L2 and L3 caches. In *swaptions*, since FORECASTER turns off 75% of L2 and 68% of L3, the actual amounts of static power saved are 67% and 61%, respectively.

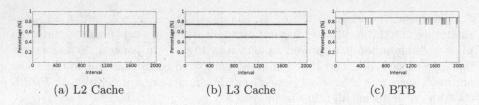

(a) L2 Cache   (b) L3 Cache   (c) BTB

Fig. 12. Average turned off amount of (a) L2, (b) L3, and (c) BTB during the execution of *swaptions*.

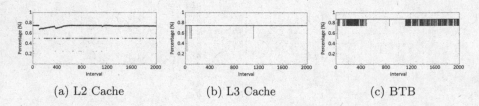

(a) L2 Cache   (b) L3 Cache   (c) BTB

Fig. 13. Average turned off amount of (a) L2, (b) L3, and (c) BTB during the execution of *combination-5*.

Runtime Overhead: The runtime cost of the proposed design can be divided into two parts: prediction/reconfiguration latency, and the DNN module power consumption. As for the latency cost, hardware telemetry reading and reconfiguration do not happen in the critical path. The hardware will continue in its old configuration till the decision is made for a new configuration. [24] shows that the reconfiguration time is negligible (tens of cycles). We use this number in our simulation. Overall, our approach manages to reduce the IPS degradation by about 44% compared to MLE-histogram, as shown in Table 5.

Table 5. IPS degradation (%) vs. baseline. Negative numbers in parentheses.

Technique	single-program	multi-program	mean
DVFS	(0.1)	0.2	0.1
Best-static	0.0	(0.8)	(0.4)
Forecaster	(0.3)	(0.7)	(0.5)
MLE-histogram	(0.4)	(1.4)	(0.9)
MLE-vanilla	(0.6)	(1.3)	(1.0)
Oracle	0.5	0.9	0.7

Table 6. Cost of different DNN hardware. This power usage is less than 3.5% of the overall system power.

PE Array	Frequency (MHz)	Latency	Slice Reg	Power (W)	
				Static	Dynamic
8*8	268	6352	79566	0.20	2.51
12*12	258	3200	93179	0.21	4.36
16*16	247	1896	109972	0.22	4.72

The main power cost of Forecaster comes from the DNN driver module and the Processing Elements (PEs). With 16×16 configuration, the PE array of Forecaster consumes a total power of 4.94 W, as shown in Table 6. For the DNN driver module, its total power consumption measured by McPAT is only 0.032W.

Altogether, the total power usage of FORECASTER is 4.97W. As the system over-all power consumption measured by McPAT is 142W for the single-program sce-nario and 153W for the multi-program scenario, the power consumption of FORE-CASTER is just 3.49% and 3.24% extra. Furthermore, since the DNN model is only used once per 0.5M instructions, its actual energy cost is minimal.

Hardware Implementation Cost. The hardware cost consists of the DNN hardware and the extra hardware used to implement the knobs. The DNN uses a four-hidden-layer fully connected neural network with the neuron configuration of *384/384/256/256*. There are also an input layer of 14 neurons and an output layer of 128 neurons. We use *ReLU* activation for the input and hidden layers and *Softmax* for the output layer. For the hardware implementation, we consider sev-eral design points as shown Table 6. We use 16*16 PE array size in our final design.

The hardware needed for the knobs is straightforward. The prefetcher is just clock-gated as the knob is on/off. The BTB also uses clock-gating depending on the configuration. We have four configurations so a small 2×4 decoder will do the job as shown in the customization logic in Fig. 7a. Clock gating the cache ways is simplified by the fact that the way-reconfiguration logic, shown in Fig. 7b, never gates a valid entry so no change to the cache controller or coherence hardware is needed. The way-reconfiguration logic is not complicated because it exploits the fact that large caches (such as L3) are usually partitioned. Therefore we have one logic circuitry per partition.

8 Conclusions

The work presents the *first* DNN-based PSC technique, called FORECASTER. FORECASTER exploits two intuitive observations to cope with the long infer-ence latency of a DNN model and boost customization impact. FORECASTER works in two phases - offline training and online reconfiguration. We provide a detailed design and implementation of FORECASTER and compare its perfor-mance against a prior state-of-the-art approach. Overall, FORECASTER provides 2.5X and 1.5X more power efficiency gain over the best static configuration and prior state-of-the-art approach.

Acknowlegement. We thanks the reviewers and the members of PALab research group for valuable feeback. This work is supported by Texas A&M University Faculty Startup Grant, and NSF Grant No. 1931078.

References

1. Agarwal, A., Li, H., Roy, K.: DRG-cache: a data retention gated-ground cache for low power. In: Design Automation Conference (2002)
2. Balasubramonian, R., Albonesi, D., Buyuktosunoglu, A., Dwarkadas, S.: Memory hierarchy reconfiguration for energy and performance in general-purpose processor architectures. In: MICRO (2000)
3. Bitirgen, R., Ipek, E., Martinez, J.F.: Coordinated management of multiple inter-acting resources in chip multiprocessors: a machine learning approach. In: MICRO (2008)

4. Chen, T., et al.: DianNao: a small-footprint high-throughput accelerator for ubiquitous machine-learning. In: ASPLOS (2014)
5. Chen, Y.H., Emer, J., Sze, V.: Eyeriss: a spatial architecture for energy-efficient dataflow for convolutional neural networks. In: ISCA (2016)
6. Choi, S., Yeung, D.: Learning-based SMT processor resource distribution via hill-climbing. In: ISCA (2006)
7. Deng, Q., Meisner, D., Bhattacharjee, A., Wenisch, T.F., Bianchini, R.: CoScale: coordinating CPU and memory system DVFS in server systems. In: MICRO (2012)
8. Dubach, C., Jones, T.M., Bonilla, E.V., O'Boyle, M.F.P.: A predictive model for dynamic microarchitectural adaptivity control. In: MICRO (2010)
9. Esmaeilzadeh, H., Sampson, A., Ceze, L., Burger, D.: Neural acceleration for general-purpose approximate programs. In: MICRO (2012)
10. Haj-Yahya, J., et al.: SysScale: exploiting multi-domain dynamic voltage and frequency scaling for energy efficient mobile processors. In: ISCA (2020)
11. Hubert, H., Stabernack, B.: Profiling-based hardware/software co-exploration for the design of video coding architectures. IEEE TCSVT **19**, 1680–1691 (2009)
12. Intel, "Profile-Guided Optimization (PGO)." https://software.intel.com/content/www/us/en/develop-/documentation/cpp-compiler-developer-guide-and-reference/top/optimization-and-programming-guide/profile-guided-optimization-pgo.html
13. Ipek, E., Mutlu, O., Martínez, J.F., Caruana, R.: Self-optimizing memory controllers: a reinforcement learning approach. In: ISCA (2008)
14. Isci, C., Buyuktosunoglu, A., Cher, C.Y., Bose, P., Martonosi, M.: An analysis of efficient multi-core global power management policies: maximizing performance for a given power budget. In: MICRO (2006)
15. Khan, T.A., et al.: Ripple: profile-guided instruction cache replacement for data center applications. In: ISCA (2021)
16. Li, S., Ahn, J.H., Strong, R.D., Brockman, J.B., Tullsen, D.M., Jouppi, N.P.: McPAT: an integrated power, area, and timing modeling framework for multicore and manycore architectures. In: MICRO (2009)
17. Li, Y., Pedram, A.: CATERPILLAR: coarse grain reconfigurable architecture for accelerating the training of deep neural networks. In: 2017 IEEE 28th International Conference on ASAP (2017)
18. Manan, A.: Efficient 16 nm SRAM design for FPGA's. In: SPIN (2018)
19. Pallipadi, V., Starikovskiy, A.: The Ondemand governor (2006)
20. Petrica, P., Izraelevitz, A.M., Albonesi, D.H., Shoemaker, C.A.: Flicker: a dynamically adaptive architecture for power limited multicore systems. In: ISCA (2013)
21. Powell, M., Yang, S.H., Falsafi, B., Roy, K., Vijaykumar, N.: Reducing leakage in a high-performance deep-submicron instruction cache. In: VLSI (2001)
22. Ravi, G.S., Lipasti, M.H.: CHARSTAR: clock hierarchy aware resource scaling in tiled architectures. In: ISCA (2017)
23. Reagen, B., et al.: Minerva: enabling low-power, highly-accurate deep neural network accelerators. In: ISCA (2016)
24. Tarsa, S.J., et al.: Post-silicon CPU adaptation made practical using machine learning. In: ISCA (2019)
25. Ubal, R., Sahuquilo, J., Petit, S., López, P.: Multi2Sim: a simulation framework to evaluate multicore-multithreaded processors. In: SBAC-PAD (2007)
26. Wiltgen, A., Escobar, K.A., Reis, A.I., Ribas, R.P.: Power consumption analysis in static CMOS gates. In: SBCCI (2013)

Computer Architectures and Operating Systems

TOSTING: Investigating Total Store Ordering on ARM

Lars Wrenger$^{(\boxtimes)}$, Dominik Töllner, and Daniel Lohmann

Systems Research and Architecture Group, Leibniz Universität Hannover,
Hannover, Germany
{wrenger,toellner,lohmann}@sra.uni-hannover.de

Abstract. The Apple M1 ARM processors incorporate two memory consistency models: the conventional ARM weak memory ordering and the *total store ordering (TSO)* model from the x86 architecture employed by Apple's x86 emulator, Rosetta 2. The presence of both memory ordering models on the same hardware enables us to thoroughly benchmark and compare their performance characteristics and worst-case workloads.

In this paper, we assess the performance implications of TSO on the Apple M1 processor architecture. Based on various workloads, our findings indicate that TSO is, on average, 8.94% slower than ARM's weaker memory ordering. Through synthetic benchmarks, we further explore the workloads that experience the most significant performance degradation due to TSO.

Keywords: TSO · Memory Ordering · Apple M1

1 Introduction

On traditional uniprocessor systems, the effects of memory accesses are observable in the same order as they were specified in the instruction stream (program order). This is still the case for multitasking on a single core. Challenges arise when the memory is shared between multiple participants who access it *concurrently*, such as other cores, processors, or accelerators. Providing a consistent *global order* in which memory accesses are visible to all observers can be particularly difficult for multiscalar processors with instruction reordering and local caches that buffer accesses.

Memory consistency models (MCMs) in shared-memory systems formalize how writes to shared memory can be observed by different participants within a shareability domain. These hardware-defined guarantees provide rules that lead to predictable results of shared memory operations [17,20,23]. These models differ in how strict guarantees they provide. Both x86 and ARM define a MCM that allows (limited) reordering of instructions [1,5,6]. x86 guarantees a globally consistent order for stores (TSO). ARM, in contrast, allows stores to different memory locations to be observed differently from the program order. While complicating the programming model, ARM's weaker memory ordering allows processors to reorder instructions more freely and potentially reduce synchronization

G. Goumas et al. (Eds.): ARCS 2023, LNCS 13949, pp. 139–152, 2023.
https://doi.org/10.1007/978-3-031-42785-5_10

overheads between caches. Seeing this tradeoff between higher performance and simpler programming models, we ask how extensive the performance benefits really are.

Apple's M1 processors implement the ARMv8.3-A *instruction set architecture (ISA)*, which specifies a weak memory ordering model. With these SoC processors, Apple transitions from Intel-based technology to ARM. Together with introducing an entirely new ISA, these Apple Silicon SoCs also significantly change the memory model the hardware now operates on [2]. To provide backward compatibility with their former x86-based devices, Apple developed a translation layer called *Rosetta 2*. This translation engine can emulate applications built for x86_64 on Apple Silicon SoCs [9]. Unfortunately, a direct translation on a per-instruction basis alone is insufficient since x86 follows a stricter memory ordering. Every memory access could potentially rely on *total store ordering (TSO)*. To produce the same behavior as under x86, each access would have to be explicitly synchronized. Instead of paying the accompanying performance costs, Apple built TSO directly into their processors. Thus, the M1 SoC has both the ARM and the x86 memory ordering models implemented in hardware, making it the ideal target for comparing these MCMs.

1.1 About This Paper

While benchmarks for comparisons between the M1 and other processor families exist [14,25], no research has yet evaluated the performance impact of TSO on M1 SoCs. Additionally, to the best of our knowledge, existing research sparsely conducts evaluations on the *M1 Ultra*, which combines two *M1 Max* dies connected by *UltraFusion*, Apple's custom packaging architecture [4].

In this paper, we evaluate the performance impact of enabling TSO on Apple's M1 Ultra by running synthetic TSO-oriented benchmarks as well as the CPU benchmarks of SPEC, a non-profit corporation to establish standardized benchmarks [12]. With our evaluation, we claim the following contributions:

(1) Apple's M1 Ultra benchmark data for the SPEC CPU benchmark suite.
(2) Quantification of TSO described by the benchmark suite and tailor-made synthetic test cases.

2 Memory Consistency Models

The *memory consistency model (MCM)* defines the correct behavior of shared memory for concurrent access. It is a contract between the developer, the compiler, and the parallel system, providing rules that, if followed, lead to predictable results of shared memory operations. Parallel systems, like x86 or ARM, usually have a relatively lax consistency model for their normal loads and stores and specific instructions to enforce stricter guarantees. With them, they can simulate a stricter MCM if needed.

2.1 Programming Model

For hardware independence, most programming languages provide an *atomics* abstraction, such as `std::atomic` in C++ or `std::sync::atomic` in Rust [8, 10]. These abstractions define their own MCMs and a set of operations (e.g., `atomic_fetch_add`) that ensure consistency independently from the hardware MCM. The compiler inserts the required instructions and fences to enforce the guarantees where necessary. Usually, *atomics* provide the three memory ordering models listed below in increasing strictness:

relaxed Only loads/stores to the same location are ordered consistently. No guarantees are provided for different memory locations.

acquire-release The acquire-release relation synchronizes accesses to different memory locations for pairs of releasing stores and acquiring loads. All other stores (to different memory) before a releasing store are guaranteed to be visible after an acquiring load of the same memory on another processor.

sequential-consistent All sequential-consistent operations are guaranteed to be visible to all processors in the same order.

2.2 Total Store Ordering on x86

1: X ← 1		X	Y		X	Y
2: Y ← 2		---	---		---	---
		0	0		0	0
		1	0		1	0
		1	2		0	2
					1	2

(a) CPU0: Store instructions   (b) CPU1: Visibility with TSO or acquire-release   (c) CPU1: Visibility with weak/relaxed ordering

Fig. 1. Observable effect of stores to different memory locations. Given that $X = 0, Y = 0$, each row in Fig. 1c and Fig. 1b represents an observable intermediary state for CPU1, when CPU0 executes the two stores from Fig. 1a.

The x86 architecture guarantees that stores are visible in a consistent order, meaning that each processor observes stores from other processors in the same order [5]. Additionally, every processor also performs stores in program order. Therefore the case that Y is updated before X is impossible, as shown in Fig. 1b. This ordering is transitive. Other processors observe stores that are causally related in an order consistent with the causality relation. This *total store ordering (TSO)* already fulfills the *acquire-release* relation for regular loads and stores; thus, no stricter instructions are needed and emitted by the compiler if using the corresponding *atomic* abstractions.

On the downside, the compiled code loses the information of which instructions are expected to be *acquire-release* and which could also be relaxed. This missing information makes it challenging to emulate x86 on systems with weaker memory ordering efficiently, as the optimal placement of fences is an undecidable problem [15]. To provide correctness, x86 emulators (e.g., QEMU) basically insert a fence after every memory instruction.

2.3 Weak Ordering on ARM

The ARM architecture, on the other hand, has a weak memory ordering model. In the ARMv8 ISA, the concurrency has been revised: In contrast to ARMv7, the architecture now has a *multicopy-atomic model (MCA)*, guaranteeing that modifications to a cache line are linearizable [6]. While this MCM is stricter than the non-MCA ARMv7 model, implementors did not exploit the latter [31]. This multicopy-atomicity guarantees a consistent order of updates to the same location. However, in contrast to x86, stores to different locations are not required to be visible consistently, meaning that every state in Fig. 1c can still be observed by other processors (CPU1). Stronger ordering guarantees can only be enforced with explicit fences or memory barriers (DMB, DSB) or load, store, compare-and-swap, fetch-add and similar instructions with *acquire-release* semantic (LDAR, STLR, LDADDAL, CASAL from ARM A64 [1]). Despite being named *load-acquire* (LDAR) and *store-release* (STLR), these instructions actually fulfill the sequential-consistent memory ordering if combined. Consequently, they are relatively slow, as discussed in Sect. 4.2. Thus, ARMv8.3 introduced LDAPR, which allows reordering before STLR to different locations [1]. Despite making acquire-release atomics more efficient, LDAPR is still not used by most compilers for *load-acquire* (instead LDAR is emitted). Recently, clang added support for LDAPR in C/C++ atomics in version 16 (March 2023), GCC in version 13 (April 2023), and for Rust, this is still only available on the nightly channel.

In general, ARMs laxer memory model gives cores more freedom to reorder instructions, potentially increasing the overall multicore performance for regular (relaxed) instructions. The downside of this is the more complex programming model. Developers have to explicitly synchronize memory accesses if their data structures might rely on the order of writes. However, this might not be a problem, as more and more programming languages have sufficient cross-platform abstractions for *atomics*.

3   The Apple M1 Architecture

Apple has disclosed only limited information regarding their custom M1 chips [4, 28]. Details on core counts, cache and memory sizes, theoretical memory bandwidth, and some performance characteristics have been made public. However, there is no official information about the processor's cache coherence, load and store buffers, micro-operations, instruction schedulers, and execution units. Insights into the microarchitecture stem primarily from reverse engineering projects [7, 24].

The M1 Ultra *system on a chip (SoC)* consists of two M1 Max chiplets connected through an UltraFusion interconnect, having a reported bandwidth of

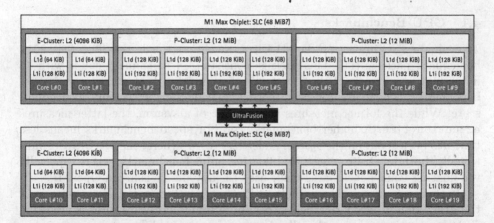

Fig. 2. Cache-Architecture of the M1 Apple Silicon Processor. The E-Clusters each contain two efficiency cores (codename "Icestorm"), while the P-Clusters consist of four performance cores (codename "Firestorm"). Each core has L1 data and instruction caches and shares the L2 cache with the rest of the cluster.

2.5TB/s [4]. A schematic representation of the chiplets and core clusters can be found in Fig. 2. The processor architecture has 16 performance cores grouped in four clusters and four efficiency cores in two clusters. Each processor encompasses separate L1 instruction (L1i) and L1 data (L1d) caches, while an L2 cache is associated with each cluster. Information about a shared last-level (or system-level) cache has not been disclosed. Experimental data indicates that the SLC sizes are 48 MB for the M1 Max and potentially 96 MB for the M1 Ultra [3]. However, these values were not corroborated by our benchmarks. It is also not known if the two SLCs are separated or combined. Regarding cache-line size, `sysctl` on macOS reports a value of 128 B, while `getconf` and the `CTR_EL0` register on Asahi Linux return 64 B, which is also supported by our measurements.

The M1 Ultra is not a conventional ARM processor. It incorporates custom instructions, accelerators, and media units, along with a hardware implementation for TSO, which can be enabled by setting the first bit of the general config register (`ACTLR_EL1`) [7]. After that, normal memory accesses show the same memory ordering behavior as under x86. Unfortunately, further details of this hardware implementation and its limitations are not publically available.

4   Evaluation

Our test system is an Apple Mac Studio with an M1 Ultra SoC, 128 GiB main memory, and 1 TiB SSD. Our software stack is based on Asahi Linux 6.1.0, a Linux port to Apple Silicon. The TSO memory ordering was toggled system-wide for all cores using a kernel module [13] before executing the respective benchmark. The SPEC benchmarks were compiled with GCC 12.1, and the synthetic benchmarks with Rust 1.69.0.

4.1 CPU Benchmarks

To evaluate TSO impact on the M1 Ultra, we choose to run the SPEC CPU 2017 benchmark package [11]. This package consists of 4 benchmark suites with 43 individual benchmarks. SPEC generally distinguishes between *rate* and *speed* benchmarks, which use different metrics to calculate a system's benchmark score. While the former measures throughput of a system, the latter measures execution time. A higher benchmark score for speed benchmarks means less time has been spent on the *system under test (SUT)* (here, the M1 Ultra). Additionally, both integrate integer and floating point benchmarks, where especially the floating point benchmarks make use of heavy parallelism via OpenMP.

In this evaluation, we focus on the *SPECspeed 2017 Floating Point* suite since the utilization of heavy parallelism results in many hardware threads accessing shared memory concurrently, allowing us to evaluate different memory ordering models properly. We utilize all CPU cores within the M1 Ultra, resulting in a total of 20 threads in execution for every benchmark issued. The benchmarks run CPU- and memory-intensive code such as 3D simulation, modeling of physical systems and their behavior, as well as image manipulation. We execute three iterations of the floating point benchmark suite and select the median of those iterations as the documentation recommends. A final score is calculated by computing the geometric mean of all selected medians of all benchmarks. While the suite provides two benchmark tuning modes *base* and *peak*, we<only show the peak version that uses more platform-specific optimizations in this paper. However, the base configuration exhibits similar trends. This whole suite is executed twice, once for enabled TSO and once for disabled TSO. The benchmark code does not contain any atomic operations, hence neither the compiler nor the hardware are hinted to emit/execute such instructions. Therefore, the application binary code is exactly the same for *weak ordering (WO)* and TSO.

The results are illustrated in Fig. 3, where the impact of different MCMs varies across individual benchmarks. For instance, in the 649.fotonik3d_s benchmark, WO achieves a score of 83.63, while TSO records a score of 83.27. Enabling TSO does not affect this benchmark. In contrast, for the 644.nab_s benchmark, WO scores 171.34, and TSO attains a significantly lower score of 137.43. In the majority of benchmarks, the weak ordering native to the ARMv8 Apple Silicon outperforms TSO. The geometric mean score for the TSO-disabled benchmarks is 86.57, whereas the TSO-enabled benchmarks yield a geometric mean score of 78.83, translating to a 8.94% decrease in performance.

4.2 Synthetic Benchmarks

We devised two synthetic benchmarks to delve deeper into the performance discrepancies observed in the SPECS benchmarks: (1) a *store* benchmark and (2) a *fetch-add* benchmark. Both benchmarks employ a shared memory buffer between two threads: a writer, responsible for updating the buffer, and a reader, tasked with observing these updates. The benchmarks vary only in the instruction utilized for buffer updates: The writer thread iterates through the buffer in 64-byte

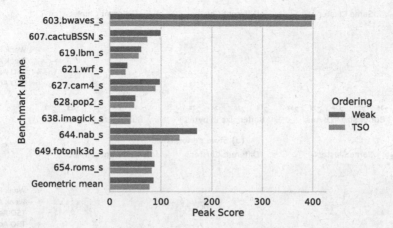

Fig. 3. SPECspeed 2017 Floating Point. Comparison of the parallel SPEC CPU benchmarks. Faster execution results in a higher score.

(cache-line) steps, executing either *stores* or *fetch-adds* to increment the numbers within the first 8 bytes of each element. Initially, all elements are zero, and in the first iteration, they are all incremented to one, then in the second iteration to two, and so forth. The *store* benchmark (1) uses a store operation to write the current iteration to all elements, while the *fetch-add* benchmark (2) uses this instruction to increment the previous values, resulting in the same general behavior.

Concurrently, the reader iterates through the buffer, loading and comparing pairs of adjacent elements. It observes and counts out-of-order updates where the second element is smaller than the first, indicating that the update operations were perceived in a different order from the writer's execution. This phenomenon only occurred under weak ordering; when TSO was enabled, no out-of-order updates were detected. Apart from the shared buffer and a boolean utilized for synchronizing the beginning and end of the measurement, the threads do not access any shared data. They also do not synchronize between iterations; thus, the reader usually finishes more iterations than the writer.

In these benchmarks, we counted the number of iterations each thread could complete within one second. This value was then multiplied by the buffer length to calculate the operations per second. The benchmarks were compiled with relaxed (LDR and STR or LDADD) and acquire-release (LDAR and STLR or LDADDAL) instructions. These exact same binaries were then executed with and without TSO enabled. The reader and writer threads were pinned to different cores of either the same cluster, sharing an L2 cache, a separate cluster on the same chiplet, or different chiplets.

Regarding the *store* benchmark, Fig. 4 shows the number of parallel stores (Fig. 4a) and loads (Fig. 4b) for varying buffer sizes. The horizontal lines indicate the cache sizes (128 KiB, 12 MiB and 96 MiB as described in Sect. 3). Our first observation is that, for all benchmarks, enabling TSO does not impact

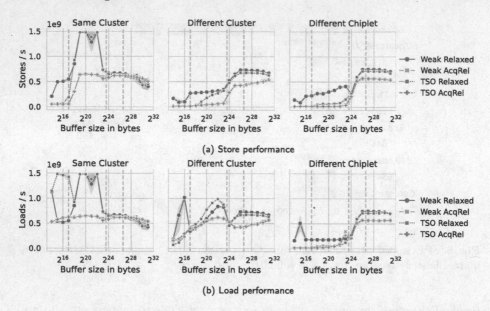

(a) Store performance

(b) Load performance

Fig. 4. Concurrent store and load operations. The writer (top) and reader (bottom) threads were pinned to different cores of the same cluster (left), separate clusters of the same chiplet (middle), and different chiplets (right). The gray horizontal lines mark the cache sizes (L1 = 128 KiB, L2 = 12 MiB and SLC = 96 MiB).

the performance of the acquire-release instructions. This outcome is to be expected, as these acquire-release instructions employ an explicit and even stricter sequentially-consistent memory ordering (Sect. 2.3), making them generally slower than weak ordering and TSO.

Looking at the store performance of the first benchmark, we see that it is pretty low for buffers that fit in the L1 cache, possibly due to cache invalidations (Fig. 4a). Meanwhile, for buffers with sizes between the L1 and L2 cache, the highest number of stores occurs on the same cluster. This performance drops significantly on different clusters where the L2 cache is not shared. For buffers larger than the L2 cache, the performance is similar regardless of the cores used. The limits of the L1 and L2 cache sizes are clearly visible, while the SLC is not so apparent. We only observe that the performance stops increasing for buffers larger than 96 MiB (the SLC size).

The read performance, with TSO enabled, is faster for buffers smaller than the L1 cache (Fig. 4b). This seems to be a pattern when comparing weak stores and loads on small buffers: The lower the store performance is, the faster loads tend to become. This inverse effect might be attributed to fewer cache invalidations, as TSO writes are considerably slower. The performance counters, shown in Fig. 5, support this observation: The number of load and store misses is higher on weak ordering, where the number of writes is also significantly higher. For buffers between the L1 and L2 cache sizes, the highest number of loads occurs on the same cluster. The performance drop is not as significant for different clus-

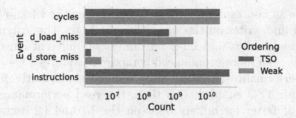

Fig. 5. Perf counters for the *store* benchmark. The benchmark was executed on the same cluster with a 2^{16} bytes buffer. The events were measured for both the writer and reader threads together.

ters on the same chiplet but is more pronounced between chiplets. Also, TSO loads are slightly faster for L2-sized buffers on different clusters. For buffers larger than the L2 cache, the performance is again very similar across different configurations.

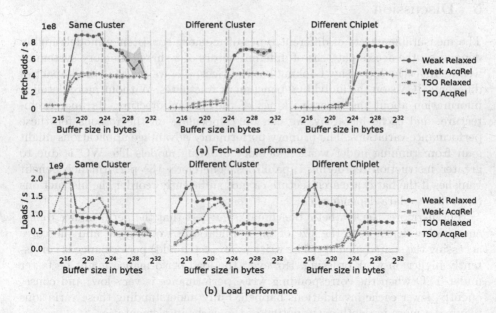

Fig. 6. Concurrent fetch-add and load operations

The second synthetic benchmark used fetch-adds (`LDADD/LDADDAL`) in the writer thread to increment the buffer elements (Fig. 6). When comparing the *ldadd* benchmark (Fig. 6a) with the *store* benchmark (Fig. 4a), we see that fetch-adds are, at best, only half as fast as stores. Also enabling, TSO decreases the fetch-add performance to or even below the acquire-release instructions. This differs from the previous benchmark, where the TSO stores were generally above their acquire-release counterparts. Meanwhile, weakly-ordered fetch-adds are almost twice as fast, especially for buffers between the L1 and L2 cache sizes with the reader and writer on the same cluster. Again, the instructions are far slower for L1-sized buffers and L2-sized buffers on different clusters. However, this difference is even more pronounced compared to stores.

The load performance (Fig. 6b) also changed significantly from the *store* benchmark. With TSO enabled, this time, the read performance is slower for small buffers but faster for buffers between the L1 and L2 cache sizes on the same cluster. On different clusters, TSO reads are now consistently slower than weakly ordered ones. We again see that lower fetch-add performance generally results in higher load performance.

In summary, our analysis of the *store* and *ldadd* benchmarks reveals several performance nuances based on buffer sizes and the relationship between the reader and writer threads. We see that stores and fetch-adds are generally and sometimes drastically slower under TSO. With a few exceptions, the load performance also seems to be faster on weak ordering.

5   Discussion

The measurable effects of different types of memory consistency models highly depend on the access patterns of different actors of a shared memory system as well as its cache hierarchy. Looking back at Sect. 4.1, we see that the impact of different MCMs on the individual benchmark fluctuates. Without more detailed information about the inner workings of the M1 architecture, its microarchitecture, and cache hierarchy, we can only speculate on the reasons for these performance variations: The primary performance advantage applications might gain from running under weaker memory ordering models like WO is due to greater instruction reordering capabilities. Therefore, the performance benefit vanishes if the hardware architecture cannot sufficiently reorder the instructions (e.g., due to data dependencies).

Furthermore, the synthetic benchmarks suggest that the performance difference highly depends on the size of the application's working set and the cores accessing the shared memory. The write (store, fetch-add) performance is consistently higher on weak ordering. However, the load performance might be faster under TSO when the corresponding write performance is very low, and consequently, fewer cache invalidations happen. Fully understanding these variations requires a more in-depth examination of the cache implementation.

Strict models like *sequential consistency (SC)* prohibit hardware from reordering instructions but make it easier for developers and compilers to reason about parallel code. Or, from another perspective, the freedom of hardware reordering instructions *requires* developers and compilers to thoroughly reason about the order in which the emitted code is executed to ensure the program's semantics remain correct. In this setting, the novel feature of the Apple M1, where the MCM is configurable at run time, provides interesting flexibility for software developers and compilers.

6   Related Work

The field of memory consistency models has been under active research for a couple of decades. With the emergence of multiprocessor systems, the sequentiality properties of those systems needed to be properly formalized. In a seminal paper from 1979, Lamport describes sequential consistency as the property of a multiprocessor system to run all instructions of all processors in some sequential order and that each processor strictly follows its program instruction order [27]. Instruction reordering, however, can provide a considerable performance benefit if the CPU can reschedule instructions to reach a higher cache hit rate. Therefore, over the following years, many different other consistency models have been established, such as WO [17], *processor consistency (PC)* [21], *partial store ordering (PSO)*, TSO, and many others. While most hardware commonly follows a specific consistency model, there are a few systems in the wild next to the M1 that allow toggling between different MCMs dynamically, during runtime and in hardware. Notably, all architectures that include a SPARC v8 Reference MMU implementation allow to switch between PSO and TSO during runtime by toggling the PSO bit in the MMU control register of a specific processor [32]. The key difference between SPARC systems and the M1 is that the latter can switch to WO as an alternative MCM, which is more relaxed compared to PSO and therefore allows further instruction reordering. With the new release of SPARC v9, the successor to SPARC v8, a new in-hardware toggleable MCM has been added: *relaxed ordering (RO)* [33]. RO under SPARC v9 is even closer to WO on ARM compared to PSO, as it allows further instruction rescheduling. SPARC v9 systems and ARM, however, provide different synchronization primitives if instruction rescheduling needs to be prohibited. While the former provides more coarse-grained, global synchronization primitives, ARM comes with smaller, distinct shareability domains to limit the necessity of synchronization.

To investigate the performance impact of these consistency models, several benchmarks have been conducted. Gharachorloo et al. [19] measured the effect of different MCMs on a simulated Stanford DASH multiprocessor architecture. Their results have shown that stricter ordering models performed significantly worse than less strict models for architectures with blocking reads. A more recent study by Naeem et al. [29] draws the same conclusion on *network-on-chip (NOC)* based distributed shared memory multicore systems, improving their system performance when transitioning from stricter to weaker memory consistency models.

Moving from stricter to weaker models shifts the responsibility of sequentiality from the hardware to the software and software toolchain. This inherently enforces research on how to express program sequentiality as a developer and how to emit appropriate instructions as a compiler. In the paper of Boehm et al. [16], the authors describe a divergence between C/C++ being single-threaded programming languages while giving additional multithread support via an additional library. Since the language itself does not provide intrinsic support for multithreaded code, it is up to the libraries to offer synchronization primitives for concurrent access to shared resources, such as a shared address space, that enforce a specific order for particular instructions. Enforcing a specific order is achieved by properly placing memory barriers, guaranteeing that certain load/store operations execute before/after surrounding instructions. Shaked et al. [18] investigate the impact of memory barriers on mixed-size memory accesses of different data widths. Today's processors commonly allow accessing memory at granularities of 1, 2, 4, or 8 bytes. Placing barriers for mixed use of those granularities should enforce the same ordering as for data accesses of equal width. This general assumption, however, proves to be wrong for ARMv8 and POWER architectures, as the authors' evaluation clarifies. While placing a strong memory barrier between every memory access of equal width for architectures implementing WO results in a sequential-consistent behavior, this is not the case for mixed-size memory accesses.

Other research regarding Apple's M1 processors is sparse. [25] benchmarked the M1 and M1 Ultra for high-performance scientific computing and compared its GPU performance against two Nvidia-equipped servers, while [14] studied their energy efficiency. ARM systems, in general, have been evaluated against x86 systems on different, primarily HPC-based workloads [22,30,34]. Kodama et al. [26] evaluated the performance of the ARM A64FX against a dual-socket Xeon using the SPEC CPU and OMP benchmarks. Nevertheless, none of these works focused specifically on memory-ordering differences.

7   Conclusion

The Apple M1 is the first processor that implements both, ARM's weak memory ordering and Intel's TSO, as a software-configurable feature. This also makes it possible for the first time to compare the performance impact of the different memory models on real hard- and software.

In our results, we see a significant effect on the multicore performance when comparing both models. Despite being more challenging to program for, the weak model is generally faster: 8.94% on average running SPEC CPU and more than twice as fast in some of our synthetic benchmarks. However, the lack of knowledge about the internals of the M1 architecture makes it hard to fully explain all effects of TSO on this SoC. Our results suggest that these are deeply entangled with the caching hierarchy and memory access path. Nonetheless, we think that this work is an essential step toward understanding the actual runtime effects of the memory ordering models.

References

1. ARM Cortex-A Series - Programmer's Guide for ARMv8-A. ARM Limited (2015)
2. Apple announces Mac transition to Apple silicon (2020). https://nr.apple.com/d2O2Y718J3. Accessed 22 Mar 2023
3. Apple's M1 Pro, M1 Max SoCs investigated: new performance and efficiency heights (2021). https://www.anandtech.com/show/17024/apple-m1-max-performance-review. Accessed 23 Mar 2023

4. Apple M1 Ultra (2022). https://www.apple.com/newsroom/2022/03/apple-unveils-m1-ultra-the-worlds-most-powerful-chip-for-a-personal-computer/. Accessed 22 Mar 2023

5. Intel 64 and IA-32 Architectures Software Developer's Manual - Combined Volumes: 1, 2A, 2B, 2C, 2D, 3A, 3B, 3C, 3D and 4. Intel (2022). https://www.intel.com/content/www/us/en/developer/articles/technical/intel-sdm.html. Accessed 30 May 2023

6. Learn the architecture - Memory Systems, Ordering, and Barriers. ARM Limited (2022). https://developer.arm.com/documentation/102336/0100. Accessed 30 May 2023

7. Asahi Linux docs wiki (2023). https://github.com/AsahiLinux/docs/wiki. Accessed 23 Mar 2023

8. C++ atomic operations library (2023). https://en.cppreference.com/w/cpp/atomic. Accessed 26 Mar 2023

9. Rosetta Translation Environment (2023). https://developer.apple.com/documentation/apple-silicon/about-the-rosetta-translation-environment. Accessed 22 Mar 2023

10. Rust standard library - module std::sync::atomic (2023). https://doc.rust-lang.org/std/sync/atomic/index.html. Accessed 26 Mar 2023

11. SPEC CPU benchmark package (2023). https://www.spec.org/cpu2017/. Accessed 27 Mar 2023

12. The Standard Performance Evaluation Corporation (2023). https://www.spec.org/. Accessed 22 Mar 2023

13. Tsoenabler for Linux (2023). https://github.com/cyyself/m1tso-linux. Accessed 26 Mar 2023

14. Ali, Z., Tanveer, T., Aziz, S., Usman, M., Azam, A.: Reassessing the performance of arm vs x86 with recent technological shift of apple. In: 2022 International Conference on IT and Industrial Technologies (ICIT), pp. 01–06 (2022). https://doi.org/10.1109/ICIT56493.2022.9988933

15. Atig, M.F., Bouajjani, A., Burckhardt, S., Musuvathi, M.: What's decidable about weak memory models? In: Seidl, H. (ed.) ESOP 2012. LNCS, vol. 7211, pp. 26–46. Springer, Heidelberg (2012). https://doi.org/10.1007/978-3-642-28869-2_2

16. Boehm, H.J., Adve, S.V.: Foundations of the c++ concurrency memory model. In: Proceedings of the 29th ACM SIGPLAN Conference on Programming Language Design and Implementation, pp. 68–78. PLDI 2008, Association for Computing Machinery, New York, NY, USA (2008). https://doi.org/10.1145/1375581.1375591

17. Dubois, M., Scheurich, C., Briggs, F.: Memory access buffering in multiprocessors. In: Proceedings of the 13th Annual International Symposium on Computer Architecture, pp. 434–442. ISCA 1986, IEEE Computer Society Press, Washington, DC, USA (1986)

18. Flur, S., et al.: Mixed-size concurrency: arm, power, C/C++11, and sc. In: Proceedings of the 44th ACM SIGPLAN Symposium on Principles of Programming Languages, pp. 429–442. POPL 2017, Association for Computing Machinery, New York, NY, USA (2017). https://doi.org/10.1145/3009837.3009839

19. Gharachorloo, K., Gupta, A., Hennessy, J.: Performance evaluation of memory consistency models for shared-memory multiprocessors. In: Proceedings of the Fourth International Conference on Architectural Support for Programming Languages and Operating Systems, pp. 245–257. ASPLOS IV, Association for Computing Machinery, New York, NY, USA (1991). https://doi.org/10.1145/106972.106997

20. Gharachorloo, K., Lenoski, D., Laudon, J., Gibbons, P., Gupta, A., Hennessy, J.: Memory consistency and event ordering in scalable shared-memory multiprocessors. SIGARCH Comput. Archit. News **18**(2SI), 15–26 (1990). https://doi.org/10. 1145/325096.325102

21. Goodman, J.R.: Cache consistency and sequential consistency (1991). http:// digital.library.wisc.edu/1793/59442. Accessed 28 Mar 2023

22. Gupta, N., Ashiwal, R., Brank, B., Peddoju, S.K., Pleiter, D.: Performance evaluation of parallex execution model on ARM-based platforms. In: 2020 IEEE International Conference on Cluster Computing (CLUSTER), pp. 567–575 (2020). https://doi.org/10.1109/CLUSTER49012.2020.00080

23. Higham, L., Kawash, J., Verwaal, N.: Defining and comparing memory consistency models (1997)

24. Johnson, D.: Apple M1 Microarchitecture Research (2023). https://dougallj. github.io/applecpu/firestorm.html. Accessed 23 Mar 2023

25. Kenyon, C., Capano, C.: Apple silicon performance in scientific computing. In: 2022 IEEE High Performance Extreme Computing Conference (HPEC), pp. 1–10 (2022). https://doi.org/10.1109/HPEC55821.2022.9926315

26. Kodama, Y., Kondo, M., Sato, M.: Evaluation of SPEC CPU and SPEC OMP on the A64FX. In: 2021 IEEE International Conference on Cluster Computing (CLUSTER), pp. 553–561 (2021). https://doi.org/10.1109/Cluster48925.2021.00088

27. Lamport: How to make a multiprocessor computer that correctly executes multiprocess programs. IEEE Trans. Comput. C **28**(9), 690–691 (1979). https://doi. org/10.1109/TC.1979.1675439

28. Mattioli, M.: Meet the famlly. IEEE Micro **42**(3), 78–84 (2022). https://doi.org/ 10.1109/MM.2022.3169245

29. Naeem, A., Chen, X., Lu, Z., Jantsch, A.: Realization and performance comparison of sequential and weak memory consistency models in network-on-chip based multicore systems. In: 16th Asia and South Pacific Design Automation Conference (ASP-DAC 2011). pp. 154–159 (2011). https://doi.org/10.1109/ASPDAC.2011.5722176

30. Ouro, P., Lopez-Novoa, U., Guest, M.F.: On the performance of a highly-scalable computational fluid dynamics code on AMD, arm and intel processor-based HPC systems. Comput. Phys. Commun. **269**, 108105 (2021). https://doi.org/ 10.1016/j.cpc.2021.108105.   https://www.sciencedirect.com/science/article/pii/ S0010465521002174

31. Pulte, C., Flur, S., Deacon, W., French, J., Sarkar, S., Sewell, P.: Simplifying ARM concurrency: multicopy-atomic axiomatic and operational models for ARMv8. Proc. ACM Program. Lang. **2**(POPL), 1–29(2017). https://doi.org/10. 1145/3158107

32. SPARC International Inc, C.: The SPARC Architecture Manual: Version 8. Prentice-Hall Inc, USA (1992)

33. SPARC International Inc, C.: The SPARC Architecture Manual (Version 9). Prentice-Hall Inc, USA (1994)

34. Xia, J., Cheng, C., Zhou, X., Hu, Y., Chun, P.: Kunpeng 920: the first 7-nm Chiplet-based 64-core ARM SOC for cloud services. IEEE Micro **41**(5), 67–75 (2021). https://doi.org/10.1109/MM.2021.3085578

Back to the Core-Memory Age: Running Operating Systems in NVRAM only

Jonas Rabenstein[1]([⊠]), Dustin Nguyen[1]([⊠]), Oliver Giersch[2]([⊠]),
Christian Eichler[3]([⊠]), Timo Hönig[3]([⊠]), Jörg Nolte[2]([⊠]),
and Wolfgang Schröder-Preikschat[1]([⊠])

[1] Friedrich-Alexander-Universität Erlangen-Nürnberg (FAU), Erlangen, Germany
{rabenstein,nguyen,wosch}@cs.fau.de
[2] Brandenburgische Technische Universität Cottbus-Senftenberg (BTU),
Cottbus, Germany
{oliver.giersch,joerg.nolte}@b-tu.de
[3] Ruhr-Universität Bochum (RUB), Bochum, Germany
{christian.eichler,timo.hoenig}@rub.de

Abstract. The classic core memory was completely non-volatile and thus kept at least part of the operating system persistently in main memory, even over power cycles. Nowadays we can repeat this approach with NVRAM, but with terabytes of main memory on a completely different scale and with parts of the operating-system state stored in volatile CPU caches. In this paper, we discuss our experiences of running large modern operating systems including their applications entirely in NVRAM. We adapted stock Linux and FreeBSD kernels to work exclusively with NVRAM by hiding all DRAM from the kernels at boot time to establish a realistic performance baseline without changing anything else. Following this entirely NVRAM-agnostic approach, we could observe an effective performance penalty of a factor of about four, but only negligible increases in whole-system power draw. For our system with two CPU sockets and 56 cores total, we also observed a reduction in power draw in several scenarios. Due to prolonged execution times, the energy consumption increased as well for these measured workloads. While this might be discouraging at first sight, this result was achieved *without any* performance tuning as to the specific characteristics of today's NVRAM technology. Therefore, we are also discussing means to mitigate the observed shortcomings by integrating NVRAM appropriately into the memory hierarchy of future robust persistent systems.

Keywords: NVRAM · Operating Systems · Energy

1 Introduction

The current trend towards fast byte-addressable *non-volatile memory* (NVM)—NVRAM for short as synonymous—with latencies and a write resistance much closer to ordinary RAM (i.e. DRAM or SRAM) than to Flash, positions this *storage class memory* (SCM [3]) as a possible replacement for the established volatile technologies. This opens up a fundamentally different approach to the resilient operation of computing systems, in which all programs, including the operating system, are regularly executed directly in NVRAM.

Completely dispensing with DRAM promises a positive effect on energy consumption, which is particularly important for the service life of mobile devices, but stationary setups would also benefit in terms of electricity costs or cooling. Such an "NVM-only" solution, however, still has to cover the volatile state stored in CPU registers and caches and keep it consistent with the counterparts held in the NVRAM.

Given such a top of the "memory pyramid" with both volatile and non-volatile features, the primary advantages of NVRAM—direct byte-addressability and persistence—are not, in fact, transparently made available to the vast majority of applications and imply major challenges, especially for the programming of such systems [10] as "using NVM for persistence requires fail-safe guarantees from application or device failures" [6]. For example, power failures in combination with NVRAM cause control flows that can unexpectedly transform a sequential process into a non-sequential process: A program has to deal with its own state from previous interrupted runs [9].

With quite simple precautions, however, these problems can be solved efficiently and functionally transparently even without special hardware support, both for the machine programs (i.e., applications) and for a large part of the operating system programs at the operating system level itself:

1. by a sporadically triggered checkpointing mechanism integrated into the exception-handling subsystem [2] and
2. by integration of this new storage class into the memory hierarchy via the virtual memory subsystem, whereby the persistence of NVRAM pages buffered in RAM is ensured by the former (point 1.., analogous to [5]).

Both concepts combined pave the way for direct execution from NVRAM for the operating system and the machine programs running on it, but especially for legacy software.

But the advantage of such a purely *software-based whole-system persistence* with direct execution from NVRAM is of little value if the resulting performance is too poor for the common use case, making this mode of operation unattractive. It is therefore essential to first compare the cost of an NVRAM-based (general purpose) operating system with that of its traditional RAM-based variant before moving on to implementing NVRAM-specific concepts for an energy-efficient transparent execution of legacy software, in order to be able to better classify the hoped-for added value—in a real environment, not by simulation or emulation.

This is exactly what this paper does: it presents a case study where Linux and FreeBSD, including machine programs, are executed from both NVRAM and DRAM, and compares the obtained performance characteristics. DRAM-based operation is nothing special, but it determines the baseline for comparison. In contrast, the NVRAM-based operation of "vanilla" Linux or FreeBSD is—to the best of our knowledge—an unprecedented act, which, as we will describe, requires some bold engineering work. The migration of Linux and FreeBSD from DRAM to NVRAM will not only show whether the higher access latencies of the latter are drowned out in the background noise of the overall system but also help to gain insights and guidelines for operating system development in general.

> *Please note again, that none of the aforementioned challenges of a persistent operating system are addressed at this early stage and that our modified operating-system kernels are still functionally volatile, only running in non-volatile main memory (i.e. NVRAM).*

We go further than [13] and supplement their work with the evaluation of systems that run entirely in NVRAM. Thus, the paper makes the following contributions:

- A field report on freeing Linux and FreeBSD from DRAM dependencies and preparing both operating systems to use NVRAM exclusively.
- A before-and-after comparison of the performance and energy efficiency of the systems in different configurations using either NVRAM or DRAM, with various benchmarks and practical, real-world workloads.
- Recommendations for transitioning to NVRAM-based operating systems that enable functionally transparent use of NVRAM for legacy software.

The rest of the paper is organised as follows: Sect. 2 introduces the hardware used for the experiments, explains the operating system configurations and briefly describes the evaluation scenarios and benchmarks. Section 3 characterises the performance and energy efficiency of the hardware and operating system platforms we use and presents a before-and-after comparison. The empirical results are then discussed in Sect. 4, followed by a presentation of relevant related work in Sect. 5. Finally, Sect. 6 gives a brief summary of our work.

2   Fundamentals and Methodology

In this Section, we present the computer hardware used for the experiments, explain the operating system configurations required for them and describe the evaluation scenarios as well as the benchmarks.

2.1   Hardware Platform

In addition to the processor system components of our test device, especially the NVRAM equipment, the raw data of the main memory regarding timing and bandwidth are interesting as a reference for the theoretical (manufacturer's specification) performance. The latter is especially significant as a baseline for the subsequent evaluation.

Processing Systems. The evaluation platform used to run and benchmark both Linux and FreeBSD is a Dell PowerEdge R650 equipped with two Intel® Xeon® Gold 6330 processors. Each processor has 28 cores and 56 threads, respectively.

Their base frequency is 2.0 GHz, even though they can boost to up to 3.10 GHz. As conventional memory, there are eight 32 GB DDR4 RDIMMs.

For NVRAM, there are eight DIMMs of Optane^{TM} Persistent Memory 200 with a capacity of 128 GB each. Both kinds of memory are distributed evenly between the CPUs, populating each memory channel with one DIMM. In total, the system has 256 GB RAM and 1024 GB NVRAM. Even though the available RAM and NVRAM support up to 3200 MT/s, both are limited by the CPUs to 2933 MT/s. The NVRAM is configured to App Direct Mode.

NVRAM Baseline. The manufacturer specifications of the memory bandwidth for the 128 GB NVRAM DIMM is quite sobering compared to DRAM. The idle average latency for 64 B accesses in App Direct Mode is given as 340 ns. Note that each load or store instruction fetches a 64-byte cache line. At the persistent memory module, this results in a read or write of 256 bytes of data accessed [4].

For the evaluation carried out here, namely running "vanilla" Linux and FreeBSD, respectively, directly from NVRAM, the access mix of 67% read and 33% write is baseline relevant. In contrast, the (to-be) NVRAM-based backup of the volatile system state will have 100% write in focus.

2.2   Operating Systems

While our modified versions themselves would allow running on an "NVM-only" platform, we can neither modify the hardware nor the firmware. Common problems tackled by both implementations revolve around x86-64's startup process, which requires physical memory below 4 GiB for switching from real mode to long mode. In addition, some legacy drivers depend on 32-bit addressable memory, while NVRAM populates physical addresses well above 4 GiB.

However, we would like to point out that once the system finished booting, all allocations are served from NVRAM only. As such, the RAM is solely used as a workaround for hardware and firmware limitations and not used for essential functionality of the operating system in execution.

Linux. NVRAM is already extensively supported by current versions of Linux and can be used as a block device (DAX), directly mapped into the address space of an application or extend the system memory. Together with the ability to dynamically on- and offline memory regions during runtime, usage of RAM could be almost eliminated for userspace applications. However, as the memory of the kernel itself can not be moved, it would remain in RAM.

To overcome this limitation, the most recent version available during the development process (*v6.1*) was modified to allow to only use NVRAM already from the early boot stages on. During bootstrapping, a stub decompresses the kernel image and allows to randomise the used kernel start addresses. To detect suitable regions, as well as later on, when initialising the memory allocation pools, a firmware-provided memory map is used. As this map also provides information about non-volatile memory regions, we introduced a kernel parameter (memtype) to allow the selection of memory types to be used on each boot.

FreeBSD. As a basis for our changes to the FreeBSD system, we have used version 13.1, which is the most recent at the time of writing. The current state of NVRAM support in FreeBSD is limited to a device driver that makes the recognized NVRAM DIMMs accessible. From there on, it can be used as a fast backing store for conventional file systems—but this does not mean that FreeBSD itself runs in NVRAM.

FreeBSD uses a custom, single-stage UEFI bootloader maintained in lockstep with the rest of the operating system for non-legacy bootstraps by default. Based on the EFI memory map, we adjusted the loader to place the kernel and modules into NVRAM. In addition, the initial virtual address mapping used during the early boot stage had to be adapted to reflect this change.

The FreeBSD kernel for x86-64 has a documented dependency on the kernel being loaded into the lower 4 GiB of memory, and many internal invariants rely on that property. We identified each of these reliant components in the kernel and modified them to work with the altered kernel placement. With the kernel placed in NVRAM, the initialisation of the memory subsystem had to be changed as well. Based on the EFI memory map, most of the RAM pages are ignored. A small, single-digit number of RAM pages in the low physical address range are set aside and stored in a separate data structure to serve the architecture-specific requirements. In addition, all NVRAM regions are assigned to the NUMA domain of their corresponding CPU in order to avoid memory accesses across domains. To satisfy the 32-bit address DMA requirements of old drivers, IOMMU-assisted DMA remapping had to be enabled as well. This required no further changes aside from setting the appropriate kernel parameter, however, the DMA remapping driver requires a single page of RAM below 4 GiB for itself. These changes by themselves suffice to fully bootstrap the kernel in NVRAM with only a single CPU core. For multi-core support the set aside memory was used to initialize a transient allocator, which can be used to satisfy any memory allocations to low-address memory. The architecture of x86-64 requires 20-bit addresses for startup and 32-bit addresses for the transition to long mode. With all cores online, all references to the transient allocator and DRAM memory are dropped, resulting in the execution of the operating system and all future allocations being served from NVRAM.

2.3   Evaluation Approach

During the evaluation, the systems were mostly isolated from any outside induced noise, by shutting down any non-evaluation–related service and disabling SSH access on the standard port.

As our modified Linux allows to select the memory region type that should be used as main memory dynamically by a command line parameter, the same binary had been used in the comparison. Our configuration is based on Debian, with some unused modules removed.

The evaluation of the FreeBSD systems is done on the same hardware with the same kernel configuration (*GENERIC*). Both kernels and loaders (original and modified) are loaded via iPXE netboot, while the whole FreeBSD userland is already installed on the local harddrive.

All our power measurements are conducted using an external measurement device, the Microchip MCP39F511N Power Monitor Demonstration Board [12]. The server's (cf. Sect. 2.1) two power-supply units (PSUs) are each connected to one of the MCP39F511N measurement channels, allowing for a realistic whole-system measurement, including the power losses in the PSUs and other hardware components. The MCP39F511N is connected to another server to ensure that the power measurement does not influence the system under test. Thus, our measurement approach provides realistic, real-world power values of the otherwise unaltered, off-the-shelf hardware platform.

Microbenchmark. To gain detailed measurements regarding the performance characteristics of NVRAM vs. RAM and placement strategies of the operating systems under test, the *sysbench* [14] test suite was used. The baseline was established by using sysbench's *memory* benchmark. To estimate the impact on overall system performance, we used *fileio*, which interacts with several subsystems such as the virtual file system, buffers, and system call handling. The sysbench version used is supplied by the operating system vendor, Debian respectively FreeBSD—in both cases version 1.0.20.

Different combinations of sysbench configurations were run multiple times to test a variety of workloads. These options for adjustment are the number of used threads, the block size of memory chunks and the kind of access. By modifying the number of threads, the operating system is forced to make NUMA-placement decisions, while different block sizes influence cache usage.

Application. In order to evaluate the systems' performance with a real-world workload, the build-system of the respective operating system is deemed as suitable. Most of the workload is comprised of source to binary translation, whereas source files are read into memory, optimised and written back as an object file. Since the option -pipe is used during translation, no intermediate files are generated, leading to greater memory consumption. During linking, all object files are read again, and merged into a single binary. In between are some transformations made by tools such as *awk* for generating header files and *gzip* for compression of build artefacts.

3   Performance Characterisation

Following [13], we measure the performance of the NVRAM hardware (Intel Optane^{TM}) underlying the experiments on the one hand and the operating systems on the other. The focus is on the timing and power requirements of Linux and FreeBSD for the conventional DRAM-based deployment and the NVRAM-based ("NVM-only") approach to be evaluated. Every measurement was repeated five times, and the presented numbers are the median thereof with a 95% confidence level.

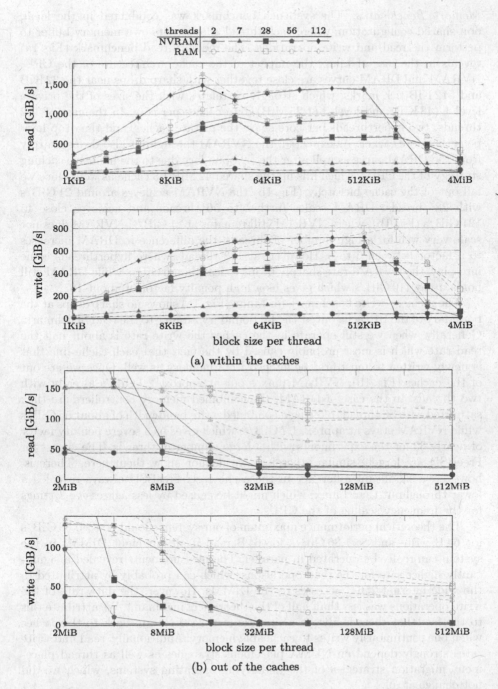

Fig. 1. sysbench memory throughput for different block sizes per thread executed on top of our modified Linux.

Memory Benchmarks. The sysbench benchmark was conducted in the local, non-shared configuration, where each thread allocates its own memory buffer to perform the read and write operations. The memory read benchmark (Fig. 1a) reveals in the case of Linux the impact of the cache architecture of the CPU. NVRAM and DRAM curves are close together with sharp drops near the 32 KiB and 512 KiB tick marks, which strongly correlates with the sizes of the private level 1 (48 KiB) and level 2 (1.25 MiB) data caches per core. In the case of 112 threads, two hyperthreads per core share the private caches, and the drop happens therefore earlier. As expected, the NVRAM throughput also drops sharply from the DRAM curve as well after the L2 boundary due to the inclusive caching strategy of the CPUs, which fills up the shared 42 MiB L3 cache as well. Once we fall out of the cache hierarchy (Fig. 1b) the NVRAM achieves around 21 GiB/s with 28 threads. DRAM scales further to 56 threads and achieves close to 121 GiB/s (Fig. 1b), where NVRAM still remains at 21 GiB/s. NVRAM does not scale very well for a high number of threads, the difference to DRAM increases to a factor between 5 to 6. However, at 112 threads where hyperthreads come into play, the NVRAM rate sharply drops to less than 6 GiB/s while DRAM still holds up at 110 GiB/s which gives us a high penalty factor of about 18.

The memory-write benchmark for Linux (Fig. 1a) shows no sharp drops at the boundary of the L1 cache but at the L2 boundary, similar to the read benchmark, Generally, when we still operate in the caches the write rate is about half the read rate which is most probably caused by the fact, that each cache line that is newly written to must first be fetched from memory as well. Once we are out of the caches (Fig. 1b), NVRAM maxes out at approx. 2.1 GiB/s already with two threads. In the case of DRAM, the combined memory controllers are then saturated with 56 threads offering a combined write bandwidth of about 56 GiB/s while NVRAM stays at approx. 1.7 GiB/s, which gives us a severe penalty factor of nearly 33 for the experiments with a large number of threads. The curves for FreeBSD are largely similar, therefore we do not show them here. There is, however, a significant difference in the cache case. FreeBSD always revealed a lower throughput than Linux, which might be caused by less aggressive settings for the frequency scaling of the CPUs.

The theoretical performance maximum of our system should be 8×0.56 GiB/s for 64 B write and 8×1.86 GiB/s for 64 B read if all our eight DIMMs in the system can really be operated in parallel. The measurements revealed a significantly higher rate for the read operations, which can probably by attributed to the wide internal 256 B accesses of the DIMMs. However, the data rate of the write operations was less than half of the theoretical maximum. We attribute this to the fact that there is always a simultaneous read stream back to the caches when one continuously writes to cacheable memory. Additionally, read and write rates strongly depend on NUMA placement strategies as well as thread placement/migration strategies of the underlying operating systems, which we did not change at all.

When the combined working sets of all applications fit mostly into the cache hierarchy, there is only a slight performance penalty for the NVRAM-based systems caused by working set changes. Memory-bound applications, however, might suffer severely, especially the low write rates are the biggest problem and can inhibit parallel execution significantly.

File Benchmarks. In Fig. 2, the results of the sequential memory read and write benchmarks using the traditional file system interface via system calls are shown for Linux and FreeBSD. In the case of NVRAM, Linux reaches its read peak of about 5.4 GiB/s already with four threads, while FreeBSD reaches its peak of nearly 4.9 GiB/s with 28 threads. From 14 threads on, however, the curves of the two systems are relatively close together. Both systems do not scale well beyond seven threads, irrespective of the type of memory used. In the case of DRAM, Linux outperforms FreeBSD by a large margin, 15.5 GiB/s achieved already with seven threads vs about 10 GiB/s with 28 threads. All in all, for the read benchmark, the performance penalty of NVRAM is about 3x in the case of Linux and approx. 2x for FreeBSD.

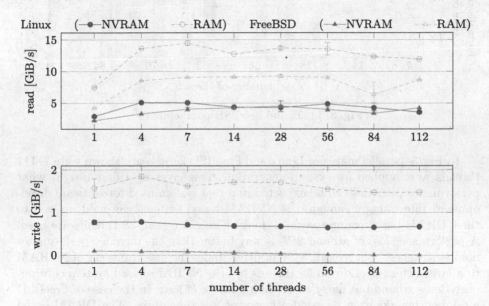

Fig. 2. sysbench fileio sequential read and write throughput

In the case of the write benchmark (Fig. 2), the throughput is way lower than in the case of read, probably because an `fsync()` operation is automatically inserted for every 100 write requests by the benchmark, that caused real write operations to storage. The scalability is very low for this benchmark, both systems are saturated with a few numbers of threads already. We strongly assume that even the occasional `fsync()` operations quickly saturated the SSDs of our system. Linux achieved slightly less than 2 GiB/s with DRAM and four threads. With NVRAM it achieved slightly less than 0.85 GiB/s with four threads as well.

The penalty for NVRAM was about 2.4x. In the case of FreeBSD, one thread already achieved the peak of 0.1 GiB/s for NVRAM and about 0.18 GiB/s for DRAM. In all cases, the penalty for NVRAM was less than 1.5x.

Parallel Make Benchmarks. For the before and after comparison, we use a parallel make on each of the system's build infrastructure to show how painful an "NVM-only" approach really is in terms of system performance and whether or not the differences in performance are lost in the system-related background noise and are no longer perceived.

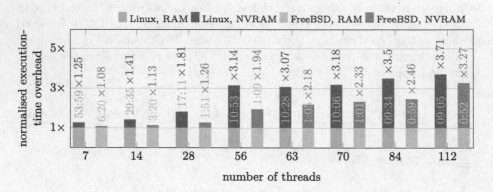

Fig. 3. Linux and FreeBSD parallel make

In Fig. 3, parallel makes of Linux and FreeBSD kernels are shown were 7–112 threads were applied for system generation. This gives us a first insight what performance penalties can be expected in a real system used for software development. Interestingly enough, the NVRAM-based systems can hold up well to their DRAM-based counterparts, as long as no more than 28 threads are used. A performance loss of around 25% is way better than the memory performance numbers suggest. The overall "system jitter" hides the disadvantages of NVRAM to a large extent here. From 56 threads on, the NVRAM-based system continuously loses ground but never more than a factor of four. In the case of FreeBSD most benchmarks even revealed a factor of less than three. The DRAM-based systems are able to continuously achieve a slight performance benefit from more threads but at a very low margin. There is only a negligible achievement from 56 threads onwards, probably due to increasing serial portions of the build process.

In absolute times, the generation of the FreeBSD system was nearly a magnitude faster than the generation of Linux, probably due to the size of the sources. The penalty factors for NVRAM are slightly better (from 1.08x to 3.27x) for any degree of parallelism than in the case of the Linux kernel. But the general observations are otherwise similar. For up to 28 threads, the NVRAM-based system keeps up well with its DRAM counterpart, with a penalty of less than 1.3x.

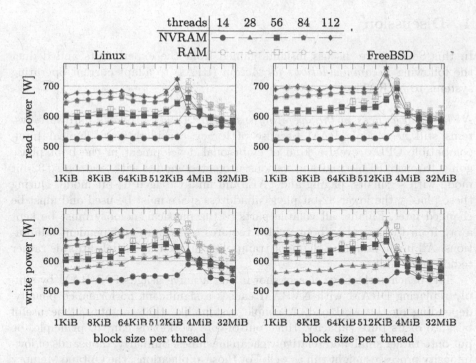

Fig. 4. Whole-system power draw for the benchmarks presented in Fig. 1.

Power Consumption. Figure 4 illustrates the average power draw for the sysbench memory evaluation scenarios presented in Fig. 1: On Linux, the power demand for reading and writing blocks of up to 512 KiB (or 1 MiB, depending on the level of parallelism) from/to NVRAM (solid shapes and lines) is almost identical compared to running the respective benchmark on DRAM (blank shapes and dashed lines). When surpassing the boundary of 512 KiB/1 MiB—the same block size the overall throughput decreases (see Fig. 1a) due to caching effects—the power draw starts to decrease alongside the throughput. As for the throughput, the power decrease is more pronounced when operating on NVRAM due to its lower performance, causing the same benchmarks running on DRAM to cause a higher power draw while exhibiting a higher throughput. This decrease in power draw is most likely caused by the CPUs becoming idle by waiting for the memory. Also, in terms of power draw, the difference between reading from and writing to memory is small: While writing to both DRAM and NVRAM draws slightly more power for small block sizes, these values begin to fall below the corresponding values for reading when surpassing the block size of 512 KiB/1 MiB.

When running the same benchmarks on FreeBSD, the observed values are very similar to the values observed on Linux.

4   Discussion

In this Section, we discuss insights gained from the experiments and deduct the following *Recommendations for Action* (RFAs) to adapt current operating systems to NVRAM:

NVRAM awareness in the operating system(RFA #1). Today's hardware systems still need some RAM because of legacy considerations. Typical Intel-compatible CPUs reveal a kind of embryonal development in the boot phase going through 16-bit real and various protected modes with segments, 32-bit mode with segments, paging and PAE, and finally, paged 64-bit mode. During these phases, the lower 32-bit physical address space must be used and must be changed later. Finally, all volatile parts of the physical memory must be kept away from the kernel to boot, which requires some system-dependent adaptations. All in all, adapting the boot trampoline and kernel initialisation is rather tedious and fiddly.

The benchmarks have clearly shown that a naive usage of NVRAM by simply replacing DRAM with NVRAM causes a significant performance penalty, depending on the workload. A simple system like that might still be useful because of its pure capacity. Huge out-of-core workloads can, in principle, be put onto rather small and relatively cheap machines. Similarly, thousands of low-intensity processes might run as well. For those applications, the Optane Memory Mode that manages some of the available DRAM as hardware-controlled cache, would probably be sufficient, for example. However, in that mode, a part of the DRAM is lost and NVRAM is treated as volatile.

Transition from DRAM to NVRAM (RFA #2). Current Linux systems can already use NVRAM following the SNIA recommendations. Furthermore, (parts of) the NVRAM can also be used by the virtual memory subsystem as a kind of overflow memory in times of high memory pressure. The NVRAM is handled as a "far away", still volatile, NUMA domain in this case without taking advantage of its persistence features at all. In contrast, we clearly want to go beyond pure capacity scaling. In further work, we want to use NVRAM truly as storage-class memory, targeting robust systems, that provide efficient whole system persistence with stock hardware and fast recovery times in exceptional cases. In the next step, we will develop a suspend-to-NVRAM mechanism, that allows us to freeze and wakeup entire systems with minimal latency on demand. Following [2,5], we will integrate this mechanism into the handling of power failures, such that systems will be able to survive power losses, ideally with low amounts of residual energy from the power supply or a low-capacity UPS.

Persistency Guarantees and Power/Energy (RFA #3). Contemporary operating systems, such as Linux and FreeBSD, are designed for running in and working with volatile main memory. Due to this volatility, the operating system conducts a variety of persistency measures—such as periodic file-system cache writebacks—just to protect from the loss of volatile data in the rare event of a power outage. Such persistency measures, however, come at the cost of computational and energetic overhead, and their implementation also increases the trusted code base.

Once the persistency of the main memory is guaranteed by the hardware, that is, the system is using non-volatile main memory instead of volatile DRAM, the software-implemented persistency measures become superfluous and can be removed. Despite the lower throughput of NVRAM, without such measures, the operating system can finally leverage the advantages of NVRAM over conventional, volatile DRAM and, thus, compensate for the lower performance at least partially—and achieve even higher performance compared to DRAM-only by implementing the subsequent RFA #4.

Architectural Changes due to NVRAM (RFA #4). Finally and most importantly, we will make virtual memory subsystems NVRAM-aware and develop a *virtual NVRAM* that will manage the DRAM only as a cache for NVRAM to mitigate the inherent performance penalties while retaining its persistence. Such a multi-level virtual memory subsystem is most likely needed anyway in the future since other memory technologies like *high-bandwidth memory* (HBM) also have to be integrated appropriately.

Apart from the memory hierarchy, NVRAM awareness offers plenty of opportunities for improvements ranging from simplistic ones to highly sophisticated schemes based on machine learning and similar techniques. For example, when a scheduler decides to move low-intensity processes to "slow" economy cores, its memory contents might be moved lazily to NVRAM as well. Program code often has a high locality of reference and fits into the internal CPU caches, thus code could always be placed into NVRAM without much performance loss, as our benchmarks show. Accessing code and data in large persistent file system caches would be possible without hard page faults but fast lazy mappings. All in all, the observed performance penalties can most certainly be overcome but require substantial changes to rather complex parts of current operating systems.

5   Related Work

There is as yet no Linux or FreeBSD that, together with all machine programs (i.e., applications), runs directly and exclusively from NVRAM. Thus, at present, our approach cannot be compared with other solutions on a level playing field.

This includes the concept of *whole system persistence* [7], which achieves the persistence of complete systems on the basis of special DIMMs that contain both DRAM and equally sized Flash memory. The content of the DRAM part is saved with the help of backup capacitors on the local Flash as soon as a power failure is detected. The same applies to NV-Hypervisor [11], where DRAM content is also hardware-based persisted. In contrast, with our "NVM-only" vision, we do not expect any special hardware support other than NVRAM to keep main memory contents persistent.

Twizzler [1] seems to be an exception to these developments: It is presented as a system from which a complete NVRAM-based operating system can be built with a data-centric design. Whether Twizzler itself can be considered an "NVM-only" system, however, remains an open question. In addition, Twizzler must be understood as a replacement for an exokernel-based operating system (implemented in Rust) and would establish Linux or FreeBSD as a guest operating system, if at all. The programming model of Twizzler unfolds its positive effect, especially when used directly by the machine programs that are then to run in NVRAM; it does not make the latter transparent for legacy software as our approach does.

6   Conclusion

We strongly argue that NVRAM needs to be integrated appropriately into the memory hierarchy to realize its true potential. Since this is a highly complex undertaking, we have first shown with our work here that state-of-the-art operating systems can be run directly from NVRAM, which is a first to the best of our knowledge. What's more: entire software stacks, including legacy software, can actually be run from NVRAM and don't have to do without the persistence properties of this memory technology.

We have now established a nearly worst-case baseline for the possible performance of such systems under heavy load. While the synthetic memory benchmarks showed a wide variety of performance penalties, *all* of the kernel build benchmarks only revealed a penalty of significantly less than 4x. Thus, the expected degradation was drowned in "system jitter" to a large extent. The power draw increased only insignificantly and even decreased for several workloads, while the overall energy consumption was proportional to the prolonged execution times of the benchmarks.

Although these measurement results may seem discouraging, one should not forget that these numbers have been achieved with systems where we performed a rigorous technology swap from DRAM to NVRAM without taking *any* special precautions for efficient NVRAM operation. When we additionally use certain amounts of DRAM as a software-controlled cache for NVRAM integrated into the virtual memory subsystem, the way is paved for robust, moderately priced servers with huge memory capacities—and which provide an efficient abstraction layer in particular for legacy software that can also be directly run from NVRAM without any change. We want to show this in further work.

Unfortunately, Intel has ceased to produce the Optane DIMMs used for our work. However, first approaches like "memory semantics SSDs" were already announced that might fill the gap and lead in a similar direction. The idea is in the world, and we strongly expect CXL-based solutions for storage class memory in the near future.

Acknowledgments. The author order corresponds to the FLAE (*first-last-author emphasis*) model. This work was funded by the Deutsche Forschungsgemeinschaft (DFG, German Research Foundation) – project numbers 465958100, 501993201, and 502615015 and by the German Federal Ministry of Education and Research (BMBF), project AI-NET-ANTILLAS 16KIS1315.

Availability. The source code developed for the work and the measurement data obtained is published via https://doi.org/10.5281/zenodo.7788760. See also [8].

References

1. Bittman, D., Alvaro, P., Mehra, P., Long, D.D.E., Miller, E.L.: Twizzler: a data-centric OS for non-volatile memory. In: Proceedings of the 2020 USENIX Annual Technical Conference (USENIX ATC 2020), pp. 65–80. USENIX Association (2020)
2. Eichler, C., Hofmeier, H., Reif, S., Hönig, T., Nolte, J., Schröder-Preikschat, W.: Neverlast: an NVM-centric operating system for persistent edge systems. In: Proceedings of the 12th ACM SIGOPS Asia-Pacific Workshop on Systems, APSys 2021, pp. 146–153. Association for Computing Machinery, New York, NY, USA (2021). https://doi.org/10.1145/3476886.3477513
3. Freitas, R.F., Wilcke, W.W.: Storage-class memory: the next storage system technology. IBM J. Res. Dev. **52**(4/5), 439–447 (2008)
4. Hady, F.T.: Faster access to more data. Intel Non-Volatile Memory Solutions Group, Intel Corporation, USA, Technology brief (2022)
5. Heiser, G., Le Sueur, E., Danis, A., Budzynowski, A., Salomie, T.l., Alonso, G.: RapiLog: reducing system complexity through verification. In: Proceedings of the 8th ACM European Conference on Computer Systems, EuroSys 2013, pp. 323–336. Association for Computing Machinery, New York, NY, USA (2013). https://doi.org/10.1145/2465351.2465383
6. Kannan, S., Qureshi, M., Gavrilovska, A., Schwan, K.: Energy aware persistence: reducing energy overheads of memory-based persistence in NVMs. In: 2016 International Conference on Parallel Architecture and Compilation Techniques (PACT), pp. 165–177 (2016). https://doi.org/10.1145/2967938.2967953
7. Narayanan, D., Hodson, O.: Whole-system persistence. In: Proceedings of the seventeenth international conference on Architectural Support for Programming Languages and Operating Systems (ASPLOS 2012), pp. 401–410 (2012)
8. Rabenstein, J., et al.: On the performance of NVRAM-based operating systems: a case study with Linux and FreeBSD. Technical report CS-2023-01, Friedrich-Alexander-Universität Erlangen-Nürnberg (FAU), Department Informatik (2023). https://doi.org/10.25593/issn.2191-5008/CS-2023-01
9. Ransford, B., Lucia, B.: Nonvolatile memory is a broken time machine. In: Proceedings of the 2014 Workshop on Memory Systems Performance and Correctness (MSPC 2014), p. 5 (2014)
10. Ren, J., Hu, Q., Khan, S., Moscibroda, T.: Programming for non-volatile main memory is hard. In: Proceedings of the 8th ACM SIGOPS Asia-Pacific Workshop on Systems (APSys 2017), pp. 1–8. no. 13, ACM Digital Library (2017)
11. Sartakov, V.A., Kapitza, R.: NV-Hypervisor: hypervisor-based persistence for virtual machines. In: 2014 44th Annual IEEE/IFIP International Conference on Dependable Systems and Networks, pp. 654–659 (2014). https://doi.org/10.1109/DSN.2014.64
12. Technology, M.: MCP39F511N power monitor demonstration board. https://www.microchip.com/en-us/development-tool/ADM00706
13. Yang, J., Kim, J., Hoseinzadeh, M., Izraelevitz, J., Swanson, S.: An empirical guide to the behavior and use of scalable persistent memory. In: Proceedings of the 18th USENIX Conference on File and Storage Technologies, FAST 2020 (2020)
14. Zaitsev, P.: sysbench (2004). https://github.com/akopytov/sysbench

Retrofitting AMD x86 Processors with Active Virtual Machine Introspection Capabilities

Thomas Dangl[1(✉)], Stewart Sentanoe[1], and Hans P. Reiser[2]

[1] University of Passau, Innstr. 43, 94032 Passau, Germany
{td,se}@sec.uni-passau.de
[2] Reykjavík University, Menntavegur 1, Reykjavík, Iceland
hansr@ru.is

Abstract. *Active virtual machine introspection* mechanisms intercept the control flow of a virtual machine running on top of a hypervisor. They enable external tools to monitor and inspect the state at predetermined locations of interest synchronous to the execution of the system. Such mechanisms, in particular, require support from the processor vendor by facilitating interpositioning. This support is missing on *AMD x86* processors, leading to inferior introspection solutions. We outline implicit assumptions about active introspection mechanisms in previous work, offer constructions for solution strategies on *AMD* systems and discuss stealthiness and correctness. Finally, we show empirically that such retrofitted software solutions exhibit performance metrics in the same order of magnitude as native hardware solutions.

Keywords: virtual machine introspection · monitoring · system security · reliability · stealthiness · cloud computing

1 Introduction

Virtual machine introspection (VMI) is a popular approach for monitoring virtual machines (VMs) at the hypervisor level. VMI is desirable for many practical purposes, including intrusion detection, malware analysis, and main memory forensics. To perform VMI, we have to provide a monitoring application with the means to access a target virtual machine's internal state.

There are two flavors of VMI: *active* and *passive*. *Passive* VMI, or polling VMI, refers to unsynchronized, read-only access to the virtual machine's state. This approach involves periodically polling the virtual machine's memory and registers to gather information about its state. *Active* VMI, or event-based VMI, involves intercepting the virtual machine's control flow and executing custom code in response to specific events. This approach allows for more fine-grained control over the target virtual machine, but can be more complex to implement.

Significant hardware differences exist between *Intel* and *AMD x86* processors, which majorly impact the use of *active* VMI. The usual approaches used by

G. Goumas et al. (Eds.): ARCS 2023, LNCS 13949, pp. 168–182, 2023.
https://doi.org/10.1007/978-3-031-42785-5_12

VMI tools and libraries on *Intel* processors do not work on *AMD* processors due to fundamental differences in their design. Specifically, *AMD* processors support hardware-assisted virtualization through their *Secure Virtual Machine* (SVM) extension and enable *Second Level Address Translation* (SLAT) using *Rapid Virtualization Indexing* (RVI). This is different from *Intel* processors, which use *Virtual Machine Extensions* (VT-x) and support SLAT with *Extended Page Tables* (EPT). Additionally, while *Intel* processors have a feature called the *Monitor Trap Flag* that simplifies single-stepping a virtual machine, *AMD* systems do not offer an equivalent capability.

It is essential to address the current lack of VMI support on *AMD* processors to expand the applicability of VMI-based tools. Notably, within the *SmartVMI* project[1], our objective is the development of VMI toolchains for generating training data sets for the next generation of VMI-based security tools, and neglecting *AMD* platforms as a valuable source of real-system data sets would severely hinder the generalizability of our outcomes. Therefore, this paper introduces a software implementation that retrofits missing hardware features onto current *AMD x86* processors, extending their introspection capabilities. Our approach seamlessly integrates with popular introspection APIs and off-the-shelf hypervisors, enabling developers of introspection applications to quickly port their existing software to *AMD* systems. Our contributions include the following key aspects:

1. We analyse two significant architectural differences between *Intel* and *AMD* *x86* processors that affect the realization of active introspection mechanisms taking into account related research.
2. We conceptualize a mechanism that addresses the shortcomings of previous approaches through retrofitting virtualization features in software. This mechanism enables virtualized single-stepping on systems that support regular, non-virtualizable single-stepping.
3. Based on this principle, we develop a proof of concept implementation for the *KVM* hypervisor and the *LibVMI* introspection library, based on KVMi [8]. We publish this implementation as an open source software.

This paper is structured as follows: Sect. 2 provides background knowledge on VMI. Section 3 summarizes existing work that targets VMI on *AMD* processors and highlights their limitations. Section 4 presents our *guided single-stepping* approach, including a proof-of-concept implementation using *KVMi*. In Sect. 5, we evaluate the correctness, stealthiness, and performance of our solution. Finally, Sect. 6 concludes the paper.

2   Background

In this section, we present relevant background on hardware-assisted virtualization for *AMD* and *Intel x86* systems as well as on virtual machine introspection.

---

[1] https://www.smartvmi.org/.

2.1   Hardware-Assisted Virtualization

The predominant approach to system virtualization on *x86* is *hardware-assisted virtualization*, which was introduced by Intel in 2005 through *VT-x/VMX* (Virtual Machine Extensions). This extension featured new processor modes for virtualization: *VMX root mode*, used as privileged mode by the hypervisor, and *VMX non-root mode*, where the guest system executes in a non-privileged mode. Our particular interest are context switches from the unprivileged to the privileged mode, i.e., from the guest virtual machine to the hypervisor, through traps, refered to as *VM exit* (the opposite direction, from the hypervisor to the virtual machine, is called *VM entry*). The configuration of the virtual machines running under *hardware-assisted virtualization*, including *VM exit* conditions, is performed in the *Virtual Machine Control Structure* (VMCS) [16].

AMD processors also support *hardware-assisted virtualization* since the introduction of the *Secure Virtual Machine* (SVM) extension[2] in 2006. In this extension, the new processor modes are called *host mode* (privileged) and *guest mode* (unprivileged). The hypervisor configures the hosted virtual machines through the *Virtual Machine Control Block* (VMBC) [17].

Starting with the second generation of processor extensions for *hardware-assisted virtualization*, the vendors implemented a concept known as *Second Level Address Translation* (SLAT). While traditional paging solely translates logical, virtual addresses to physical addresses, SLAT extends capabilities of the *Memory Management Unit* (MMU) by another dimension: The translation of the physical address within the virtual machine to the physical address on the host machine. For *Intel* processors, the SLAT implementation is called *Extended Page Tables* (EPT). *Intel* refers to the top-level paging structure in the guest that translates from *guest virtual addresses* (GVA) to *guest physical addresses* (GPA) as *Page Map Level 4* (PML4). For the new dimension, the corresponding paging structure is called EPT PML4 and translates from GPA to *host physical addresses* (HPA) [5]. The CR3 register references the PML4, while the VMCS stores the EPT PML4 in the EPT Pointer (EPTP) field.

AMD x86 processors implement SLAT with *Rapid Virtualization Indexing* (RVI) or *Nested Paging* (NP). In this implementation, the *guest page tables* (gPT) translate *guest linear addresses* (GLA) to *guest physical addresses* (GPA). For the second level address translation, *nested page tables* (nPT) are used to convert GPA to *system physical addresses* (SPA) [18]. The CR3 register in the guest is referred to as *guest CR3* (gCR3) and holds the reference to the gPT. The hypervisor loads the nPT value into the *nested CR3* (nCR3) field in the VMBC [1]. Besides completely different terminology, there are also significant implementation differences between AMD's RVI and Intel's EPT.

2.2   Virtual Machine Introspection

Virtual machine introspection is the "approach of inspecting a virtual machine from the outside for the purpose of analyzing the software running inside it."

---

[2] Newer publications refer to the same extension as *AMD Virtualization* (AMD-V) [18].

Garfinkel and Rosenblum characterize VMI by three main properties [4]: Isolation (between monitoring and monitored system), introspection (monitoring software has a full, untampered view of the whole system), and interposition (interception of operations in the virtual machine).

VMI-based monitoring mechanisms can be categorized as either *passive (or polling)*, which means they analyze the main memory of the virtual machine based on external triggers, or as *active (or event-triggered)*, which means they interposition themselves with the control flow of the virtual machine, e.g., by placing breakpoints [6]. The active interpositioning allows introspection applications to perform their introspection task at specific, predetermined locations in the control flow of applications running inside the guest virtual machine.

In our work, we investigate two forms of *active* VMI: The first type of introspection mechanism is memory access tracing based on the SLAT feature of modern processors. For such mechanisms, first, the VMI application modifies the memory access permissions of a page within the SLAT. Second, accessing these pages triggers a trap to the hypervisor, which then emits an event to the introspection application. Besides these two basic steps, there are also mechanisms that involve additional actions, such as creating new views (top-level paging structures for SLAT) and dynamically switching between these views [9].

The second kind of introspection mechanism involves the use of hyper-single-stepping functionality. Unlike regular single-stepping, which transfers control to the guest kernel after each instruction and can be used, e.g., by guest-level debuggers, hyper-single-stepping executes a single instruction in the guest and then traps to the hypervisor, which then can notify the VMI tool. When combined with a software hyper-breakpoint [14], this mechanism is particularly valuable. This combination involves replacing an instruction in the guest with a breakpoint instruction. Upon reaching this instruction, the guest traps to the hypervisor. The VMI tool handles this breakpoint by restoring the original instruction and activating single-stepping. After the guest executes the original instruction, the single-step triggers another hypervisor trap and the VMI tool re-inserts the breakpoint.

3   State of the Art

While VMI is a promising technique for practically any efficiently virtualizable architecture, current industry and academia work focuses mainly on the *x86* architectures. Yet as we have alluded to in earlier parts of this work, there are several architectural differences between the two main *x86* vendors, namely *Intel* and *AMD*, that limit the applicability of previous active introspection research on *AMD* processors. These limitations exist because most works in the literature conducted their development on *Intel* processors with the *Intel VT-x* processor extensions. Subsequently, we will describe the two main architectural differences and summarize the state of the art regarding addressing the open problems arising from them.

3.1 SLAT-Based Mechanisms

Zhang and Zonouz have shown that the combination of SLAT controls and events is suitable for hiding injected code from the guest [20]. By maintaining a set of complementary paging structures for read/write/execute operations and switching between them dynamically, it is possible to have a different mapping for reads to a page compared to an instruction fetch. Hence, injected code practically becomes invisible to the guest. While their approach used a hypervisor to perform the code hiding, we do not consider their approach as virtual machine introspection due to the non-flexible design. Instead, they created the technique specifically for rootkits.

The first hypervisor to offer support for a wide range of options to manipulate the SLAT for introspection purposes was Xen with the altp2m mechanism [9]. It allows the introspection application to manage multiple *guest-physical* to *machine-physical* mappings for a single virtual machine, manipulate these mappings, switch between them, and directly handle the related events. However, as of now, altp2m is only available on *Intel* processors.

Tanda was the first to identify the realization of SLAT memory access permissions on *AMD* processors as an issue regarding implementing the usual code hiding technique [13]. Whereas *Intel EPT* allows configuring read, write, and execute permissions of access to a specific page, *AMD RVI* merges the read and execute permissions. Hence, it is not possible to set them separately, which adversely affects the earlier-mentioned code-hiding technique. Tanda has also outlined two partial workarounds for this problem. However, when used with virtual machine introspection, these partial solutions rely on the availability of hyper-single-stepping, which, as we will see in the following, is also missing. Furthermore, neither of the approaches he proposed reaches performance characteristics close to utilizing the hardware implementation on *Intel*.

Therefore, we can conclude that SLAT-based introspection mechanisms on *AMD* processors are equally powerful to those on *Intel* if and only if hyper-single-stepping is available. Henceforth, this paper will focus on realizing this requirement and thus provide adequate support for active introspection mechanisms on *AMD64*.

3.2 Hyper-Single-Stepping

The prevalent way to realize hyper-single-stepping for VMI architectures in environments based on hardware-assisted virtualization is through virtualized processor capabilities. For example, *Intel* processors feature the *Monitor Trap Flag*, which can be set in the VMCS by the hypervisor. When this flag is enabled, the processor will trigger a *VM exit* after each execution of an instruction.

The two most popular open-source hypervisors with VMI support for hyper-single-stepping – *Xen*[3] [2] and *KVMi* [8] – employ this functionality. However,

---

[3] https://xenbits.xen.org/gitweb/?p=xen.git;a=blob;f=xen/arch/x86/hvm/vmx/int r.c;h=80bfbb478782446cb17b53004435e41206f993b8;hb=556c2e817c9cf23b675eb4ea a2dc091f7bb3039f#l250.

as mentioned earlier, this requires support from the architecture and, ultimately, the processor vendor. Currently, an equivalent of the *Monitor Trap Flag* does not exist on AMD. Hence, the feature is unavailable on *AMD* processors.

Yet, some debuggers such as GDB [7,19] offer limited single-stepping support for virtual machines even on *AMD*. They accomplish this by using the non-virtualized single-stepping feature of the processor. Therefore, they incur severe drawbacks: the single-stepping is trivially detectable from within the guest, malicious actors can easily disable the mechanism, and the guest cannot do any single-stepping on its own. All of these reasons make this approach unsuitable for VMI, where solutions are bound to be isolated from the guest and stealthy. The challenges to achieving these properties in an adverse environment are the topic of this paper.

Finally, Sato et al. discuss ensuring stealthiness and correctness of retrofitted virtual machine introspection mechanisms [12]. Their work mainly focuses on retrofitted hardware breakpoints. However, we believe we can draw relevant lessons for a much broader range of mechanisms, including hyper-single-stepping, see Sect. 4.2.

4   Introspection on the AMD64 Architecture

As the realisation of the solutions presented by Tanda [13] rests on the availability of hyper-single-stepping, and one can implement the outlined approaches at the level of the introspection application with existing APIs, we focus solely on the hyper-single-stepping functionality for the remainder of this paper. In our work, the trust model assumes the hypervisor and the host system, which runs the VMI application, to be trusted. Furthermore, we consider the hardware and its firmware to be untampered. All other entities are untrusted. Finally, we assume that the attacker does not directly attack the hypervisor or other trusted entities, for example, through VM escapes.

4.1   Design

A naive approach to address the lack of the monitor trap flag on *AMD* machines is to emulate instead of virtualizing the instructions in question. The approach of falling back to emulation when hardware-assisted virtualization is unsuitable is a common technique for similar problems. Regrettably, it comes with two significant shortcomings: First, the emulation is often prone to errors due to the high complexity and heterogeneity of processors. Second, it may sacrifice the performance gains of efficient virtualization and can therefore slow down the execution of the virtual machine significantly.

Another potential solution is to disassemble the current instruction and insert a hyper-breakpoint directly following this instruction on-the-fly [11]. This approach reduces the susceptibility to errors compared to the emulation since the only requirement to execute the strategy is to determine the correct length of

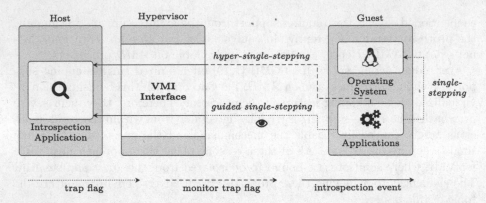

Fig. 1. Concept of *guided single-stepping* contextualized with other approaches

any instruction. However, it still can be considered significantly slower than virtualization with the monitor trap flag because every single-step now requires mapping, reading, and length-disassembling the next instruction through VMI.

Instead of these slow and error-prone approaches, we rely on the regular trap flag in the guest to generate the trap. Then, we elevate this trap to the hypervisor by configuring the processor to perform exception intercepting on the respective exception vector [1]. As we will see later, this retrofitting of single-stepping for introspection applications comes at practically no cost and is resistant to both errors and malicious insiders.

Figure 1 shows our approach called *guided single-stepping* alongside single-stepping and hyper-single-stepping. We refer to it as *guided* since we guide the guest's execution from the outside to avoid manipulation and detection of the monitoring. Our approach offers a way to realise the benefits of virtual machine introspection, namely isolation, and interposition, for a single-stepping mechanism targeting virtual machines. Hence, it provides the same guarantees as hyper-single-stepping, even when not explicitly supported by the hardware.

However, an important design decision remains. Like many other introspection mechanisms, our approach can be implemented at different levels, i.e., in the hypervisor, an introspection library, or the guest itself. We decided to place our solution in the hypervisor and the introspection library *LibVMI*.

Operating at multiple levels in the introspection stack enables a particularly small footprint: Since our implementation is implemented transparently at the hypervisor level, existing introspection applications, in general, do not need to be modified for operation on *AMD* systems when using *guided single-stepping*. As single-stepping in a VMI context is often used only selectively, e.g., to step over a single instruction, counterintuitively, an implementation at the level of the introspection library reduces the overhead. Hence, the introspection application can determine partial emulation functions ahead of time and potentially even cache them.

4.2   Implementation

As mentioned in the beginning, our proof-of-concept implementation[4] builds upon the open-source introspection API *KVMi* based on the *KVM* hypervisor. Since it operates at multiple layers in the introspection stack, we will discuss the challenges and concrete realisation separately for each affected layer.

Hypervisor Layer. The core responsibility of the part of our solution that resides in the hypervisor is to configure the virtual machine such that regular hardware single-stepping is enabled and the generated traps end up in the hypervisor. In particular, this requires the following three steps that must occur transactionally and are started by the KVMI_VCPU_CONTROL_SINGLESTEP command:

1. Exception intercepting must be enabled for the #**DB** (Debug Exception) vector. We implement this using the set_exception_intercept helper function[5] during update_bp_intercept.
2. We must save off the original RFLAGS of the vCPU to determine whether to reinject the exception and to set the trap flag correctly upon exit. Our solution stores the guest's RFLAGS within the vcpu_svm struct using the svm_get_rflags function.
3. Finally, we must force the trap flag on within the guest for the duration of the *guided single-stepping*. Our solution performs this manipulation within __kvm_set_rflags[6].

To disable the *guided single-stepping* after reaching the target instruction, we have to perform the inverse of these three steps in reverse order. In this case, we can omit step 2. Enabling and disabling the *guided single-stepping* is only possible when the vCPU is currently not running, i.e., it is halted by either an active mechanism or paused.

After setting up the virtual machine in this way, single-step operations in the guest trap to the hypervisor. In *KVM*, they eventually reach the exit handler called db_interception[7]. In this handler, we can convert the exception to a VMI event and send it to the introspection application for further processing.

Since our retrofitted approach utilizes the regular trap flag, we need to consider the edge case that the virtual machine itself is already single-stepping, e.g., for debugging purposes. To account for this issue, we need to reinject the interrupt into the virtual machine if the trap flag was already set by the guest. Hence, we have saved the guest's original value of RFLAGS in step 2. Reinjecting the debug exception is as simple as calling kvm_queue_exception with DB_VECTOR after delivering the event to the introspection application. Thereby, the operating system in the guest can correctly handle the single-step on its own.

---

[4] Available at: https://github.com/smartvmi/VMI-on-AMD.

[5] https://elixir.bootlin.com/linux/v5.4.217/source/arch/x86/kvm/svm.c#L591.

[6] https://elixir.bootlin.com/linux/v5.4.217/source/arch/x86/kvm/x86.c#L10104.

[7] https://elixir.bootlin.com/linux/v5.4.217/source/arch/x86/kvm/svm.c#L2783.

Our implementation currently does not handle a change to the trap flag in the guest during single-stepping. This situation can, for example, occur when a self-debugging program in the guest sets the trap flag on itself to obfuscate its control flow. Addressing this problem would require sophisticated emulation at the level of the hypervisor. However, we consider this a niche technique that remains outside the scope of our current work.

Finally, the single-step may clobber the debug-status register (DR6). As the processor sets bit 14 of DR6 when a #**DB** exception occurs due to single-stepping, the guest could detect this value and conclude that it is being monitored. To avoid this situation, we clear this bit if and only if we have not reinjected the single-step into the guest.

Application Layer. At the level of the introspection library or the application layer, we will exclusively deal with implementation details that are cheaper to implement at this level than in the hypervisor. In particular, we apply partial emulation on top of some critical instructions. As the application, in many cases, e.g., when using hyper-single-stepping together with hyper-breakpoints, knows the instruction ahead of time, the resulting overhead can be limited. Not only can we avoid mapping and reading the page of the currently executed instruction, but we can also eliminate all superfluous emulation for the statistically dominant instructions that do not require intervention.

As our retrofitted approach uses the guest's trap flag to generate the interrupts, malicious insiders could potentially interfere with the monitoring by manipulating the RFLAGS in the guest. To address this, we guide the execution in the guest. The instruction we have to worry about the most is the POPF instruction that loads new flags from the stack. We manipulate the execution of this instruction by dynamically rewriting the stack contents upon execution. Before the guest executes this instruction, we force the trap flag onto the top-most value on the stack:

```
1  ACCESS_CONTEXT(ctx,
2          .translate_mechanism = VMI_TM_PROCESS_DTB,
3          .addr = event->x86_regs->rsp + 8,
4          .pt = event->x86_regs->cr3 & ~0x1000ull);
5
6  uint64 eflags, eflags_new;
7  if (VMI_SUCCESS == vmi_read_64(vmi, &ctx, &eflags))
8  {
9          eflags_new = eflags | X86_EFLAGS_TF;
10         vmi_write_64(vmi, &ctx, &eflags_new);
11 }
```

As the value remains on the stack after the execution, we have to write back the original value after the instruction executes to hide the presence of the monitoring. To this end, we must account for the fact that this value lies beyond the stack pointer after the execution of the instruction.

The counterpart to the POPF instruction is the PUSHF instruction. This instruction places the flags on top of the stack. As it is also available in user mode, it is an ideal candidate to detect our monitoring. Again, we can avoid detection by rewriting the stack after its execution:

```
1  ACCESS_CONTEXT(ctx,
2          .translate_mechanism = VMI_TM_PROCESS_DTB,
3          .addr = event->x86_regs->rsp + 8,
4          .pt = event->x86_regs->cr3 & ~0x1000ull);
5
6  uint64 eflags;
7  if (VMI_SUCCESS == vmi_read_64(vmi, &ctx, &eflags))
8  {
9          eflags &= ~X86_EFLAGS_TF;
10         vmi_write_64(vmi, &ctx, &eflags);
11 }
```

Finally, we have to deal with the *CLI* instruction that clears the interrupt flag. With interrupts disabled, the single-stepping mechanisms will no longer work. Luckily, most modern kernels nowadays are fully or mostly preemptible. Therefore, we should not encounter this instruction for the most part when using *guided single-stepping*. Assuming the execution reaches this instruction, we propose two different approaches based on where it is located: In case it occurs in a trusted location, i.e., one of the few places in the kernel that are not preemptible, we ignore it. If we encounter the instruction in an untrusted position, i.e., a driver or code not belonging to the kernel image, we propose to halt the virtual machine for manual inspection.

5   Evaluation

In the following, we assess our *guided single-stepping* proof-of-concept implementation regarding its correctness, stealthiness, and performance.

5.1   Correctness

Our work relies on the correctness of the trap flag in the guest and the interception of the #**DB** exception. Since all existing debuggers for the *x86* architecture use the trap flag, we can assume the feature to be working correctly.

However, there are critical differences to the hyper-single-stepping facilitated by the monitor trap flag. In particular, the behavior between the two can differ when delivering interrupts. First, our solution does not yet consider that the trap flag can be reset from an *Interrupt Service Routine* (ISR), e.g., through the IRET instruction. We could address this weakness by applying the flag to the stack when encountering such an instruction, much like for the PUSHF instruction. Since most introspection applications use single-stepping selectively, e.g., for stepping over a single instruction, we currently do not regard this as a problem.

Second, it is theoretically possible to use hardware multitasking to turn off the trap flag from within the guest. The necessary procedure requires stripping the flag from the EFLAGS field in the active *Task State Segment* (TSS). We must note that this is not possible from long mode since hardware multitasking is not available in this mode and the TSS only holds the stack pointers and the *Interrupt Stack Table* (IST). Therefore, exploiting this weakness would require the attacker to switch the processor back to protected mode. For this reason, we consider this possibility very unlikely. However, we could solve this issue by trapping writes to the EFER (Extended Feature Enable Register) MSR (Model-specific Register). By checking against a write of 0 to bit 8 (Long Mode Enable), we can detect this behavior and halt the machine for manual inspection.

What we should note for both cases, however, is that this only disables single-stepping until the next VM exit since our implementation in the hypervisor makes sure to reapply the flag before entering the guest.

Finally, all instructions covered in our proof-of-concept implementation are single-byte instructions (POPF, PUSHF, and CLI). Therefore, we generally do not require sophisticated disassemblers to identify them accurately from the intro-spection application. However, a malicious guest could append prefixes such as the REX prefix to the instruction that does not have any effect, and thus no sensible assembler would generate [1]. Hence, we caution against simply checking the opcode for security-critical applications.

5.2   Stealthiness

As is the case with many VMI-based systems, our solution is not entirely invisible to the guest. Active introspection can be detected from within the guest in numerous ways. The most primitive approach that is often present in malware is the detection of the hypervisor. This detection is possible due to the enforced isolation, which requires privileged instructions to be emulated [10]. By comparing the execution time of these instructions with their native unvirtualized counterparts, it is easy to determine if the system is currently executing under virtualization.

However, there are also much more sophisticated methods that not only can determine the presence of the hypervisor but also ongoing active introspection [15]. These can include timing attacks on various exit conditions, such as our interception of the #**DB** exception. Therefore, our *guided single-stepping approach* is detectable from within the guest. However, we should consider that the same is true for hyper-single-stepping.

While discussing our implementation, we addressed other detection methods, such as reading out the trap flag. To verify the effectiveness of these measures, we attempted to detect the presence of our monitoring with the application shown below. As expected, our solution can successfully hide the presence of the trap flag from the guest.

```
1  uint64_t eflags = __builtin_ia32_readeflags_u64();
2  fprintf(stdout, "X86_EFLAGS_TF: %lu\n", !!(eflags &
       ↪ X86_EFLAGS_TF));
```

5.3   Performance

To evaluate the performance of our solution, we use an *ASUS PN51* fitted with an *AMD Ryzen 5 5500U* Hexa-core CPU, 32 *GiB* of *DDR4-2666* main memory, and 1 *TiB* of non-volatile memory on an *Kingston A2000* NVMe SSD. We use Debian 11 for both the host and guest operating systems in our evaluation. The virtual machine used in the following experiments has 2 *GiB* of main memory assigned to it. We take comparative measurements for *Intel* processors on a machine with similar characteristics. This machine is an *ASUS PN62* equipped with a *Intel Core i7-10510U* quad-core CPU, 32 *GiB* of *DDR4-3200* main memory, and 1 *TiB* of non-volatile memory on an *Kingston A2000* NVMe SSD.

Microbenchmarks. To assess the performance of our retrofitted software solution, we measure breakpoint and single-stepping performance by placing a breakpoint on the `getpid` system call. Upon execution of this breakpoint, we replace it with the original instruction, single step over it, and restore the breakpoint. We chose this way of evaluating the performance of our solution because it resembles how VMI is usually used in real-world applications. We include the source code of this benchmark in the repository. Our setup measures 1,000 system call invocations from user mode. We present the results of this measurement with a sample size of 10 in Fig. 2.

As expected, the native solution implemented in hardware and microcode on *Intel* outperforms our retrofitted software solution for *AMD*. However, both in terms of overhead and absolute execution time, the approaches are within one order of magnitude of each other. The overhead of this mechanism is around 2.6 times higher on *AMD* than on *Intel*. In absolute terms, the difference amounts to a factor of 1.9. The error of our measurement was below 10% in both cases.

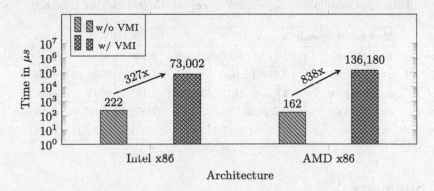

Fig. 2. Execution time with breakpoint on `__x64_sys_getpid` (less is better)

A limitation of this measurement is the jointness of the breakpoint and single-stepping mechanism. Hence, it is not evident if the difference we observe can be attributed entirely to the single-stepping or if the breakpoint implementation exhibits some overhead caused by architectural differences. However, we still argue for this way of determining the performance as it is closest to real-world applications of the proposed mechanism.

UnixBench. The initial microbenchmark focused on assessing the worst-case scenario for VMI. It involved a loop executing a lightweight system call, `getpid`, which merely returns the process's PID and has minimal execution time. VMI introduced a trap to the monitoring application in each iteration. To provide a more realistic understanding of VMI's impact on the performance of a target VM, we conducted additional tests using selected system calls traced during the execution of various *UnixBench* [3].

Table 1 lists the results obtained from these tests. The performance figures indicate the number of iterations completed within a fixed time interval. The *spawn* test repeatedly invoked the `clone` system call, and the *execl* test invoked the `execl` function, which translates to the `execve` system call. Despite tracing each system call invocation in these tests, due to the higher execution time of the system calls itself, the relative overhead imposed by VMI was significantly lower. The *syscall* (system call overhead) test resembled our microbenchmark and produced similar results. The *pipe* throughput test focuses on communication via a pipe, and we.traced all `write` system calls during the test, with significant overhead. Lastly, the pipe-based context switching test *context1* is "more like a real-world application" [3] and measures switches between two processes engaged in a bidirectional pipe conversation. When tracing the `pipe` system call, which is called only once at the beginning, no noticeable overhead was observed. We omitted the *DhryStone* and *WhetStone*, as they do not use system calls, and thus their runtime performance is not influenced by VMI-based system call tracing.

Table 1. Consolidated *UnixBench* scores on *AMD64* (higher is better)

Test	Monitored Syscall	w/o VMI	w/ VMI	Unit
spawn	sys_clone	18,050 ($\pm$475)	3,548 ($\pm$817)	processes/s
execl	sys_execve	5,168 ($\pm$101)	1,880 ($\pm$553)	calls/s
syscall	sys_getpid	17,758,288 ($\pm$339,741)	7,435 ($\pm$911)	calls/s
pipe	sys_write	2,639,602 ($\pm$49,713)	7,472 ($\pm$1,057)	calls/s
context1	sys_pipe	259,947 ($\pm$1,272)	261,195 ($\pm$3,612)	calls/s

6 Summary

In this paper, we have identified the causes of the limited availability of active introspection mechanisms on *AMD x86* processors impacting many introspection applications and remedied some of the more pressing concerns. Thus, we have improved the state of the art of VMI-based approaches and enabled their use on previously inaccessible systems.

First, we have highlighted two architectural differences that affect the implementation of introspection tools and the applicability of previous research. Active mechanisms such as hyper-breakpoints often use SLAT-based controls and events to realize code hiding. However, the specific implementation of SLAT with *AMD RVI* does not allow to set read and execute permissions independently. Hence, we cannot use the usual code-hiding technique. Previous research has proposed alternative approaches, which rely on the availability of hyper-single-stepping. Yet, due to the missing support of the monitor trap flag on *AMD* processors, these approaches have not been realized for introspection-based solutions.

Second, we have focused on remedying this lack of hyper-single-stepping with our *guided single-stepping* approach. Instead of relying on hardware support through the *Monitor Trap Flag*, we retrofit the capabilities using software and interception intercepting. We guide the execution of the guest from the hypervisor and the introspection application to ensure the correctness and stealthiness of the monitoring.

Third, we have implemented the approach of *guided single-stepping* in the *KVM* hypervisor and the *LibVMI* introspection library. The evaluation of this novel software-based approach demonstrates that its performance is in the same order of magnitude as comparable hardware implementations on *Intel* processors. Hence, we claim that our solution increases the portability of introspection applications for *AMD* processors.

Finally, we release our proof-of-concept implementation as free software and work towards integrating it into the relevant open-source projects.

Acknowledgement. This work has been funded by the Bundesministerium für Bildung und Forschung (BMBF, German Federal Ministry of Education and Research) – project 01IS21063A-C (SmartVMI).

References

1. Advanced Micro Devices: AMD64 Architecture Programmer's Manual, Volume 2 (2019)
2. Barham, P., et al.: Xen and the art of virtualization. In: Proceedings of the Nineteenth ACM Symposium on Operating Systems Principles, SOSP, pp. 164–177. Association for Computing Machinery, Bolton Landing, NY, USA (2003). https://doi.org/10.1145/945445.945462
3. Byte Magazine: byte-unixbench (1983). https://github.com/kdlucas/byte-unixbench. Accessed 20 Apr 2023
4. Garfinkel, T., Rosenblum, M.: A virtual machine introspection based architecture for intrusion detection. In: NDSS, vol. 3, pp. 191–206 (2003)
5. Intel Corporation: Intel® 64 and IA-32 Architectures Software Developer's Manual, Volume 2A (2009)
6. Jain, B., Baig, M.B., Zhang, D., Porter, D.E., Sion, R.: SoK: introspections on trust and the semantic gap. In: IEEE Symposium on Security and Privacy, pp. 605–620 (2014). https://doi.org/10.1109/SP.2014.45
7. Kiszka, J.: Debugging kernel and modules via GDB (2023). https://www.kernel.org/doc/Documentation/dev-tools/gdb-kernel-debugging.rst. Accessed 31 Mar 2023

8. Lazăr, A.: KVMi subsystem v7 for KVM. KVM mailing list (2021). https://lore.
   kernel.org/kvm/20200207181636.1065-1-alazar@bitdefender.com/. Accessed 24
   Mar 2023
9. Lengyel, T.K.: Stealthy monitoring with Xen altp2m (2016). https://xenproject.
   org/2016/04/13/stealthy-monitoring-with-xen-altp2m/. Accessed 24 Mar 2023
10. Pék, G., Buttyán, L., Bencsáth, B.: A survey of security issues in hardware virtu-
    alization. ACM Comput. Surv. **45**(3), 1–34 (2013)
11. Proskurin, S., Lengyel, T., Momeu, M., Eckert, C., Zarras, A.: Hiding in the shad-
    ows: empowering ARM for stealthy virtual machine introspection. In: Proceedings
    of the 34th Annual Computer Security Applications Conference, ACSAC, pp. 407–
    417. Association for Computing Machinery, New York, NY, USA (2018). https://
    doi.org/10.1145/3274694.3274698
12. Sato, M., Nakamura, R., Yamauchi, T., Taniguchi, H.: Improving transparency
    of hardware breakpoints with virtual machine introspection. In: 12th Interna-
    tional Congress on Advanced Applied Informatics (IIAI-AAI), pp. 113–117 (2022).
    https://doi.org/10.1109/IIAIAAI55812.2022.00031
13. Tanda, S.: AMD-V for hackers. Hypervisor Development Hands On for Security
    Researchers on Windows, Workshop, VXCON (2019). http://tandasat.github.io/
    VXCON/AMD-V_for_Hackers.pdf. Accessed 24 Mar 2023
14. Taubmann, B.: Improving digital forensics and incident analysis in production envi-
    ronments by using virtual machine introspection. Ph.D. thesis, Faculty of Com-
    puter Science and Mathematics, University of Passau (2019)
15. Tuzel, T., Bridgman, M., Zepf, J., Lengyel, T.K., Temkin, K.J.: Who watches the
    watcher? detecting hypervisor introspection from unprivileged guests. Digit. Invest.
    26, S98–S106 (2018)
16. Uhlig, R., et al.: Intel virtualization technology. Computer **38**(5), 48–56 (2005)
17. Van Doorn, L.: Hardware virtualization trends. In: ACM/Usenix International
    Conference On Virtual Execution Environments, vol. 14, pp. 45–45 (2006)
18. VMWare Inc.: Performance Evaluation of AMD RVI Hardware Assist
    (2008). https://www.cse.iitd.ernet.in/~sbansal/csl862-virt/2010/readings/RVI_
    performance.pdf. Accessed 24 Mar 2023
19. Wessel, J.: Using kgdb, kdb and the kernel debugger internals (2022). https://
    www.kernel.org/doc/Documentation/dev-tools/kgdb.rst. Accessed 31 Mar 2023
20. Zhang, M., Zonouz, S.: How to hide a hook: a hypervisor for rootkits. Phrack Mag.
    15(69) (2016)

Organic Computing Applications 1 (OC)

Abstract Artificial DNA's Improved Time Bounds

Aleksey Koschowoj$^{(\boxtimes)}$ and Uwe Brinkschulte

Goethe University Frankfurt, Frankfurt am Main, Germany
{koschowoj,brinks}@es.cs.uni-frankfurt.de

Abstract. The Artificial DNA (ADNA) is a powerful tool for designing self-organizing, self-healing and self-configuring distributed embedded systems. However, a large amount of knowledge on the targeted hardware, available sensors, is required, thus limiting the reusability and adaptability of an already composed ADNA. Recently, the *abstract ADNA* (A^2DNA) has been proposed as a countermeasure to this problem. In an A^2DNA, sensor elements are replaced by so-called *abstract sensors* describing properties of the required sensory input. Only when the A^2DNA is initialized on the target hardware, these abstract sensors are specified by a combination of actual sensors available. In addition, a semantic knowledge base provides knowledge on the hardware's sensors and their relations. In order to convert an A^2DNA to a hardware specific ADNA, knowledge about how to calculate a required sensor value that cannot be directly measured by the hardware from other available sensors is required. In this paper, we present and analyze two algorithms that determine this knowledge.

Keywords: Artificial DNA · Semantics · Organic Computing · Virtual Sensors · Embedded Systems

1 Introduction

The research field of Organic Computing has been established by [1] and [13] in order to master both the growing complexity of real-time embedded systems equipped with sensors and actuators and their spread into our day-to-day environment. In order to achieve this, OC aim to adapt principles found in biological systems, like self-organization, to technical systems. Together with self-configuration, self-improvement/self-optimization, self-description/self-explaining, self-protecting and self-healing, self-organization forms the so-called self-* properties as described in [14]. An example for a mechanism that adapts the self-* properties onto a technical system is the Artificial Hormone System (AHS) [15] with the Artificial DNA (ADNA) developed by [3]. Recently, [12] introduced another expansion level the abstract ADNA (A^2DNA) extending

Funded by the Deutsche Forschungsgemeinschaft (DFG, German Research Foundation) - project number 445555232.

the knowledge available to the system by a semantic knowledge base on sensors, actuators and their interdependencies. However, the algorithms operating on this new knowledge leave room for improvement and more rigorous analysis. The initial implementation, with its worst-case execution time of $\mathcal{O}(n^8)$, is not suitable for real-time system operation. Consequently, it cannot be utilized to promptly compensate for the loss of hardware, e.g. sensors, by providing an alternative realization.

In this paper, we present and analyze two algorithms utilizing this knowledge to infer more knowledge on the available and realizable sensors. The first is an improved version of the approach described in [12]. The second, a novel approach utilizing preprocessing and auxiliary data structures resulting in even better time bounds.

The paper is structured as follows: First, we provide a brief overview of related research and a short introduction into both the AHS and the ADNA. Second, we summarize the A^2DNA's core concepts. Next, we describe and analyze both algorithms. Finally, we describe how our new approach can be used in conjunction with current research on the ADNA and provide some closing remarks.

2   Related Work

For several years, researchers have focused on enhancing a system's knowledge by adding semantics. While previous work, such as [9], has explored the use of ontologies for sensors and their measurements, the proposed ontology places greater emphasis on the measurements themselves and treats the underlying system as a singular block, in contrast to the granular structure found in the ADNA. Other ontologies, including [2] and [8], focus on physical quantities and their relations, but their relations are limited to the relationships between units of measurement rather than the physical quantities themselves. Only [7] has shifted its focus on physical quantities and fundamental concepts in physics. Since it is in its early stages, it can only serve as an orientation. Therefore, ADNA will require its own ontology which is part of the A^2DNA.

In addition to the A^2DNA, other proposals, such as [6] and [11], deal with the semantic description of the ADNA, with a stronger focus on the building blocks, their behavior, and classification. [5] also discusses the combination of ADNA and online diagnosis using semantics. Finally, [10] proposes the concept of the conditional ADNA, which extends the range of available tasks by using condition elements. These elements enable the denial of certain task sets while allowing the assignment of other tasks based on the input signals from the condition elements, thus enabling a change between different predefined substructures at runtime.

3   AHS and ADNA

As described in [3] and [4], the AHS is a self-organizing, self-improving, self-configuring, self-healing and decentralized mechanism that allocates tasks to so-called *processing elements* (PEs) in embedded real-time systems. Akin to the hormone system of higher mammals where cells communicate via the bloodstream by exchanging hormones, the PEs send short messages, so-called *hormones*, to communicate and decide the task assignment among themselves. These hormones consist of *eager values, suppressor* hormones and *accelerator* hormones. Each PE has its own set of *local eager values*, that indicate a PE's default suitability, for each task. Suppressor hormones inhibit a PE's eagerness to acquire a task either because that task is already taken or the PE does not have the computational capacity to carry out that task anymore. In contrast, accelerator hormones raise the PE's eagerness to acquire a task. When a PE acquires a new task T_i, it disperses accelerator hormones to its neighboring PEs for tasks related to task T_i.

Figure 1 shows the whole underlying communication control loop the so-called *hormone loop* for a processing element PE_γ. For each task PE_γ receives eager values, accelerator hormones and suppressor hormones from all other PEs. Then PE_γ calculates its own eager values utilizing the received hormones and sends its new *modified eager values* to the other processing elements. If PE_γ has the highest eager value for task T_i then it will acquire this task and sends suppressor hormones that convey this acquisition, and possible accelerator hormones to the other processing elements.

On its own, the AHS lacks any knowledge of the system whose tasks it has to allocate. This knowledge, including the required tasks, their communicative interconnections and the PEs' initial suitability for each task, is provided by the ADNA. When a task is assigned to a PE, the PE derives the parametrization from its local copy of the ADNA. The corresponding process is shown in Fig. 2. The ADNA is based on the observation that most embedded systems can be assembled from a limited number of basic elements, e.g. sensors, actuators, arithmetic/logic units, etc. Thus, it is possible to compose a given embedded system by combing a sufficient multiset of these elements and providing a fitting parameterization for each element. An exemplary control loop build from basic elements and its netlist are given in Fig. 3 and Fig. 4 respectively.

4 A^2DNA

4.1   Relation to the ADNA

Just as the ADNA describes the parameterization and interconnections of building blocks, adding a new descriptive layer to the AHS, the A^2DNA functions as an additional layer of abstraction in relation to the ADNA. The A^2DNA introduces semantic knowledge on the building blocks[1] and enables the description of a building block based on its requirements such as the measured physical quantity. Depending on the available knowledge and hardware, a concrete specification of this block must be determined to adapt the A^2DNA into a system-specific ADNA.

---

[1] At this stage the knowledge is limited to knowledge on the sensors and actuators.

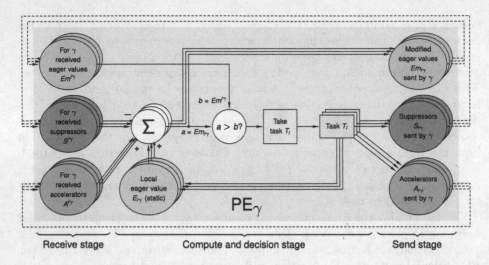

Fig. 1. Hormone Cycle, [4]

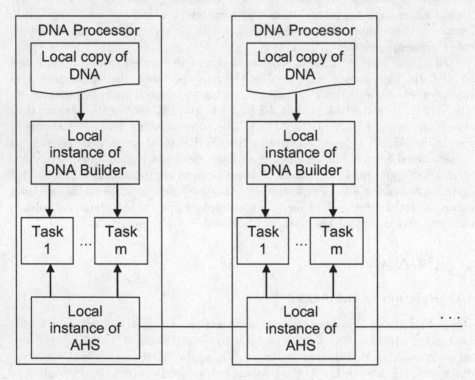

Fig. 2. ADNA architecture, [3]

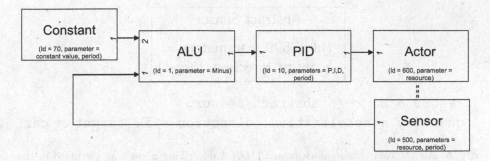

Fig. 3. A closed control loop consisting of basic elements, [6]

```
1  = 70   (1:2.2) 100 25    // constant setpoint value, period 25 msec
2  = 1    (1:3.1) -         // ALU, control deviation (minus)
3  = 10   (1:4.1) 4 5 6 25  // PID (4, 5, 6), period 25 msec
4  = 600          1         // actor, resource id = 1
5  = 500  (1:2.1) 2 25      // sensor, resource id = 2, period 25 msec

ADNA line:           linenumber = id destinationlink parameters //comment
destinationlink:     (destchannel:destlinenumber.sourcechannel...)
```

Fig. 4. Netlist and parameterization of the closed control loop shown in Fig. 3, [6]

4.2 Fundamental Idea

The A^2DNA is a generalized form of the ADNA. A sensor block no longer refers to a specific piece of hardware, but describes an *abstract sensor*.

Definition 1 (Abstract sensor). *Let $\mathcal{Q}$, $\mathcal{D}$ and $\mathcal{T}$ be three disjoint sets. Their elements (values) describe a physical quantity $q_s \in \mathcal{Q}$, a direction $d_s \in \mathcal{D}$, and which target $t_s \in \mathcal{T}$ an abstract sensor $s := (q_s, d_s, t_s) \in \mathcal{Q} \times \mathcal{D} \times \mathcal{T}$ measures.*

Example 1. A system (car) may have an abstract sensor (v, x, c) that describes a real sensor measuring the car's (c) velocity (v) in the x-axis direction (x). But our A^2DNA in Fig. 5 requires the abstract sensor $(a, \overline{x}, c)$ that measures the car's acceleration a in the negative x-axis $(\overline{x})$.

A meaning to the attribute's values and their relations, e.g. acceleration being the temporal derivation of velocity or what directions are each others inverses, are given by so called equations.

Definition 2 (Equation). *For $j \geq 1$, let $(k_0, k_1, \ldots, k_j)$ be a tuple, such that $\{k_0, k_1, \ldots, k_j\}$ is a $(j+1)$-element subset of either $\mathcal{Q}$ or $\mathcal{D}$ or $\mathcal{T}$. An equation $eq := k_0 = \mathrm{OP}_{i=1}^{j} k_i$ describes the relation between an attribute value k_0 and the sequence of attribute values $(k_1, \ldots, k_j)$. The j-nary operator OP denotes a specific building block[2] that derives the output k_0 from the input $k_1, \ldots, k_j$.*

---

[2] The block's exact structure must not be known in the equation, just what block or set of blocks will be needed.

```
          Abstract Sensor
     (Id = 599, parameters =
     quantity, direction, target)
```

```
1 = 599 a nx c // abstract sensor,
  quantity = acceleration, direction = x̄, target = car
```

Fig. 5. An abstract sensor block in an A^2DNA describing a car's acceleration in the negative x-axis

We also refer to $k_1, \ldots, k_j$ as an equation's right-hand side. Further, let $|eq| := j$ be the length of eq.

Remark 1. A given set of equations $\mathcal{E}$ can be separated into three disjoint sets depending on the affected attribute $\mathcal{Q}$, $\mathcal{D}$ or $\mathcal{T}$. These sets are denoted as $\mathcal{E}_{\mathcal{Q}}$, $\mathcal{E}_{\mathcal{D}}$ or $\mathcal{E}_{\mathcal{T}}$ respectively.

Example 2. To our car system in Example 1 we can convey both the relation between velocity and acceleration and the relation between a direction and its reverse with the equations:

$$\bar{x} = (-1) \cdot x \tag{1}$$

$$a = \dot{v} \tag{2}$$

The equations serve as the backbone of the knowledge base.

Definition 3 (Knowledge base). *A knowledge base $\mathcal{K} := (\mathcal{S}, \mathcal{E})$ consists of a set $\mathcal{S}$ of sensors available on the system's hardware and a set $\mathcal{E}$ of known relations (equations).*

Remark 2. The sets $\mathcal{Q}$, $\mathcal{D}$ and $\mathcal{T}$ are implicitly given by the values that appear in the available sensors and known equations. Therefore, each of their sizes are asymptotically $\mathcal{O}(n)$ in regards to the input size $n = |\mathcal{K}|$.

Example 3. Combining the abstract sensors and equation from Examples 1 and 2, the car system might have a simple knowledge base:

$$\mathcal{K} = (\underbrace{\{(v, x, c)\}}_{\mathcal{S}}, \underbrace{\{\bar{x} = (-1) \cdot x, a = \dot{v}\}}_{\mathcal{E}}).$$

In order to build an ADNA, abstract sensors in the A^2DNA must be specified by a *determinator* when initializing the system. This whole process is shown in Fig. 6.

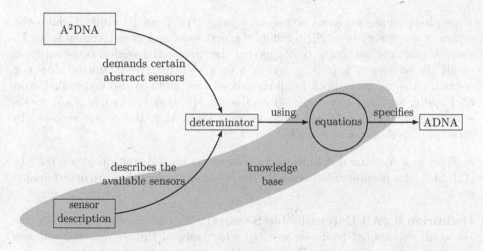

Fig. 6. Specification process, [12]

4.3 Determinability

Before we focus on the specification, we must know which sensors are implicitly given on a knowledge base $\mathcal{K}$. This is done by applying an equation to a set of sensors and adding the yielded sensor to that set.

Definition 4 (Applying equations). *Let S be a set of sensors and $eq :=$ $k_0 = \mathrm{OP}_{i=1}^{j}\, k_i$ be an equation. We say that the set of sensors yields the sensor z by applying the equation eq on the set S, denoted as $z \models eq(S)$, if one of the following cases holds[3]:*

- *If there exists a set $Z_{(d,t)} = \{(k_i, d, t)|1 \leq i \leq j\} \subseteq S$, fixed by $k_1, \ldots, k_j$ in eq, $eq(S)$ yields $z = (k_0, d, t)$.*
- *If there exists a set $Z_{(q,t)} = \{(q, k_i, t)|1 \leq i \leq j\} \subseteq S$, fixed by $k_1, \ldots, k_j$ in eq, $eq(S)$ yields $z = (q, k_0, t)$.*
- *If there exists a set $Z_{(q,d)} = \{(q, d, k_i)|1 \leq i \leq j\} \subseteq S$, fixed by $k_1, \ldots, k_j$ in eq, $eq(S)$ yields $z = (q, d, k_0)$.*

Example 4. Recall the car system from Example 1 and its knowledge base from Example 3. Applying Eq. 1 on the set S yields $z_1 = (v, \overline{x}, c)$. Applying Eq. 2 on S yields $z_2 = (a, x, c)$.

Now, we can better define when a sensor is implicitly given, we call this *determinable*.

Definition 5 (Determinable). *We say a sensor s is determinable on a given knowledge base $\mathcal{K} = (\mathcal{S}, \mathcal{E})$ iff $s \in \mathcal{S}$ or there is a set Z of sensors determinable on $\mathcal{K}$ and an equation $eq \in \mathcal{E}$, such that $z \models eq(Z)$ and $z \notin Z$.*

---

[3] Since all attribute values in an equation are from the same set, we only have these three cases.

Example 5. Again we focus on the knowledge base from Example 3. Since the sensor $s = (v, x, c)$ is in $\mathcal{S}$, it fulfills the first case and is determinable on $\mathcal{K}$. From Example 4, we know that applying the first or the second equation on $\mathcal{S}$ yields the sensors $z_1 = (v, \overline{x}, c)$ and $z_2 = (a, x, c)$ respectively. Since $\mathcal{S}$ does not contain either z_1 or z_2, both fulfill the second case and are also determinable on $\mathcal{K}$. Finally, applying any equation on the set $\{(v, x, c), (v, \overline{x}, c), (a, x, c)\}$ yields a new sensor $z_3 = (a, \overline{x}, c)$. Thus, we now know that the sensor required in Example 1 is determinable on $\mathcal{K}$.

This is a condensed definition, for a more rigorous definition please refer to [12]. Still, this is enough to define $\mathcal{P}_\mathcal{K}$ the set of all sensors that are determinable on $\mathcal{K}$.

Definition 6 (All Determinable Sensors). *We call a set of sensors $\mathcal{P}_\mathcal{K}$ the set of all sensors determinable on $\mathcal{K}$ iff all sensors in $\mathcal{P}_\mathcal{K}$ are determinable and applying any equation eq to $\mathcal{P}_\mathcal{K}$ yields only a sensor s in $\mathcal{P}_\mathcal{K}$.*

Example 6. In Example 5 we reached the set of sensors determinable on $\mathcal{K}$

$$\mathcal{S}' = \{(v, x, c), (v, \overline{x}, c), (a, x, c), (a, \overline{x}, c)\}.$$

Applying any equation on $\mathcal{S}'$ yields only a sensor in $\mathcal{S}'$. Thus, $\mathcal{S}' = \mathcal{P}_\mathcal{K}$ is the set of all sensors determinable on $\mathcal{K}$.

5   Determinability Algorithms

For a more precise analysis, we require two more definitions.

Definition 7 ($\mathcal{F}$). *The set $\mathcal{F}$ consists of all triples having an equation eq and a pair of values from the two sensor attributes unaffected by eq.*

$$\mathcal{F} := \mathcal{E}_\mathcal{Q} \times \mathcal{D} \times \mathcal{T} \cup \mathcal{E}_\mathcal{D} \times \mathcal{Q} \times \mathcal{T} \cup \mathcal{E}_\mathcal{T} \times \mathcal{Q} \times \mathcal{D}$$

Definition 8 (J_M). *For a set of equations M we define the sum over the length of all right hand sides as*

$$J_M := \sum_{eq \in M} |eq|.$$

5.1   Naive Algorithm

While [12] shows that a polynomial time algorithm exists, the provided asymptotic worst case execution time of $\mathcal{O}(n^8)$ is not feasible for use at the system's run time. Some small improvements can be achieved using a dictionary to represent the set of all already determined sensors $\mathcal{P}$. The adapted algorithm is shown in Algorithm 1[4]. Since all sensors in $\mathcal{S}$ are determinable, we initialize the set $\mathcal{P}$ of

---

[4] For better readability, the iteration over $\mathcal{E}$ is written as a sequential one over the sets $\mathcal{E}_\mathcal{Q}, \mathcal{E}_\mathcal{D}, \mathcal{E}_\mathcal{T}$ instead of using a switch case structure.

Algorithm 1: Determinability check

Input: Knowledge base $\mathcal{K}$ consisting of $\mathcal{S}$ and $\mathcal{E}$.
Output: Set $\mathcal{P}_\mathcal{K}$ of all sensors determinable in $\mathcal{K}$.
$\mathcal{P} := \mathcal{S}$;
do

    foreach $eq := k_0 = \mathrm{OP}_{i=1}^{j} k_i \in \mathcal{E}_\mathcal{Q}$:
        foreach $(d, t) \in \mathcal{D} \times \mathcal{T}$:
            if $((k_0, d, t) \notin \mathcal{P})$:
                counter $= 0$;
                for $i = 1$ *to* j: **if** $((k_i, d, t) \in \mathcal{P})$: counter $+= 1$;
                if *counter* $== j$: $\mathcal{P}$.Add((k_0, d, t));

    foreach $eq := k_0 = \mathrm{OP}_{i=1}^{j} k_i \in \mathcal{E}_\mathcal{D}$:
        foreach $(q, t) \in \mathcal{Q} \times \mathcal{T}$:
            if $((q, k_0, t) \notin \mathcal{P})$:
                counter $= 0$;
                for $i = 1$ *to* j: **if** $((q, k_i, t) \in \mathcal{P})$: counter $+= 1$;
                if *counter* $== j$: $\mathcal{P}$.Add((q, k_0, t));

    foreach $eq := k_0 = \mathrm{OP}_{i=1}^{j} k_i \in \mathcal{E}_\mathcal{T}$:
        foreach $(q, d) \in \mathcal{Q} \times \mathcal{D}$:
            if $((q, d, k_0) \notin \mathcal{P})$:
                counter $= 0$;
                for $i = 1$ *to* j: **if** $((q, d, k_i) \in \mathcal{P})$: counter$+=1$;
                if *counter* $== j$: $\mathcal{P}$.Add((q, d, k_0));

while *new sensor found*;
return $\mathcal{P}$

---

already determined sensors with $\mathcal{S}$. While we find new sensors in the previous iteration, we continue the search for new sensors. In each iteration, we check for every triple $(eq, a, b) \in \mathcal{F}$ if the yielded sensor is already in $\mathcal{P}$. If it is not, we check if all sensors in the set $Z_{(a,b)}$ fixed by eq are in $\mathcal{P}$. If this is the case, we can apply eq and add the yielded sensor to $\mathcal{P}$.

Theorem 1. *Let I be the number of while loop iterations and set N as $N := \max\{|\mathcal{Q}|, |\mathcal{D}|, |\mathcal{T}|\}$, then Algorithm 1's time complexity is bounded by*

$$\mathcal{O}\Big(I(|\mathcal{F}| + J_\mathcal{E} N^2) + |\mathcal{P}_\mathcal{K}|\Big).$$

Proof. First, we analyze the operations unaffected by the number of iterations I. These are the additions to the set $\mathcal{P}$: Over the whole algorithm, we will add each sensor $p \in \mathcal{P}_\mathcal{K}$ exactly once to $\mathcal{P}$. If $p \in \mathcal{S}$, then this will be done when we initialize $\mathcal{P}$. Otherwise, the first application that yields p will add it to $\mathcal{P}$. Therefore, we have $|\mathcal{P}_\mathcal{K}|$ steps unaffected by the while loop.

In each of the while loops iterations, we will go over all triples $(eq, a, b) \in \mathcal{F}$ and check if they may yield a new sensor. Independent from the result, this already costs $|\mathcal{F}|$ steps. For the cases which yield a new sensor, we will focus without loss of generality on the triples $(eq, d, t) \in \mathcal{E}_Q \times \mathcal{D} \times \mathcal{T}$. In the worst case, each pair $(d, t) \in \mathcal{D} \times \mathcal{T}$ will trigger this check for each $e \in \mathcal{E}_Q$, therefore producing $J_{\mathcal{E}_Q}$ steps per pair, resulting in $J_{\mathcal{E}_Q} |\mathcal{D}| \cdot |\mathcal{T}|$ steps per iteration. Thus, we have asymptotically $\mathcal{O}(J_{\mathcal{E}_Q} N^2)$ steps for those triples. Therefore, all those checks require asymptotically

$$\mathcal{O}((J_{\mathcal{E}_Q} + J_{\mathcal{E}_D} + J_{\mathcal{E}_T}) N^2) = \mathcal{O}(J_{\mathcal{E}} N^2)$$

steps.

All in all, each iteration has $\mathcal{O}(|\mathcal{F}| + J_{\mathcal{E}} N^2)$ steps and for I iterations we have $\mathcal{O}(I(|\mathcal{F}| + J_{\mathcal{E}} N^2))$. Therefore, we have a time complexity of

$$\mathcal{O}\left(I(|\mathcal{F}| + J_{\mathcal{E}} N^2) + |\mathcal{P}_\mathcal{K}|\right). \qquad \square$$

Corollary 1. *For an input $\mathcal{K}$ with $n := |\mathcal{K}|$, Algorithm 1 has a time complexity of $\mathcal{O}(n^6)$.*

Proof. By Definition 7, $\mathcal{F}$ consists of triples of equations and the two unaffected attributes. Each of these sets is implicitly contained in $\mathcal{K}$. Therefore, we have

$$|\mathcal{F}| = |\mathcal{E}_Q| \cdot |\mathcal{D}| \cdot |\mathcal{T}| + |\mathcal{E}_D| \cdot |\mathcal{Q}| \cdot |\mathcal{T}| + |\mathcal{E}_T| \cdot |\mathcal{Q}| \cdot |\mathcal{D}| = \mathcal{O}(n^3).$$

Since the equations are part of the input, their length $J_{\mathcal{E}}$ is $\mathcal{O}(n)$. Thus, $J_{\mathcal{E}} N^2 = \mathcal{O}(n^3)$.

In the worst case, we may only add at most one sensor[5] per iteration to $\mathcal{P}$. Therefore, $I \leq |\mathcal{P}_\mathcal{K}| - |\mathcal{S}| + 1$ which is $\mathcal{O}(|\mathcal{P}_\mathcal{K}|)$. Finally, $\mathcal{P}_\mathcal{K}$ may be any subset of $\mathcal{Q} \times \mathcal{D} \times \mathcal{T}$. Thus, $|\mathcal{P}_\mathcal{K}| = \mathcal{O}(|\mathcal{Q} \times \mathcal{D} \times \mathcal{T}|) = \mathcal{O}(n^3)$. Therefore, Algorithm 1 has a time complexity of $\mathcal{O}(n^6)$. $\qquad \square$

5.2   Towards Preprocessing

There are two sections in this algorithm we can improve further. First, we only get one possible construction for each determined sensor because we skip a triple once the yielded sensor is added to $\mathcal{P}$. We can get this information if we use a dictionary F that stores for each triple $(eq, a, b) \in \mathcal{F}$ if it has already yielded a sensor. Since we do these checks each iteration, they have asymptotically no extra cost.

Second, in each iteration we have to check anew for each triple (eq, a, b) if all sensors in $Z_{(a,b)}$ are in $\mathcal{P}$ to apply eq. It would be more convenient to calculate the number of hits once and to update the values when a new sensor is added to $\mathcal{P}$ that affects the triple. A sensor $s = (q_s, d_s, t_s)$ only affects a triple (eq, a, b) if either q_s, d_s or t_s appears in eq's right-hand side and (a, b) are respectively (d_s, t_s), (q_s, t_s) or (q_s, d_s). Since q_s, d_s and t_s are all fixed when processing a newly added sensor, we only need a list of affected equations for each value in

---

[5] Only in the last iteration, we do not add a new sensor.

Algorithm 2: Determinability check with preprocessing

Input: Knowledge base $\mathcal{K}$ consisting of $\mathcal{S}$ and $\mathcal{E}$.

Output: Set of all determinable sensors $\mathcal{P}_\mathcal{K}$ in $\mathcal{K}$.

$R := \{(x, [])|x \in \mathcal{Q} \cup \mathcal{D} \cup \mathcal{T}\};$

foreach $eq := k_0 = \mathrm{OP}_{i=1}^j k_i \in \mathcal{E}$: **foreach** $i \in \{1, \ldots, j\}$: $R[k_i].\mathrm{Add}(eq)$;

foreach $(q, d, t) \in \mathcal{S}$: $U.\mathrm{Enqueue}((q, d, t));$

while U *not empty*:

> $(q, d, t) = U.\mathrm{Dequeue}();$
>
> **if** $(q, d, t) \notin \mathcal{P}$:
>
> > $\mathcal{P}.\mathrm{Add}((q, d, t));$
> >
> > **foreach** $eq := k_0 = \mathrm{OP}_{i=1}^j k_i \in R[q]$:
> >
> > > **if** $(eq, d, t) \notin F.Keys$: $F.\mathrm{Add}(((eq, d, t), j));$
> > >
> > > $F[(eq, d, t)]\ \text{-}= 1;$
> > >
> > > **if** $F[(eq, d, t)] == 0$: $U.\mathrm{Enqueue}((k_0, d, t));$
> >
> > **foreach** $eq := k_0 = \mathrm{OP}_{i=1}^j k_i \in R[d]$:
> >
> > > **if** $(eq, q, t) \notin F.Keys$: $F.\mathrm{Add}(((eq, q, t), j));$
> > >
> > > $F[(eq, q, t)]\ \text{-}= 1;$
> > >
> > > **if** $F[(eq, q, t)] == 0$: $U.\mathrm{enqueue}((q, k_0, t));$
> >
> > **foreach** $eq := k_0 = \mathrm{OP}_{i=1}^j k_i \in R[t]$:
> >
> > > **if** $(eq, q, d) \notin F.Keys$: $F.\mathrm{Add}(((eq, q, d), j));$
> > >
> > > $F[(eq, q, d)]\ \text{-}= 1;$
> > >
> > > **if** $F[(eq, q, d)] == 0$: $U.\mathrm{Enqueue}((q, d, k_0));$

return $\mathcal{P}$;

$\mathcal{Q} \cup \mathcal{D} \cup \mathcal{T}$. These lists can be constructed in $\mathcal{O}(|\mathcal{E}| + J_\mathcal{E}) = \mathcal{O}(n)$ by inverting the equations.

We can combine both ideas by using the dictionary F to store the values at run time and using an additional queue U to keep track of all yielded sensors. All in all, these ideas result in Algorithm 2 which we will now discuss in detail.

5.3 Algorithm with Preprocessing

As a small average case improvement, we add entries to F while executing the algorithm. Instead of generating F with possibly many unused entries, we check before an access if we a triple $(eq, a, b) \in \mathcal{F}$ has already an entry. If it does not, we only then add the entry to the dictionary. This improvement adds an extra step before each access to $\mathcal{F}$, but has asymptotically no influence on the worst case. Since we already analyzed the preprocessing in the previous subsection, we will only focus on processing the queue U.

By Definition 5, all sensors in $\mathcal{S}$ are determinable. Therefore, we initialize U by enqueuing all sensors in $\mathcal{S}$. Then, we repeat the following until U is empty: First, we dequeue a sensor $s = (q_s, d_s, t_s)$ from U. If this sensor is already in $\mathcal{P}$, we proceed with the next sensor. If the sensor has been determined for the first time, we add it to $\mathcal{P}$ and reduce the counter of all affected triples in F by one.

We get these by iterating over $R[q_s], R[d_s]$ and $R[t_s]$ while fixing $(d_s, t_s), (q_s, t_s)$ and (q_s, d_s) respectively. If a triple (eq, a, b) with $eq := k_0 = \mathrm{OP}_{i=1}^j k_j$ has no corresponding value in F, we add this triple to F and initialize the value[6] with j. If any counter reaches 0, we enqueue the resulting sensor in U.

Theorem 2. *Let N be defined as $N := \max\{|\mathcal{Q}|, |\mathcal{D}|, |\mathcal{T}|\}$, then Algorithm 2 has a time complexity of*

$$\mathcal{O}\Big(\min \big(|\mathcal{F}| + J_\mathcal{E} N^2, |\mathcal{E}| \cdot |\mathcal{P_K}|\big)\Big).$$

Proof. An upper bound for the number of steps can be defined in two ways. First, focusing on the number of operations performed by adding a new sensor. Each sensor in $\mathcal{P_K}$ triggers the operation sequence within the outermost if only once. In each step of each loop over the respective equations, only a fixed number of operations are executed. Namely, two comparisons, one counter manipulation and sometimes an addition to a dictionary or an enqueue. In the worst case, a sensor may appear in all equations resulting in at most $5|\mathcal{E}|$ operations for each sensor. Therefore, we have asymptotically $\mathcal{O}(|\mathcal{E}| \cdot |\mathcal{P_K}|)$ for this sequence.

Finally, we have to analyze how many sensors are enqueued in U since each entry must be dequeued and checked for membership in $\mathcal{P}$. Besides the initial $|\mathcal{S}|$ sensors, we can enqueue at most $|\mathcal{E}| \cdot |\mathcal{P_K}|$ sensors. Thus, we have up to $2(|\mathcal{E}| \cdot |\mathcal{P_K}| + |\mathcal{S}|)$ for the entries in U[7]. Overall, we have

$$7|\mathcal{E}| \cdot |\mathcal{P_K}| + |\mathcal{P_K}| + 3|\mathcal{S}| + |\mathcal{E}| + J_\mathcal{E} = \mathcal{O}(|\mathcal{E}| \cdot |\mathcal{P_K}|)$$

operations.

For the second upper bound, we analyze the number of operations in relation to F. With the exception of adding a sensor to $\mathcal{P}$, all operations within the while loop can be separated into two categories. The first one consists of all operations that depend on the size of F. Each entry in F is created once, will trigger at most one enqueue that results in a dequeue and a membership check down the line. Thus, we have 4 operations in this category. Therefore, each of these operations is bound by the size of F. The second category consists of all operations that depend on the number of manipulations on the counters in F. Each counter can be reduced, then follows a check if the counter has reached 0. Furthermore, each reduction forces a prior check on the existence of the required key. Thus, we have 3 operations in this category. At most, we can reduce all values in F to 0, therefore limiting these operations by the sum of the initial values in each entry in F. This is at most

$$J_{\mathcal{E}_\mathcal{Q}}|\mathcal{D}| \cdot |\mathcal{T}| + J_{\mathcal{E}_\mathcal{D}}|\mathcal{Q}| \cdot |\mathcal{T}| + J_{\mathcal{E}_\mathcal{T}}|\mathcal{Q}| \cdot |\mathcal{D}|$$

which is bound above by $J_\mathcal{E} N^2$.

---

[6] Thus, we only have to check if any counter has reached 0, instead of checking for different js.

[7] Since we have dequeue every enqueued entry the number of operations doubles.

All in all, these observations result in a second upper bound of

$$4|\mathcal{F}| + 3J_\mathcal{E} N^2 + 3|\mathcal{S}| + |\mathcal{P}_\mathcal{K}| + |\mathcal{E}| + J_\mathcal{E} = \mathcal{O}(|\mathcal{F}| + J_\mathcal{E} N^2).$$

We can combine both upper bounds to

$$\mathcal{O}\Big(\min\big(|\mathcal{F}| + J_\mathcal{E} N^2, |\mathcal{E}| \cdot |\mathcal{P}_\mathcal{K}|\big)\Big).$$

□

Corollary 2. *For an input $\mathcal{K}$ with $n := |\mathcal{K}|$, Algorithm 2 has a time complexity of $\mathcal{O}\big(n^3\big).$*

Proof. Since our upper bound is the minimum of two upper bounds, we have to determine which is the smaller in which case. The bound $|\mathcal{E}| \cdot |\mathcal{P}_\mathcal{K}|$ depends on $|\mathcal{P}_\mathcal{K}|$ in relation to n. For $|\mathcal{P}_\mathcal{K}| = \mathcal{O}(n^2)$, $|\mathcal{E}| = \mathcal{O}(n)$ still keeps the complexity in $\mathcal{O}(n^3)$. For $|\mathcal{P}_\mathcal{K}| = \omega(n^2)$, the overall bound is dominated by the second bound.

As argued in Corollary 1, $|\mathcal{F}| + J_\mathcal{E} N^2 = \mathcal{O}(n^3)$. This bound is true for any $|\mathcal{P}_\mathcal{K}|$. Therefore, it is worse for $|\mathcal{P}_\mathcal{K}| = \mathcal{O}(n^2)$, but imposes the required limit on $|\mathcal{P}_\mathcal{K}| = \mathcal{O}(n^2)$. All in all, we have a complexity of $\mathcal{O}(n^3)$. □

Since Algorithm 2 creates during its execution auxiliary data structures, a space analysis is necessary. The set $\mathcal{P}$ is the algorithm's output, therefore we do not consider its space as auxiliary.

Theorem 3. *Algorithm 2 requires $\mathcal{O}(|\mathcal{F}|)$ auxiliary space.*

Proof. During the algorithm's execution, we have to keep at worst one counter for every entry in $\mathcal{F}$ accessible in F. Each such entry may enqueue at most one element into the queue U. Therefore, both require $\mathcal{O}(|\mathcal{F}|)$ auxiliary space. Since the inverted equations in R are a similar to reordering the equations, they require asymptotically the same space of $\mathcal{O}(|\mathcal{E}| + J_\mathcal{E})$. This auxiliary space is asymptotically dominated by $\mathcal{O}(|\mathcal{F}|)$. Therefore, requiring $\mathcal{O}(|\mathcal{F}|)$ overall. □

Corollary 3. *For an input $\mathcal{K}$ with $n := |\mathcal{K}|$, Algorithm 2 requires $\mathcal{O}(n^3)$ auxiliary space.*

Proof. As argued in Corollary 1, $|\mathcal{F}| = \mathcal{O}(n^3)$. □

5.4 Specification

As described in [12], we can expand $\mathcal{P}$ to a dictionary which uses the determined sensor as key and the equation that yielded the sensor as value. Then, this dictionary can be used to recursively specify an abstract sensor. In case of Algorithm 2, we can further expand this to a sensor referencing a list of equations that yield the sensor. These lists can be filled during Algorithm 2's execution by enqueuing a sensor s with the yielding equation eq. Thereby, we can add eq to the sensor's list, after performing the check whether $s \in \mathcal{P}$. Therefore, Algorithm 2 allows to construct a sensor using different structures whereas Algorithm 1 only finds a single structure.

6   Conclusion and Future Work

6.1   Conclusion

In this paper, we have introduced and analyzed two improvements, one without and one with auxiliary data structures, for the determinability algorithm described in [12]. The Algorithm 1 without auxiliary structures improves the worst-case time bound from $\mathcal{O}(n^8)$ to $\mathcal{O}(n^6)$. On top of these improvements, Algorithm 2 uses auxiliary structures and reduces the worst case time bound to $\mathcal{O}(n^3)$ while requiring an auxiliary space of $\mathcal{O}(n^3)$, it also finds more possible structures for an abstract sensors specification.

6.2   Future Work

Future work will focus on algorithms utilizing the knowledge provided by Algorithm 2. This includes efficient algorithms that specify the abstract sensors with one of their constructions. For this, we will also develop and evaluate heuristics to decide which possible construction fits further aspects like using less building blocks or using only simple building blocks. Such a heuristic may also be a pretrained neural network.

Both algorithms are described using a centralized approach, which contrasts with the decentralized nature of the AHS and ADNA. Future work will involve the development and analysis of more decentralized versions. An approach inspired by the AHS's task distribution shows promise. In this approach, each PE possesses a portion of the knowledge base and initiates the determination process based on its own knowledge base. If a PE determines a new sensor, it shares this information with other PEs through a message, allowing them to expand their sets of determinable sensors.

If we keep track of every possible construction, we can integrate them with the conditional ADNA proposed in [10]. This would seamlessly provide emergency structures for the same abstract sensor. These alternate structures also provide a system's diagnosis unit with reference values that can be used to analyze an abstract sensor's output.

References

1. Allrutz, R., et al.: POSIPAP organic comp - VDE (2003). https://www.vde.com/resource/blob/932548/bfcfaa9bae199aa27f888319c396d6ed/fa-6-1-organic-computing-download-akkordeon-data.pdf
2. Borst, R., Akkermans, H., Pos, A., Top, J.: The PhysSys ontology for physical systems. In: Proceedings Workshop Qualitative Reasoning 1995, Amsterdam, NL, pp. 11–21 (1995)
3. Brinkschulte, U.: Technical report: artificial DNA - a concept for self-building embedded systems. arXiv abs/1707.07617 (2017)
4. Brinkschulte, U.: An artificial DNA for self-descripting and self-building embedded real-time systems. Concurr. Comput. Pract. Experience **28**, 3711–3729 (2015)

5. Brinkschulte, U., Obermaisser, R., Meckel, S., Pacher, M.: Online-diagnosis with organic computing based on artificial DNA. In: 2019 First International Conference on Societal Automation (SA), pp. 1–4 (2019). https://doi.org/10.1109/SA47457.2019.8938032

6. Brinkschulte, U., Pacher, M.: Semantic description of artificial DNA for an organic computing middleware architecture. In: Proceedings of the 1st International Workshop on Middleware for Lightweight, Spontaneous Environments, MISE 2019, pp. 1–6 (2019)

7. Cvjetkovic, V.: Web physics ontology: online interactive symbolic computation in physics. In: 2017 4th Experiment@International Conference (exp.at 2017), pp. 52–57 (2017). https://doi.org/10.1109/EXPAT.2017.7984405

8. FAIRsharing Team: Fairsharing record for: quantities, units, dimensions and types (2015). https://doi.org/10.25504/FAIRSHARING.D3PQW7

9. Haller, A., et al.: The SOSA/SSN ontology: a joint W3C and OGC standard specifying the semantics of sensors, observations, actuation, and sampling. Semant. Web-Interoperability Usability Applicability IOS Press J. **56**, 1–19 (2019)

10. Homann, P., Pacher, M., Brinkschulte, U.: Evaluation of conditional tasks in an artificial DNA system. In: 25th IEEE International Symposium on Real-Time Distributed Computing, ISORC 2022, Västerås, Sweden, 17–18 May 2022, pp. 1–10. IEEE (2022). https://doi.org/10.1109/ISORC52572.2022.9812764

11. Koschowoj, A.: Towards a semantic description of artificial DNA using ontologies. In: Tomforde, S., Krupitzer, C. (eds.) Organic Computing, pp. 32–46. Universität Kassel (2022). https://doi.org/10.17170/KOBRA-202202215780. https://kobra.uni-kassel.de/handle/123456789/14004

12. Koschowoj, A., Pacher, M., Brinkschulte, U.: The next step in the evolution of artificial DNA: the abstract ADNA. In: 10th Edition in the Evolution of the Workshop Series on Autonomously Learning and Optimizing Systems (SAOS) (in press)

13. Schmeck, H.: Organic computing - a new vision for distributed embedded systems. In: Eighth IEEE International Symposium on Object-Oriented Real-Time Distributed Computing (ISORC 2005), pp. 201–203 (2005). https://doi.org/10.1109/ISORC.2005.42

14. Tomforde, S., Sick, B., Müller-Schloer, C.: Organic Computing in the Spotlight. CoRR abs/1701.08125 (2017). http://arxiv.org/abs/1701.08125

15. von Renteln, A., Brinkschulte, U., Pacher, M.: The artificial hormone system–an organic middleware for self-organising real-time task allocation. In: Müller-Schloer, C., Schmeck, H., Ungerer, T. (eds.) Organic Computing—A Paradigm Shift for Complex Systems, pp. 369–384. Springer, Basel (2011). https://doi.org/10.1007/978-3-0348-0130-0_24

Evaluating the Comprehensive Adaptive *Chameleon* Middleware for Mixed-Critical Cyber-Physical Networks

Melanie Feist[✉], Mathias Pacher, and Uwe Brinkschulte

Goethe University Frankfurt, Frankfurt am Main, Germany
{feist,m.pacher,brinksch}@em.uni-frankfurt.de

Abstract. Cyber Physical Systems (CPS) are growing more and more complex due to the availability of cheap hardware, sensors, actuators and communication links. A network of cooperating CPSs (CPN) additionally increases the complexity. Furthermore, CPNs are often deployed in dynamic, unpredictable environments and safety-critical domains, such as transportation, energy, and healthcare. In such domains, usually applications of different criticality level exist. As a result of mixed-criticality, applications requiring hard real-time guarantees compete with those requiring soft real-time guarantees and best-effort application for the given resources within the overall system.

This poses challenges as well as it offers chances: the increasing complexity makes it harder to design, operate, optimize and maintain such CPNs. However, on the other side an appropriate use of the increasing resources in computational nodes, sensors, actuators can significantly improve the system performance, reliability and flexibility. Hence, Organic Computing concepts like self-X features (self-organization, self-adaptation, self-healing, etc.) are key principles for such systems.

Therefore, the comprehensive adaptive middleware *Chameleon* has been developed which applies such principles for CPNs. In this paper, the self-adaptation mechanism of *Chameleon* based on a MAPE-K loop and learning classifier systems is examined and evaluated. The results show its effectivity in autonomously handling the system resources to keep the required constraints of the applications with respect to their criticality.

Keywords: adaptive middleware · mixed-criticality · cyber-physical systems · cyber-physical networks · MAPE-K · learning classifier systems

1 Introduction

The rapid growth of Cyber-Physical Systems (CPS) due to the availability of cheap hardware, sensors, actuators and communication links, has led to an

G. Goumas et al. (Eds.): ARCS 2023, LNCS 13949, pp. 200–214, 2023.
https://doi.org/10.1007/978-3-031-42785-5_14

increased system complexity. In the automotive area e.g. the number and capabilities of these components in a car is constantly rising during the last years. This complexity arises due to the interdependence of physical processes, sensing and actuation, communication networks, and computing resources. The combination of these factors creates a multitude of issues that must be addressed, such as task allocation, scheduling, fault tolerance and communication. As the number of heterogeneous components in such a system rises, the complexity of the interactions between them also increases. A network of cooperating CPSs - a so-called Cyber Physical Network (CPN) - makes the situation even more complex, since information between the CPSs in the network has to be exchanged and actions have to coordinated and deployed. Cooperating or platooning vehicles, in which several autonomous vehicles drive in a convoy with small inter-vehicle distances and coordinate their inter-vehicle gaps via IEEE 802.11p communication, can be an example for such a CPN. Additionally, CPNs are often deployed in dynamic, unpredictable environments and safety-critical domains, such as transportation, energy, and healthcare. In such domains, usually applications of different criticality level exist. In an automotive environment for example, the brake has a higher criticality level regarding safety as the infotainment. As a result of mixed-criticality, applications requiring hard real-time guarantees compete with those requiring soft real-time guarantees and best-effort application for the given resources within the overall system. This leads to the need to accommodate multiple levels of criticality while ensuring safety and reliability, which increases the already high complexity even more.

A main idea of Organic Computing is to improve the operation of highly complex systems by transferring operation decisions from design-time to runtime. Self-X features like self-organization, self-adaptation and self-healing are a key principles for such systems since the increasing complexity cannot be handled effectively and efficiently by the system developer without the assistance of the system itself any longer. This paper presents and evaluates a *comprehensive adaptive mixed-criticality supporting middleware for Cyber-Physical Networks* (*Chameleon*) which efficiently handles safety-related non-functional real-time requirements with regard to the mixed-criticality aspect. The entire system consisting of applications, computing nodes, communication channels, sensors, actuators and the middleware itself is considered. In such a comprehensive approach, the key parameters of each of these components (e.g. scheduling parameters, scheduling schemes, task parameters, communication parameters and protocols, data compression, monitoring rates,) as well as the structure itself (task allocation) are subject of adaptation. While the basic architecture of *Chameleon* have already been introduced in [2] and [5], this paper mainly focuses on the evaluation of the adaptation process. It is organized as follows: After this introduction, related work is presented in Sect. 2. Then, the basic architecture and the self-adaptation mechanism of *Chameleon* are introduced in Sect. 3. Following, Sect. 4 presents extensive evaluation results. Finally, Sect. 5 concludes this paper.

2 Related Work

Self-organization has been a research focus for several years. In particular, the Organic Computing Initiative can be listed here. Its basic aim is to improve the controllability of complex embedded systems by using principles found in organic entities [15]. Organization principles which are successful in biology are adapted to embedded computing systems and used to ácquire self-X properties

Self-Organization is often encapsulated into a middleware. Several projects related to Organic Computing use this approach. In the frame of the DoDOrg project, e.g. the Artificial Hormone System (AHS) was introduced [13]. The AHS has been later extended by the Artificial DNA (ADNA) [3]. Other self-organizing middlewares arise from the field of Wireless Sensor Networks (WSN), e.g. [19,20]. Here, the focus lies on energy-efficiency rather than on safety-related real-time constraints. Additionally, all the middlewares mentioned above mainly deal with self-organizing task allocation. In *Chameleon*, task allocation is one adaptation possibility in a wider range of other self-organizing adaptation capabilities.

Chameleon is intended to allow CPNs to maintain real-time constraints with regard to the mixed-criticality aspect. There are various general research trends related to mixed-critical CPNs. First, there are several approaches dealing with the handling of mixed-criticality. Those are in general based on different scheduling strategies to ensure the sound execution of critical system tasks. Hu *et al.* introduces an adaptive real-time scheduling algorithm to handle dynamic multiple-criticality applications based on a least-laxity first ·strategy. Thereby, a mode-switch scheme and virtual deadlines to meet the different requirements of multiple-criticality applications are used [8]. *ASDYS* is a dynamic scheduling approach using active strategies· where the mixed-criticality is actively treated throughout the scheduling process. The aim of the approach is to minimize the deadline miss rate ratio [1]. On the other hand, *GoodSpread* is a framework that statically allocates multi Quality-of-Service (QoS) resources to a set of control applications so that each of them meets its performance requirements in all scenarios while using the minimum amount of high-QoS resources [14]. All of those papers address mixed-criticality in terms of scheduling. *Chameleon*, however, considers scheduling as one but not the only part of the adaptation possibilities.

An approach for a self-organizing task allocation with respect to mixed criticality is presented in [9]. This approach extends the AHS mentioned above by so-called task assignment priorities. These priorities enable self-healing in overload situations by gradually dropping low-priority tasks. In comparison to our approach, the system view is limited to the nodes and adaptation to handle overload situations is limited to task dropping.

Ratasich *et al.* present a self-healing framework for building resilient CPS which achieves self-healing through structural adaptation [12]. In contrast, our approach is not limited to structural adaptation. Instead also parametric adaptation to modify the behavior of the system is applied.

[7] provides an initial-architecture for a CPS middleware. Thereby, the target is on subsystems where timing deadlines are not hard nor safety critical. Thus, this architecture is not suitable for the goal of our work.

3 Middleware Architecture and Implementation

In the following, the basic middleware architecture including the adaptation mechanism and its implementation are briefly presented. For more details on the middleware architecture and underlying system model, please refer to [5].

3.1 Middleware Architecture

A middleware in a mixed-critical CPN is responsible for transparent operation of the distributed system. It handles all the interactions of applications, sensors and actuators within a single CPS and the entire CPN. It also manages the resources like computation nodes and communication channels to enable distributed operation. Therefore, the middleware is the ideal place to provide self-adaption which affects the entire CPN. Figure 1 shows the architecture of the *Chameleon* middleware. The middleware is structured in a modular way and can be divided into

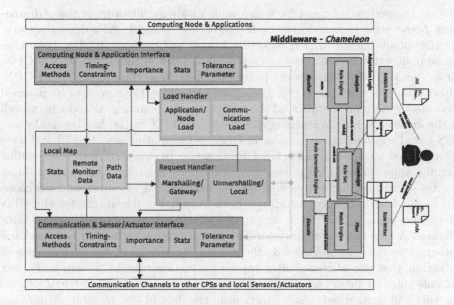

Fig. 1. Middleware Architecture

two major parts: the **Basic Middleware** part shown on the left side of the figure and the **Adaptation Logic** shown on the right sied. The **Basic Middleware** part is responsible for the basic middleware operations to provide distributed system interaction and transparency. It consists of several sub-parts: The *Interfaces* connect the middleware to the computing node and applications on one side and to the communication network and sensors/actuators on the other side. The *Local Map* contains information about the location of applications, sensors and actuators and how they can be reached using the communication network.

It is filled automatically by analyzing the incoming network traffic. The *Request Handler* is responsible for the management of messages between the application and the communication side and the transformation of application requests to messages and vice versa. The *Load Handler* finally handles the load management of applications. It can modify the computational and communication load by starting, stopping, relocating, tuning (changing e.g. the periods and priorities of) applications as well as changing data compression or scheduling schemes.

Mixed-criticality is introduced by defining an *Importance* parameter (cf. interfaces in Fig. 1), which expresses the level of criticality for a component[1]. This cardinal valued parameter allows to express the criticality of a component on a fine grain level. By introducing a cardinal valued *Importance* parameter, the criticality of a component can be expressed on a fine-grained level independent of its priority.

3.2 Adaptation

The core ingredient of the *Chameleon* middleware architecture is the **Adaptation Logic part** shown in grey on the right side of Fig. 1. As a design pattern, the commonly known MAPE-K feedback loop architecture [10] has been chosen to realize the desired self-adaptation capabilities in the mixed-critical CPN. First, the **Monitor** samples the parameter data from the mixed-critical CPN. Afterwards, this data needs to be analyzed and adaptations need to be planned if necessary. As representation of the analyzing and planning component as well as the knowledge base, a learning classifier system (LCS) [18] has been selected. LCS-based approaches are popular in Organic Computing (cf. [16,17]) and have been applied for approaches in the CPS domain. In comparison to other online learning approaches, LCS are less computationally complex. Therefore, training can be performed on devices with low computational resources and decisions can be made in real-time, which are both essential requirements for the CPN adaptation process. LCS use a set of *rules* that represent potential adaptations schemes. A rule thereby mainly consists of a condition clause, an action clause and an expected *reward*. Based on the measured reward, i.e., the effectiveness of an action, that was observed after applying a certain rule, LCS learn and select suitable rules for future adaptations. In *Chameleon*, the **Analyzer** first derives abstract and normalized *health values* from the data of the *Monitor*. *Health values* range from 1 (best healthy state) to 0 (least healthy state) down to negative (unhealthy state). This enables a unified concept for defining conditions for LCS rules. Such *health values* are for example retrieved from parameters like load (of a communication channel or a computational network node) or deadline misses (of an application). After deriving the *health values*, the *Analyzer* uses its *Rule*

---

[1] *Importance* must not be confused with priority. Regarding real-time scheduling, components with short periods often result in high priorities (e.g. rate monotonic scheduling). However these components might be less important for the system than components with longer periods and resulting lower priority. In case of overload or lack of resources the lower priority component then has to be preferred.

Engine to trigger an adaptation if necessary. Therefore, it compares the current system condition to the condition clauses of the *Rule Set* stored in the **Knowledge** base. Thereby, the rules are expressed in *Rango*—a generic and flexible rule language—which is dedicated to systematically and formally create set-based adaptation rules for mixed-critical CPNs in an intuitive way [6]. The rules are parsed from a rule file (.rul) and automatically integrated into the knowledge base. Also, *Rango* offers a rule writer, which exports rules modified by learning into a human-readable form (.rulx) which makes the learning process persistent and allows the user to inspect the learning result. All rules that are currently applicable are included in the *match set*. The **Planner** collects all action clauses from the match set into the action set. Then, it selects the action that is expected to lead to the highest reward[2].

In the next step, the **Execute** stage deploys the selected action to the mixed-critical CPN.

As the final step in the LCS-based MAPE-K cycle, the *Analyzer* determines the measured reward of an executed action and updates the *Rule Set* accordingly.

An LCS-based feedback loop may additionally contain a *Rule Generation Engine* which evolves the rule set automatically at runtime, e.g., with genetic algorithms [18], but this is not implemented yet and part of future work.

3.3 Middleware Implementation

For the realization of *Chameleon*, the modules of the basic middleware architecture and the LCS-based MAPE-K *Adaptation Logic* shown in Fig. 1 have been prototypically implemented in C++ 11.

Table 1 summarizes the *Lines of Codes* and *Code Size* of all *Chameleon* modules. The modules were compiled using *clang* version 5.0.1, target x86-w64-windows-gnu. It can be seen that the basic middleware itself is rather small with an overall code size far less than 100kBytes. Also, the adaptation logic doesn't occupy much code space. The biggest module is the *Rule Parser* and *Rule Writer* with 93kBytes. However, this module may not necessarily be included in each *Chameleon* instance since the *Rule Set* can be compiled offline and loaded directly into the local *Knowledge* base in binary format. Also, for the *Rule Writer*, the *Rule Set* modified by learning can be exported in binary form and written back in human readable form offline.

To simulate the environment, OMNet++ (Objective Modular Network Testbed in C++) [11] has been used. OMNet++ is a commonly known and well reputed event-based simulator for network processing. It offers many features and pre-defined modules to precisely simulate communication networks and sensor/actuator systems. Furthermore, it has been extended by modules to simulate applications and computing nodes.

---

[2] This can be done value based like in classical LCS or precision based (where the best match of measured reward and expected reward are considered) in extended learning classifier systems (XCS).

Table 1. Lines of Codes and Code Size [kBytes] of *Chameleon* modules.

	Lines of Code	Code Size		Lines of Code	Code Size
Basic Middleware:			Adaptation Logic:		
Interfaces	716	22	Monitor	1170	24
Local Map	832	25	Analyze and Plan	1940	56
Load Handler	616	17	Execute	720	19
Request Handler	176	2	Rule Parser and Rule Writer	3835	93

4   Evaluation

For the practical evaluation of *Chameleon*, an automotive scenario has been chosen because it offers a wide range of criticality and timing constraints (comfort functions, driving assistants, driving functions) as well as dynamics (e.g. turning on or off assistants or comfort functions at runtime, processor failures). In more recent car configurations, different functionalities share more powerful processors. This reduces the costs and eases redundancy, since functionalities now can be moved between processors. It also offers opportunities for adaptation. Thus, *Chameleon* has been integrated into a simulated networked car environment (based on OMNeT++, cf. Sect. 3.3).

The simulated environment offers the opportunity to deeply look inside the adaptation processes while deficiencies will not cause physical harm. As network computing nodes, 4 processors ($Node_A$ .. $Node_D$) with a capacity of 10 Mips each have been chosen. The processors are interconnected with each other and the sensors and actuators via a CAN like bus system with 500 kBits/sec transmission capacity supporting message priorities. The applications and their major parameters[3] used for the evaluation are shown in Table 2. Applications marked with * are started on driver demand, all the others are activated at system start. Important parameters for the timing behavior of the rule evaluation are the evaluation period (rules are evaluated periodically), the reward delay (to measure the reward after an action is executed) and the monitoring periods (the periods in which parameters of m components are monitored). Based on the application periods, an evaluation period of 100 ms and a reward delay of 2000 ms has been chosen. The local monitoring period is set to 5-times the application period, while the global monitoring period is 2-times the local monitoring period. These values are a suitable compromise between monitoring resolution (as lower the values as better) and overhead (as higher the values as better). A basic *Rule Set* consisting of 17 rules for handling of failures, overload situations, scheduling issues, recovery and connection losses has been applied. This *Rule Set* as well as a complete definition of the *Rango* syntax can be found in [4]. In the following, major evaluation results are presented.

---

[3] higher values indicate higher *Importance* and priority.

4.1   Evaluation 1: Handling of Dynamic Load Changes

For the first experiment, several events have been injected to change the overall load of the system. Those are summed up in Table 3. Thereby, the first two columns of the table show the time of the event and the event itself. First, the system load is gradually increased: After 10 s the performance of computing $Node_A$ is slowed down from 10 Mips to 7.5 Mips due to thermal issues. At 25 s the *Cruise Control* application is started by the driver. The *Infotainment* system and the *Navigation* are started after 40 s respectively 55 s. Beginning with second 70 the load now is gradually decreased back to its initial value. By this, it shall be evaluated how the adaptation mechanism not only reacts on increased but also on decreased load. Therefore, at 80 s the original performance of $Node_A$ is restored. Afterwards, the *Cruise Control*, *Infotainment* and *Navigation* are stopped at 80, 90 and 100 s.

Table 2. Application Parameters

Application	Importance	Priority	Period [ms]	Max Period [ms] (tune)
Steering	7	4	50	50 (–)
Brake	7	4	50	50 (–)
Passenger Safety	7	5	25	25 (–)
Powertrain	6	5	25	25 (–)
Lights	6	1	500	1000 (2)
Stability	5	4	50	100 (2)
Data Repository	5	*inherits*	–	– (–)
*Cruise Control**	4	4	50	100 (2)
Driver Warning	3	2	250	500 (2)
*Navigation**	2	3	100	500 (5)
*Infotainment**	1	4	50	500 (10)

Column 3 of Table 3 shows the actions selected by the autonomous adaptation mechanism. Additionally, adaptation actions selected manually by a human developer[4] are listed in column 4. Columns 5 show the component affected by an action.

Thus, this evaluation not only validates the effectivity of the action portfolio (cf. Sect. 3 *Load Handler*), but also can serve as a comparison between the effectivity of the autonomous adaptation mechanism versus manual adaptation by a human developer. Although not being a strict evidence, it gives a good impression on the quality and capability of the selected autonomous self-adaptation mechanism in conjunction with its *Rule Set*.

---

[4] The manually selected adaptation actions have been performed as a proof of concept before the implementation of the autonomous adaptation mechanism was finished.

Figure 2 compares the number of unhealthy applications (applications which violate their constraints) with manual, autonomous and without the adaptation. As well, the number of the overall activated and running applications, the events and the adaptation actions as reference to Table 3 column 3 and 4 are shown.

It can be seen, that without adaptation a large number of unhealthy applications occur. The manual and autonomous adaptation keeps the system healthy (meet the real-time constraints) by relocation, tuning, data compression and pausing of the least important application. While the autonomous adaptation succeeds to keep the system healthy without pausing any application by efficiently combining the other actions (e.g. actions A5-A7) the human developer did not find this solution and paused one application instead. Overall, the autonomous adaptation performs significantly better than the manual adaptation since it reacts quickly to unhealthy applications in the system (A1-A7) and the adaptation actions are more fine grain and less restrictive. The last actions of the autonomous adaptation (A8-A13) react to the decreased load by undoing previous adaptation measures. This was not in the focus of the manual adaptation experiment.

Table 3. Events and adaptation actions (manual and autonomous).

time [s]	Event	Actions (*Chameleon*)	Action (manual)	Components
10	Slow down $Node_A$ (10 to 7.5 Mips)			
10.3		Relocate (A1)		*Stability and Drive Dynamics*: $Node_D$
15			Relocate (M1)	*Stability and Drive Dynamics*: $Node_D$
25	Start *CruiseControl* ($Node_C$)			
25.41		Tune (A2)		*Driver Warning*: Factor 2
27.81		Tune (A3)		*Cruise Control*: Factor 2
30			Tune (M2)	*Cruise Control*: Factor 1.5
40	Start *Infotainment* ($Node_D$)			
40.25		Compress (A4)		*Infotainment*: Factor 0.8
45			Compress (M3)	*Infotainment*: Factor 0.75
			Tune (M4)	*Infotainment*: Factor 2
55	Start *Navigation* ($Node_D$)			
55.55		Compress (A5)		*Navigation*: Factor 0.8
57.65		Tune (A6)		*Navigation*: Factor 5
59.65		Relocate (A7)		*Navigation*: $Node_A$
60			Pause (M5)	*Infotainment*
			Tune (M6)	*Navigation*: Factor 3
70	Speed up $Node_A$ (7.5 to 10 Mips)			
80	Stop *Cruise Control*			
90	Stop *Infotainment*			
90.26		Untune (A8)		*Navigation*: Factor 4.5
		Untune (A9)		*Driver Warning*: Factor 1.5
92.27		Untune (A10)		*Navigation*: Factor 4
		Untune (A11)		*Driver Warning*: Factor 1
94.28		Untune (A12)		*Navigation*: Factor 3.5
96.28		Untune (A13)		*Navigation*: Factor 3
98.28		Untune (A14)		*Navigation*: Factor 2.5
100	Stop *Navigation*			

Figure 3 compares the execution time of the high important *Brake* application to its constraint given by the period. The start of the *Cruise Control* leads to a slight violation of the execution time constraint. This is due to the fact that in the chosen initial configuration of the evaluation scenario both applications reside on $Node_C$. The autonomous adaptation mechanism reacts to this violation by tuning the least important application in the system (A2). The second violation about two seconds later is counteracted by tuning the next least important application (A3). This leads to the restoration of the initial valid execution times. Also, the further load changes can be noticed in the diagram but do not cause any further violation of the constraint. In contrast, without adaptation the constraint is heavily violated especially after the start of the *Infotainment*.

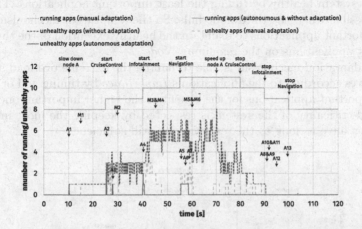

Fig. 2. Comparison of unhealthy applications (apps) with manual, autonomous (*Chameleon*) and without adaptation.

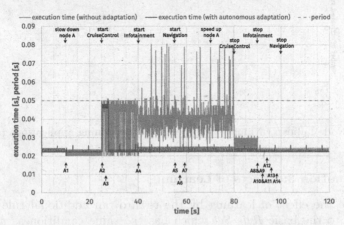

Fig. 3. Execution time and period of the *Brake* application with autonomous (*Chameleon*) and without adaptation.

4.2   Evaluation 2: Handling of Failures

This evaluation investigates the handling of failures by the autonomous adaptation mechanism. To maximize the pressure and load on the system, node failures are successively injected unless only a single node is left. A node failure causes the middleware instance and all applications running on this node to crash. It will be examined how the system reacts on such failures. The aspect of mixed-criticality and the influence of the *Importance* is of particular interest here. Figure 4 shows the number of unhealthy, running and activated applications while Fig. 5 displays the allocation of the applications on the nodes ordered by *Importance*. The adaptation mechanism is able to compensate two node failures completely by restarting the affected applications on other nodes and keeps the system healthy by tuning the least important applications. This is no longer possible when the third node fails. So the adaptation mechanism pauses lower important applications to maintain the healthy execution of the three most important applications on the remaining $Node_A$.

The adaptation mechanism is able to handle the extreme overload situation and behaves according to the application's *Importance* by tuning and or pausing of less important applications for the benefit of the higher important ones. Thus, the mixed-criticality of the system is respected by keeping the most important application alive as long as the resources are still sufficient.

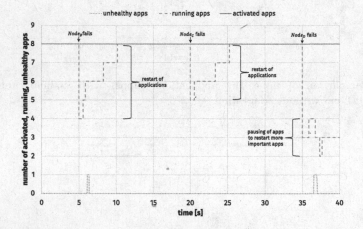

Fig. 4. Node failures - Number of unhealthy and running applications (apps).

4.3   Evaluation 3: Effects of Learning

To evaluate the effect of learning by the reward, an additional rule has been introduced to the basic *Rule Set* which has the same condition as an already existing rule but a different action. While the original action decreases the period and priority of an unhealthy application, the new action increases both values. The *Rule engine* can now learn which of both rules performs better under this condition and therefore has to be preferred.

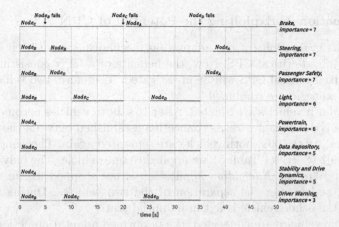

Fig. 5. Node failures - Allocation of applications on nodes ordered by *Importance*

In the chosen evaluation scenario (same as for evaluation 1), the newly added rule is executed first at time 57.65 causing a strongly negative reward. This is reflected in the peak of unhealthy applications at that time in Figs. 6. Therefore, the new rule is never applied again. Instead, the original rule with the same condition is used to bring the system back into a healthy state.

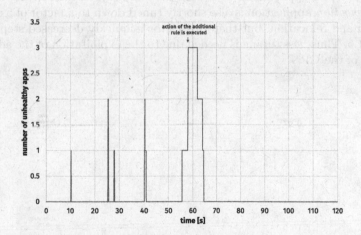

Fig. 6. Learning - Number of unhealthy applications (apps).

Thus, this evaluation shows that *Chameleon* is able to learn from past experience. If a rule has not the desired effect, the reward decreases and thus is no longer applied.

4.4   Evaluation 4: Exploiting the Potential of CPN

The previous evaluations of the adaptation mechanisms have been conducted on a single mixed-critical CPS. Now, the benefits of a CPN consisting of more than one mixed-critical CPS will be investigated. Therefore, two vehicles of the application scenario are combined.

Initially, both vehicles are isolated. After 15 s, both vehicles become interconnected. This is done via a wireless connection established between the $Node_D$ of both vehicles. After 100 s, both vehicles are separated again. The same events as in evaluation 1 (Sect. 4.1 Table 3) are applied to one vehicle. The only difference is that after 100 s the *Navigation* application is not stopped like in evaluation 1, but kept active after the separation of the two vehicles. During the whole evaluation, the other vehicle is left in its initial state.

Before the vehicles are connected, the performed adaptation actions of evaluation 1 and evaluation 4 are identical. Afterwards, vehicle V_1 uses local adaptation actions first. This results in almost the same actions as in evaluation 1. After 59.53 s, a *Chameleon* instance in V_1 exploits the potential of the additional resources due to the connection to V_2 (CPN) and relocates the *Navigation* application to a node of vehicle V_2. Figure 7 shows the benefit of this inter-CPS adaptation by comparing the period of the *Navigation* application in evaluation 1 (CPS) and evaluation 4 (CPN). In evaluation 1, the *Navigation* is tuned down to a factor of 5 after the activation until the system load is decreased (speed up of $Node_A$, stop of applications *Cruise Control* and *Infotainment*). In evaluation 4, the *Navigation* application is also shortly tuned down to a factor of 5 after the activation and relocation, but then this factor is quickly decreased step by step down to 1.5. Thus, less tuning is needed due to the exploitation of the additional resources of the CPN.

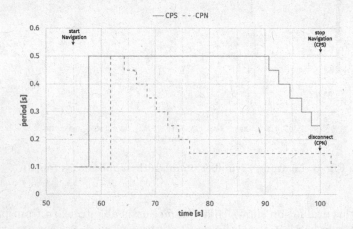

Fig. 7. Comparison of the period of the *Navigation* application in evaluation 1 (CPS) and evaluation 9 (CPN) while *Navigation* is running in both evaluations

After the disconnection of the vehicles at 100 s, the *Navigation* application of V_1 is relocated back to its origin. Since the load in vehicle V_1 meanwhile has decreased (see events at 70, 80 and 90 s in Table 3), the *Navigation* application is able to continue its operation at its original period.

Thus, the adaptation mechanism can use the resources of CPNs and adapt the system through global and local adaptation actions. The exploitation of abilities and resources of the whole CPN leads to more adaptation options and better results.

Many more experiments and evaluations have been conducted which could not be shown here due to page limitations, e.g. healing of scheduling issues, communication overhead, analysis of the real-time behavior, the usability and usability of *Rango*, etc. All these evaluations have shown that *Chameleon* is well able to efficiently manage mixed-critical CPNs to maintain to keep the system within the constraints while respecting the mixed-criticality aspect.

5 Conclusions

Chameleon is a middleware architecture dedicated to autonomously manage CPNs with mixed-critical applications. It uses an LCS-based realization of the MAPE-K loop to provide system adaptation and learning from the outcome of adaptation actions. System constraints can be expressed by normalized *health values* while the rule language *Rango* is used to define adaptation rules in a flexible and intuitive way. The evaluation showed that, having a suitable basic *Rule Set*, *Chameleon* is able to keep the system within the constraints while respecting the mixed-criticality aspect. It can handle overload situations (even better as the human developer was able to), properly react to node failures, learn from the payoff and exploit the additional resources offered by CPNs. Future work will focus on the design of a rule generation engine to automatically define and generate new and improved rules.

References

1. Bai, Y., Huang, Y., Xie, G., Li, R., Chang, W.: ASDYS: dynamic scheduling using active strategies for multifunctional mixed-criticality cyber-physical systems. IEEE Trans. Ind. Inform. **17**(8), 5175–5184 (2021)
2. Brinkschulte, M., Becker, C., Krupitzer, C.: Towards a QoS-aware cyber physical networking middleware architecture. In: 1st International Workshop on Middleware for Lightweight, Spontaneous Environments, MISE 2019, pp. 7–12. Association for Computing Machinery, New York (2019)
3. Brinkschulte, U.: Prototypic implementation and evaluation of an artificial DNA for self-descripting and self-building embedded systems. EURASIP J. Embed. Syst. (2017)
4. Chameleon: Basic Rule Set and Rango Grammer (2023). https://github.com/GrammarRango/Rango.git
5. Feist, M., Becker, C.: A comprehensive approach of a middleware for adaptive mixed-critical cyber-physical networking. In: Proceedings of the PerCom Workshops. IEEE (2022)

6. Feist, M., Breitbach, M., Trotsch, H., Becker, C., Krupitzer, C.: Rango: an intuitive rule language for learning classifier systems in cyber-physical systems. In: 2022 IEEE International Conference on Autonomic Computing and Self-Organizing Systems (ACSOS), Los Alamitos, CA, USA, pp. 31–40. IEEE Computer Society (2022)
7. García-Valls, M., Baldoni, R.: Adaptive middleware design for CPS: considerations on the OS, resource managers, and the network run-time. In: Proceedings of the ARM. ACM (2015)
8. Hu, B., Cao, Z., Zhou, L.: Adaptive real-time scheduling of dynamic multiple-criticality applications on heterogeneous distributed computing systems. In: Proceedings of the CASE. IEEE (2019)
9. Hutter, E., Brinkschulte, U.: Handling assignment priorities to degrade systems in self-organizing task distribution. In: Proceedings of the ISORC. IEEE (2021)
10. Kephart, J.O., Chess, D.M.: The vision of autonomic computing. Computer **36**(1), 41–50 (2003)
11. OMNet++: Discrete Event Simulator (2023). https://omnetpp.org/
12. Ratasich, D., Hoftberger, O., Isakovic, H., Shafique, M., Grosu, R.: A self-healing framework for building resilient cyber-physical systems. In: Proceedings of the ISORC. IEEE (2017)
13. von Renteln, A., Brinkschulte, U., Pacher, M.: The artificial hormone system—an organic middleware for self-organising real-time task allocation. In: Müller-Schloer, C., Schmeck, H., Ungerer, T. (eds.) Organic Computing—A Paradigm Shift for Complex Systems. ASYS, vol. 1, pp. 369–384. Springer, Basel (2011). https://doi.org/10.1007/978-3-0348-0130-0_24
14. Roy, D., Ghosh, S., Zhu, Q., Caccamo, M., Chakraborty, S.: GoodSpread: criticality-aware static scheduling of CPS with multi-QoS resources. In: Proceedings of the RTSS. IEEE (2020)
15. Schmeck, H.: Organic computing - a new vision for distributed embedded systems. In: 8th IEEE International Symposium on Object-Oriented Real-Time Distributed Computing (ISORC 2005), Seattle, USA, pp. 201–203 (2005)
16. Sommer, M., Tomforde, S., Hähner, J.: An organic computing approach to resilient traffic management. In: McCluskey, T.L., Kotsialos, A., Müller, J.P., Klügl, F., Rana, O., Schumann, R. (eds.) Autonomic Road Transport Support Systems. AS, pp. 113–130. Springer, Cham (2016). https://doi.org/10.1007/978-3-319-25808-9_7
17. Stein, A., Maier, R., Rosenbauer, L., Hähner, J.: XCS classifier system with experience replay. In: Proceedings of the GECCO. ACM (2020)
18. Urbanowicz, R.J., Moore, J.H.: Learning classifier systems: a complete introduction, review, and roadmap. J. Artif. Evol. Appl. (2009)
19. Yang, J., Zhang, H., Ling, Y., Pan, C., Sun, W.: Task allocation for wireless sensor network using modified binary particle swarm optimization. Sens. J. **14**(3), 882–892 (2014)
20. Yin, X., Dai, W., Li, B., Chang, L., Li, C.: Cooperative task allocation in heterogeneous wireless sensor networks. Int. J. Distr. Sens. Netw. **13**(10) (2017)

CoLeCTs: Cooperative Learning Classifier Tables for Resource Management in MPSoCs

Klajd Zyla[✉][iD], Florian Maurer[iD], Thomas Wild[iD],
and Andreas Herkersdorf[iD]

Chair of Integrated Systems, Technical University of Munich, Munich, Germany
{klajd.zyla,flo.maurer,thomas.wild,herkersdorf}@tum.de

Abstract. The increasing complexity and unpredictability of emerging applications makes it challenging for multi-processor system-on-chips to satisfy their performance requirements while keeping power consumption within bounds. In order to tackle this problem, the research community has focused on developing dynamic resource managers that aim to optimize runtime parameters, such as clock frequency, voltage and task mapping. There is a large diversity in the approaches proposed in this context, but a class of resource managers that has gained traction recently is that of reinforcement learning-based controllers. In this paper we propose CoLeCTs, a resource manager that enhances the state-of-the-art resource manager SOSA by employing a joint reward assignment function and enabling collaborative information exchange among multiple learning agents. In this manner we tackle the suboptimal determination of local performance targets for heterogeneous applications and allow cooperative decision making for the learning agents. We evaluate and quantify the benefits of our approach via trace-based simulations.

Keywords: MPSoCs · Resource management · DVFS · Reinforcement learning · LCTs · Cooperation

1 Introduction

As applications become more computationally complex and process larger amounts of data, they put higher demands regarding performance on multi-processor system-on-chips (MPSoCs). This comes at the cost of higher power consumption, which increases the failure rate and accelerates the aging process of electronic components. In order to achieve the performance target of an application while fulfilling the power constraints of the platform (MPSoC) where it runs, dynamic frequency scaling (DFS) [29], dynamic voltage and frequency scaling (DVFS) [12] and optimization of task distribution among CPU cores [9] are commonly used. However, it is challenging to effectively employ these methods

We acknowledge the financial support from the DFG Grant HE4584/7-2.

G. Goumas et al. (Eds.): ARCS 2023, LNCS 13949, pp. 215–229, 2023.
https://doi.org/10.1007/978-3-031-42785-5_15

because MPSoCs run different applications with variable workloads and individual goals. Consequently, it is difficult to develop controllers that can build accurate models of the system that take into account the microarchitecture of the MPSoC, device variations, emerging workloads and can then determine the optimal clock frequency, voltage and task distribution at runtime.

In order to solve this problem, ongoing research presents approaches which are **(1) robust** against environmental changes and corner cases [8,26,27], **(2) model-independent** to adapt to emerging workloads [7–9], **(3) scalable** for many-core architectures [8,25,26], and provide **(4) coordination** between the per-core low-level controllers to ensure stable operation [8,11,24].

Coordination helps to distribute the workload between CPU cores by assigning local targets for each core. However, each low-level controller individually attempts to achieve its local optimization target without awareness of the behavior of its peers. This may lead to unstable and globally suboptimal behavior. Furthermore, a suboptimal assignment of the local targets could prevent the resource manager from achieving the common goal (e.g., a video-decoding application runs three tasks on different cores, which are required to process the whole frame).

In order to tackle these issues, we propose cooperative learning classifier tables (CoLeCTs), a resource manager for MPSoCs which builds on SOSA [8], a state-of-the-art reinforcement learning (RL)-based resource manager, and employs cooperation. Cooperation enables the low-level controllers to jointly achieve the requirements of an application without active workload distribution by a supervisory entity. To this end, the optimization targets of the low-level controllers are application-specific and not core-specific (e.g., an application's overall performance target for all cores instead of dividing it into core-specific targets). We evaluate the global impact of control decisions and allow the controllers to constructively work together by exchanging information.

CoLeCTs fulfills the aforementioned properties (1)–(4) in the same way as SOSA [8], but is more optimal by introducing cooperation to the resource manager. We evaluate our design via trace-based simulations in Matlab in a packet processing scenario. The results show that, by using our resource manager, the MPSoC drops no packets, processes packets up to 95.77% faster and needs up to 23.32% less queue space for temporary storage of incoming packets compared to SOSA.

2   Related Work

Classical control-theoretic approaches [20,21,25] deliver optimal behavior in well-defined scenarios with multiple objectives, but are not able to handle changing applications. They also require the definition of a model, on the basis of which control decisions are made.

Heuristic solutions [1,15,18] are model-independent, but likewise lack the ability to adapt to workload changes. Furthermore, coming up with an optimal heuristic, even in a static environment, is challenging.

Machine-learning approaches [2,4,19] have been proven to solve problems with large configuration spaces and can build and update their models at runtime. However, some of them are dependent on the definition of a model and their decisions are usually difficult to interpret. A subclass of machine-learning approaches that has gained traction recently are RL resource managers [8,10,17,30].

Moreover, RL has been applied to enable energy-efficient deep learning inference at the edge [13] and to jointly adjust application- and system-level parameters at runtime to satisfy the Quality-of-Service (QoS) of multi-user High Efficiency Video Coding (HEVC) streaming in power-constrained servers [5]. Other recent fields of application of RL are runtime control of configuration parameters on coarse-grained reconfigurable architectures (CGRA) for sparse linear algebra operations [22], the optimization of the performance of machine learning workloads on mobile and embedded platforms [32] and the design of energy-efficient memory subsystems [16].

In contrast to control-theoretic and heuristic approaches, RL approaches are able to adapt to environment changes and can be model-independent due to their generalizability. Compared to other machine-learning approaches, they do not necessarily need a model of the dynamics of the environment and the decisions are explainable in some approaches. However, they often leave designers with the conundrum of having to make a trade-off between optimality and scalability. This comes as a result of the exponential growth of the state-action space as the complexity of the resource management problem increases with more CPU cores and parameters. Intelligent design decisions are required to address this issue. Moreover, applying RL to MPSoC control with distributed decision making (e.g., one RL agent per core, as in SOSA [8]) results in a multi-agent system. These often lack cooperation between the agents toward achieving the common goal, thus leading to locally optimal, globally suboptimal decisions [23].

3 Background

In this section we describe the resource manager SOSA [8], focusing on the learning process that occurs in the low-level controllers attached to the CPU cores. Then we elaborate on the challenges in SOSA that motivated our work and describe a cooperation method that could be effectively employed to address these challenges.

3.1 SOSA

Figure 1 shows a hierarchical representation of SOSA and its interaction with the MPSoC. Its main components are the *supervisor* in SW and the *learning classifier tables (LCTs)* in HW. The LCTs act as the above-mentioned low-level controllers.

Supervisor. The supervisor, which was introduced in SPECTR [26], provides *self-adaptivity* to the resource manager by exploiting supervisory control theory

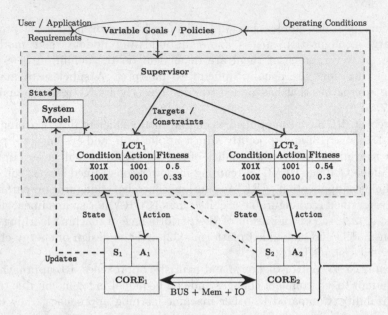

Fig. 1. Hierarchical representation of SOSA [8] on an MPSoC. SOSA components in the shaded region.

(SCT) [28]. This is enabled by translating the user and application requirements (e.g., packets per second in a packet processing scenario) into per-core hardware-related targets and constraints (e.g., an instructions per second (IPS) target and a power constraint). These can be adjusted based on the MPSoC's current state (e.g., high temperature due to defective fan), which is provided by an abstract model of the MPSoC. This system model is updated based on the current sensor values of the real hardware.

LCTs. The hardware-related targets and constraints are used by the *self-optimizing* LCTs, which were initially introduced in ASoC [33]. LCTs make decisions based on a set of rules. Each rule has a *condition*, an *action* (e.g., increase/decrease frequency) and a *fitness*. The condition represents a state or a set of states of the corresponding CPU core. The fitness is an indicator of the rule's effectiveness toward achieving the low-level objective and it corresponds to the action-value function in a typical RL agent. In order to optimize the MPSoC operation with respect to the targets and constraints given by the supervisor, each LCT first senses the current state (e.g. current frequency, utilization, power consumption) of its corresponding core and compares the state to the conditions of the rules. Rules whose conditions match the current state build the match set. Afterwards the LCTs decide which rule of the match set gets applied based on the fitness values. Possible selection strategies are highest fitness wins and roulette wheel (the probability of a rule to be selected is proportional to its fitness value). The action of the selected rule gets forwarded to the actuators. Once an action is applied, its effect gets evaluated based on the received immediate reward. The reward is determined based on the change of the system's state toward the low-level target and the fulfillment of the low-level constraints: '0' for deviating from the target or violating the constraint and '1' for approaching the target and simultaneously fulfilling the constraint. The reward R changes the fitness f of the applied rule, so that past experiences are considered in future decisions: $f(s,a) \leftarrow f(s,a) + \beta (R - f(s,a))$. β represents the impact of the latest reward.

3.2 Challenges in SOSA

As mentioned in Sect. 3.1, the supervisor derives per-core targets and constraints from the application requirements, while the LCTs attempt to independently achieve their local targets through learning. An example would be an image processing application that requires the MPSoC to process incoming images at a frame rate of 30 frames per second (fps). The supervisor figures out that the MPSoC must process 3000 *million instructions per second (MIPS)* in order to achieve the required frame rate. However, the supervisor is not aware of the degree of parallelism of the application, the complexity of the individual threads, etc. Therefore, the overall performance requirement is only combined with the knowledge of available cores (and potentially their individual maximum compute performance, e.g. Arm Big.LITTLE). In order to achieve the required performance while optimizing power consumption, the supervisor attempts to distribute the workload among the CPU cores uniformly/proportional to the compute performance. In our image processing example with three identical cores, the required processing rate of 3000 *MIPS* (global target) gets divided by three. Consequently, each LCT manages its CPU core, such that it achieves a performance of 1000 *MIPS* (local target). The idea behind this approach is that the LCTs will by chance discover the workload distribution that allows each core to achieve its local target and thus the global performance requirement. The division of global goals into subgoals makes use of emergent behavior [17], which causes two problems.

The first problem is the potentially suboptimal determination of per-core low-level targets by the supervisor. While the assignment of the same performance target to every CPU core might be optimal for fully parallelizable homogeneous applications, it's not efficient for other types of applications. For instance, single-threaded applications are composed of tasks that run on only one CPU core at a time. If all three cores of a CPU have the same target, two of them will have nothing to do and thus won't reach their target, while the one where the task is running will meet its target, but this won't be sufficient to reach the global performance target. In order to solve this problem, SOSA would need a more complex supervisor that is aware of several low-level application metrics, like the degree of parallelism. These are often not available. Another scenario where the supervisor makes a suboptimal assignment of targets are heterogeneous applications with a mixture of compute- and memory-intensive tasks where no task allocation results in an equal workload distribution. E.g., let's assume a three-core CPU where a core runs a compute-intensive task, while the other two run memory-intensive tasks. The latter perform few computations and thus find it difficult to reach their performance targets. Hence, their agents will probably increase their clock frequencies, which might lead to a significant increase in power consumption with little or no performance improvement if more access contentions to the shared bus and memory occur. As a result, the MPSoC again won't reach the global performance target. Furthermore, the LCTs receive feedback only regarding the achievement of their local targets. This could result in the development of greedy local behaviors that are globally suboptimal due to the lack of incentive to help other agents achieve their local goals [23].

The second problem is that in many cases emergent behavior is unstable [6] and globally suboptimal. In our case this means that the agent's policies might be unstable and they might not converge to a globally optimal policy. The reason is that an agent could misinterpret the rewards it receives because the effect of its action on the environment depends on the unknown states of the other agents and the actions they take due to the access to shared resources, such as interconnect and memory. Even if the agents find the optimal workload distribution by chance, they might not realize it and thus their policies won't necessarily converge to it. A simple example that illustrates this point is when an agent in a deterministic environment receives different reward values for the same action it applies in a certain state, because the joint state of the other agents and the joint action that the other agents apply is different in each learning step. Furthermore, since the other agents continually change their policies, the environment appears nonstationary to the agent under observation. This might cause the policy of this agent to oscillate or to converge to a globally suboptimal policy.

3.3   Cooperation in LCTs

Cooperation methods directly address the need for cooperation in decentralized systems with shared resources. Tan identified and studied three general cooperation methods between learning agents [31]. First, agents can share instantaneous information, such as states, actions and rewards. Secondly, agents can share information about past experiences in the form of episodes, which are defined as sequences of $\langle state, action, reward \rangle$ previously encountered by the agent that others may not have experienced yet. Thirdly, agents can share learned policies. Although inter-agent communication can increase their learning rates and optimize their policies, it incurs costs in terms of computational resources and power consumption. Hence, a cost-benefit trade-off is necessary. We employ a modified version of *immediate action notification* [31] because it's effective, simple and does not impair the explainability of the LCTs.

In regular immediate action notification we assign ordinal numbers to the agents. In every learning step the first agent takes an action and informs the other agents about it. The second agent selects its action by taking into account the action selected by the first agent, so the second agent basically adapts to the first one. Then, it informs the remaining agents about the selected action and so on. Every agent is aware of the current individual states of the other agents. Figure 2 illustrates a decentralized system that consists of three learning agents and applies immediate action notification.

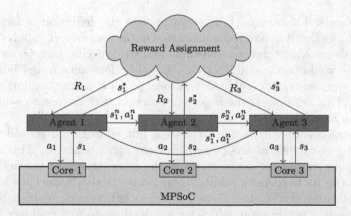

Fig. 2. Decentralized multi-agent system that consists of three learning agents and applies immediate action notification: s_i/a_i denotes an individual state/action of agent i; s_i^* denotes the part of the state that is directly related to the achievement of the goal of agent i; R_i denotes the reward that the reward assignment function allocates to agent i

4 Design

In this section we elaborate on the design changes that we made to the resource manager presented in SOSA [8]. They address the two main challenges mentioned in Subsect. 3.2. In principle there are two solutions to the first problem of suboptimal determination of local low-level objectives for single-threaded and heterogeneous applications.

The first solution is to equip the supervisor with knowledge of the type of tasks that run on each CPU core. This would allow it to assign different performance targets to each core based on the computational intensity of the tasks it executes. This approach has some issues. First, this knowledge is often not available. The supervisor usually receives a high-level goal, such as a frame rate in image processing applications, and it translates it into a global performance target. Secondly, even if the processing demands of each task are known, a CPU core usually does not continuously execute a single task, but it switches between tasks with different computational intensities. Hence, the supervisor would have to change the local performance target whenever the currently executed task changes. Dynamically determining the performance target is inefficient due to the additional delay that the software implementation of the supervisor introduces.

The second solution to the first problem is to let the supervisor simply translate the high-level goal into a global performance target and derive no local performance targets. In CoLeCTs this solution is the first modification we apply to the resource manager presented in SOSA. In this manner we remove the restriction imposed by the local performance targets and reward any combination of CPU-core performance values that leads to the achievement of the global performance target. This approach does not prevent the definition of local targets or constraints when it makes sense to do so. On the contrary, it enables a combination of system-wide targets/constraints and core-specific targets/constraints. An example would be the definition of a global performance target bounded by a global power constraint combined with local power constraints allotted to each CPU core. This example is the objective function that we use to evaluate our approach in Sect. 5.

The above-mentioned modification does not address the second problem, which is the instability of the principle of emergent behavior. This is caused by the missing awareness of the states of the other agents or the actions they take. This can be tackled by adding cooperation methods, such as immediate action notification. For CoLeCTs we propose a lightweight, scalable version of immediate action notification, which we add to the resource manager.

As in immediate action notification, we assign ordinal numbers to the agents. The agents operate sequentially according to these numbers. This sequential operation is affordable since it takes about an order of magnitude less than the decision-making period of our hardware-based LCTs. In multi-core architectures with shared bus/memory, the overall memory access rate as well as the overall power consumption are highly correlated with the operating frequencies of the cores. Therefore, forwarding the future operating frequencies of the cores allows the ordinally following agents to apply beneficial DVFS decisions toward achieving the overall performance target without violating the power constraints.

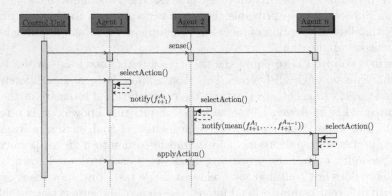

Fig. 3. Lightweight version of immediate action notification

As depicted in Fig. 3, in every learning step each agent selects a frequency change as an action $(a_t = \Delta f_t)$, computes the mean value over the future frequencies $\left(f_{t+1}^{A_i} = f_t^{A_i} + a_t^{A_i}\right)$ of the cores of all the ordinally preceding agents and of its core and forwards it to the ordinally following agents. The ordinally following agents take this value into account when selecting their actions. The idea behind the choice of the mean value instead of the individual frequencies is that it contains the essential information, but scales significantly better with the increasing amount of cores in terms of the potential state space.

We can illustrate the benefit of this cooperation method for the performance of the multi-core architecture with an example. Memory access conflicts degrade the performance of the CPU. Hence, when the third agent knows that the CPU cores of the first two agents are going to operate at a high frequency in the next period and thus probably access the shared memory very often, it eventually learns via RL to decrease the frequency of its CPU core in order to reduce access conflicts. One can think of a scenario where the first two agents always keep their CPU-core frequencies high and the third agent has to keep its core frequency low in order to adapt to them. This would in turn cause the first two CPU cores to consume more power and process their tasks faster. Such a scenario is very unlikely to happen for two reasons. First, we limit the extent to which load imbalances might occur by defining local power constraints. Second, since the agents use the roulette-wheel selection algorithm to choose the actions, exploration of equally or even more beneficial states is very likely to occur, thus making such conditions temporary.

5   Evaluation

In this section we evaluate CoLeCTs via trace-based simulations in Matlab based on these properties: optimality, robustness and reproducibility.

5.1   Simulation Setup

We assume that the MPSoC, which contains three LEON3 CPU cores [3], processes incoming packets in real time in a network node. Each packet requires the processing of three types of tasks: (1) *IntMM* [14] is a memory-intensive Stanford benchmark that multiplies integer matrices; (2) *FloatMM* [14] is a memory-intensive Stanford benchmark that multiplies floating-point matrices; (3) *CPUIntensive* is a compute-intensive benchmark that adds two integer values in every clock cycle. Each packet is assigned to an application that is composed of the following sequential task graph: $(1) IntMM \rightarrow (2) CPUIntensive \rightarrow (3) FloatMM \rightarrow (4) CPUIntensive \rightarrow (5) FloatMM \rightarrow (6) IntMM$. Each unit of the task graph is statically mapped to a CPU core in design time. In our experiments we do not employ task migration as a possible action in order to demonstrate the ability of the resource manager to cope with scenarios where no ideal task distribution among CPU cores can be found. Each core has its own FIFO task queue and we ensure that a task can be processed only after its predecessor has been processed. We set the queue size to 1000 entries.

We evaluate CoLeCTs by employing two different task mappings. In the first scenario each CPU core processes two different tasks, while in the second one each of them executes the same task. In both cases we set power constraints relative to the maximum power consumption, i.e. core-specific constraints equal to 85% and a system-wide constraint equal to 75%. We also define a system-wide performance target based on the mean inter-packet gap and the number of instructions that the application that is assigned to the packet requires.

The individual state of each agent is composed of the current frequency, utilization and performance of the CPU core that it controls. The actions that each agent can take are: increase/decrease frequency by one/two step(s) and do nothing.

We use six use-case-oriented metrics as indicators of the optimality of CoLeCTs:

- Mean amount of dropped packets
- Mean amount of processed packets
- Mean amount of processing time per packet
- Mean queue fill level
- Mean amount of system-wide power constraint violations
- Mean amount of core-specific power constraint violations

We show the robustness of our resource manager by periodically varying the inter-packet gap to random values up to 20 ms around the mean, which we set at 95 ms. We keep the performance target constant, thus showing that our resource manager can handle short-term workload fluctuations. A supervisor as in SOSA is necessary only for long-term variations. We show the reproducibility of the results by performing 20 simulation runs for each scenario and computing the standard deviation of each optimality indicator. We inject around 2500 packets in each run and simulate a period of 237,5 s.

5.2   Results

Figure 4 depicts the performance of SOSA and CoLeCTs regarding the aforementioned optimality metrics when mapping two different tasks to the same CPU core. CoLeCTs outperforms SOSA in five metrics, while performing worse in one of them – the mean amount of system-wide power constraint violations.

In this scenario core 1 and core 2 have a higher processing workload than core 3 (CPUIntensive is one of the tasks they execute), but SOSA assigns the same performance target, which is derived from the processing workload of the application, to all CPU cores. This means that core 1 and core 2 process at a slower rate than they should, which leads to the total IPS being far below the global performance target, as shown in Fig. 5a. As a result, their task queues fill up and incoming tasks are eventually dropped. When a task is dropped, the corresponding packet is also dropped. In contrast to SOSA, CoLeCTs defines a global performance target based on the processing demands of the application. This allows the CPU cores to tailor their processing rate to the workload of the assigned tasks and jointly achieve the global target, as shown in Fig. 5b. The simulation results show that by using CoLeCTs, the MPSoC drops no packets, processes packets on average 90.91% faster and the queue fill levels are on average 21.5% lower compared to SOSA. Moreover, our resource manager leads to 50.8% more processed packets and 0.667% less core-specific power constraint violations, but 0.665% more system-wide power constraint violations.

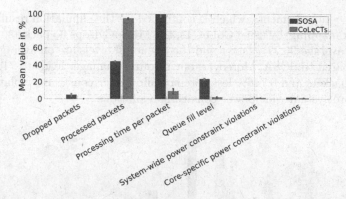

Fig. 4. Performance of SOSA and CoLeCTs regarding six use-case-oriented optimality metrics while mapping different tasks to the same CPU core. The processing time includes the queuing time. The mean values are computed over 20 simulations runs. The error bars indicate the standard deviation of each optimality metric. In order to obtain a metric that can be measured in %, we set the mean amount of processing time per packet that SOSA achieves to 100%.

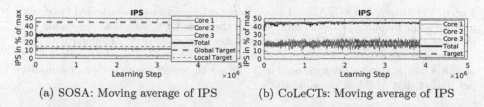

(a) SOSA: Moving average of IPS   (b) CoLeCTs: Moving average of IPS

Fig. 5. Moving average of the IPS achieved by the CPUs managed by SOSA and CoLeCTs during a simulation run for the first task mapping

Figure 6 illustrates the performance of SOSA and CoLeCTs regarding the aforementioned optimality metrics when mapping twice the same task to the same CPU core. As in the first scenario, CoLeCTs outperforms SOSA in five metrics, while performing worse in one of them - the mean amount of system-wide power constraint violations.

In this scenario core 2 processes the compute-intensive task CPUIntensive, while the other cores process memory-intensive tasks. Since SOSA allocates the same performance target to all CPU cores, core 2 processes at a slower rate than it should, which again leads to the total IPS being far below the global performance target, as shown in Fig. 7a. On the other hand, CoLeCTs allows the CPU cores to tailor their processing rate to the workload of the assigned tasks and cooperatively achieve the global target, as shown in Fig. 7b. Since different tasks impose different processing workloads on the CPU cores, assigning the same task to the same core leads to larger discrepancies in processing workloads among the CPU cores. This results in a less optimal determination of core-specific performance targets by SOSA than in the first task mapping. Consequently, it is reasonable to expect that our resource manager delivers larger performance improvements, which is confirmed by the simulation results. In the second task mapping, by using CoLeCTs, the MPSoC drops no packets, processes packets on average 95.77% faster and the queue fill levels are on average 23.32% lower compared to SOSA. Moreover, our resource manager leads to 71.2% more processed packets and 0.746% less core-specific power constraint violations, but 0.058% more system-wide power constraint violations.

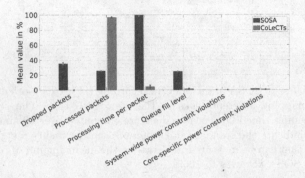

Fig. 6. Performance of SOSA and CoLeCTs regarding six use-case-oriented optimality metrics while mapping twice the same task to the same CPU core. The processing time includes the queuing time. The mean values are computed over 20 simulations runs. The error bars indicate the standard deviation of each optimality metric. In order to obtain a metric that can be measured in %, we set the mean amount of processing time per packet that SOSA achieves to 100%.

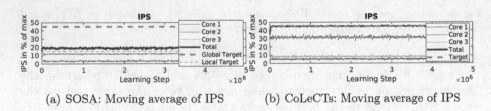

(a) SOSA: Moving average of IPS   (b) CoLeCTs: Moving average of IPS

Fig. 7. Moving average of the IPS achieved by the CPUs managed by SOSA and CoLeCTs during a simulation run for the second task mapping

In both scenarios the amount of processed packets and the amount of dropped packets do not add up to 100% of all the injected packets because there are still tasks in the queues when the simulation ends. Furthermore, the standard deviation of SOSA and CoLeCTs over all simulation runs for each metric is similarly low with a mean of 0.79% and 0.67% respectively.

6   Conclusion and Outlook

In this paper we propose CoLeCTs, a cooperation-enhanced resource manager with a joint reward assignment function that addresses the challenges in SOSA.

In order to tackle the suboptimal allocation of low-level objectives to the CPU cores, we translate the system goal into a system-wide performance target and define no local performance targets. This design change allows the CPU cores to tailor their processing rate to the workload of the assigned tasks. We also introduce cooperation to the resource manager by employing a lightweight version of immediate action notification that scales well. The simulation results show that CoLeCTs is superior to SOSA in almost all optimality metrics, while retaining key features of state-of-the-art resource managers - robustness, model-independence, scalability and reproducibility.

Future work could address the implementation and evaluation of our resource manager on an FPGA to confirm the simulation results. Moreover, one could extend the existing system with other types of actions, such as task migration. In this context, a promising idea is to apply multi-step RL to consider the long-term influence of the applied actions. An interesting research area is the investigation of model-based RL algorithms, which could increase the optimality of the resource manager by allowing the agents to not just learn by trial and error, but also to plan their actions depending on the running application.

Acknowledgement. We thank our IPF project partners at TU Braunschweig and UC Irvine, Rolf Ernst, Fadi Kurdahi, Nikil Dutt and their teams, as well as our colleagues at TUM for their valuable feedback and suggestions during our discussions.

References

1. Askarizade Haghighi, M., Maeen, M., Haghparast, M.: An energy-efficient dynamic resource management approach based on clustering and meta-heuristic algorithms in cloud computing IaaS platforms. Wirel. Pers. Commun. **104**(4), 1367–1391 (2019)
2. Beckmann, N., Sanchez, D.: Maximizing cache performance under uncertainty. In: 2017 IEEE International Symposium on High Performance Computer Architecture (HPCA), pp. 109–120. IEEE (2017)
3. Cobham Gaisler AB: GRLIB IP Library User's Manual (2022). https://www.gaisler.com/products/grlib/grlib.pdf, version 2022.2
4. Costero, L., Iranfar, A., Zapater, M., Igual, F.D., Olcoz, K., Atienza, D.: MAMUT: multi-agent reinforcement learning for efficient real-time multi-user video transcoding. In: 2019 Design, Automation & Test in Europe Conference & Exhibition (DATE), pp. 558–563. IEEE (2019)
5. Costero, L., Iranfar, A., Zapater, M., Igual, F.D., Olcoz, K., Atienza, D.: Resource management for power constrained HEVC transcoding using reinforcement learning. IEEE Trans. Parallel Distrib. Syst. **31**(12), 2834–2850 (2020)
6. Cucker, F., Smale, S.: Emergent behavior in flocks. IEEE Trans. Autom. Control **52**(5), 852–862 (2007)
7. Deng, Q., Meisner, D., Bhattacharjee, A., Wenisch, T.F., Bianchini, R.: CoScale: coordinating CPU and memory system DVFS in server systems. In: 2012 45th Annual IEEE/ACM International Symposium on Microarchitecture, pp. 143–154. IEEE (2012)

8. Donyanavard, B., et al.: SOSA: self-optimizing learning with self-adaptive control for hierarchical system-on-chip management. In: Proceedings of the 52nd Annual IEEE/ACM International Symposium on Microarchitecture, pp. 685–698 (2019)

9. Donyanavard, B., Mück, T., Sarma, S., Dutt, N.: SPARTA: runtime task allocation for energy efficient heterogeneous manycores. In: 2016 International Conference on Hardware/Software Codesign and System Synthesis (CODES+ ISSS), pp. 1–10. IEEE (2016)

10. Dutt, N., Kurdahi, F.J., Ernst, R., Herkersdorf, A.: Conquering MPSoC complexity with principles of a self-aware information processing factory. In: Proceedings of the Eleventh IEEE/ACM/IFIP International Conference on Hardware/Software Codesign and System Synthesis, pp. 1–4 (2016)

11. Gupta, U., et al.: Adaptive performance prediction for integrated GPUs. In: 2016 IEEE/ACM International Conference on Computer-Aided Design (ICCAD), pp. 1–8. ACM (2016)

12. Kim, W., Gupta, M.S., Wei, G.Y., Brooks, D.: System level analysis of fast, per-core DVFS using on-chip switching regulators. In: 2008 IEEE 14th International Symposium on High Performance Computer Architecture, pp. 123–134. IEEE (2008)

13. Kim, Y.G., Wu, C.J.: Autoscale: energy efficiency optimization for stochastic edge inference using reinforcement learning. In: 2020 53rd Annual IEEE/ACM International Symposium on Microarchitecture (MICRO), pp. 1082–1096. IEEE (2020)

14. LLVM: LLVM "test-suite" repository (2022). https://github.com/llvm/llvm-test-suite/tree/main/SingleSource/Benchmarks/Stanford

15. Ma, Y., Zhou, J., Chantem, T., Dick, R.P., Wang, S., Hu, X.S.: Online resource management for improving reliability of real-time systems on "Big-Little" type MPSoCs. IEEE Trans. Comput.-Aided Des. Integrated Circuits Syst. **39**(1), 88–100 (2018)

16. Maity, B., Donyanavard, B., Dutt, N.: Self-aware memory management for emerging energy-efficient architectures. In: 2020 11th International Green and Sustainable Computing Workshops (IGSC), pp. 1–8. IEEE (2020)

17. Maurer, F., Donyanavard, B., Rahmani, A.M., Dutt, N., Herkersdorf, A.: Emergent control of MPSoC operation by a hierarchical supervisor/reinforcement learning approach. In: 2020 Design, Automation & Test in Europe Conference & Exhibition (DATE), pp. 1562–1567. IEEE (2020)

18. del Mestre Martins, A.L., da Silva, A.H.L., Rahmani, A.M., Dutt, N., Moraes, F.G.: Hierarchical adaptive multi-objective resource management for many-core systems. J. Syst. Architect. **97**, 416–427 (2019)

19. Mishra, N., Imes, C., Lafferty, J.D., Hoffmann, H.: CALOREE: learning control for predictable latency and low energy. ACM SIGPLAN Not. **53**(2), 184–198 (2018)

20. Moazzemi, K., Maity, B., Yi, S., Rahmani, A.M., Dutt, N.: HESSLE-FREE: heterogeneous systems leveraging fuzzy control for runtime resource management. ACM Trans. Embed. Comput. Syst. (TECS) **18**(5s), 1–19 (2019)

21. Mück, T., Donyanavard, B., Moazzemi, K., Rahmani, A.M., Jantsch, A., Dutt, N.: Design methodology for responsive and robust MIMO control of heterogeneous multicores. IEEE Trans. Multi-Scale Comput. Syst. **4**(4), 944–951 (2018)

22. Pal, S., Amarnath, A., Feng, S., O'Boyle, M., Dreslinski, R., Dubach, C.: SparseAdapt: runtime control for sparse linear algebra on a reconfigurable accelerator. In: 54th Annual IEEE/ACM International Symposium on Microarchitecture, MICRO-54, pp. 1005–1021 (2021)

23. Panait, L., Luke, S.: Cooperative multi-agent learning: the state of the art. Auton. Agent Multi-Agent Syst. **11**(3), 387–434 (2005)

24. Pothukuchi, R.P., Ansari, A., Voulgaris, P., Torrellas, J.: Using multiple input, multiple output formal control to maximize resource efficiency in architectures. In: 2016 ACM/IEEE 43rd Annual International Symposium on Computer Architecture (ISCA), pp. 658–670. IEEE (2016)

25. Pothukuchi, R.P., Pothukuchi, S.Y., Voulgaris, P., Torrellas, J.: Yukta: multilayer resource controllers to maximize efficiency. In: 2018 ACM/IEEE 45th Annual International Symposium on Computer Architecture (ISCA), pp. 505–518. IEEE (2018)

26. Rahmani, A.M., et al.: SPECTR: formal supervisory control and coordination for many-core systems resource management. In: Proceedings of the Twenty-Third International Conference on Architectural Support for Programming Languages and Operating Systems, pp. 169–183 (2018)

27. Rahmani, A.M., Haghbayan, M.H., Miele, A., Liljeberg, P., Jantsch, A., Tenhunen, H.: Reliability-aware runtime power management for many-core systems in the dark silicon era. IEEE Trans. Very Large Scale Integration (VLSI) Syst. **25**(2), 427–440 (2016)

28. Ramadge, P.J., Wonham, W.M.: The control of discrete event systems. Proc. IEEE **77**(1), 81–98 (1989)

29. da Rosa, T.R., Larréa, V., Calazans, N., Moraes, F.G.: Power consumption reduction in MPSoCs through DFS. In: 2012 25th Symposium on Integrated Circuits and Systems Design (SBCCI), pp. 1–6. IEEE (2012)

30. Sadighi, A., et al.: Design methodologics for enabling self-awareness in autonomous systems. In: 2018 Design, Automation & Test in Europe Conference & Exhibition (DATE), pp. 1532–1537. IEEE (2018)

31. Tan, M.: Multi-agent reinforcement learning: independent vs. cooperative agents. In: Proceedings of the Tenth International Conference on Machine Learning, pp. 330–337 (1993)

32. Xun, L., Tran-Thanh, L., Al-Hashimi, B.M., Merrett, G.V.: Optimising resource management for embedded machine learning. In: 2020 Design, Automation & Test in Europe Conference & Exhibition (DATE), pp. 1556–1561. IEEE (2020)

33. Zeppenfeld, J., Herkersdorf, A.: Applying autonomic principles for workload management in multi-core systems on chip. In: Proceedings of the 8th ACM International Conference on Autonomic Computing, pp. 3–10 (2011)

Hardware Acceleration

Improved Condition Handling in CGRAs with Complex Loop Support

Ramon Wirsch[✉] and Christian Hochberger

Computer Systems Group, Technische Universität Darmstadt,
Merckstr. 25, 64283 Darmstadt, Germany
{wirsch,hochberger}@rs.tu-darmstadt.de

Abstract. Coarse Grained Reconfigurable Arrays (CGRA) have become a popular technology to realize compute accelerators. CGRAs can be found in High-Performance systems and also in embedded systems. In order to provide the highest speedup, they need to support conditional statements and nested loops. This requires a management of conditions within the CGRA. This management can be done in different ways. In this contribution, we compare two such concepts and evaluate the impact that these concepts have on the achievable clock frequency, the required resources and the change of schedules. It turns out, that with our new condition management and the accompanying advanced schedule, we can save more than 20% of runtime.

Keywords: CGRA · Scheduling · Compute Accelerator · Nested Loops

1 Introduction and Motivation

Coarse Grained Reconfigurable Arrays (CGRA) have become a wide spread technology to speed up applications. The part of the application that is mapped to the CGRA is called kernel. CGRAs contain an array of processing elements (PE) that work in parallel and can exchange data with neighboring PEs. The exact definition of neighbors can be very different depending on the nature of the CGRA. Typically, CGRAs are also able to access the main memory autonomously (either through address generators/memory access units or by including caches in some PEs). Control of PEs can either be centralized (providing context numbers/addresses to the PEs) or it can be realized distributed as a kind of program in the PEs. Most CGRAs allow switching the context from cycle to cycle and thus enable larger kernels. Few CGRAs limit the execution to a single context, such that all computations must be spatialy distributed.

Since CGRAs execute the kernels in parallel, there are some natural competitors: Superscalar and VLIW processors. In contrast to superscalar processors, CGRAs offer more flexibility to control the operations that are executed in parallel. At the same time, they are more efficient than VLIW processors, as no central bottleneck like a single register file is present.

G. Goumas et al. (Eds.): ARCS 2023, LNCS 13949, pp. 233–247, 2023.
https://doi.org/10.1007/978-3-031-42785-5_16

We believe that the most efficient type of CGRA allows the mapping of nested loops and also allows control flow in the loop body. Thus, conditions for these decisions must be computed, aggregated and stored. To this end, different concepts in the CGRAs can be found.

In this contribution, we compare two such concepts for condition management with each other. We evaluate the impact on the clock frequency, the consequences they have on scheduling and the overall impact on whole kernels.

The paper is structured as follows. Section 2 presents how conditional code and loops are handled by various types of CGRAs. Two alternative concepts for handling conditions are described and compared in Sect. 3. These two concepts are then evaluated in Sect. 4. Ultimately, we give a conclusion and outlook onto future work in Sect. 5.

2   Related Work

Some CGRAs, like [1,9] forgo any conditional execution or control flow on PEs entirely. DySER [4,5] as CGRA architecture is similar to our CGRA in terms of the spatial operating principles and its ability to predicate single operations, so that multiple alternative branches of sequential code can be scheduled in parallel. Since DySER targets being an "in-core" accelerator, it can rely on the host processor for handling loops and control flow. The accelerator itself can only handle predicating operations as a form of speculatively executing all branches in parallel and only using the correct result further. It only maps the contents of excerpts of loops onto the architecture. It does not need the temporal configuration that lets the CGRA execute different operations over time. ADRES [7,8] also only handles loops and complex logic by virtue of being the part of a VLIW processor with a shared register file.

HiPREP [6] has PEs more akin to RISC cores. They can operate quite independently, using their own register file and instruction/context memory. Each PE can handle its own control flow and operate completely independently of others. The architecture includes synchronization mechanisms to let diverging PEs cooperate with another. Memory accesses are handled by separate Address-Generator-Units. While our PEs can also be configured with enough internal operand ports to execute operations autonomously, without the input from neighbors and theoretically have the hardware for diverging control flow, they lack synchronization facilities. The CGRA is intended to operate in lock-step, with the scheduler assigning each PE actions for a shared timestep. Conditions are thus handled centrally and distributed to all PEs from there. The hardware's ability to have diverging control flow on each PE is only used to compress idle steps. A single PE can idle without this taking up an explicit NOP context, but it will still remain in lock-step with all other PEs. Other than that, our context memories have a lot more entries to contain larger kernels encompassing many loops and entire loop-hierarchies. Memory accesses are handled from within the CGRA. The addresses are calculated using the regular integer operations and used by a subset of PEs that have additional access to their own cache or memory port.

CGRA-ME [2,3] has a similar integration with a host-processor to us. It also requires predication as means to replace control flow in the schedulers input representation. While CGRA-ME supports temporal configuration with different contexts over time, it does not support any control flow in regard to those different contexts and can therefore not map complex loop structures.

Previously mentioned architectures share that they are designed for static generation of kernels. A kernel's scope is either determined manually or chosen without knowledge of their dynamic behavior. On the other hand, this approach typically provides more type information and can be integrated into existing compilers and reuse existing vectorization methods. The time to map and generate binary contexts for the target CGRA is much less relevant and a more optimal scheduling approach can be used.

AMIDAR-CGRA [12,13] takes a very different approach to generating kernels. It was designed for dynamic binary translation, integrated into the AMIDAR processor. Kernels are to be generated only from the binary instructions the host processor would normally execute. This motivates changes to the CGRA architecture. A quicker and more simple mapping to the target CGRA is important, as kernels are only discovered at runtime and all translation efforts take away processing power from the host processor, much like Just-In-Time optimization popularized by Java Virtual Machines. The PE architecture is geared towards temporal configuration of longer kernels spanning hundreds of contexts with support for very regular nested loops as they can occur in standard Java Byte Code. Like most CGRAs if-else constructs are still represented using predication, branching support is only present to the extend needed to map regular do-while loops. Our CGRA is based on this original work, but our goal to develop a host-architecture-agnostic CGRA [11], requires it to be more flexible in handling loop control flow and conditions. Modern, optimizing compilers, such as GCC and LLVM will output code that does not hold to the simplistic loop structures present in Java Byte Code.

3   Condition Handling in CGRAs

Figure 1 shows the general structure of the CGRA HW, based on [13] and [12]. Each PE by default has its own context unit that has an individual context counter (i.e. active context). This is done to localize storage and to allow compressing idle contexts. If a single PE will idle multiple timesteps, those contexts do not to take up a full context cach, but can be combined into an *idle count* that is stored with the last active context. The context units are generic and multiple PEs could easily share one, if idle compression is not desired or both PEs tend to idle at the same time. While technically, each PE could operate relatively independently, the CGRA is missing synchronization mechanisms for diverging PEs and schedules all PEs in lockstep. Our PEs themselves support predicated execution of operations while the context units support relative jumps and conditional branches. The hardware could reproduce arbitrary, direct control flow, just no indirect control flow.

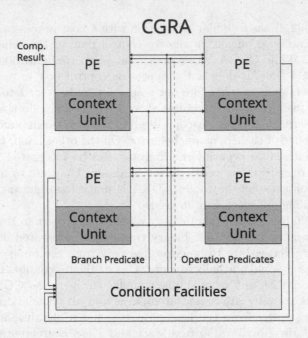

Fig. 1. Shows condition facilities, PEs of a CGRA that can achieve predication of operations and arbitrary control flow capable of nested loop structures

3.1 CBox

Previous work used a centralized, so-called Condition Box, *CBox* in short, for all handling of conditions and supplying predication signals to PEs and the context units. The CBox collects all results of comparisons from all PEs. It contains a 1-bit wide register file of configurable size to store conditions, integrates logic operations such as AND, OR and NOT. It also has one or more predicate outputs that can be used to predicate branches to different contexts or as operation inputs to predicate/influence single operations on the various PEs. Internally, the CBox consists of multiple *EvalBlocks*, shown in Fig. 2 that each contain the logic operations, access to all inputs and producing one regular predicate, but share the same register file. The gate structure of the EvalBlock was originally designed to handle the kinds of operations that occur in Java Byte Code. Due to the short-circuiting behavior of the code, arbitrary combinations of operations cannot occur as a single operation. In Byte Code they will always be split by branches and thus essentially form a hierarchy of nested if-operations. The Eval-Block structure is very efficient at handling those. It can take condition logic stemming from nested if-operations and compute the conditions needed for the if- and else-cases in the same timestep as the underlying comparison operation computes its result. Our CGRA is however no longer constrained to Java Byte Code. In optimized assembly code, logic operations can get more complicated, which requires replicated comparisons in order to still be mappable to the Eval-

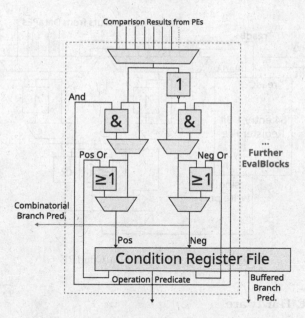

Fig. 2. Shows internals of CBox/one EvalBlock. In both *combinatorial branch predication* and *buffered branch predication* variants

Block. Memory address aliasing checks also consist of a more complex tree of logic operations that would map perfectly to the parallel PEs of a CGRA and are penalized heavily by needing to find a sequential order of the comparisons. The existing EvalBlock implementation can never and-combine two arbitrary conditions. One of the inputs needs to be precomputed and already stored, while the other input must be newly produced by a comparison that finishes in the same timestep.

The limited ability to supply predicates to PEs of only 1 per EvalBlock was already observed [11] to pose a bottleneck for larger CGRAs, where ideally operations from both if- and else-branch will execute simultaneously, requiring more than one predicate in the same timestep. Simply increasing the count of EvalBlocks, as intended by the original designer does not scale well, as each EvalBlock already requires 2 write ports and at least 3 read ports of the shared register file. Such a register file is not efficiently mappable to common FPGAs, which are used for prototyping.

The original CBox was designed with both, the combinatorial and buffered branch predicate, but the buffered predicate was not used by the scheduling, since the input format into the schedule was not designed for it and this always incurred one unnecessary timestep penalty for every branch operation.

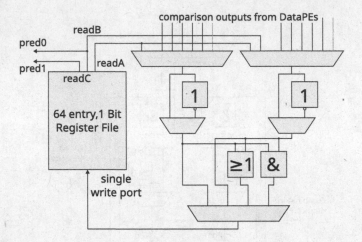

Fig. 3. Shows internals of a CondPE

3.2   CondPE Hardware

To overcome the previously described limitations of the CBox, we propose a new structure for implementing the condition facilities of our CGRA as a replacement. The new implementation is based on the main principles of the PEs and are thus named ConditionPEs or CondPE in short, as opposed to the traditional DataPEs. The proposed replacement shown in Fig. 3 still fits the overall structure shown in Fig. 1. It requires only changes internal to the handling and scheduling of conditions. A single CondPE is intended to be a replacement for a CBox with a single EvalBlock. More CondPEs can be added to the CGRA as needed. Each CondPE will have its own register file and will be part of a "condition-interconnect" much like the DataPEs are. This may require routing of conditions from one CondPE to another, like is already required for DataPEs, that often require their neighbors to supply operands. Consequently, our scheduling approach already supports routing of any irregular interconnect where every PE is reachable from every other unit by some number of routing hops. Furthermore, we designed the CondPE to be paired with a commonly available and optimized 3-read-1-write register file. We swap the specialized structure of the EvalBlock with a generic condition logic unit that can forward, and-combine and or-combine any 2 operands, each of which can either be supplied from the internal register file, a neighboring CondPE or a DataPEs comparison result. Each operand can also be inverted independently of the other. Since more registers can be added by adding more CondPEs, we also fix the register file size to 64 entries, which is efficiently mapped to the distributed memory modern Xilinx FPGAs support. Because all supported logic operations are actually commutative, the operand multiplexers do not each need to have every comparison result from every DataPE or every predicate output from every neighboring CondPE available. We instead distribute those inputs from external sources evenly across the two operands to reduce the size of those MUXs. The scheduler will need to swap operands during scheduling in order to map every combination of locally stored condition with every newly produced comparison result. The new hardware allows many actions, the previous one was not capable of. Combinatorially available comparison results from DataPEs can now be stored directly and processed further at a later time. There are no intermediary results that cannot be stored in the register file when a combination of logic operations is required. Both where found to be big limitations in previous work. Two separate comparisons can even be combined combinatorially in the same timestep, if the comparisons are bound to DataPEs in a way where they arrive via separate operands.

The CondPEs allow a more distributed architecture which also enables new kinds of CGRA compositions. CondPEs could be localized to only a partition of DataPEs. Each partition could execute independently of others, as long as at least a single CondPE is present in the partition. This partitioning concept could be evaluated in future work, but is of no immediate concern for this work, as the current scheduling approach cannot fully utilize CGRAs large enough, that partitioning would make a meaningful difference. This work targets a single CGRA partition, where every CondPE has access to all comparison results combinatorially, with 1-hop routing/full interconnect between all CondPEs and where every DataPE has access to all predicates of all CondPEs.

3.3   Scheduler Application Representation - SCAR

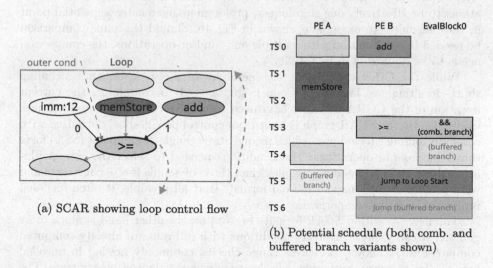

(a) SCAR showing loop control flow

(b) Potential schedule (both comb. and buffered branch variants shown)

Fig. 4. CBox SCAR Format and scheduling

Kernels are first expressed as conventional Control Flow Graphs (CFGs), which can be optimized and are then converted into the data-flow-centric Scheduler Application Representation (SCAR) format. Even though the hardware is already capable of arbitrary direct control flow, the current SCAR format cannot express branches explicitly. Rather it groups operations / nodes into loops, which will start at the top and name a single "loop-controller" to be the decider whether to exit the loop or continue until the bottom of the loop and jump back to the beginning for the next iteration. The loop-controller represents the computation of the loop-condition as well as the point in time when the branch exiting the loop would be placed. This structure is shown in Fig. 4a and can be arbitrarily nested to represent any regular loop structure. If-else constructs are currently all mapped to predicated execution. The hardware's branch-capabilities are still only used for loops and switching between different kernel variants (assuming aliasing-free memory accesses or total store order).

Figure 4a also shows how the previous hardware was paired with scheduler input that directly and explicitly expressed the original CBox operations. The loop-controller ">=" node maps exactly to what a single EvalBlock can accomplish in a single timestep. The two or-operations the EvalBlock can also execute simultaneously are not depicted in the example, but would also be represented by the same comparison node. Besides being difficult to read, the approach to handle loop-conditions and points of control flow as one causes inefficiencies. In most loops, there are operations with side effects that must either finish before control flow leaving the loop or are only valid after a loop-exit was not taken (which implies condition-outcome that the old SCAR cannot otherwise express with loop conditions). While the addition of a *buffered branch* improved the critical path of the hardware considerably, it caused the loop control flow operations to be effectively one step longer, prolonging this mostly sequential point in the schedule. An example is shown in Fig. 4b. Should the same comparison be needed in combination with multiple and- and or-operations, the comparison needs to be replicated in its totality.

While the CBox can realize any hierarchy of if-else statements including short-circuiting, as Java Byte Code is guaranteed to contain it, the current iteration of the CGRA and toolchain need to work for any input-architecture. Consequently the SCAR graph is built from control flow graphs, optimized with common compiler techniques, which means Static Single-Assignment (SSA) form that contains phi operations. The conditions needed to select the correct phi-input differ and can be more complex than those of simple if-else constructs and were problematic to map to the old format. If at all possible, it often included replicating a lot of comparisons.

The new *Condition SCAR* format (Fig. 5a) on the other hand is much more generic. It can express arbitrary conditions with full reuse of already computed comparisons. It allows to express range checks, commonly needed in unrolled loops or for memory overlapping checks, as efficient, balanced binary trees. The cost of this change is that a chain of conditions that was mappable to the CBox will take more time steps to compute. Figure 5b shows, why this is often not a limitation in practice. Loop variables and conditions needed for control flow decisions are often available much earlier than the side effects complete. They can simply be spread throughout a loop without causing any schedule length increases. Complicated and error-prone logic optimizations during the creation of SCAR could be dropped, as the new format can express any combination of conditions. Operations that previously were only valid after the loop-exit branch can now be simply predicated, giving the scheduler more choices in ordering those nodes. Had enough resources been free, the predicated operation from Fig. 5b could even have been scheduled before the exiting branch.

Lastly, the Java-style branch-to-exit, jump-to-iterate behavior shown in Fig. 4a can be replaced with a single do-while branch. Most compilers will seek to reorder assembly code into this form to save an additional instruction. This was already the case in our CFG representations, but can only now be expressed in SCAR and used by the scheduler. Multiple exit-points per loop are now also supported by the scheduler. While this lays the groundwork for expressing if-else constructs as well, deciding between branching and simply predicating alternative paths is difficult. Due to the lockstep nature of the CGRA it is difficult to overlap branches and already ongoing operations efficiently at low scheduling overhead.

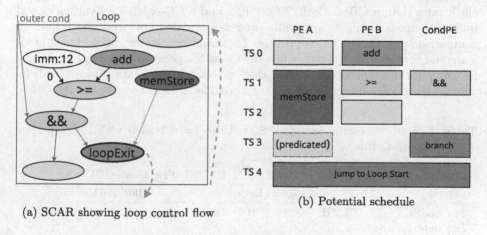

(a) SCAR showing loop control flow

(b) Potential schedule

Fig. 5. Condition SCAR Format and scheduling

3.4   Scheduler Improvements

The old format required to make static decisions on the order of comparisons that are and- or or-combined. The new scheduler can make this decision during scheduling and potentially fuse the logic-operation into the same timestep as the operand that was produced last. This feature is used in Fig. 5b to schedule the and-operation into the same timestep as the comparison. Without it, the comparison-result would be stored unaltered, to be processed in another timestep. The scheduler was extended with multiple of such fusing optimizations that depend on the actual scheduling order and resource availability. It is also capable of scheduling multiple logic operations in the same timestep as a shared comparison input. Due to the ability to quickly invert CondPE inputs, the scheduler can even decide to store some intermediary conditions in inverted form from SCAR at very low overhead. With this newly added fusing support, it was also possible to extend the scheduler to also support scheduling for CBox hardware with buffered branches from the new format. While a successful mapping cannot be guaranteed, as the CBox only supports chains and not arbitrary trees of logic, it can be made to work for most benchmarks with only slight changes to the SCAR graph and helps avoiding the wasted timesteps for buffered branches, that made this CBox variant previously uninteresting for scheduling.

4   Evaluation

4.1   HW Synthesis

Our efforts focus on implementing the CGRA on Xilinx Virtex-7-485 and Artix-7-200 FPGAs. The much simpler structure of the CondPE internals, especially the register file is expected to have reduced resource usage, yet still achieve higher clock rates than a CBox. Both, 2 CondPEs and a CBox with 2 EvalBlocks and buffered branch predicate are synthesized as standalone projects. Both have 16 comparison inputs. The CBox provides 2 operand predicates and a branch predicate and contains 64 registers, while the CondPEs provide 4 operand predicates in total, the first of which is also used as branch predicate. Since CondPEs contain 64 condition registers each, they provide twice the storage as the CBox.

Table 1. Synthesis results for CondPE vs. CBox on xc7vx485 with 16 comparison inputs & context units

Condition Unit	Frequency	LUTs		DMEM	FFs	Context Width	
		Total	Logic			BlockRAMs	Bits
2x CondPE 2x Context Units	201 MHz	206	194	12	38	2x6.5	2x 57 Bit
2x EvalBlocks 1x Context Unit	168 MHz	1026	1026	0	83	12	106 Bit

The Tables 1 and 2 show that the CondPEs are synthesizable at higher frequencies and save a significant amount of logic resources while providing more registers and predicates. LUTs for a single CondPE cannot be given exactly, as the synthesis optimizes across module boundaries. Because the context is delivered combinatorially between the context unit and PEs, these optimizations are desirable. CondPEs require orders of magnitude less LUTs than the CBox with its 4 write-port, 7 read-port register file, which is on the critical path. Analysis of the paths reading from the register files show that the CondPEs can deliver register file outputs about 1ns faster than the CBox. Solely the context consumption increases, but this is due to effects outside of the CondPE itself. By

Table 2. Synthesis results for CondPE vs. CBox on xc7a200 with 16 comparison inputs & context units

Condition Unit	Frequency	LUTs		DMEM	FFs	Context Width	
		Total	Logic			BlockRAMs	Bits
2x CondPE 2x Context Units	117 MHz	241	229	12	38	2x6	2x 57 Bit
2x EvalBlocks 1x Context Unit	101 MHz	1128	1128	0	83	12	106 Bit

default every PE has its own context unit that each consumes 20 Bits of context for its internal branching and compression logic. The remaining context is less than what the CBox requires. The context unit could be shared to save an additional 20 Bits of context width. This is not further evaluated, as the resulting difference in BlockRAMs is negligable. The synthesis found some solutions with identical amount of BlockRAMs and others using more. The critical paths up until the outputs of the context units are identical in either case, for CBox and CondPE. Targeting the smaller Artix-7 FPGA shows similar results, with just slightly higher LUT usage and reduced frequencies. The relative difference between CondPE and CBox remains similar.

Table 3. Achieved frequencies for whole 4x4 CGRAs, with homogenous Int&FP operations or just basic integer operations and only 2 division units

Config.	Target FPGA	Frequency	Crit. Path
hom., 1 CondPE	xc7vx485	125.5 MHz	data ops
hom., 2 CondPE	xc7vx485	125.6 MHz	data ops
hom., 1 EvalBlock, comb.	xc7vx485	107 MHz	comb. branch
hom., 1 EvalBlock, buf.	xc7vx485	123.6 MHz	data ops
hom., 2 EvalBlock, comb.	xc7vx485	110.3 MHz	comb. branch
hom., 2 EvalBlock, buf.	xc7vx485	123.9 MHz	buf. branch, data ops
het. int., 2 CondPE	xc7a200	91.1 MHz	data ops
het. int., 2 EvalBlock, buf.	xc7a200	87.8 MHz	buf. branch

When synthesizing a whole CGRA, Table 3 shows that the CondPE never limits the maximum frequency, while the combinatorially branching CBox is a strong limitation. The DataPE operators currently prevent the CondPE hardware from showcasing its full frequency potential. Large CGRAs with many operators per DataPE may in the worst case achieve ±1 MHz of the CBox implementation. A few operations could already be slightly optimized to achieve the advantages for the CondPE shown in the table.

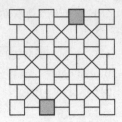

Fig. 6. PE configuration of evaluated CGRA

4.2 Scheduling

We compare three different main versions. The original CGRA hardware, including a CBox, scheduled from the original CBox SCAR. Then CBox with buffered branching, scheduled from the new Condition SCAR. This version also includes the improved scheduling of phi instructions, now that the conditions this requires can be safely expressed in SCAR. Lastly, the CBox is replaced with CondPEs on top of using Condition SCAR. All benchmarks target a two-dimensional grid-based 4x4 CGRA with matrix-star interconnect, shown in Fig. 6. All configurations support all arithmetic operations (standard integer and single precision float operations) homogeneously and have 2 PEs with memory access.

To evaluate the scheduling, the PolyBench Benchmark suite [10] with mini datasets is used, similar to [11]. PolyBench provides a collection of kernels that can be compiled for various platforms without code changes, do not use File-IO and has one kernel per program, which makes it easy to check, whether a program could be mapped, even when selecting kernels automatically. Benchmarks were compiled for RISC-V with -Og and -O3 compiler options, resulting 2x 28 benchmarks. The *deriche* and *jacobi-1D* benchmarks are excluded, because they contain the *RISC-V FCLASS.S* operation, which is still unsupported by the toolchain or require soft-float double precision math. Only the intended kernel of each benchmark is captured in CFG form, unrolled, otherwise optimized and scheduled for the CGRA. The resulting schedules can then be simulated. The *trmm* and *gramschmidt* benchmarks compiled with -O3 cannot be mapped to the CGRA, because they contain irregular loop structures, that are not currently supported by either the SCAR format or the scheduler. The CGRA hardware itself could theoretically handle them, thanks to full direct branching support Though they would likely not result in good utilization, as it is also not possible to unroll and thereby increase the parallelism of irregular loops with the current suite of CFG optimizations.

The simulated behavior of the CGRA itself is accurate, only cache- & memory-latencies are not accurately simulated. The scheduling behavior with regard to memory operation binding and scheduling is identical over all three compared variants, so this does not influence results.

Table 4. Scheduling & Simulation results of PolybenchSuite

Condition Facility	SCAR	geo.mean sched. length	geo.mean cycles
CBox, 1 Block, comb. branch	old/CBox	207.5	221576.8
CBox, 1 Block, buf. branch	old/CBox	211.6	224975.7
CBox, 1 Block, buf. branch	new/Condition	195.2	211231.7
CBox, 2 Block, buf. branch	new/Condition	191.3	209918.5
1 CondPE	new/Condition	192.1	207954.6
2 CondPE	new/Condition	188.8	208007.3

Table 4 shows, that the biggest overall improvement is afforded by the switch to the new SCAR format, because it enabled more efficient representations of phi instructions and the required condition logic. The fact that the CBox hardware cannot map all possible combinations of boolean logic, whereas the CondPE can, does not come into play in any of the benchmarks. Increasing EvalBlocks or CondPE count increases the amount of predicates that can be delivered in the same timestep. Predicate-limited benchmarks can benefit greatly, but still inefficient binding causes routing overhead between CondPEs which can make the schedule longer at critical points, while overall still reducing its length.

EvalBlocks suffer no similar disadvantages in scheduling, because they share a register file and require no routing. These inefficiencies for CondPEs can be improved with better binding, while there are no such options for the CBox.

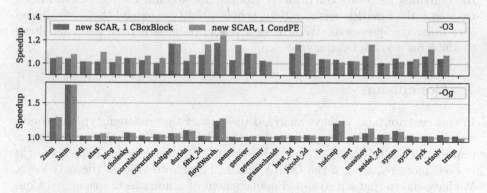

Fig. 7. Relative speedup simulated of cycles of new variants over baseline for each benchmark

Figure 7 shows that the majority of benchmarks benefit from the new format as well as CondPEs. Scheduling results are noisy, because only simple heuristics are used to guide binding. When multiple choices remain, the scheduler uses a pseudo-randomizer to spread out utilization. This can mostly lead to binding multiple variables to the same PE, which prevents parallel access later in the schedule. With smaller speedups, this noise can dominate runtime differences.

Og benchmarks often have a simple while-structure, which forces early evaluation of conditions. This simultaneously benefits the new format, that can express conditions more efficiently, but is a disadvantage for CondPEs, as they take longer to compute complex conditions and can not use their superior implementation of do-while control flow. Optimizing nested conditions in SCAR could alleviate at least some of the compute-overhead.

4.3   Combined Evaluation

Table 5. Geom. mean of projected runtimes at respective max. frequency achieved by matching hardware on xc7vx485 (as shown in Table 3)

Condition Facility	SCAR	geom. mean runtime on HW (ms)
CBox, 1 Block, comb. branch	old/CBox	2.071
CBox, 1 Block, buf. branch	old/CBox	1.820
CBox, 1 Block, buf. branch	new/Condition	1.709
CBox, 2 Block, buf. branch	new/Condition	1.694
1 CondPE	new/Condition	1.657
2 CondPE	new/Condition	1.656

The change in clock frequency and the change in scheduling can be combined. Table 5 shows the geom. mean of schedule runtimes scaled by the frequency the matching hardware can achieve. Taking into account the increases in clock frequency the CondPE configurations achieve, they can extend their overall lead over other configurations. We achieve a reduction of 20% from 2.071 ms down to 1.656 ms over all benchmarks.

5   Conclusion

In this contribution, we have analyzed the impact that different types of condition handling have on the performance of a CGRA. Such condition handling is required, if the CGRA shall be able to execute conditional code sequences or it is even more required, if the CGRA should be able to execute (nested) loops. We have shown that a distributed management of conditions in specialized Condition PEs can achieve higher clock frequencies as a centralized approach. At the same time, the distributed approach is more efficient in terms of resources. Also, this change can have a positive effect on the scheduling of applications. In total, the improvement from previously existing solution to our improved solution combining the better hardware with the better scheduling reduces the execution time by up to 20%. Since we already know how to improve some parts of our new scheduling, we believe that higher reductions are possible.

5.1   Outlook

We plan to investigate other uses of the benefits of the CondPE hardware. Since the predicate outputs now have more slack, but do not benefit the achievable frequencies of the whole CGRA much, options, such as on-the-fly inversion of predicates should be investigated. This could further reduce the amount of logic operations that take up a timestep and would also allow the scheduler to place branches to jump over operations that currently would just be predicated, but still take up valuable timesteps. Introducing such short-circuit branches, when multiple alternative chains of data operations are scheduled in parallel, requires the scheduler to dynamically obtain predicates depending on which path finishes earlier than the other. The ability to invert already existing predicates as needed, without additional hardware usage, could close this gap at low overhead for scheduler and achievable frequency.

References

1. Adhi, B., Cortes, C., et al.: Exploration framework for synthesizable CGRAs targeting HPC: initial design and evaluation. In: IPDPSW, pp. 639–646 (2022)
2. Anderson, J., Beidas, R., Chacko, V., et al.: CGRA-ME: an open-source framework for CGRA architecture and CAD research (invited). In: ASAP, pp. 156–162 (2021)
3. Chin, S.A., Sakamoto, N., Rui, A., Zhao, J., Kim, J.H., et al.: CGRA-ME: a unified framework for CGRA modelling and exploration. In: ASAP, pp. 184–189 (2017)
4. Govindaraju, V., Nowatzki, T., et al.: Breaking SIMD shackles with an exposed flexible microarchitecture and the access execute PDG. In: PACT, pp. 341–352 (2013)
5. Hoy, C.H., Govindarajuz, V., Nowatzki, T., Nagaraju, R., et al.: Performance evaluation of a DySER FPGA prototype system spanning the compiler, microarchitecture, and hardware implementation. In: ISPASS, pp. 203–214 (2015)
6. Käsgen, P., Messelka, M., Weinhardt, M.: HiPReP: high-performance reconfigurable processor - architecture and compiler. In: FPL, pp. 380–381 (2021)
7. Mei, B., Vernalde, S., Verkest, D., De Man, H., Lauwereins, R.: ADRES: an architecture with tightly coupled VLIW processor and coarse-grained reconfigurable matrix. In: Y. K. Cheung, P., Constantinides, G.A. (eds.) FPL 2003. LNCS, vol. 2778, pp. 61–70. Springer, Heidelberg (2003). https://doi.org/10.1007/978-3-540-45234-8_7
8. Mei, B., Vernalde, S., et al.: Exploiting loop-level parallelism on coarse-grained reconfigurable architectures using modulo scheduling. In: DATE, p. 10296 (2003)
9. Podobas, A., Sano, K., Matsuoka, S.: A template-based framework for exploring coarse-grained reconfigurable architectures. In: ASAP, pp. 1–8 (2020)
10. Pouchet, L.N.: Polybenchc-4.2.1 beta. https://github.com/MatthiasJReisinger/PolyBenchC-4.2.1
11. Wirsch, R., Hochberger, C.: Towards transparent dynamic binary translation from RISC-V to a CGRA. In: Hochberger, C., Bauer, L., Pionteck, T. (eds.) ARCS 2021. LNCS, vol. 12800, pp. 118–132. Springer, Cham (2021). https://doi.org/10.1007/978-3-030-81682-7_8
12. Wolf, D., Engel, A., Ruschke, T., Koch, A., Hochberger, C.: UltraSynth: insights of a CGRA integration into a control engineering environment. J. Signal Process. Syst. 93(5), 463–479 (2021). https://doi.org/10.1007/s11265-021-01641-7
13. Wolf, D., Jung, L., Ruschke, T., Li, C., Hochberger, C.: AMIDAR project: lessons learned in 15 years of researching adaptive processors. In: ReCoSoC, pp. 1–8 (2018)

FPGA-Based Network-Attached Accelerators – An Environmental Life Cycle Perspective

Fritjof Steinert[1,2] and Benno Stabernack[1,2(✉)]

[1] Fraunhofer for Telecommunications, Heinrich Hertz Institute (HHI),
Einsteinufer 37, 10587 Berlin, Germany
`fritjof.steinert@hhi-extern.fraunhofer.de,`
`benno.stabernack@hhi.fraunhofer.de`
[2] Embedded Systems Architectures for Signalprocessing, University of Potsdam,
August-Bebel Straße 89, 14469 Potsdam, Germany

Abstract. Homogeneous computing systems are reaching their limits with the growing demands of current applications. Accelerating compute-intensive applications ensures manageable computing times and boosts energy efficiency, which is an important lever as part of ongoing efforts to tackle global climate change. Field Programmable Gate Array (FPGA) accelerators are well-known for increasing throughput and, in particular, energy efficiency for many applications. FPGA accelerators connected directly to the data center high-speed network are ideal for integration into a heterogeneous data center, avoiding the energy and resource overhead of a carrier system. The standalone Network-attached Accelerators (NAAs) further benefits from low latency and predictable line-rate network throughput, as well as an interoperable communications interface. For selected use cases, we compare a heterogeneous computing cluster extended by NAAs with a homogeneous CPU-based cluster not only in terms of computing performance and energy efficiency, but also considering resource efficiency. For this purpose, we perform a Life Cycle Assessment (LCA) for both systems based on the Key Performance Indicators for Data Center Efficiency (KPI4DCE) indicator set, which takes into account the manufacturing phase in addition to the usage phase. The KPI4DCE tool has been extended to include modeling of NAAs. This allows us to show that NAAs are not only more energy-efficient, but also more resource-efficient for the selected applications, leading to a strong improvement of the environmental impact of the manufacturing phase.

Keywords: FPGA · Network-attached Accelerator · Data Center · Life Cycle Assessment · Reconfigurable Computing · Heterogeneous Computing

This work is part of the NAAICE project, which is funded by the German Federal Ministry of Education and Research under reference 16ME0624.

G. Goumas et al. (Eds.): ARCS 2023, LNCS 13949, pp. 248–263, 2023.
https://doi.org/10.1007/978-3-031-42785-5_17

1   Introduction

With ever-increasing compute requirements of applications such as Machine Learning (ML), image and video processing (e.g. video transcoding for social media), distributed databases and the like, the need for energy-efficient acceleration in Data Centers (DCs) is growing. Classical processor-based architectures are reaching their limits, especially after the end of Dennard scaling. Homogeneous computing systems are accompanied by Graphics Processing Units (GPUs), Field Programmable Gate Arrays (FPGAs) and Application Specific Instruction Processors (ASIPs) like a Tensor Processing Unit (TPU) to provide the required processing capabilities in an energy-efficient manner. In this heterogeneous landscape, the challenge is to find the appropriate compute node for a workload. Energy efficiency in the usage phase has become the most important design parameter in this regard, as it helps lessen the enormous greenhouse impact of global DCs. Although ASIPs are to be preferred for energy efficiency and performance reasons, long development times and in particular the lack of flexibility outside a specific domain are an obstacle to their deployment in DCs.

Escobar et al. conducted an extensive study to determine which application groups are suitable for which kinds of accelerators and are consequently the most efficient [6]. They distinguish 4 groups:

1. High arithmetic demand and relatively regular memory access patterns → on GPU.
2. High arithmetic demand and irregular regular memory access patterns → on FPGA.
3. Low arithmetic demand and sophisticated memory management → on multi-core processors.
4. Low arithmetic demand and operators are mapped directly to hardware → on FPGA.

While the study provides an initial guide to selecting an accelerator, it does not consider the communication interface. Microbenchmarks indicate that hardware-based network implementations offer line-rate throughput as well as low variance and deterministic latencies, unlike typical software stacks [3,23]. The implementation of Network Interface Controller (NIC) directly in FPGA also saves the communication detour via the host when the data is delivered via network to the compute node. In a DC architecture with compute nodes and storage nodes, this is always the case resulting in a latency reduction. Therefore, network-coupled FPGAs are well suited e.g. for latency-critical tasks.

Connecting the FPGA directly to the DC network degrades the host to a power-only enclosure. By using a standalone, network-attached FPGA accelerator, called Network-attached Accelerator (NAA), as proposed in [20,24], the baseline energy requirements of the system can be greatly reduced without sacrificing performance, thereby boosting the energy efficiency. NAAs are treated as distinct and fully equal nodes in the DC.

However, in addition to the operational phase, the environmental aspects of the manufacturing phase, transportation, installation, and disposal should also be included in a Life Cycle Assessment (LCA), as these phases can have a significant impact. Not just a single component (as one NAA), but the entire system (whole DC) should be considered in order to exclude undesirable interactions. It is evident that the NAA approach also performs well in the extensive environmental analysis as the reduced number of components in an NAA architecture decreases the impact of the manufacturing phase on the environmental footprint, in tandem to energy consumption.

Our main contribution is to perform and evaluate an environmental life cycle analysis for a heterogeneous cluster accelerated by standalone NAA nodes and its comparison with a homogeneous CPU-based cluster.

The following paper is structured as follows: In Sect. 2, the background and related work regarding an optimal NAA communication model, LCA for DCs and NAA use cases is presented. Section 3 describes our FPGA hardware framework for NAA, which incorporates one-sided Remote Direct Memory Access (RDMA) communication. It also introduces a flexible and scalable energy measurement system for DCs. A review of the environmental impacts over the complete life cycle of an NAA cluster compared to a homogeneous cluster is conducted in Sect. 4. Section 5 summarizes and gives an outlook on our future developments.

2   Related Work

2.1   Communication Model for Network-Attached Accelerators

In the past, high-speed interfaces were usually used for coupling the appropriate accelerators, such as Peripheral Component Interconnect Express (PCIe). For coupling in a multiprocessor configuration, even more tightly coupled processor interfaces such as QuickPath Interconnect (QPI), which provide cache coherence, have been used. Due to their high data rates, these interfaces allow very close coupling with the program flow of the main process and are suited for communication-bound compute problems. However, the decisive factor for selecting an adequate compute accelerator is not only the question of the available bandwidth of the interfaces, but the speedup including the communication time over the compute time on the host. It can be observed that there is a class of computing problems that require only a small amount of data, and thus a small bandwidth for actual communication, which very quickly become compute-bound instead of communication-bound.

This relationship can be visualized by the so-called Roofline model [14]. Figure 1 shows the relationship between achieved computational complexity and required computational complexity. In the figure, applications that are in the right area of the graph of the Roofline model are particularly well suited, e.g. the MobileNetV2 inference kernel used in the analysis.

2.2   Environmental Life Cycle Assessment for Data Centers

To evaluate the environmental impact of a DC, numerous indicators based on a literature review are presented in [17]. The indicators describe the impacts at different system levels and are classified according to the objectives: energy consumption, Global Warming Potential (GWP), raw materials and others such as water consumption. Some indicators include more than one objective. The most common efficiency indicator is Power Usage Effectiveness (PUE), which describes the efficiency of building services as the ratio between the used energy of the whole DC and the consumed energy of Information Technology (IT) devices like compute nodes, storage servers and switches. Whether IT systems perform relevant tasks with the energy consumed is not part of the PUE and thus a weak point of this indicator.

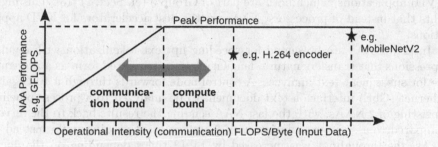

Fig. 1. NAA communication Roofline model.

At the level of the entire DC, which includes building services and IT equipment, only 8 indicators are applicable, of which only Data Center Performance Per Energy (DPPE) takes into account energy demand, GWP and raw material demand. Moreover, almost all indicators including DPPE consider only the usage phase, which is insufficient for a comprehensive LCA.

$$\text{KPI} = \frac{\text{benefit [e.g. ops]}}{\text{effort [e.g. kg Sb.eq./a]}} \tag{1}$$

Therefore, the study [17] developed the indicator set Key Performance Indicators for Data Center Efficiency (KPI4DCE) as a quotient of benefit to effort (cf. Eq. (1)), where the benefit metric is throughput in operations per second (ops). It relates the generic benefit of the DC to the environmental effort in the sub-areas computing power of the nodes, utilized storage capacity, external data traffic as well as infrastructure of the DC for Cumulative Energy Demand (CED), GWP, Abiotic Depletion Potential (ADP) and water consumption. Hence, 16 sub-indicators exist. As a simplification, only the manufacturing and usage phases are considered for KPI4DCE, since the influence of the transportation and disposal phases is marginal according to the case studies in [8,17]. In [8], the indicator set was developed further, and the database was updated. The KPI4DCE effort indicators in detail are:

- **ADP**: usage of non-renewable raw materials and minerals in kg of antimony equivalents per year [*kg Sb.eq./a*].

- **CED**: consumption of non-renewable and renewable energy resources in mega-joules per year $[MJ/a]$.
- **GWP**: effect on global warming in kilograms of carbon dioxide equivalents per year $[kg\ CO_2\ eq./a]$.
- **Water**: Water consumption in cubic meters per year $[m^3/a]$.

2.3   Use Cases for Network-Attached Accelerators

The survey by Kachris et al. shows significant performance and energy efficiency gains for FPGA-based Map Reduce and FPGA-based Key-value Database (KVD) applications, which both are part of Group 3 (cf. Sect. 1) [13]. This highlights that instead of processors, NAAs are the best accelerators for KVD applications.

In [24], NAAs are presented for speeding up text tokenization with regular expressions that transfers natural language into a structured form as a prerequisite for subsequent text analyzes. A control node forwards through a 10 Gigabit Ethernet (GbE) interface a text document to be analyzed to a process pipeline consisting of 2 NAAs, with the last NAA sending the results back to the server. Compared to a software solution with 2 servers as processing units instead of NAAs, the throughput was increased by 14–18 times depending on the document size, the latency was reduced 12–40-fold and the response time variance was reduced to 0.5 ms from 3–4 ms. Compared to employing tightly-coupled FPGAs in the nodes, the NAAs were able to increase the throughput by 10.8–14.8, the latency was reduced up to 1.11x, and the variance of the response times was reduced to the same extent as in the software solution. The server system consumes a total of 600 W and the tightly-coupled FPGA solution requires overall 650 W. The NAA architecture, on the other hand, requires only 250 W with increased throughput, which improves energy efficiency by 33.6x–43.2x compared to the software solution. Tightly-coupled FPGA increase energy efficiency by only 10x–14x.

The acceleration of a Jacobi 2D Stencil is shown for an upgrade of the NAA approach of [24] in a cluster with up to 31 NAAs (each with 10 GbE) and one CPU [15]. The application is automatically synthesized for the FPGA using Message Passing Interface (MPI) transpilation and communication is based on a MPI/User Datagram Protocol (UDP) stack. For data sizes from 16×16 to 1024×1024, speedups over a homogeneous CPU cluster of 1.96–5.55 are achieved for different cluster sizes. The energy efficiency increases by 5.74–31.31.

In [5], the authors investigate the acceleration of Monte-Carlo European Option Pricing (MCE), which is applied in the financial community for the pricing of an option with multiple uncertainties, for NAAs among others. The high-end GPU A100 with 7 nm node technology achieves the highest throughput, however, the end-to-end response time of the NAA (mid-range FPGA) with 20 nm node technology for cold runs, which is particularly important in the financial industry, is 3 orders of magnitude better. A more recent and performant FPGA can certainly improve the throughput significantly. This is underlined by the fact that a 3 times larger tightly-coupled FPGA with 16 nm achieves 7–8

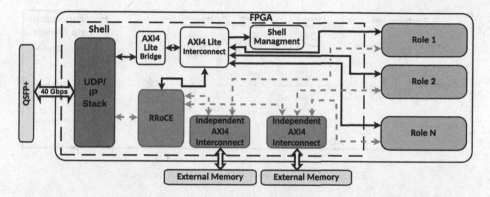

Fig. 2. Exemplary NAA hardware framework.

times the throughput of the NAA due to more parallel MCE cores. However, the cold start time of the tightly-coupled FPGA is worse, so the authors do not investigate this solution further.

In [2], a comparison of a network protocol load balancer between Virtual Machine (VM)-based software and NAA, which needs an extra serial port for control purposes, is shown. The VM already experiences packet drops and latency variance starting at 25 MBps. In contrast, the NAA can operate up to 100 MBps without losses and constant latency variance.

In addition, there are some applications that have not been implemented on standalone NAAs, but can probably be easily adapted. Due to space limitations, they are not presented in detail such as tightly-coupled accelerators with direct network access [4,12] or FPGA-based switches for In-Network data Processing (INP) [9].

The presented use cases for the NAAs reveal the throughput, latency, and energy efficiency advantages of the distributed NAA architecture in a heterogeneous DC for certain problems, which motivates us to also investigate this architecture in terms of resource efficiency and manufacturing phase impact.

3   Exemplary NAA Framework

For the NAAs, we adopt the hardware abstraction layer described in [20] as an exemplary hardware framework that divides the FPGA into a static shell and up to N roles (cf. Fig. 2). The shell provides a 40 GbE with UDP/IP stack as communication interface and Routable RDMA over Converged Ethernet (RRoCE) protocol stack based on it, which is introduced in more detail in [16]. RRoCE is intended for reliable, connection-oriented RDMA communication via one-sided WRITE transfers, especially between servers and NAAs. This permits scalable and interoperable communication in a heterogeneous DC with a low processor load on the server side. A 512-bit Advanced eXtensible Interface Bus (AXI)-4 interconnect is used to access external memory. The roles are managed by a

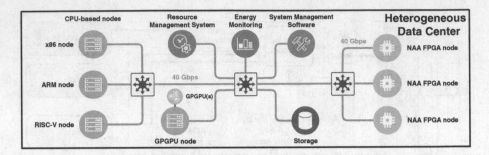

Fig. 3. Heterogeneous DC with NAA nodes.

lightweight AXI-4-Lite system, that can only be controlled by a manager from within the shell to prevent unwanted control of one role by another. Further possibilities of the framework such as partial reconfiguration or streaming communication of the network stack with the roles are not used for performance reasons, even though these functionalities are important in a real DC environment.

4   Environmental Life Cycle Assessment of NAA Nodes

4.1   Initial KPI4DCE Observations

For the LCA, a heterogeneous cluster accelerated by NAA nodes (cf. Fig. 3) is compared against a homogeneous cluster as baseline architecture, which relies on classical CPU-based nodes typically found in DCs. The comparison is based on the indicator set KPI4DCE and the advancements in [8]. KPI4DCE applies the integer portion of the Standard Performance Evaluation Corporation (SPEC)-2006 benchmark as a measure of *beneficial computing power*. This benchmark contains 12 individual benchmarks [19], which are not readily executable on an application-specific FPGA accelerator. Instead of abstract benchmarks, we apply real life benchmarks that represent relevant applications, as described below. According to [8], the adoption of own benchmarks instead of SPEC-2006 provides comparable results as long as the benchmarks are adopted on all compared systems.

MobileNetV2: MobileNetV2, as a current Deep Neural Network (DNN) for image classification on 224 × 224 images, is part of an important application category and was thus considered as benchmark. We rely on the work introduced in [16] with two MobileNetV2 roles per NAA. The images to be classified are aggregated and transmitted via RRoCE to the NAA nodes for classification. From there, the results are sent back to a server via RRoCE for further processing. For our tests we used the Imagenet Large Scale Visual Recognition Challenge 2012 (ILSVRC2012) validation data set with 50000 images.

H.264 Encoder: Video transcoding is needed for internet video platforms or social media to adapt video resolution and quality to different devices. Encoding with for example H.264/Advanced Video Coding (AVC) is the computationally intensive part, which is an element of SPEC-2006. The employed NAA implementation with two parallel H.264 High Definition (HD) encoders running at 30 frames per second (fps) is based on the work presented in [21]. The decoded video data is transmitted via 40 GbE using RRoCE to the NAAs, where they are encoded and then sent to a server via RRoCE for further playout. The functionally identical C reference software is used as the software encoder. As test sequence (SteamLocomotive) with 1920 × 1080 pixels, YUV 4:2:0, 8-bit color depth and 300 frames targeting 5 Mbps was encoded.

The total manufacturing expenses in all categories (CED, GWP, ADP and water consumption) are distributed over the expected service periods in years given in Tables 1 and 2 [8,17]. In the majority of DCs examined in both studies, the ADP is dominated by the manufacturing phase, even when excluding significant portions of building services due to their low impact in the analysis [8,17]. The remaining ADP in the usage phase is caused by the combustion of fossil fuels to generate electricity. To increase resource efficiency, it is advisable to maximize the lifespan of IT equipment. But this creates a trade-off with energy footprint, as more efficient IT devices help reduce that consumption. However, in the other categories (CED, GWP, and water consumption), the usage phase dominates.

In an LCA for electronic products, just 10% of the components contribute 90% to the GWP, which is used as a simplified indicator in [22]. Therefore, the consideration of the main contributions is particularly relevant, which are in descending order in a DC context [22]:

1. Integrated Circuits (ICs): active semiconductors like memory (DRAM, Solid-State Drive (SSD), HDD) or logic (CPU, GPU, FPGA).
2. Printed Circuit Board (PCB): material (substrate, finish and solder).
3. Ports: power and communication interfaces such as electrical/optical connectors and cables.
4. Chassis: housing materials plus cooling.

Despite numerous uncertainties, such as the assessment of the benefit of IT operations, the usage of accelerators, the neglect of internal network traffic or, in particular, the very incomplete data basis for the resource consumption of IT components, the authors in [17] consider KPI4DCE as robust and reliable in trend. The authors of [8,17] see further research required to improve the database, especially for the determination of ADP, since the number of data sets in the electronic area is small, complex to create, and they also quickly become outdated. For the calculation of KPI4DCE, an Excel-based tool has been published [7], which is subsequently used in version 2.5.

4.2   CPU-Based Nodes

For the examination of the homogeneous CPU-based cluster as a baseline architecture, the resources shown in Table 1 are assumed. Due to the absence of

Table 1. CPU-based cluster resources.

#	Qty.	Type	Lifetime	Description
1	80	compute nodes	5 years	Intel Xeon Silver 4114, 10C@2.2 GHz, 13.75 MiB L3 Cache, 6 × 8 GiB DDR4 SDRAM, 1 TB HDD, 40 GbE, 2×PWS-1K43F-1R power supply
2	1	control server	5 years	same as #1
3	1	storage server	6 years	same as #1 but 8 × 4 TB HDD
4	3	40 GbE switch	7 years	with 32 ports

a server cluster, the software implementations are run on a single node (running a bare metal Ubuntu 20.04.5 LTS) and the results are extrapolated. In our experience, this extrapolation leads to a negligible error for the application type used, since the applications are embarrassingly parallel. In addition, the energy requirements of the infrastructure were taken into account with PUE=1.2 according to a typical PUE of an energy-efficient DC [10]. For modeling the GWP of electricity consumption, the medium-voltage electricity mix of Germany is assumed based on environmental LCA database Ecoinvent V3.5 (published 2018) [8]. The power measurement of the servers was carried out via the Power Management Bus (PMBus) of the power supply via the Baseboard Management Controller (BMC). The measured idle power of a computing node is 100 W. A typical power consumption of 150 W with passive copper cabling is reported per switch [18]. For classical DCs without accelerators, we believe that the KPI4DCE tool can be applied well. No additional assumptions had to be taken regarding the servers, the storage servers or the network infrastructure.

MobileNetV2: The CPU-based MobileNetV2 runs on 10 physical cores, using thread pinning, by means of ONNX runtime. Using more cores did not result in more throughput due to hyperthreading overhead. Per compute node, using a batch size of 20 frames, MobileNetV2 classifies 182.67 fps (measured with 10 iterations), which is the benefit. This yields a system performance of 14613.6 fps or 414.77 billion frames/year assuming a cluster utilization over the year of 90% The energy consumption amounts to 111 MWh per year. With the DC components and infrastructure, this adds up to a demand of 142.84 MWh, resulting in an electrical energy expenditure of 1239.78 mJ per frame during the usage phase.

H.264 Encoder: Each compute node encodes 20 parallel HD video streams employing all CPU cores. The benefit is defined as the number of encoded fps. A frame rate of 4.06 fps per node is achieved and 166 W is consumed during encoding measured with 10 iterations. The 80 nodes thus encode 9.21 billion images/year at an assumed average CPU utilization of 90%, consuming 112.92 MWh during this time. The remaining components of the cluster increase the energy consumption along with an energy consumption of 24 MWh to simulate the PUE to 145.24 MWh per year. Per image, this corresponds to an electrical energy expenditure of 56718.4 mJ in usage phase.

Table 2. Resources of NAA-accelerated cluster.

#	Qty.	Type	Lifetime	Description
1	1	control server	5 years	Intel Xeon Silver 4114, 10C@2.2 GHz, 13.75 MiB L3 Cache, 6 × 8 GiB DDR4 SDRAM, 1 TB HDD, 40 GbE, 2×PWS-1K43F-1R power supply
2	1	NAA	5 years	8 NAAs (10AX115N3F40E2SG), each with 2×4GiB DDR3 SDRAM and 40 GbE, ASPOWER R2A-DV0800-N with 2 redundant power supplies
3	1	storage server	6 years	same as #1 but 8 × 4 TB HDD
4	1	40 GbE switch	7 years	with 12 ports

4.3 NAA-Based Nodes

The heterogeneous cluster accelerated with NAA-based nodes consists of the components shown in Table 2. Compared to Table 1, the compute nodes have been replaced by 8 NAAs in a chassis equipped with simple backplanes (just 2 layers) and components for power supply and cooling. The same assumptions regarding PUE and electricity supply of the DC are made as in Table 1. The idle power averages at 260 W after a few minutes of runtime. The 385A PCB from Bittware was selected as NAA [1]. The switches were substituted with a scaled-down model with a measured average power of 40 W, since the NAA cluster requires fewer ports. A more detailed description of the NAA node can be found in [16].

For the adaptation of KPI4DCE to standalone NAA chassis, some assumptions have to be stated for the application of the KPI4DCE tool. To determine the effort in the manufacturing phase for logic ICs, KPI4DCE applies the formula Eq. (2), which takes the number of CPU cores as a measure of the die size [8]. The die size is used to infer the effort using manufacturing data from an Intel factory in Ireland from 2017 and 2018.

$$\text{CPUDieSize}[\text{cm}^2] = 0.24584 \cdot \text{CoresNumberPerCPU} + 0.49157 \qquad (2)$$

When modeling the NAA architecture for KPI4DCE, it should be noted that an FPGA as a spatial architecture cannot be compared with the invariant cores of a CPU. However, to enable modeling nevertheless, we have inferred an equivalent number of CPU cores based on the die size of the FPGA according to the formula Eq. (3);

$$\text{CoresNumberPerCPU} = (\text{CPUDieSize}[\text{mm}^2]/100 - 0.49157)/0.24584 \qquad (3)$$

The die area of FPGAs is usually not publicly known, in contrast to the package size. However, for the 10AX115N3F40I2SGES FPGA, which is part of the Arria 10 GX family, this information was published in a forum by the manufacturer [11]. This FPGA is the equivalent of the 10AX115N3F40E2SG used in the environmental assessment except for the temperature range and that it is an engineering sample. Neither factor should affect the die area. The stated die area is 337.9 mm^2, which results in an equivalent number of 11.7 CPU cores, rounded up to 12, according to Eq. (3). The estimate is subject to large uncertainties due to insufficient data, since other process technologies are applied for FPGA manufacturing, so equating them with CPUs is only a rough approximation. Also, even the database for manufacturing CPUs based on only one fab from 2 years is very poor. The influence of the external memory on the FPGA PCB is modeled by specifying it as a RAM module, and the flash memory for booting the FPGA is modeled as an SSD.

The influence of the FPGA PCB, each with 115.48 cm^2 and unknown number of layers [1], is not modeled by the chosen approach. However, the impact can be modeled approximately through the backplane, which is considered with the fixed area 1006.5 cm^2 and 6 layers for all server types in the KPI4DCE tool [8,17]. Together with our backplane, which is 508.5 cm^2 in area with 2 layers, this gives a total PCB area of 1432.3 cm^2. To accurately reflect the impact of the PCBs, a correction factor for the PCB area compared to the static PCB area of the modeled servers was added to the KPI4DCE tool and set to 1.423 for the PCBs of the NAA chassis including 8 NAAs.

The power distribution is modeled through the NAA enclosure, which corresponds to a server enclosure. Network cables are not part of the calculation tool [17], but since the required number for the NAA-accelerated DC is lower due to the smaller node count, this simplification is slightly unfair towards the heterogeneous DC. No further assumptions need to be made for the NAA chassis regarding housing and cooling compared to the modeled server chassis, since it consists of the same components as the latter.

Overall, we can only agree with the authors of [8,17] and see major research required in the adoption of accelerator technologies such as GPUs and FPGAs.

MobileNetV2: The classification performance of the 8 NAAs is 10340 fps employing a batch size of 128 at a consumption of 420 W. Due to the higher throughput, the classification was carried out in a continuous loop and the measurement was performed over a period of 15 min after a startup phase of 5 min. This results in an annual output of 293.5 billion frames/year at 90% utilization with an electrical energy consumption of 140.6 mJ/frame including the DC overhead (classification only needs mJ/frame). Compared to the CPU-based classification, the energy consumption per frame in the utilization phase was reduced by a factor of 8.82.

H.264 Encoder: The 8 NAAs, with an assumed power consumption of 450 W, can encode 480 HD frames per second. At an expected workload of 90%, this corresponds to 13.6 billion frames/year and an electrical energy consumption of 3098,6 mJ per encoded frame, which equates to an efficiency increase of 18.31 in the usage phase.

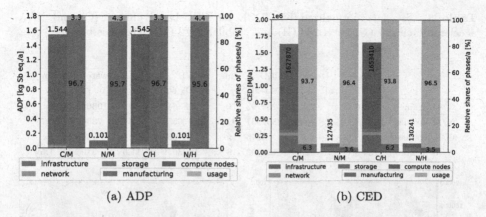

Fig. 4. Absolute ADP and CED for CPU-based cluster (C) and NAA-accelerated cluster (N) for H.264 (H) and MobileNetV2 (M). Relative shares of the manufacturing and usage phases per year.

4.4 KPI4DCE Evaluation

The PUE is assumed to be constant at 1.2 for both clusters, since the infrastructure of the DC can potentially be reduced to the same extent due to the lower requirements of fewer computing nodes. The simplification is not relevant for the comparison of the two clusters with each other. The same service life is assumed for NAAs as for servers for better comparability. However, due to the typically lower energy consumption in the usage phase and the slower product cycle for FPGAs, longer lifetimes are reasonable. It is evident from Fig. 4a that the heterogeneous cluster accelerated with NAAs (cf. Table 2) has a reduced absolute ADP compared to the homogeneous CPU-based cluster (cf. Table 1). Note that the CPU-based cluster provides higher benefit for MobileNetV2, but lower benefit for H.264. Normalizing the indicators to effort following Eq. (1) restores comparability, as seen in Table 3. Thus, for MobileNetV2, the ADP of the NAA-accelerated cluster is 10.8x better and H.264 even 22.6x. Due to the high system performance of the NAAs and the high energy efficiency, a targeted performance can be achieved with a lower node number. The smaller compute node number as well as the generally smaller resource requirements of a NAA node, caused by saving the host server, are the main reasons for the improvement of the resource efficiency. The same compute resources are used for both benchmarks (H.264, MobileNetV2), which explains why the ADP is nearly identical. It differs only by the ADP part of the electrical supply. The relative allocation of the ADP to the manufacturing and usage phase for one year is also shown in Fig. 4a. It can be seen that the manufacturing phase dominates for all use cases. This is consistent with the initial considerations presented in Sect. 4.1.

In Fig. 4b, the CED of the clusters is shown for the different use cases. It is evident that the NAA-accelerated cluster consumes significantly less energy due to the much improved energy efficiency as well as the infrastructure adapted to the smaller node number. In contrast to ADP, CED is dominated by the usage

Table 3. To effort normalized KPI4DCE for CPU-based cluster (C) and NAA-accelerated cluster (N) for H.264 (H) and MobileNetV2 (M). Higher is better.

#	[effort]							
	ADP [kg Sb eq./a]	Im.	CED [MJ/a]	Im.	GWP [CO$_2$ eq./a]	Im.	water [m^3]	Im.
C/M [frames]	268.6 G	1x	254793	1x	3983644	1x	103692 M	1x
N/M [frames]	2905.7 G	10.8x	2302931	9x	21876557	5.5x	73369 M	0.7x
C/H [frames]	6.0 G	1x	5576	1x	87266	1x	2305 M	1x
N/M [frames]	134.9 G	22.6x	104603	18.8x	1003059	11.5x	3406 M	1.5x

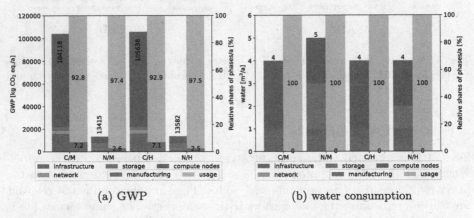

(a) GWP   (b) water consumption

Fig. 5. Absolute GWP and water usage for CPU-based cluster (C) and NAA-accelerated cluster (N) for H.264 (H) and MobileNetV2 (M). Relative shares of the manufacturing and usage phases per year.

phase in all cases. The clarity of the relative distribution is due to the high utilization of the DC, which optimally exploits the fixed effort of the manufacturing phase.

In Fig. 5a the GWP of the clusters is depicted, which is fed from coolant leakages and from the fossil shares of the DC energy supply according to the applied electricity mix. Compared to the homogeneous cluster, the NAA-accelerated cluster emits fewer greenhouse gases due to lower CED. From the normalized numbers in Table 3, it is evident that the unchanged rate of coolant leakage decreases the GWP for the NAA accelerated cluster less than the CED. As expected, the usage phase dominates the GWP in all cases. In order to reduce the CED and thus the GWP, it is particularly worthwhile to optimize the usage phase, for example by taking advantage of energy-efficient sleep states for unused components both at the system level (energy-saving mode for complete nodes) and within a node (e.g., shutting down unused DRAM).

Figure 5b reports the direct water consumption of the DC. This is determined by the cooling systems, which is allocated by the KPI4DCE tool (with rounding errors) into the categories infrastructure, network, storage systems and compute nodes on a percentage basis. Therefore, the water consumption for the NAA-accelerated cluster tends to be overestimated. The reduced number of nodes is expected to result in lower cooling requirements and thus, after adjusting the cooling capacity, in reduced water consumption.

5   Conclusion

For the given examples, we can summarize that the NAA-accelerated cluster performs significantly better than the homogeneous cluster with CPU-based compute nodes in terms of resource efficiency (improved by up to 22.6), energy efficiency (improved by up to 18.8), and greenhouse gas emissions (improved by up to 11.5), as evident in Table 3. Therefore, we consider standalone NAA as an ideal addition to a heterogeneous DC to increase energy and resource efficiency and thus reduce GWP.

Our future work will focus on the development of a software framework with hardware support for energy measurement of NAAs. In addition, we will investigate further use cases, possibly with other FPGAs, such as Agilex, using KPI4DCE.

References

1. Bittware 385a. https://www.bittware.com/fpga/385a/. Accessed 06 Apr 2023
2. Byma, S., Steffan, J.G., Bannazadeh, H., Leon-Garcia, A., Chow, P.: FPGAs in the cloud: booting virtualized hardware accelerators with OpenStack. In: 2014 IEEE 22nd FCCM. IEEE (2014). https://doi.org/10.1109/fccm.2014.42
3. Caulfield, A.M., Chung, E.S., Putnam, A., Angepat, H., et al.: A cloud-scale acceleration architecture. In: 2016 49th IEEE/ACM MICRO, Taipei, Taiwan, pp. 1–13. IEEE (2016). https://doi.org/10.1109/MICRO.2016.7783710
4. Chung, E., Fowers, J., Ovtcharov, K., Papamichael, M., et al.: Serving DNNs in real time at datacenter scale with project brainwave. IEEE Micro **38**, 8–20 (2018). https://doi.org/10.1109/MM.2018.022071131
5. Diamantopoulos, D., Polig, R., Ringlein, B., Purandare, M., et al.: Acceleration-as-a-μService: a cloud-native Monte-Carlo option pricing engine on CPUs, GPUs and disaggregated FPGAs. In: 2021 IEEE 14th CLOUD, Chicago, IL, USA, pp. 726–729. IEEE (2021). https://doi.org/10.1109/CLOUD53861.2021.00096
6. Escobar, F.A., Chang, X., Valderrama, C.: Suitability analysis of FPGAs for heterogeneous platforms in HPC. IEEE TPDS **27**, 600–612 (2016). https://doi.org/10.1109/TPDS.2015.2407896
7. Gröger, J., Liu, R.: Green cloud computing. https://www.oeko.de/publikationen/p-details/green-cloud-computing. Accessed 29 Mar 2023
8. Gröger, J., Liu, R., Stobbe, L., et al.: Green cloud computing. Technical report, UBA (2021). https://www.umweltbundesamt.de/sites/default/files/medien/5750/publikationen/2021-06-17_texte_94-2021_green-cloud-computing.pdf
9. Hartmann, M., Weber, L., Wirth, J., Sommer, L., Koch, A.: Optimizing a hardware network stack to realize an in-network ML inference application. In: 2021 IEEE/ACM H2RC, St. Louis, MO, USA, pp. 21–32. IEEE (2021). https://doi.org/10.1109/H2RC54759.2021.00008

10. High-Performance Computing Data Center Power Usage Effectiveness. https://www.nrel.gov/computational-science/measuring-efficiency-pue.html. Accessed 06 Apr 2023
11. How tall is the die for the 10ax115n3f40i2sges? https://community.intel.com/t5/Programmable-Devices/How-tall-is-the-die-for-the-10AX115N3F40I2SGES/m-p/592124. Accessed 05 Apr 2023
12. Javaid, H., Yang, J., Santoso, N., Upadhyay, M., et al.: Blockchain machine: a network-attached hardware accelerator for hyperledger fabric. In: 2022 IEEE 42nd ICDCS, Bologna, Italy, pp. 258–268. IEEE (2022). https://doi.org/10.1109/ICDCS54860.2022.00033
13. Kachris, C., Soudris, D.: A survey on reconfigurable accelerators for cloud computing. In: 2016 26th IEEE FPL. IEEE (2016). https://doi.org/10.1109/fpl.2016.7577381
14. Ofenbeck, G., Steinmann, R., Caparros, V., Spampinato, D.G., Püschel, M.: Applying the roofline model. In: 2014 IEEE ISPASS, pp. 76–85 (2014). https://doi.org/10.1109/ISPASS.2014.6844463
15. Ringlein, B., Abel, F., Ditter, A., Weiss, B., et al.: Programming reconfigurable heterogeneous computing clusters using MPI with transpilation. In: 2020 IEEE/ACM H2RC, GA, USA, pp. 1–9. IEEE (2020). https://doi.org/10.1109/H2RC51942.2020.00006
16. Schelten, N., Steinert, F., Knapheide, J., Schulte, A., Stabernack, B.: A high-throughput, resource-efficient implementation of the RoCEv2 remote DMA protocol and its application. ACM Trans. Reconfigurable Technol. Syst. 1–23 (2022). https://doi.org/10.1145/3543176
17. Schödwell, B., Zarnekow, R., Liu, R., Gröger, J., Wilkens, M.: Kennzahlen und Indikatoren für die Beurteilung der Ressourceneffizienz von Rechenzentren und Prüfung der praktischen Anwendbarkeit. Technical report, UBA (2018). https://www.umweltbundesamt.de/sites/default/files/medien/1410/publikationen/2018-02-23_texte_19-2018_ressourceneffizienz-rechenzentren.pdf
18. Sn2700 open ethernet switch. Technical report, Mellanox Technologies (2019)
19. SPEC CINT2006: Integer component of spec CPU2006 (2006). https://www.spec.org/cpu2006/CINT2006/
20. Steinert, F., Schelten, N., Schulte, A., Stabernack, B.: Hardware and software components towards the integration of network-attached accelerators into data centers. In: 2020 23rd Euromicro DSD, Kranj, Slovenia, pp. 149–153. IEEE (2020). https://doi.org/10.1109/DSD51259.2020.00033
21. Steinert, F., Stabernack, B.: Architecture of a low latency h.264/AVC video codec for robust ML based image classification. J. Sign. Process. Syst. **94**(7), 693–708 (2022). https://doi.org/10.1007/s11265-021-01727-2
22. Stobbe, L.: Workshop: Grundlagen der Ökobilanzierung und methodisches vorgehen für die umweltpotenzialbewertung. Technical report, Fraunhofer IZM (2023). https://owncloud.fraunhofer.de/index.php/s/IzOQHShUbTMbMX5#pdfviewer
23. Weerasinghe, J., Abel, F., Hagleitner, C., Herkersdorf, A.: Disaggregated FPGAs: network performance comparison against bare-metal servers, virtual machines and Linux containers. In: 2016 IEEE CloudCom, Luxembourg, Luxembourg, pp. 9–17. IEEE (2016). https://doi.org/10.1109/CloudCom.2016.0018
24. Weerasinghe, J., Polig, R., Abel, F., Hagleitner, C.: Network-attached FPGAs for data center applications. In: 2016 IEEE FPT, Xi'an, China, pp. 36–43. IEEE (2016). https://doi.org/10.1109/FPT.2016.7929186

Optimization of OLAP In-Memory Database Management Systems with Processing-In-Memory Architecture

Shima Hosseinzadeh[1]([⊠]) [iD], Amirhossein Parvaresh[2] [iD], and Dietmar Fey[1] [iD]

[1] Department Computer Science, Chair of Computer Architecture,
Friedrich-Alexander-Universitat Erlangen-Nürnberg (FAU), 91058 Erlangen, Germany
{shima.hosseinzadeh,dietmar.fey}@fau.de
[2] Ilmenau University of Technology, Ilmenau, Germany
amirhossein.parvaresh@tu-ilmenau.de

Abstract. With the growing popularity of Processing-In-Memory (PIM) technology, many sectors of the industry are willing to take advantage of this new technology. However, the state-of-the-art applications are not optimized to fully utilize the PIM capabilities. In this paper, an in-memory database is analyzed and its functions whose executions cause the majority of CPU clock cycles are identified. Factors such as running time and cache locality are studied and processes causing long running times are accelerated with the PIM technology. The results show that by utilizing the proposed optimization methods, there is an overall speedup of 110.94% in the selected functionalities in the database management system. Furthermore, a deep analysis of the results is provided, summarizing key observations and programming recommendations for the in-memory database developers, and providing guidelines on where to take advantage of this new memory technology, and where to avoid it.

Keywords: In-Memory Database · Processing-In-Memory · Profiling · 3D-stacked Memory · Benchmarking · Workload Characterization · Memory Systems

1 Introduction

In-memory databases are designed to accumulate the entire data in the main memory. With the increasing storage capacity of Dynamic Random Access Memory (DRAM), it is now affordable to have a hardware system that can store a very large amount of data. The main downside of the in-memory databases is that the latency and bandwidth of DRAM have become a bottleneck in data centers; a problem better known as the "memory wall" [2]. In fact, in a traditional database system, on average half of the execution time is spent on memory stalls [4].

Although DRAM's cost-per-bit has been decreasing at a rapid rate, its latency has remained almost constant. An emerging technology to tackle these

G. Goumas et al. (Eds.): ARCS 2023, LNCS 13949, pp. 264–278, 2023.
https://doi.org/10.1007/978-3-031-42785-5_18

challenges is the 3D-stacked memory, such as High Bandwidth Memory (HBM) [13] and Hybrid Memory Cube (HMC) [12]. The basic idea of this technology is to stack up DRAM and logic dies with Through-Silicon Vias (TSVs), which, in nature, implements the idea of Processing-In-Memory (PIM). This technology enables designers to build a low-power, high-performance in-memory system that potentially moves the data-intensive computation to the memory side.

From the application point of view, a PIM in the computer system does not boost performance, unless the application is adjusted to take advantage of the new memory features. Therefore, it is necessary to scrutinize the functionality of the application and specify the areas in the code that cause long running time, in order to instruct the system to execute the functions with long running time, known as hot spots, inside the memory.

One of the key applications in database management systems is query processing. This area has gained a lot of attention recently due to the exponential growth of data and its diversity, and the fact that it should be handled efficiently. As a result, PIM has been used to improve the performance of query processing. In particular, [26] designed a ReRAM-based PIM architecture based on the dot-product computation of crossbar ReRAM that mainly supports three query operations: aggregation (mainly for GROUPBY and SUM methods), restriction, and projection (for SELECT function). In [10], pointer chasing inside the memory is implemented. One of the areas where pointer chasing is heavily used is in B/B+-trees which can effectively index large data sets. High memory access in this work is alleviated by traversing linked data structures inside the memory instead of sending the data to the CPU and waiting to receive it. Note that only the final node is sent to the CPU for decreasing data movement between RAM and CPU.

The study [19] investigates the challenges posed by data movement between CPU and main memory in computer systems and compares traditional and emerging techniques for mitigating data movement bottlenecks, and involves a large-scale characterization of applications.

In this paper, a thorough analysis of an Online Analytical Processing (OLAP) in-memory database is presented to find its functions with a long running time. These functions are further studied and accelerated by using in-memory processing technology. The results show that by optimizing the database management systems with in-memory processing, an overall speedup of 110.94% is achieved in comparison with the case where all the processing is performed on the CPU. Moreover, functions that cannot be accelerated with the PIM technology are identified. Finally, guidelines are presented for the database developers about how to use the new PIM technology in the best way possible.

The remainder of this paper is organized as follows. In Sect. 2, the terms and technologies used in this paper are described. Section 3 describes the database setup and how the experiment is done using the simulation environment. In Sect. 4, the experimental data is investigated, and some key observations are discussed. In Sect. 5, the results are demonstrated and their behavior are justified. Finally, in Sect. 6, a quick summary of the observations made in this paper are presented.

2 Preliminaries

2.1 3D-DRAM

The 3D high-capacity memories were designed by stacking DRAM dies on top of each other, in order to provide higher capacity and bandwidth for the era of big data. Bandwidth barriers and parallelism capability of Double Data Rate (DDR) interface for high-speed computing motivated memory manufacturers to develop high-performance RAM by utilizing TSV-stacked DRAM. There are some good examples of manufactured 3D-DRAM, such as Micron's HMC [6], and Samsung's HBM-PIM [13].

Most 3D-DRAM devices consist of multiple DRAM dies plus one logic die stacked on top of each other. These dies are connected via TSVs and there are vaults that are vertical memory organizations within each cube. The vaults comprise a set of memory portions from various DRAM dies that are connected with a vault controller within the logic die.

There are numerous advantages that come with 3D-DRAM when compared with conventional DRAM. These advantages can be summarized as follows:

- **Capacity**: In stacked DRAM dies, one cube can hold more capacity with the same package footprint as the traditional DRAM device.
- **Aggregated bandwidth and parallelism**: A 3D-DRAM accomplishes its high bandwidth by combining numerous TSVs in each cube with a high transfer rate.
- **Energy efficiency**: Shorter TSV buses trim the capacitance and length of connections between the memory controller and DRAM devices, making the 3D-DRAM more efficient than DDRx memories. The work [27] has demonstrated that 3D-stacked memories, such as HBM and HMC, can be up to 15× more energy efficient than an equivalent DDRx manufactured by Micron.
- **Abstracted interface**: In contrast to DDRx-based systems, a generalized protocol is necessary to communicate with single or multiple cubes, separating the memory controller function from the CPU. By employing a logical layer within the cubes, the CPU can issue read and write commands instead of device-specific CAS (Column Address Strobe) and RAS (Row Address Strobe) commands, effectively concealing silicon variation and bank conflicts within each cube.
- **Near-memory computation**: With regards to HMC [6] and HBM-PIM [13] specifications, the logic die is not only used as the vault controller but also supports some atomic operational instructions. The instructions operate in read-modify-write sequence, in the sense that they operate on 16-bytes memory operands and they write back the results to DRAM layers.

2.2 Processing-In-Memory (PIM)

One of the bottlenecks in conventional computing systems is the data movement between processing units and memory devices. The state-of-the-art PIM technique has recently emerged as a promising solution to this challenge [3,5,21,30] by a range of technologies from 3D memory technology to within memory computation logic such as PIM in nonvolatile memories [9].

Classification of PIM Logic. There are two main categories of processing units with regard to their execution model, namely, fully programmable PIM, and fixed-function PIM [16].

In fully programmable PIM logic, a processor fetches, decodes, and executes instructions from the code loaded onto the PIM accelerator. This approach enables compatibility with conventional compilers but requires the programmer to manage communication between the host processor and the PIM unit.

Fixed-function PIM involves a defined processing unit or established operations based on memory access instructions. This method can encode PIM operations in modified LOAD and STORE instructions or through special prefixes in a general-purpose processor's ISA. It further categorizes into Bounded-operand PIM Operation (BPO), applying a fixed number of operations to data, and Compound PIM Operation (CPO), involving a changing number of operations and memory locations.

2.3 PIM Simulation Environment

HMC-Sim is one of the first HMC simulators that feature cycle-accurate simulation, but it lacks scalability for PIM support. PIMSim [28] is a trace-based simulator for PIM architecture that supports both host-side and memory-side simulation. It allows users to configure PIM units and offers three input types to accommodate varying simulation requirements. PIMSim aims to support new memory types, such as HMC and HBM.

Another tool for 3D-DRAM simulation is Ramulator-PIM which is a combination of ZSim [24] and Ramulator [14] for a design space exploration of general-purpose PIM architectures. In this simulation framework, a host CPU is considered alongside PIM cores that are located in the logical layer of 3D stacked memory. This tool has the ability to simulate the host CPU and PIM cores in order to compare their performance on parts of or on the entire application. This is a trace-driven simulation, in which a modified version of ZSim provides memory traces for feeding the Ramulator.

3 Experimental Setup

In this work, a thorough experiment on the PIM for query processing acceleration is conducted, which sheds light on how this technology can be used to make database management systems faster.

Fig. 1. Specifying Region Of Interest (ROI) in Code

3.1 Database Management System

In this paper, DuckDB is used in the experiments, which is an embedded OLAP database management system [22]. For benchmark execution, DuckDB has a built-in benchmark runner that takes the query name of the benchmark, generates TPC-H [1] data tables, loads them into the database, and runs the query on them. The TPC-H benchmark is a decision support benchmark that measures the performance of database systems in executing ad-hoc analytical queries against a realistic and scalable dataset. It consists of a set of standardized queries that represent typical business operations. In this study, a scaling factor (SF) of 0.01 was used, which means the dataset used for the benchmark represents 1% of the full TPC-H dataset.

3.2 Profiler

To conduct the experiment for profiling purposes, Perf [7], a Linux-based performance analysis and profiling tool, is selected. Perf offers a comprehensive set of functionalities for measuring and analyzing various aspects of system performance. For this study, two specific events are utilized. Firstly, the `cpu-clock` event is employed to measure the program's execution time, providing insights into different code segments and aiding in identifying performance bottlenecks. Secondly, the `page-fault` event captures the occurrence of page faults during program execution, helping analyze memory usage and identifying potential optimization opportunities by minimizing disk I/O-induced performance degradation.

With the general knowledge acquired about the execution time and the number of page faults, the next step is to find the "hot spots" in the program. Hot spots are regions of code that take the most execution time and optimizing them has a huge impact on the overall performance. These regions are executed inside the memory. Since this analysis deals with the execution time, the `cpu-clock` event can be utilized for this purpose.

3.3 Profiling the Database

A *profile* is an annotated code that indicates hot spot execution time. It also indicates the parts of code in which specific hardware/software events occur. In order to have accurate results, the number of samples in the recorded file should be high enough, so that a correct judgment on the hot spot can be made. There are usually two ways to increase the number of samples; either by enlarging the execution time or by increasing the resolution at which samples are taken.

3.4 Simulation Environment

In the Ramulator-PIM simulation environment, a computer system is considered that consists of host CPU cores and general-purpose PIM cores. Since the HMC model is chosen for the PIM simulation, PIM cores are designated in the logic layer of the HMC 3D-stacked memory. This type of simulation enables us to simulate both host CPU cores and PIM cores, with the aim of comparing the performance of both for a specific application, or even a part of an application.

With hot spot regions identified in the profiling step, these regions, which are also known as offload regions in PIM simulation, are executed in PIM cores. ZSim provides a library that facilitates the instrumentation and can be used by adding its header to the program we want to test. Then, the region of interest (ROI) is marked in the code using hooks (see Fig. 1).

4 Analysis

4.1 Finding the Hot Spots

The profiling procedure was done in a non-virtualized environment, mainly due to the high potential for value contamination, which can negatively impact the reliability and accuracy of the collected performance data. Easy access to program counters and performance registers may not be readily available in such environments, further complicating the profiling process.

4.2 Observations and Discussion

Based on the profiling results, it can be seen that most of the speed bottlenecks in the database execution are caused by data movement between the main memory and the CPU. Two important functions that cause high data movement are memcpy() and memset(), which are the focus of acceleration in this paper. Figure 2 shows the result of running each TPC-H query and verifies the percentage of cache misses caused by functions used to implement SELECT.

The result in Fig. 2 indicates that a large portion of cache misses in most TPC-H queries are caused by either the Linux kernel or function calls for the SELECT operator. While it is true that cache misses caused by the Linux kernel are prevalent, it is important to note that they are not entirely inevitable. The kernel's behavior is largely influenced by user mode programs through system calls, implying that cache misses can be influenced and potentially minimized by optimizing the interaction between user programs and the kernel[1].

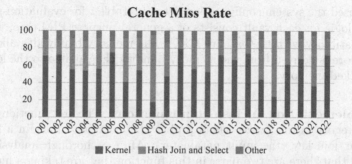

Fig. 2. Cache Miss Rate With TPC-H Workload

---

[1] Q1, Q2, etc. represents the query names in the TPC-H workload.

Note that a multi-level cache hierarchy is beneficial for applications that have hierarchical reuse patterns, in which higher and smaller cache levels respond to most accesses to later levels. However, it is worth mentioning that in conventional systems, where data processing predominantly occurs within processor cores, data often necessitates traversal through the memory hierarchy before it can undergo processing. In such systems, only applications whose data can be fitted in small caches can benefit from speed-ups, whereas other applications with large data footprints should spend a large portion of their time shuffling data to and from cache levels.

4.3   Analysis of the Bottlenecks

After scrutinizing the functions that cause bottlenecks in each query, they are classified into three main categories:

- **Hash Join functions**: Functions such as `Probe`, `InsertHashes`, `ApplyBitmask`, `SerializeVectorData`, etc. are all members of this category.
- **Select functions**: Consists of functions such as `Copy` in vector utility class, `Select`, and `AppendData` in vector operations class, which are used implicitly in the `SELECT` operation.
- **Other functions**: The functions that could not fit into the other two categories fall under this one. These are functions for string analysis and manipulation, and time and date settings. Examples of this category are `Analyze` in the UTF8 utility class, `FromCString` in the date utility class, and `string_t`.

In the following section, some of the important functions mentioned above are further analyzed and are designed to be executed inside the memory. Afterward, the performance of PIM and non-PIM execution are compared to verify PIM enhancements.

5   Results

5.1   PIM Implementation

We have used the system configuration listed in Table 1 for evaluation purposes. The PIM logic for each vault consists of a general-purpose PIM core, which has ISA compatibility with the baseline CPU. The memory bandwidth allocated to the PIM core is derived from the memory bandwidth available to the logic layer of 3D-stacked memory.

PIM Implementation in Hash Join Functions. The first function analyzed in this category is the `Probe` which probes the engaging tables in a hash join using their join key (the input parameter). After a thorough analysis, it was concluded that there are two parts in this function that are taking a huge chunk of CPU clocks, namely the `ApplyBitmask` function utilized for initializing the pointers of the scan structure based on the hashes, and a for loop for creating

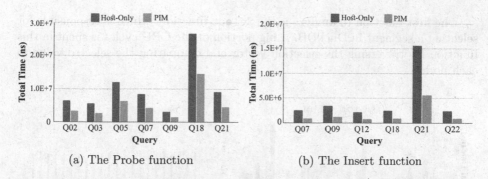

(a) The Probe function   (b) The Insert function

Fig. 3. Total Running Time Comparison of the Hash Join functions

Table 1. Evaluated System Configuration

Host CPU	4 Out-of-Order Cores at 2.2 GHz, 22 nm, x86_64 ISA
Baseline Caches	L1 I/D Cache, 32 KB, 4-cycle; L2 Cache, 256 KB, 8-way, 4-cycle; L3 Cache, 6 MB, 12-way, 27-cycle
Baseline Memory	16 GB DDR3-1600, Bus Bandwidth 25.6 GB/s
PIM Core	1 Out-of-Order processing unit per vault at 2.4 GHz, L1 I/D Cache 32 KB 8-way, L2 Cache 256 KB 8-way
3D-Stacked Memory	8 GB total size, 32 vaults (per cube), DRAM with 166 MHz Frequency

the selection vector. According to the `Perf` report on Query, 18.87% of the CPU clocks were dedicated to these two parts in the `Probe` function.

Figure 3a demonstrates the total time of running the `Probe` in host-only and PIM mode. It should be noted that only Q02, Q03, Q05, Q07, Q09, Q18, and Q21 were chosen for benchmarking since the `Probe` function was heavily utilized in these queries.

The results show that on average **96.9%** speedup is gained when the `Probe` function is executed inside the memory. By analyzing the `Probe` function, it can be seen that the bottlenecks of this function were mostly simple, yet repetitive, operations such as linked-list pointer chasing and simple addition, and running them inside the memory resulted in an acceptable speedup. From the other point of view, the `Probe` function does not fully utilize cache locality, which makes it more compelling to be executed inside the memory.

Next in this category, the `InsertHashes` function is verified. As the name implies, this function is used to add a new entry in the hash table, and the bottleneck consists of a call to `ApplyBitmask` function to get the appropriate position to add, and a for loop to adjust pointers in the vector when the new item (node) is added. After running Q07, Q09, Q12, and Q18 TPC-H queries they showed high running time in `Perf`, as depicted in Fig. 3b.

The PIM results in the `InsertHashes` were promising, due to their ease of operation, and low cache locality. Based on the results, **278.6%** speedup was achieved when this function was executed inside the memory.

PIM Implementation in Select Functions. In this section, bottleneck functions that were used in the process of the `SELECT` operation will be examined. These functions are mainly used to scan through a table, copy the results, and add them to the final data structure.

The first function to analyze is the `Select` function, which is responsible for selecting a segment in DuckDB. A big portion of the CPU cycles is spent in this function for traversing the selection vector and comparing the selected value to each node.

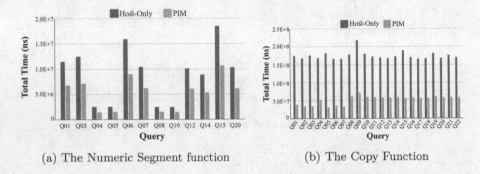

(a) The Numeric Segment function   (b) The Copy Function

Fig. 4. Total Running Time Comparison of Select functions

Because of the similar nature of this function with the ones already discussed, the speedup was expected, which is on average **69.1%**.

The next function is the `Copy` in the vector operations class, which is heavily used in the `SELECT`, and other database operations. The main duty of this function is to copy the content of one vector to another, and it is used in a variety of use cases in DuckDB. As can be seen in Fig. 4b, a significant speedup was achieved when the `Copy` function was executed in the PIM mode. Functions such as `Copy`, which spend a large number of CPU cycles on memory latency, can benefit from PIM by eliminating the data movement from CPU to RAM and vice versa. The average speedup achieved in this experiment is **351.3%**.

Finally, the last function is the `AppendData` in the string segment class. Although this function is not a specific function used in the `SELECT` operation,

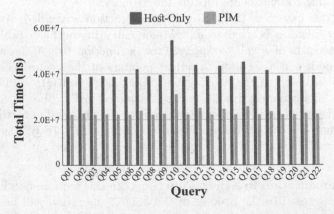

Fig. 5. Total Running Time Comparison of the AppendData function in String Segment

according to the `Perf` analysis, it is heavily used implicitly in the `SELECT` operation. This function consists of pointer manipulation, verification on added value (if it is null or not), verification on overflow block, and finally appending the data to the desired vector or dictionary. The comparison result of running time when this function is executed in PIM and host-only mode can be seen in Fig. 5.

The average speedup achieved in running `AppendData` in PIM mode is **75.2%**. It is notable to mention that the speedup here is not as great as the one achieved in `Copy` since the operations in the `AppendData` are more complex and they benefit more from cache locality.

PIM Implementation in Other Functions. In this section, other functions that could not be fitted in either of the previous two categories but still are bottlenecks are verified.

The example here is the `FromCString` function in the date utility class, which as its name implies, is used to convert the C-formatted date strings into the Date class. The result of the simulation can be seen in Fig. 6a.

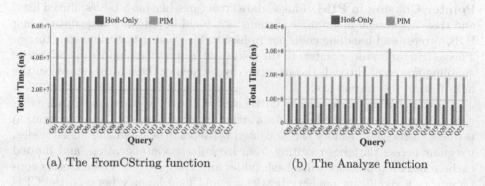

(a) The FromCString function   (b) The Analyze function

Fig. 6. Total Running Time Comparison of other functions

Not only this function did not gain any benefits from the PIM mode, but also it lost on average **−53.2%** of its performance. The reason behind this negative result could be justified by the way this function works; its operations are complex and after cache analysis, it could be seen that it benefited from cache locality. As a result, running it inside the memory caused performance degradation.

The other function chosen for this category is the `Analyze` function in the UTF utility class. The function consists of an algorithm to check if a string is a valid UTF8. Based on the analysis done with `Perf`, it seems that this function benefits from the cache hierarchy. The results can be seen in Fig. 6b.

Due to the complex algorithm and high cache locality, some degradation in speed compared to the host-only scenario can be seen. On average, **−41.3%** speed loss was achieved when the code was executed inside the memory.

The last function in this category is the `string_t` function. This is the member function of the proprietary string type in the DuckDB that uses low-level functions such as `memset()` and `memcpy()` for efficient creation and modification of strings in DuckDB. In order to accelerate this function, the underlying `memset()` and `memcpy` are executed inside the memory so that the overhead of moving data to the CPU and back to the memory is eliminated. The results of running this function in host-only and PIM mode are demonstrated in Fig. 7. It can be seen that the speed up is about **76.0%** when running this function inside the memory.

5.2   Database Design Considerations with PIM

Looking at the results achieved by database system analysis and the simulation results on Ramulator-PIM, there are many interesting facts learned from this simulation. Among them, there are three important points that can be very helpful for database designers. These points are elaborated in this section.

Pointer Chasing in PIM. Linked data structures like hash tables, linked lists, and trees are crucial in database systems. They aid in indexing large data (using B/B+ trees) and handling collisions in hash tables (using key-value structures). These structures store pointers to the next (and/or previous) nodes in each node, enabling traversal through the structure by retrieving the address stored in the next field of the current node.

Pointer chasing, performed by CPU cores within an application thread, experiences degradation as the linked data structure grows larger. This deterioration is due to serialized memory access caused by dependencies among linked nodes, irregular access patterns resulting from irregular node allocation, and limited cache reuse in applications like hash tables and B/B+ trees. These factors contribute to a significant memory bottleneck and long latency between the CPU and memory during linked data structure traversal [8,17,18].

The PIM mechanism can be used here to avoid moving data to the CPU. PIM has the advantage of reducing the latency, as an address does not need to be brought to the CPU before de-referencing, and also the process of node traversal would not rely on caching and pre-fetching. Since database systems heavily use linked data structures, PIM can bring a huge performance boost as is proven by the results of this section.

Bulk Bitwise Operations Using PIM. One of the bottlenecks of the database system that is verified in this section is the bit-wise operation (AND, OR, NOT, etc.) on large bit vectors. The example of a bulk bitwise operation in this study is the `ApplyBitmask` function, which caused a bottleneck for both `Probe` and `InsertHashes` functions. In fact, many modern databases are utilizing bulk bitwise operations to support bitmap indices. As an example, the recent work called "WideTable" [15] designed the complete database system geared around a technique called BitWeaving [29], which speeds up the scan operation

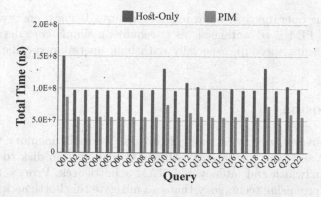

Fig. 7. Total Running Time Comparison of the string_t

using bulk bitwise operation. In commodity systems, a bulk bitwise operation needs a large amount of data to be transferred to the memory channel. This high-volume data transfer could result in high energy and bandwidth consumption, and high memory latency. Although there have been some studies on accelerating bulk bitwise operation using GPUs and field-programmable gate arrays (FPGAs), their throughput is limited due to the limited memory bandwidth.

The benefit of using a 3D-stacked memory such as HMC is that thanks to its high memory bandwidth between its banks, and a logic layer, processing bulk bitwise operations would be significantly accelerated. According to the results of the experiments done on the `ApplyBitmask` function, it is evident that running a bulk bitwise operation inside memory can achieve high acceleration.

Bulk Data Copy and Initialization with PIM. There are numerous operations in database systems that trigger bulk data copy and data initialization. Although these types of operations do not need any sort of computation, with the current system, a large amount of data must be transferred back and forth to the memory controller to perform these operations. All the bulk data operations can result in high energy, bandwidth, and latency consumption, which in turn degrades system performance and energy efficiency.

There are two reasons behind this inefficiency caused by the bulk data operations. First, current systems perform these operations one word or cache line at a time, which directly results in high latency. Second, due to a large amount of data transfer across memory channels caused by bulk operations, a significant amount of bandwidth is consumed, leaving less bandwidth for other operations, which consequently results in high latency [25].

Accelerating bulk data copy and initialization is crucial for improving overall database system performance. Previous studies [20,23] have demonstrated that a significant amount of time is wasted in the operating system due to these operations. Despite some enhancements, such as enhanced copy and move instructions (ERMSB) in x86 ISA [11], the underlying architecture remains largely unchanged, resulting in limited improvements.

Performing operations in main memory reduces latency, energy, and bandwidth issues. PIM is advantageous as it requires a simple core design and can achieve significant speedup, especially with bulk operation-specific cores ([25], Fig. 7).

6   Conclusion

Modern databases are transitioning from disk to main memory, due to low DRAM price and their low latency. All the transition from disk to DRAM has made the bandwidth and latency of DRAM a bottleneck. Processing In Memory is a new promising technology that can mitigate this bottleneck by avoiding bulk data migration to CPU and backward and also is able to handle simple operations in the main memory.

In this study, first, a thorough database profiling was performed to find the hot spots in the DuckDB database. Then, a PIM simulator was used to accelerate these bottlenecks. The hot spots were caused by three types of functions; SELECT functions, Hash Join functions, and other functions such as string creation and manipulation.

This paper showed how a database designer can benefit from PIM technology to achieve the best out of this technology. Pointer chasing is one of the areas that is widely used in the database systems, such as in B/B+ trees, key-value data structures, and hash tables. It was demonstrated that running pointer chasing inside the memory can significantly accelerate database operations. In addition, bulk bitwise operations such as AND, OR, and NOT can be well performed inside the memory, as was seen in functions such as ApplyBitmask. Finally, bulk data initialization and copy can benefit from PIM, since the data does not have to move to the CPU and back to perform such operations.

Acknowledgement. We would like to acknowledge Dr. Seyyed Ali Hashemi for his valuable feedback and suggestions that improved this work.

References

1. TPC-H Benchmark. http://www.tpc.org/tpch/. Accessed 11 Dec 2022
2. Wulf, W.A., McKee, S.A.: Hitting the memory wall: implications of the obvious. ACM SIGARCH Comput. Archit. News **23**, 20–24 (1995)
3. Ahn, J., Hong, S., et al.: A scalable processing-in-memory accelerator for parallel graph processing. In: Proceedings of the 42nd Annual International Symposium on Computer Architecture, pp. 105–117 (2015)
4. Ailamaki, A., DeWitt, D., et al.: DBMSs on a modern processor: where does time go? In: VLDB 1999, Proceedings of 25th International Conference on Very Large Data Bases, 7–10 September 1999, Edinburgh, Scotland, UK, pp. 266–277 (1999)
5. Akin, B., Franchetti, F., et al.: Data reorganization in memory using 3D-stacked dram. ACM SIGARCH Comput. Archit. News **43**, 131–143 (2015)
6. Hybrid Memory Cube Consortium: HMC specification 2.0 (2015)

7. De Melo, A.: The new Linux 'perf' tools. In: Slides from Linux Kongress, pp. 1–42 (2010)
8. Ebrahimi, E., Mutlu, O., et al.: Techniques for bandwidth-efficient prefetching of linked data structures in hybrid prefetching systems. In: 2009 IEEE 15th International Symposium on High Performance Computer Architecture, pp. 7–17 (2009)
9. Hosseinzadeh, S., Klemm, M., et al.: Optimizing multi-level ReRAM memory for low latency and low energy consumption. it-Inf. Technol. **65**(1–2), 52–64 (2023)
10. Hsieh, K., Khan, S., et al.: accelerating pointer chasing in 3D-stacked memory: challenges, mechanisms, evaluation. In: 2016 IEEE 34th International Conference on Computer Design (ICCD), pp. 25–32 (2016)
11. Intel: Intel 64 and IA-32 architectures optimization reference manual. Intel Corporation (2014)
12. Jeddeloh, J., Keeth, B.: Hybrid memory cube new dram architecture increases density and performance. In: 2012 Symposium on VLSI Technology (VLSIT), pp. 87–88 (2012)
13. Kim, J., Kang, S., et al.: Aquabolt-XL: Samsung HBM2-PIM with in-memory processing for ML accelerators and beyond. In: 2021 IEEE Hot Chips 33 Symposium (HCS), pp. 1–26 (2021)
14. Kim, Y., Yang, W., et al.: Ramulator: a fast and extensible DRAM simulator. IEEE Comput. Archit. Lett. **15**, 45–49 (2015)
15. Li, Y., Patel, J.: Widetable: an accelerator for analytical data processing. Proc. VLDB Endow. **7**, 907–918 (2014)
16. Loh, G., Jayasena, N., et al.: A processing in memory taxonomy and a case for studying fixed-function PIM. In: Workshop on Near-Data Processing (WoNDP), pp. 1–4 (2013)
17. Luk, C., Mowry, T.: Compiler-based prefetching for recursive data structures. In: Proceedings of the Seventh International Conference on Architectural Support for Programming Languages and Operating Systems, pp. 222–233 (1996)
18. Mutlu, O., Kim, H., et al.: Address-value delta (AVD) prediction: increasing the effectiveness of runahead execution by exploiting regular memory allocation patterns. In: MICRO 2005, pp. 12-pp (2005)
19. Oliveira, G., Gómez-Luna, J., et al.: DAMOV: a new methodology and benchmark suite for evaluating data movement bottlenecks. IEEE Access **9**, 134457–134502 (2021)
20. Ousterhout, J.: Why aren't operating systems getting faster as fast as hardware. In: Summer USENIX 1990 (1990)
21. Pugsley, S., Jestes, J., et al.: NDC: analyzing the impact of 3D-stacked memory+ logic devices on MapReduce workloads. In: 2014 IEEE International Symposium on Performance Analysis of Systems and Software (ISPASS), pp. 190–200 (2014)
22. Raasveldt, M., Mühleisen, H.: DuckDB: an embeddable analytical database. In: Proceedings of the 2019 International Conference on Management of Data, pp. 1981–1984 (2019)
23. Rosenblum, M., Bugnion, E., et al.: The impact of architectural trends on operating system performance. ACM SIGOPS Oper. Syst. Rev. **29**, 285–298 (1995)
24. Sanchez, D., Kozyrakis, C.: ZSim: fast and accurate microarchitectural simulation of thousand-core systems. ACM SIGARCH Comput. Archit. News **41**, 475–486 (2013)
25. Seshadri, V., Kim, Y., et al.: RowClone: fast and energy-efficient in-DRAM bulk data copy and initialization. In: Proceedings of the 46th Annual IEEE/ACM International Symposium on Microarchitecture, pp. 185–197 (2013)

26. Sun, Y., Wang, Y., et al.: Energy-efficient SQL query exploiting RRAM-based process-in-memory structure. In: 2017 IEEE 6th Non-Volatile Memory Systems and Applications Symposium (NVMSA), pp. 1–6 (2017)
27. Weis, C., Wehn, N., et al.: Design space exploration for 3D-stacked DRAMs. In: 2011 Design, Automation Test in Europe, pp. 1–6 (2011)
28. Xu, S., Chen, X., et al.: PIMSim: a flexible and detailed processing-in-memory simulator. IEEE Comput. Archit. Lett. **18**, 6–9 (2018)
29. Li, Y., Patel, J.: Bitweaving: fast scans for main memory data processing. In: Proceedings of the 2013 ACM SIGMOD, pp. 289–300 (2013)
30. Zhang, D., Jayasena, N., et al.: TOP-PIM: throughput-oriented programmable processing in memory. In: Proceedings of the 23rd International Symposium on High-Performance Parallel and Distributed Computing, pp. 85–98 (2014)

Organic Computing Applications 2 (OC)

Real-Time Data Transmission Optimization on 5G Remote-Controlled Units Using Deep Reinforcement Learning

Nikita Smirnov[✉][iD] and Sven Tomforde[iD]

University of Kiel, Christian-Albrechts-Platz 4, 24118 Kiel, Germany
{nsm,st}@informatik.uni-kiel.de
https://www.ins.informatik.uni-kiel.de/

Abstract. The increasing demand for real-time data transmission for the remote-controlled units and the complexity of 5G networks pose significant challenges to achieving optimal performance in device-based scenarios, when the 5G network cannot be controlled by its users. This paper proposes a model-free Deep Reinforcement Learning approach for this task. The model learns an optimal policy for maximizing the data transmission rate while minimizing the latency and packet loss. Such an approach aims to investigate the applicability of the environment-agnostic agents driven purely by the transmission statistics of the acknowledged packets. The evaluation is done with the help of a 5G simulation based on the OMNeT++ network simulator and the obtained results are compared to a classic throughput-based adaptive bitrate streaming approach. Multiple questions and challenges that arose on the way to the final model and evaluation procedure are highlighted in detail. The resulting findings demonstrate the effectiveness of Deep Reinforcement Learning for optimizing real-time data transmission in 5G networks in an online manner.

Keywords: deep reinforcement learning · data transmission · adaptive bitrate streaming · 5G networks · remote-controlled unit · organic computing

1 Introduction

Organic Computing (OC) is a research field that aims to maintain the controllability of technical systems in the face of ever-increasing complexity by shifting tasks from the developer to the system itself [10]. The result is typically collectives of self-adaptive and self-organizing systems using machine learning technology that makes independent decisions based on objective functions. Especially learning technology from the field of Deep Learning (DL) and Deep Reinforcement Learning (DRL) has been proven as key-enablers for OC-capabilities.

A highly topical area of application for OC technology is autonomous systems, such as those found in the context of autonomous shipping. In this paper,

G. Goumas et al. (Eds.): ARCS 2023, LNCS 13949, pp. 281–295, 2023.
https://doi.org/10.1007/978-3-031-42785-5_19

we consider the scenario of an autonomous ferry navigating within the overloaded maritime areas, see e.g. [19]. As full autonomy is currently restricted due to legal issues, either an onboard or a remote control by a human is required. As part of current research projects, the unmanned ferry (see Fig. 1) is equipped with fifth-generation (5G) wireless communication technology to transfer its sensor data such as video and 3D point cloud flows to the shore-based remote control center.

The rapid development of 5G technology has increased the potential reliability of remote-controlled units (RCUs). The real-time data transmission in 5G-based RCUs is crucial for ensuring seamless communication between the operator and the unit, which demands low latency, high reliability, and efficient use of network resources. Since in our ferry scenario, dramatically more data is generated than 5G capacity is available, the system has to select and adapt the communicated data at runtime based on changing conditions.

The main contribution of this paper is the application, setup and testing of a general-purpose Deep Reinforcement Learning (DRL) for optimizing the real-time data transmission on the RCUs in 5G networks, where DRL agent learns to make optimal decisions based on the network conditions while so far avoiding using 5G environmental data and any knowledge about the problem. A simulation-based testbed is developed to verify the proposed approach while using both simulated and real data. This paper contributes to the growing body of research on OC and the application of DRL to wireless communication networks and it provides insights into the potential benefits of using DRL solutions in 5G networks or OC systems in general.

This paper is organized as follows: Sect. 2 shortly reviews the related work, Sect. 3 presents the optimization problem, Sect. 4 describes the proposed approach, Sect. 5 addresses evaluation and results and Sect. 6 briefly recaps the content of previous parts and concludes the paper with possible future work.

Fig. 1. Design of a 5G remote-controlled passenger ferry "Wavelab" for the Bay of Kiel.

2   Related Work

Considering optimization problems in 5G networks with machine and/or deep learning applications, there is a huge trend towards network-based solutions [14]. Unlike device-based problems, it is assumed that a developer has partial or even full control over a 5G network and may change the hardware or software parts of it so that optimization problems are more concentrated on the network-management aspects rather than on the data transmission ones. Typical examples of such problems could be network slicing, power allocation and control, scheduling, handover management, etc. [16].

A standard approach to optimize data transmission is known as adaptive bitrate streaming (ABR). Current edge- and cloud-solutions are very diverse and are massively used in everyday streaming, especially by popular video streaming services like YouTube, Netflix and other popular services. Standard techniques are based on controlling two main features: a) video bitrate, i.e., the amount of data send in the current period and b) playback stability, i.e., how smooth and continuous is the video playing on the consumer side [3].

Intelligent solutions enhance standard techniques with smart retransmission mechanisms [12], with DL-based predictive assistance [1] and also with DRL integration by introducing an agent with a state including bitrate, downloading time of the previous stream chunks and buffer occupancy [2,8]. Almost all of the existing approaches for adaptive bitrate streaming assume that the data is **on-demand** and is transmitted over the popular contemporary streaming protocols like MPEG-DASH, HLS, WebRTC and others [7] so that they try to optimize both throughput and playback smoothness. A pure bitrate-based approach with DRL assistance is used in [15] without directly taking into account latency and packet loss factors, which are very important in 5G networks.

Another important factor is that the sensors on remote-controlled units are usually heterogeneous, not only cameras but often other remote sensing devices like LiDARs and RADARs that produce 3D point clouds. Although there is a way how to reduce point clouds to a video flow by using classic MPEG video encoders as a compression tool [18], the most popular approach still involves space-partitioning trees [4], so that a generalization of adaptive bitrate streaming solutions for all possible types of data with their encoding options is needed.

3   Real-Time Data Transmission Problem

Improving performance for real-time data transmission is a more complicated and challenging task in comparison to a standard adaptive bitrate streaming since the consumer's buffer cannot be filled for some time in advance, otherwise, a human operator of the controlled unit will deal with outdated data and playback delays. Therefore, the only way is to try to optimize the bitrate directly. Due to this constraint, it is not possible to use standard HTTP algorithms like throughput-based FESTIVE [6] or buffer-based BOLA [20], since they all presuppose that: a) the consumer's buffer is used and could be manipulated, b) it is possible to have simultaneous streams with different bitrate presets. While the second condition can be so far neglected since the data, especially video data, can be encoded on-the-fly relatively fast, the first one remains unfeasible.

Given the above, the optimization problem designated in this article as "real-time data transmission" could be formulated as follows:

> try to **maximize the uplink goodput (GPT)** while at the same time **minimize the round-trip-time (RTT)** and **minimize the packet loss rate (PLR)** *by* selecting a proper bitrate for one or multiple streams for a certain period *without* holding the data in some buffer neither on the sender nor the receiver side.

It is assumed that goodput, as well as RTT, are measured at the application level, and the processing delays for unpacking and decoding the data are neglected. It is also assumed that **all optimization happens directly on the RCU**, therefore, there is no information about the packet as long as the receiver's acknowledgment does not come back. A unit uses "best-effort" transport protocols (UDP-based ones) since retransmission mechanisms are not required.

There is no ready-made formula for selecting the optimal bitrate for the next period based on the previously used bitrate and collected network feedback. *It may be even unfeasible in general due to the complexity of relations between these parameters.* The only known connection between throughput, RTT and PLR is Mathis formula for TCP congestion algorithm [9]:

$$\text{BW} < \frac{\text{MSS}}{\text{RTT}} \frac{1}{\sqrt{p}} \tag{1}$$

where BW is a bandwidth of a TCP connection, MSS is the maximum segment size (usually equals to 1460 bytes considering IP MTU of 1500 bytes) and p is a probability of a packet loss. This formula only gives an upper bound in realistic scenarios, requires a predictable loss rate and is tailored for a TCP congestion window.

There is a wide range of interconnected factors that can impact the overall performance of the data transmission and the network feedback and not all of them could be controlled by a unit itself. For example, RTT can vary depending on the uplink or downlink congestion induced by other 5G devices as well as the number of network hops in between, while PLR is strongly influenced by the distance and the orientation towards the nearest 5G base stations and physical channel quality at the moment. And since all optimization happens on a unit and a public 5G network is used, the middle layers of the core network as well as the intern computations of the base stations are hidden. Temporal relations between GPT, RTT and PLR could be studied only by observing the transmission behavior.

In summary, the absence even of an approximate formula in the general case that describes complex relationships between the key parameters and the overall complexity of a problem was the initial motivation to try to learn it with a model-free DRL approach: to investigate how far the agent could discover these relations, how well it responds to their changing behavior and can optimize its own decisions based on the observed experience of real-time data transmission in the 5G network.

4 Approach: Deep Reinforcement Learning

As mentioned above, model-free DRL was chosen as the main approach in this paper. The main advantage in comparison to the supervised learning is that it does not require any labeled data or the expert knowledge, which are both hard to be obtained for this problem. As a disadvantage, the results are dependent on the manual fine-tuning of agent's behavior control encoded through the reward function. It was also so far consciously decided not to use any device-available 5G information to help to train the agent to investigate the limits of applicability of **environment-agnostic feedback-driven approach**, i.e., the agent learns so far independently from the actual communication technology, location, etc. so that the achieved knowledge is easier to be transferred to other scenarios.

4.1 Background and Model

Reinforcement Learning is a type of machine learning that involves training an agent to learn through interaction with the environment. The agent receives feedback in the form of rewards or penalties for each action it takes. Markov Decision Process (MDP) is a mathematical framework used to model decision-making problems. It assumes that the current state of the environment contains all relevant information necessary to make a decision and that the environment follows the so-called Markov property, meaning that the process is memoryless: the probability of selecting the next state depends only on the current one. DRL is a further development of this strategy that utilizes deep neural networks (DNN) to approximate the agent's policy and value functions in MDP, see Fig. 2.

Proximal Policy Optimization (PPO) [17] was selected as a primary model among different contemporary DRL algorithms. It is an on-policy algorithm that employs a clipped surrogate objective function that constrains policy updates to prevent large policy changes that could negatively impact learning stability. One

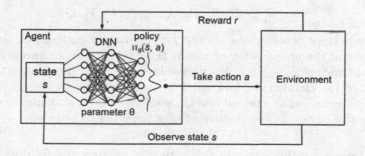

Fig. 2. Deep Reinforcement Learning workflow.

big advantage is its ability to handle both discrete and continuous action spaces. Furthermore, PPO is commonly used not only with fully-connected DNNs but also with Long Short-Term Memory (LSTM) layers, which could increase the ability to learn complicated temporal relations in sequential data and opens a perspective for further improvements.

4.2   Setup and Hyperparameters

Real-time data transmission could be always formulated as a single-agent problem by fixing the interval between two consecutive actions (transition). If a remote-controlled unit has multiple sensors and consequently multiple simultaneous streams, they could be seen as a single flow, where the current common bitrate is spread between the streams either equally or according to some prioritization scheme. It was found after some experiments that the interval equal to one second provides the best trade-off between a) a sufficient amount of sent packets together with received transmission feedback and b) a sufficiently frequent reaction of the DRL model. The first point eliminates a credit assignment problem, which would inevitably arise if the next action is applied too early, even maybe before the acknowledgments for the previous packets are delivered through a congested network. The second point provides enough flexibility for the DRL agent to control the transmission process.

The only negative drawback of this approach is the time it takes to train the agent. Since the agent waits some time to observe enough transmission with selected action, the training cannot be accelerated with modern GPUs. Even in the simulated environment, it is needed around 20–30 s to train the agent for 100 steps with one second transition period because a simulation consumes only CPU resources. On the other hand, it could be easily parallelized horizontally by training several different DRL setups simultaneously on a multi-CPU system. This drawback additionally highlights the importance of fine-tuning the DRL setup.

State. A state represents the most essential agent's parameters and the current agent's perception of the data transmission. It contains both values for a current period as well as global average values for the whole run:

$$S = \{G_p^{rx}, G_g^{rx}, R_p, R_g, J_p, J_g, P_p, P_g, V_p, Q\} \tag{2}$$

where low indexes denote either a value for the current period, p or the global average g, and the upper index rx means the receiver side. G means goodput, R - round-trip-time, J - jitter, P - packet loss rate, V is the relative standard deviation of the chunks, i.e., how much is the difference between the sizes of generated chunks within a period and Q means the quality stability, it measures how often the bitrate has been changed over the previous ten steps.

Action Space. Action space in this article is discrete and fixed so far to a size of six to compare it with standard ABR solutions: five values correspond to meaningful bitrate values and the last action turns the transmission completely off, it is the "last hope action". A set of bitrate values in kilobits per second could look like that for one video stream: $\{800, 1500, 3000, 6500, 10000\}$ reflecting typical presets from SD to 4K. It should be noted that real-world encoders cannot guarantee that they will precisely fit into the set bitrate value, there are always oscillations. This peculiarity is also transferred to the simulated streams, they may exceed with some chance an average packet size assumed for that bitrate.

Reward Function. Designing a reward function (RF) was the most challenging task due to the complex and dynamic nature of the network environment. RF needs to balance the competing objectives, such as maximizing GPT and minimizing RTT and PLR. Additionally, it should be robust to changes in network conditions and should adapt to new situations and scenarios. The function takes the current state as an argument and consists of three subparts, each of which is "responsible" for regulating one of the main optimization targets (GPT, RTT, PLR):

$$R(S) = 0.33R_{gpt}(S) + 0.33R_{rtt}(S) + 0.33R_{plr}(S) \tag{3}$$

Below is an explanation of all the parts presented in Eq. 3:

$$R_{gpt} = 0.33\frac{G_p^{rx}}{G_{max}} + 0.33\frac{G_g^{rx}}{G_{max}} + 0.33\min(\frac{G_p^{rx}}{G_g^{rx}}, 1) \tag{4}$$

$$0.5 \leq V_p < 0.75 \rightarrow R_{gpt} = 0.95R_{gpt}, V_p \geq 0.75 \rightarrow R_{gpt} = 0.9R_{gpt}$$

$$R_{gpt} = R_{gpt}(1 - \frac{Q}{10}),$$

R_{gpt} in Eq. 4 is a combination of three parts, first two examine a current global and periodic goodput at the receiver side in comparison with the maximum possible, and the last part estimates how good the agent *intents* not to perform worse than it already has. Having all three parts allow to control the goodput from all the sides and adjusting weights 0.33 were found to be the most optimal during the training. Two additional regulative mechanisms reduce the price for a goodput if a relative standard deviation of packet sizes is too big (compensates a key-frame difference) and if a bitrate is switched too often.

$$R_{rtt} =: \begin{cases} 1 - 5R_p & 0 < R_p \leq 0.1 \\ 0.6 - R_p & 0.1 < R_p \leq 0.5 \\ 0 & 0.5 < R_p < 0.9 \\ -1 & \text{otherwise} \end{cases}$$

$$J_p \geq 0.1 \wedge R_{rtt} > 0 \rightarrow R_{rtt} = 0.9R_{rtt} \tag{5}$$

R_{rtt} in Eq. 5 is built on the top of "expert knowledge". Specifications for RTTs are very tight to maintain reliability: zero is given for the RTT below half a second, and for more than 0.9 it is a constant maximum punishment. The idea is to give an extremely high reward for RTT below 100 ms., proportional reward for the RTT that is considered to be enough to provide a "good" quality of experience and harshly punish otherwise. The additional punishment is added for having a too-big jitter.

$$R_{plr} = 1 - 2P_p$$

$$\text{if no packets received} \rightarrow R = -0.25 \qquad (6)$$

R_{plr} in Eq. 6 is a linear function over a PLR, which is very vulnerable to a changed loss rate allowing to quickly punish in case of big packet drops. The last condition controls a case, when there are no packets received. It could be due to the turned-off stream as well as due to extreme congestion. It also softens the punishment from the RTT part to encourage the agent to select lower qualities.

Finally, RF is clipped in the interval $[-1, 1]$ and is equally weighted over each of the three subparts. This makes it easier to analyze and interpret a cumulative reward over multiple episodes as well as to analyze a reward distribution itself.

Hyperparameters. Hyperparameters were adjusted during multiple experiments. The main idea was to encourage the model for more exploration while still keeping a good balance. Therefore values for learning rate, entropy and clip range are changed from default ones. The size of one update was chosen to be equal to the number of steps in a single episode, the latter was chosen to be long enough (more than 10 min of data transmission) while also divisible by a batch size of 64. Network architecture is the same for both actor and critic with two hidden layers each consisting of 128 neurons. The PPO implementation was taken from stable-baselines3 library [13]. The full list of hyperparameters and the default values are presented in Table 1.

Table 1. Selected hyperparameters for the PPO model in comparison to default values.

Hyperparameter	Value	Default Value
Episodes	100	10
Steps	640	2048
Batch Size	64	256
Learning Rate	0.00025	0.0003
Gamma (discount factor)	0.99	0.99
GAE λ	0.95	0.95
Clip Range	0.1	0.2
Entropy Coef	0.01	0.0
Value Coef	0.5	0.5
Max Grad Norm	0.5	0.5
Policy Network Architecture	MLP (2 layers, 128 units each)	MLP (2 layers, 64 units each)
Value Network Architecture	MLP (2 layers, 128 units each)	MLP (2 layers, 64 units each)

4.3   Challenges

To overcome the survivorship bias, this sub-section presents the main challenges that arose on the way to the final design resulting also in rejected DRL setups that showed worse results. Some are caused by the environment, and some by the DRL setup itself:

- Stochasticity of the environment. The 5G network itself is very volatile, the next state of the DRL agent might depend not only on its actions but also on how the network behaves as a whole. That is why it has been decided to start with simulations - to minimize this factor at the beginning considering the more predictable behavior of other 5G devices.
- Low actions variation, i.e., the agent doesn't show an adaptation. It might be stuck with the maximum quality even facing extreme congestion with the hope of compensating current punishments with forthcoming rewards for maximizing a goodput or it might be too careful by not increasing the quality when the network is free. The reward function presented in this paper tries to neutralize this problem.
- "Irrational behavior" due to the cumulative nature of DRL. The agent learns a policy to maximize the cumulative reward over an episode, so it elaborates a strong bias towards certain actions or strategies, which may seem not optimal in current circumstances and may be even considered "irrational" by a human expert. An underrepresentation of "good" or "bad" network situations during the training also belongs to this problem.
- Downlink congestion. RCU waits until the package makes the full round to register it as "received" and update the statistic. If there is strong congestion in the downlink direction, the agent may misinterpret the quality of current data transmission.

5   Evaluation

5.1   5G Simulation and Scenario

The evaluation of the presented approach was conducted by developing a 5G playground using the open-source Simu5G library: the OMNeT++-based 3GPP-compliant 5G simulation written in C++ [11]. Additional modules were developed to enable working with real video and point cloud data together with encoding/decoding on-the-fly. Another implemented feature is the inter-process communication of a simulation in C++ with DRL modules from stable-baselines3 library in Python [13]. Such an approach allows to bring together multiple advantages: a) use OMNeT++ discrete events and message scheduling infrastructure, b) leverage well-developed python DL-stack, c) case further transfer to the real RCUs, where the inter-process communication with C++-based simulation will be replaced with the external communication with the real world, leaving all other parts unchanged.

The main scenario represents a sandbox, where a unit transmits the data to a server within the 5G network. The setup is adapted to a maritime field: a unit is a ferry, which sends the data from its cameras and LiDAR sensors, and a server is a shore-based station. The other 5G devices are spread over the base stations. There are also background cells imitating 5G base stations from other providers in the area, producing signal interference and noise. A full run configuration is given in Table 2, a schematic illustration of a sandbox is given in Fig. 3.

The idea of the presented sandbox scenario is to train the DRL agent with different network experiences from almost perfect to loss rates of over 70% by increasing the number of devices and their data rates as well as selecting the areas, where the agent is moving during the run. If it moves towards the bottom and right-bottom areas, then it suffers from strong congestion. On the contrary, it enjoys perfect 5G coverage, minimal delays and scheduling priority in the top and top-left areas.

Simulated streams were used during the training of the DRL model to speed up the process. Apart from saving time on reading and visualizing, they differ from the real data only by skipping the encoding, the bitrate is regulated numerically. However, the real video and LiDAR data are often used during the testing phase to verify the transmission "tolerance level" through the visualization. Sometimes "bad" transmission may be even acceptable if it still allows a human operator to adequately perceive the situation. For example, the artifacts of lost frames could be more tolerable than prolonged stalling. This process is illustrated in Fig. 4.

Table 2. A full configuration for the "sandbox" 5G scenario for DRL training.

Parameter	Value	Description
Number of gNBs	2	Number of 5G base stations (gNBs)
Number of BgCells	3	Number of background cells (BgCells)
Number of UEs	80–130	Number of other 5G devices (UEs)
Mobility Model	Random waypoints	Random trajectories for UEs
Playground area	1.5 km^2	The area for a playground
UL traffic main UE	[2.5, 20] mbit/s	Uplink traffic range for a DRL-controlled device
UL traffic other UEs	[4, 8] mbit/s	Uplink traffic range for other UEs
DL traffic other UEs	[2, 6] mbit/s	Downlink traffic range for other UEs
Simulation time	640 sec	Maximum length of one simulation run in seconds
Carrier frequency	3.6 GHz	Frequency used for transmission and reception
Bandwidth	100 MHz	Amount of frequency spectrum
Scheduling discipline	MAX C/I	Allocate resources according to signal-to-noise ratio
Antenna configuration	2 × 2 MIMO	Antenna configuration
NR scenario	Urban macro-cellular	3GPP-based 5G scenario for outdoor urban areas

The repeating OMNeT++ seeds were used to provide a reproducibility of a simulation process. The maximum bitrate was set to 10 mbit/s and constant bitrate mode (CBR) was turned on. However, PPO model itself is stochastic and always estimates actions' probability and then samples accordingly. To overcome this, it is instructed to take the *argmax* on each step. It does not make a

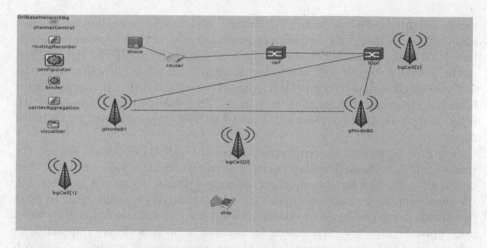

Fig. 3. OMNeT++ visualization of the "sandbox" scenario.

learned policy deterministic, on the contrary, it shrinks the variability of possible decisions, which often results in worse predictions [5], however for the first proof-of-concept it was considered an acceptable reduction.

5.2 Results

The analysis of obtained results consists of several stages. First, the training results are analyzed. Next, the agent is tested on three unseen validation sce-

Fig. 4. Visualization of a test run with one video and one LiDAR stream. The data is taken from a regular ferry and loaded into a simulation. **1** illustrates a segment loss in LiDAR stream, **2** demonstrates an artifact, **3** is a blurring effect originating from a too-big delay. One can see on **4** a console with the current transmission statistic.

narios roughly labeled as "easy", "moderate" and "hard" depending on the area
and workload. Finally, its performance is compared with the simple throughput-
based ABR algorithm, which selects the next bitrate by analyzing the goodput
of the previous step. If it is stable for three steps in a row, it selects the next
available higher quality until the maximum one is reached and downgrades it
immediately in case the goodput is reduced. The idea is to compare: a) a DRL
solution with an ABR one, and b) a model-free DRL approach with a rule-based
one.

Figure 5 illustrates a mean episodic reward (MER) collected during the
training. It is a classic learning curve: first MER explodes exponentially, then
decreases a bit and finally stabilizes on some plateau. As stated in Sect. 4.2,
the maximum step reward is equal to 1, then taking an episode equal to 640 s
(see Table 1) results in the maximum reward for one episode being 640. However, episodes are very diverse, and for some of them it is simply impossible to
achieve even half of the reward due to the extreme network conditions. Figure 6
shows the cumulative rewards collected during the three validation cases, which
makes it clear that MER from training is mostly influenced by the scenario's
complexity and the network's unpredictability.

ABR and DRL solutions were tested on the three validation scenarios and the
average outcomes were compared, see Fig. 7. DRL outperforms ABR in terms of
RTT and PLR in each of the three scenarios by sacrificing some bitrate. However,
for the "Moderate" and "Hard" scenarios DRL lowers GPT not so much in
percentage as improves the other two parameters. It is also worth saying that an
improvement of average RTT from, e.g., 80 to 60 ms is more valuable than the
proportional decrease in GPT from 5 to 4 mbit/s since the RCU is controlled
more reliably.

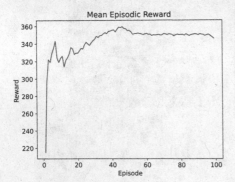

Fig. 5. Mean episodic reward during the training.

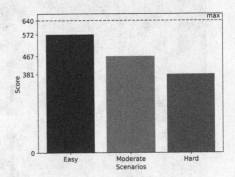

Fig. 6. Rewards for each validation scenario.

The only problem occurs with the "Easy" scenario: the agent sacrifices here
too much bitrate without a need. It could be explained that the environment-
agnostic agent learns more about how to find trade-offs in problematic cases:

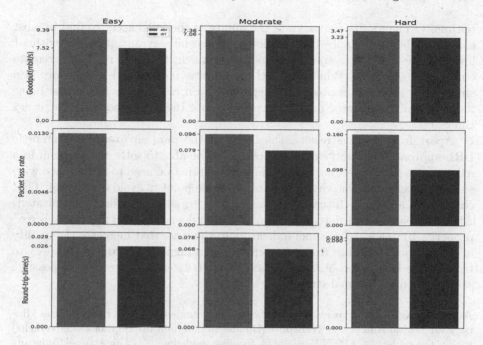

Fig. 7. The results of comparison between ABR (red) and DRL (blue) solutions on "easy", "moderate" and "hard" scenarios. (Color figure online)

if there is no loss and no strong congestion, then two of three optimization parameters (RTT, PLR) are already almost at minimum, the algorithm just needs to concentrate on keeping the transmission at the maximum rate. Such scenarios happened during the training, but they are rare because if the agent is trained on "Easy" scenarios too much, it starts losing its adaptive knowledge too fast and always selects the highest bitrate. As the result, the agent has some sort of a "fear" in "Easy" scenarios: it trembles between the two highest bitrates expecting the packet loss that may come if it stays at the maximum rate too long which will result in penalties. It is concluded that it requires adding some additional expert knowledge in its state to both perceive the adaptivity and to behave at the most optimal in all cases. This knowledge could be learned via behavioral cloning on the expert dataset.

6   Summary

The main goal of this paper was to apply the environment-agnostic and model-free DRL agent in an attempt to learn the real-data transmission problem in 5G networks and to perform better than rule-based ABR solutions without imitating their behavior. As an example problem for OC technology, it is the first step towards a data management system that could adapt to every possible network condition and control the data flow between an RCU and a human operator most optimally. The results demonstrate the ability of the DRL agent to find in most cases an effective balance between lowering the latency and loss rate without lowering the amount of transferred data too much, therefore making a remote control more reliable. While the DRL model was trained and tested only in a simulation, its design enables easy deployment on real devices in the assistance mode: a human operator might accept or ignore the suggested action at every time step.

Apart from positive results, the limits of the pure environmental-agnostic DRL approach were also clearly indicated. To be able to solve the problem in a more general way, the agent's state and reward function need to be enriched with some environmental knowledge but only to some point to avoid overfitting. That constitutes a possible future work, namely: a) to add some form of (imitated) ABR rule-based strategy to the reward function deviating from the "model-free" property, b) to add 5G channel indicators to the state that increases the quality of predictions deviating from the "environment-agnostic" property, and c) to transfer the task to a continuous action space to extend the diversity of possible actions for more optimal strategies.

Acknowledgment. This research has been partly funded by the German Federal Ministry for Digital Affairs and Transport (Bundesministerium für Digitales und Verkehr) within the project "CAPTN Förde 5G", funding guideline: "5G Umsetzungsförderung im Rahmen des 5G-Innovationsprogramms", funding code: 45FGU139_H. The authors acknowledge the financial support of the BMDV.

References

1. Biernacki, A.: Improving streaming video with deep learning-based network throughput prediction. Appl. Sci. **12**(20), 10274 (2022). https://doi.org/10.3390/app122010274
2. Cui, L., Su, D., Yang, S., Wang, Z., Ming, Z.: TCLiVi: transmission control in live video streaming based on deep reinforcement learning. IEEE Trans. Multimedia **23**, 651–663 (2021). https://doi.org/10.1109/TMM.2020.2985631
3. Dao, N.N., Tran, A.T., Tu, N.H., Thanh, T.T., Bao, V.N.Q., Cho, S.: A contemporary survey on live video streaming from a computation-driven perspective. ACM Comput. Surv. **54**(10), 1–38 (2022). https://doi.org/10.1145/3519552
4. Feng, Y., Liu, S., Zhu, Y.: Real-time spatio-temporal lidar point cloud compression (2020)
5. Huang, S., Dossa, R.F.J., Raffin, A., Kanervisto, A., Wang, W.: The 37 implementation details of proximal policy optimization (2022). https://iclr-blog-track.github.io/2022/03/25/ppo-implementation-details/. Accessed 08 Aug 2023
6. Jiang, J., Sekar, V., Zhang, H.: Improving fairness, efficiency, and stability in HTTP-based adaptive video streaming with FESTIVE. In: Proceedings of the 8th International Conference on Emerging Networking Experiments and Technologies, pp. 97–108 (2012). https://doi.org/10.1145/2413176.2413189
7. Kaur, A., Singh, S.: A survey of streaming protocols for video transmission. In: Proceedings of the International Conference on Data Science, Machine Learning and Artificial Intelligence, pp. 186–191. Association for Computing Machinery, New York (2022). https://doi.org/10.1145/3484824.3484892

8. Mao, H., Chen, S., Dimmery, D., Singh, S., Blaisdell, D., Tian, Y., et al.: Real-world video adaptation with reinforcement learning (2020)

9. Mathis, M., Semke, J., Mahdavi, J., Ott, T.: The macroscopic behavior of the TCP congestion avoidance algorithm. SIGCOMM Comput. Commun. Rev. **27**(3), 67–82 (1997). https://doi.org/10.1145/263932.264023

10. Müller-Schloer, C., Tomforde, S.: Organic Computing - Technical Systems for Survival in the Real World. Birkhäuser (2017)

11. Nardini, G., Sabella, D., Stea, G., Thakkar, P., Virdis, A.: Simu5G-An OMNeT++ library for end-to-end performance evaluation of 5G networks. IEEE Access **8**, 181176–181191 (2020). https://doi.org/10.1109/ACCESS.2020.3028550

12. Nguyen, M., Lorenzi, D., Tashtarian, F., Hellwagner, H., Timmerer, C.: DoFP+: an HTTP/3-based adaptive bitrate approach using retransmission techniques. IEEE Access **10**, 109565–109579 (2022). https://doi.org/10.1109/ACCESS.2022.3214827

13. Raffin, A., Hill, A., Gleave, A., Kanervisto, A., Ernestus, M., Dormann, N.: Stable-baselines3: reliable reinforcement learning implementations. J. Mach. Learn. Res. **22**(268), 1–8 (2021)

14. Rekkas, V.P., Sotiroudis, S., Sarigiannidis, P., Wan, S., Karagiannidis, G.K., Goudos, S.K.: Machine learning in beyond 5G/6G networks - state-of-the-art and future trends. Electronics **10**(22), 2786 (2021). https://doi.org/10.3390/electronics10222786

15. del Río Ponce, A., Serrano Romero, J., Jimenez Bermejo, D., Contreras, L., Alvarez, F.: A deep reinforcement learning quality optimization framework for multimedia streaming over 5G networks. Appl. Sci. **12**, 10343 (2022). https://doi.org/10.3390/app122010343

16. Santos, G.L., Endo, P.T., Sadok, D., Kelner, J.: When 5G meets deep learning: a systematic review. Algorithms **13**(9), 208 (2020). https://doi.org/10.3390/a13090208

17. Schulman, J., Wolski, F., Dhariwal, P., Radford, A., Klimov, O.: Proximal policy optimization algorithms (2017)

18. Schwarz, S., Preda, M., Baroncini, V., Budagavi, M., Cesar, P., Chou, P.A., et al.: Emerging MPEG standards for point cloud compression. IEEE J. Emerg. Sel. Top. Circ. Syst. **9**(1), 133–148 (2019). https://doi.org/10.1109/JETCAS.2018.2885981

19. Smirnov, N., Tomforde, S.: Navigation support for an autonomous ferry using deep reinforcement learning in simulated maritime environments. In: 2022 IEEE Conference on Cognitive and Computational Aspects of Situation Management (CogSIMA), pp. 142–149 (2022). https://doi.org/10.1109/CogSIMA54611.2022.9830689

20. Spiteri, K., Urgaonkar, R., Sitaraman, R.K.: BOLA: near-optimal bitrate adaptation for online videos. IEEE/ACM Trans. Networking **28**(4), 1698–1711 (2020). https://doi.org/10.1109/TNET.2020.2996964

Autonomous Ship Collision Avoidance Trained on Observational Data

Raphael Schwinger$^{(\boxtimes)}$ (ID), Ghassan Al-Falouji (ID), and Sven Tomforde (ID)

Christian-Albrechts-Universität zu Kiel, Kiel, Germany
{rsc,gaf,st}@informatik.uni-kiel.de

Abstract. Marine Autonomous Surface Ships (MASS) are gaining interest worldwide with the potential to reshape mobility and freight transport at sea. Collision avoidance and path planning are central components of the intelligence of a MASS. While Deep Reinforcement Learning (DRL) techniques often learn these abilities in a simulated environment, this article explores an alternative approach: learning collision avoidance and path planning solely from observational data, thus minimizing the need for simulator-based training. A state-action dataset of ship trajectories is constructed from recorded Automatic Identification System (AIS) messages. Using this data, we examine the application of the Prediction and Policy-learning Under Uncertainty (PPUU) technique, which involves training an action-conditional forward model and learning a policy network by unrolling future states and back-propagating errors from a self-defined cost function. To evaluate the learned policy, *FerryGym*, a Gymnasium environment is developed for evaluating the policy network using observational data.

Keywords: Interwoven Systems · Autonomous navigation · Reinforcement learning · Self-supervised learning · Autonomous vessels

1 Motivation

Maritime transportation has long been a crucial element in global trade and commerce, facilitating the movement of goods, people, and resources across the seas and oceans of the world [14]. However, in the era of globalisation, the maritime industry has been facing numerous challenges, including the increasing demand for goods [18], safety concerns [15], and environmental issues [11]. To address these challenges, there has been growing interest in developing autonomous maritime operations, driven by efforts from fields such as Organic Computing [12].

More than 80% of marine collision accidents are caused by or mediated through improper human decisions due to a lack of situational awareness and

This research has been partly funded by the German Ministry for Transport and Digital Infrastructure within the project "CAPTN FördeAreal - Erprobung einer (teil-)autonomen, emissionsfreien Fährschifffahrt im digitalen Testfeld" (45DTWV007B).

G. Goumas et al. (Eds.): ARCS 2023, LNCS 13949, pp. 296–310, 2023.
https://doi.org/10.1007/978-3-031-42785-5_20

failure to comply with the Convention on International Regulations for Preventing Collisions at Sea (COLREG) [24]. COLREG outlines enforceable marine traffic rules that ships must adhere to in order to avoid collisions.

The operation of Marine Autonomous Surface Ships (MASS) in the context of collectives of marine vessels can be considered as an Interwoven System (IwS). An IwS is a complex multiplex of interconnected, self-organized systems, operating independently of central control and characterized by interactively coupled components. The openness and heterogeneity of the networked system components can lead to constant changes in the topology and structure of IwS components from a system-wide perspective. According to Tomforde et al. [21], the key characteristics of an Interwoven System (IwS) can be summarized as follows: (i) The ability of the system components and their federations to self-organize. The challenges associated with the networked components and federations align with the Organic Computing (OC) initiative, cf. [22] (ii) The existence of diverse administrative domains, as individual system components do not fall under a single authority. (iii) The geographical separation of IwS components, which defines their spread within the system. (iv) The operational independence (i.e. self-organisation) and local interaction of system components can result in unforeseen (emergent) behaviour [3]. IwS can recognise this emergent behaviour and act accordingly. (v) The evolutionary development of the IwS system due to the continuous change of its components during runtime. (vi) The uncertainty in the system's behaviour and decision-making results from the system heterogeneity, self-organisation, and continuous evolution.

The operation of Marine Autonomous Surface Ships (MASS) requires integration within a constantly evolving, time-varying environment that comprises heterogeneous components. Accordingly, the characteristics of Interwoven Systems (IwS) are highly relevant to the design, development, and operation of MASS. A key aspect of this integration is ensuring safe navigation within the marine environment, encompassing both voyage planning from a global perspective and collision avoidance with static and dynamic obstacles. This article presents the adaptation of the Prediction and Policy-learning Under Uncertainty (PPUU) method [4] for learning collision-free path planning in dense marine environments from observational data.

The remainder of this paper is organized as follows: Sect. 2 provides background information on collision avoidance in MASS. Section 3 presents the adaptation of PPUU for MASS collision avoidance. Subsequently, Sect. 4 illustrates the experimental setup and evaluates the results, followed by a discussion in Sect. 5. The final section summarizes the approach adopted for developing MASS navigation.

2   Background

MASS can be considered as mobile robots with six degrees of freedom [20], i.e. three translational degrees (surge, sway and heave) and three rotational degrees (roll, pitch and yaw). In the context of autonomous navigation, the architecture of autonomous robots can, according to [26], be categorized into

Traditional Architectures and *Learning Architectures.* Learning Architectures use machine learning techniques to create a representation of the world model. The trained model enables the mapping of input features into a sequence of navigation actions. In the context of path planning for mobile robots, including MASS, navigation plans generated by traditional algorithms often reach their limits as problem complexity increases. Machine learning-based path planners, in contrast, are notable for their adaptability to environmental changes, their ability to handle uncertainty in complex environments, and their capacity for multi-objective optimization. As a result, they provide enhanced generalization.

2.1 Learning Based Strategies

With an emphasis on *Learning Architectures*, Zhao et al. [24,25] proposed a method that directly maps the states of encountered ships to the rudder angle steering of the autonomous (own) ship (OS) using a deep neural network model trained over trajectories of multiple ships using a policy-gradient-based deep reinforcement learning (DRL) algorithm. This approach assumes that the states of all agents have homogeneous manoeuvrability capabilities and are fully observable by OS at every time step.

Zhai et al. [23] employ a single-agent Double Deep Q-learning network (DDQN) model-free RL technique to steer a ship in a simulated environment. The agent is trained on synthetic data for collision-free manoeuvres. However, this model is not trained on other obstacle types than vessels, such as waterway restrictions. As a result, this approach can be applied in open waters, but not in coastal or harbour areas.

While these reinforcement learning (RL)-based methods have demonstrated impressive results [17,26], they primarily rely on simulated environments with synthetic or simulated scenarios for learning. This allows the trained agents to manoeuvre and adapt within these confines. However, such an approach can prove exhaustive and potentially unfeasible when applied to real-world scenarios, given the wide array of uncertainties and unpredictable elements inherent in these environments.

Behaviour cloning (BC) and RL are two popular techniques used for achieving autonomy in maritime vessels. While both techniques have their own advantages and disadvantages, BC has emerged as a promising approach for training navigational models for autonomous vessels. A key advantage is that it is a supervised learning technique and only depends on the availability of labelled training data. This makes it relatively straightforward to implement and allows it to adapt to the context of complex environments. It's capable of encoding the knowledge of experts by imitating their actions for a given status. BC has proven to be effective in handling complex tasks such as navigation and collision avoidance [1,8,16], where it can leverage the vast amounts of data available from human expert demonstrations. In contrast, RL may struggle to achieve optimal performance in complex tasks due to the trial-and-error nature of its training. As such, training an RL agent can be time-consuming and requires careful design of the RL model, including the actions, states, policy, environment, and perhaps most challenging of all, the appropriate reward functions.

Both BC and RL come with unique advantages and challenges. However, a distinguishing strength of BC lies in its ability to learn policies - mappings from states to actions - directly from observational data. This bypasses the RL requirement of designing an appropriate environment and reward function to train a policy. Therefore, BC presents a compelling pathway towards autonomous maritime vessels, especially in intricate scenarios where human experts can provide labelled training data. Nevertheless, the performance of models trained using a BC approach heavily depends on the quality of expert demonstrations. As a result, BC can suffer from issues like distribution mismatch and lack of exploration [10].

Prediction and Policy learning under Uncertainty (PPUU) developed by Henaff et al. [4] is a technique to learn a policy in an RL setting from observational data. PPUU tries to address both the issues of RL and BC by learning an *action-conditional forward model* that predicts future states depending on past states and actions. This mitigates the need for a simulator. A policy then can be learned by unfolding a couple of future states in the forward model and back-propagating the gradients of a computed cost function to efficiently improve the policy parameters. While training, the model can explore states not included in the observational data and therefore reduce potential distribution mismatch. However, PPUU has mostly been considered in the context of vehicular traffic and not in maritime environments.

3   Approach

This section discusses the methodology used for adapting PPUU to generate navigational paths for MASS using observational data. The anticipated result is a policy capable of mapping the current state of the agent to an action that navigates a collision-free route. The actions in this model are defined as straightforward accelerations and changes in direction. This approach does not account for specific ship controls like rudder angle or propeller speed, or factors such as weather conditions.

3.1   Automatic Identification System (AIS) as Training Data

The Automatic Identification System (AIS) is a system for broadcasting information to other ships and shore stations. It has become an integral part of maritime navigation and safety. AIS enables real-time monitoring of vessels, providing critical information such as their identity, position, speed, and course. This information is used by vessel operators to avoid collisions [6]. The International Maritime Organisation (IMO) has made AIS mandatory for vessels above a certain size [5,7]. However, AIS can still be subject to errors and cyberattacks. The accuracy and integrity of positions transmitted by AIS are, for example, examined in [2]. Nonetheless, AIS continues to be used in many studies as the most cost-effective source for tracking maritime vessels [13,19].

3.2   MASS Collision Avoidance Using PPUU

Navigation MASS can be defined as an RL problem. The agent under control, the own ship (OS), receives information about its state s from the environment. This state needs to encapsulate all the necessary information to steer the ship successfully towards its target. Hence, s is structured to include the following attributes: (1) The *position* of the agent on a 2D plane, its *velocity*, and *direction*, represented as a vector $u = (p_x, p_y, v, d) \in \mathbb{R}^4$. This vector encompasses the attributes that the agent can directly control with its actions. (2) The surrounding neighbourhood of the agent, which includes waterways, obstacles, and the positions and sizes of other vessels within the environment. The neighbouring vessels are anticipated to adhere to the International Regulations for Preventing Collisions at Sea (COLREGs) to avoid collisions. As OS is the only controllable agent, the other ships within the environment are presumed to follow their trajectories as observed in the Automatic Identification System (AIS) training set.

The design of the neighbourhood is relative to the ship's position, to include only the most pertinent information for navigation. An RGB image of fixed size $3 \times w \times h$ with width $w \in \mathbb{N}_{>0}$ and height $h \in \mathbb{N}_{>0}$ encodes the necessary information. The agent is placed in the middle of the image in the blue channel while considering its size in the representation. The red channel encodes parts of the environment that the agent is restricted to traverse. The green channel encodes other vessels and obstacles. In summary, a tuple of the state vector u and the neighbourhood image i, represent the state $s = (u, i)$. Figure 1 provides an example of a neighbourhood image from the training dataset.

To encapsulate the dynamic behaviours of other vessels, a sequence of k states $s_{k:t}$, rather than a single state s_t, is utilised. In this manner, the movements of other vessels are implicitly captured. Here, k signifies the number of past states from the temporal index t, and $s_{k:t}$ defines the sequence of states from s_{t-k} through to s_t. Given this sequence of states, the policy π calculates the subsequent action $a_t = \pi(s_{k:t})$ that the agent should take to reach its destination. The action space is represented by a two-dimensional vector $a = (\Delta v, \Delta d)$, which encodes both acceleration and change in direction.

Action-Conditional Forward Model. An action-conditional forward model f_θ, with parameters θ, is learned from observational data. This model predicts the subsequent state s_{t+1} given a sequence of prior states $s_{k:t}$, an action a_t, and a latent variable z_t. Training is carried out in a self-supervised fashion, contrasting the network's outcomes with observed samples from the training set, with a particular emphasis on predicting the position, and thus the movement, of vessels in proximity to the OS agent. As such, the forward model aims to learn and understand the dynamics of the other ships.

Given the uncertainty surrounding the potential trajectories of neighbouring vessels, the latent variable z_t is used to encode the exact trajectory. Averaging all possible trajectories is not beneficial, as the result can become imprecisely blurry and unreliable for decision-making after just a few time steps. During

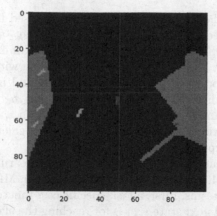

Fig. 1. Example of a neighbourhood image, encoding the agent ship in blue, other vessels in green and the restrictions of the waterway in red. (Color figure online)

training, the latent variable z_t is sampled from a distribution, the parameters of which are computed by a posterior network. The network parameters are trained in tandem with the other components of the forward model. Consequently, the latent variable used during training depends on the actual next state in the training set, allowing the trained forward model to predict trajectories as observed in the training set. In subsequent model usage, the latent variable is sampled from a prior distribution that is independent of the next state, facilitating the computation of different trajectories for the neighbouring vessels.

In the dataset, different actions are not evenly distributed across the entire positional state space. For example, sharp turns are rare in the middle of the waterway but quite common near a ferry terminal. The network might learn this bias to follow commonly observed paths, and as a result, may not respond appropriately to the actions. Since it's necessary to internally link the state vector u and the image i to predict the next state s_{t+1}, it was observed that the network fails to learn the straightforward state integration of the action for computing the next state. Henaff et al. [4] did not encounter this issue as their neighbourhood images are not detailed enough to deduce the agent's position from them.

To counter this, it is essential to train the model to integrate the action into the current state to calculate the next state. Additional training is performed on synthetic data. Here, a random position, velocity, and direction in the training set space are sampled, and random actions are applied for random durations. The target states can then be calculated using the same state integration that the network is intended to learn. The inclusion of synthetic data has the advantage of providing additional trajectories in a uniformly distributed manner, which can reduce the bias effect in the training data. A hyperparameter is introduced to control the frequency of training on synthetic data. As synthetic trajectories do not include a proper image which the agent could infer its position from, this technique is called *image dropout*.

Policy Learning. The forward model can then be used to train a policy network π_ψ with parameters ψ. Random state sequences $s_{k:t}$ are sampled from the training set. Here, t represents a specific index of the training set, and $s_{k:t}$ represents the sequence of $k \in \mathbb{N}_{>0}$ consecutive states ending with state s_t. An action from the policy network $a_t = \pi_\psi(s_{k:t})$ is computed and used as input for the forward model to predict the next state $s_{t+1} = f_\theta(s_{k:t}, a_t, z_t)$. In this case, the latent variable z_t is sampled from the prior distribution $z_t = p(z)$. This process is repeated $T \in \mathbb{N}_{>0}$ times, and a scalar cost value is calculated to update the parameters ψ by backpropagation.

To define a cost function, Model Predictive Policy learning with Uncertainty Regulation (MPUR) [4] is adapted for MASS navigation. MPUR uses a cost function consisting of two terms. First, a task-specific cost function $C(\hat{s}_{t+1})$ evaluates how bad the predicted next state s_{t+1} is for reaching the agent's objectives. This includes three objectives: The target cost $t(\hat{s}_{t+1})$, which results in a lower cost for states that are closer to the target. The proximity cost $p(\hat{s}_{t+1})$ penalises the agent if it gets close to other ships. Lastly, the land cost function $l(\hat{s}_{t+1})$ quantifies a high penalty cost if the agent gets near land or other obstacles in the waterway. The task-specific cost function is then computed as the weighted sum, with hyperparameters $\tau, \rho, \iota \in [0, 1]$, of the individual parts.

$$C(\hat{s}_{t+1}) = \tau t(\hat{s}_{t+1}) + \rho p(\hat{s}_{t+1}) + \iota l(\hat{s}_{t+1}) \tag{1}$$

The second term of the cost function is the uncertainty cost $U(\hat{s}_{t+1})$. This term quantifies the uncertainty of the forward model by the variance of outputs when predicting the state $\hat{s}_{t+1}$ on the same inputs with different dropout masks.

This results in minimising the following term to update the parameters of the network:

$$\underset{\psi}{\text{argmin}} \left[\sum_{i=1}^{T} C(\hat{s}_{t+i}) - \lambda U(\hat{s}_{t+i}) \right],$$

$$\text{such that:} \begin{cases} z_{t+i-1} \sim p(z) \\ a_{t+i-1} \sim \pi_\psi(\hat{s}_{k:t+i-1}) \\ \hat{s}_{t+i} = f(\hat{s}_{k:t+i-1}, \hat{a}_{t+i-1}, z_{t+i-1}) \end{cases} \tag{2}$$

The hyperparameter λ controls the influence of the uncertainty cost compared to the task-specific cost.

4   Evaluation

This section describes the experimental setup, followed by results and discussion.

4.1   Experimental Setup

In order to train a policy with PPUU, a dataset of state-action pairs is required. Therefore, AIS messages within a specific time interval for the region of the Fjord of Kiel were collected using a proprietary antenna, as AIS data is not freely available. These filtered data were then interpolated at one-second intervals. Speed and direction were calculated from the position data. The action a vessel took to reach its next state was inferred from the difference between the current and the next state, thereby calculating acceleration and change in direction. The resultant dataset covers an observation period of 24 h, comprising a total of 336,752 messages. For each of these messages, a neighbourhood image was generated, as exemplified in Fig. 1, yielding a dataset size of 11 GB.

FerryGym[1], a Gymnasium environment modelling the path planning problem in the Kiel Fjord is developed to test trained policies. The environment is initialised with a starting- and destination position, as well as a dataset containing trajectories of vessels. The state of the environment at a given time step includes attributes of the agent ship, other vessels, the target, and the waterway. Each vessel is modelled as an object with position, velocity, direction, length, and width attributes. Figure 2 presents a screenshot of the simulator environment.

Action-Conditional Forward Model. To train an action-conditional forward model, the dataset is processed in batches. Initiated with a data frame, a data loader computes statistics for normalization and partitions the dataset into training, testing, and validation sets. Following this, it constructs batches of training data.

The same architecture as from Henaff et al. [4], consisting of three main components: an encoder network, a hidden network, and a decoder network, is used. The encoder encodes state sequences and actions into a hidden representation. The hidden network receives this representation and outputs a tensor of the same dimensionality. The decoder computes the prediction from the hidden representation. Two types of forward models are deployed. A deterministic DNN, and a stochastic variational autoencoder (VAE) model with a sampled latent variable. During training, the VAE model is initialised with the DNN and continues training. A selection of important hyperparameters is presented in Table 1. The Adam optimiser [9] is used.

Policy Learning. For the policy network, the same architecture as from Henaff et al. [4] is used again. This network consists of an encoder network, with the same architecture as in the forward model, a linear layered network, and another linear layered network to output the two-dimensional action.

The MPUR adaptation approach uses a task-specific cost function. One component is the *target cost* function that compares the direction of the agent with the optimal direction towards the target. It also penalises the agent for not mov-

---

[1] https://github.com/raphaelschwinger/FerryGym
https://github.com/raphaelschwinger/PPUU-FerryGym

Table 1. A selection of hyperparameters used for training the forward model.

Hyperparameters		
Parameter name	Description	Default value
ncond	Number of input states	10
npred	Number of predicted states	20
batch_size	Batch size	8
synthetic	Fraction of synthetic training data	0.5

ing at the desired speed. The hyperparameter $v_{desired}$ controls the influence of the speed penalty. The target cost is calculated by the function $t(\hat{s}_{t+1})$:

$$\Delta d(\hat{s}_{t+1}) = |\hat{s}_{t+1}[d_{opt}] - \hat{s}_{t+1}[v]|$$
$$d_{cost}(\hat{s}_{t+1}) = |\sin(0.5 \cdot \Delta d(\hat{s}_{t+1}))|$$
$$v_{cost}(\hat{s}_{t+1}) = |-\frac{1}{v_{desired}} * \hat{s}_{t+1}[v] + 1| \tag{3}$$
$$t(\hat{s}_{t+1}) = \min(d_{cost}(\hat{s}_{t+1}) + v_{cost}(\hat{s}_{t+1}), 1)$$

In the notation above, $\hat{s}_{t+1}[d_{opt}]$ symbolizes the optimal direction towards the target, $\hat{s}_{t+1}[d]$ signifies the direction of the agent, and $\hat{s}_{t+1}[v]$ denotes the speed of the agent.

The *proximity cost* function $p(\hat{s}_{t+1})$ penalises the agent for getting close to other ships using a 2D Gaussian kernel, as shown in Fig. 3. It is applied to the green channel of the neighbourhood state's image.

Finally, the *land cost* function $l(\hat{s}_{t+1})$ penalises the agent for getting close to land, using the state's image red channel encoding the waterway restrictions:

$$p(\hat{s}_{t+1}) = \max \hat{s}_{t+1}[image][1] * mask \tag{4}$$
$$l(\hat{s}_{t+1}) = \max \hat{s}_{t+1}[image][0] * mask \tag{5}$$

4.2   Results

Action-Conditional Forward Model. The action-conditional forward model is tested on a validation dataset. It can predict states closely matching the target states. However, anomalies can be observed where the ship is not responding to given actions and instead follows trajectories commonly observed in the training set. For instance, when the task is to predict the trajectory of doing a strict turn in the middle of the waterway, the predicted states do not respond to the action and follow the same path as in the training set, as shown in Fig. 5a. This is a problem for our policy learning approach, as we need a correct response to our actions to judge the actions for policy learning. For this reason, the *image dropout* technique is used. As Fig. 5b demonstrates, this improves the performance of

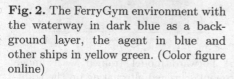

Fig. 2. The FerryGym environment with the waterway in dark blue as a background layer, the agent in blue and other ships in yellow green. (Color figure online)

Fig. 3. The Gaussian 2D mask used for proximity and land cost function.

the forward model. The predicted neighbourhood images, as shown in Fig. 4, demonstrate that the forward model predicts future neighbourhood images with decent precision. Also, the turning movement where the waterway restrictions move around OS is captured. Other ships are not present in this sample example.

As shown in Fig. 6, the forward model fails to predict the position of other ships in the dataset. It is suspected that the reason for this is that the other ships are sparsely present in the training dataset. Utilising a substantially larger dataset and dedicating more training time will likely improve the predictions of the forward model for the positions of other ships. An improvement by using the VAE model compared to the DNN could not be observed.

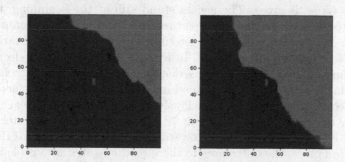

Fig. 4. Neighbourhood images of the ship getting closer to the ferry terminal. The ship is shown in blue, restrictions of the waterway are in red. (Color figure online)

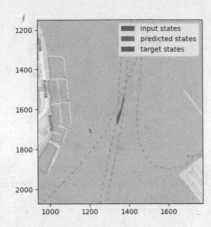 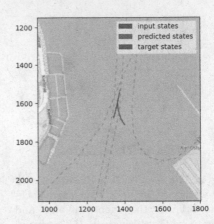

(a) Forward model trained without image dropout.

(b) Forward model trained with image dropout - trained alternating on the training set and synthetic data.

Fig. 5. Forward model predicting the next states when performing a left turn with the actions $(0, -5)$. The target states of the dataset with a different action are shown in purple. OpenSeaMap data is used as a background layer.

Policy Learning. All experiments with the trained policies are assessed in the FerryGym simulator environment. The environment is initialised by a start position, speed and direction of the OS agent. The environment loads the trajectories of other vessels from the dataset and updates their position accordingly.

Figure 7a visualises five trajectories of an agent steered with a trained MPUR policy. The start position is set near a ferry terminal and an initial heading toward the target is given. The agents stand still at the beginning, then they accelerate towards the target. One agent reaches the target, two agents miss by a few meters, and two sail past the target and then turn towards the target again. The latter four are running aground. In Fig. 7c, the target cost is decreasing at the beginning of the trajectory. This matches with the agents accelerating at the beginning until reaching the defined maximal speed. After the acceleration, the target cost is kept at a relatively low level. The heading of the agent directs towards the destination. As seen in Fig. 7d, the agent is constantly steering right and left to keep the optimal angle towards the target. Contrary to the plotted trajectory in Fig. 7a, the differences in the direction states are visible in Fig. 7b. When the agent is getting closer to the target, the land cost increases. Also, in the first third of the trajectory, an increase in land cost is visible. The proximity cost, indicating other vessels nearby, is not changing within the trajectory, other ships are not close, and therefore, no collision had to be avoided.

(a) Prediction image of the forward model, no other ships are present.

(b) Target image of the validation dataset, other ships are present.

Fig. 6. Forward model predicting neighbourhood images with other ships in the neighbourhood. The ego ship is shown in blue, the other ships in yellow-green and the restrictions of the waterway in red. (Color figure online)

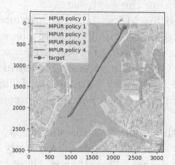

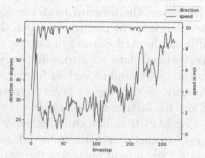

(a) Trajectories of five policy runs.

(b) Speed and direction states of the agent in the first trajectory.

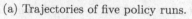

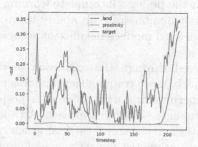

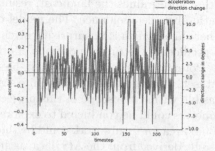

(c) Target, proximity and land cost in the first trajectory.

(d) Acceleration and direction change actions in the first trajectory.

Fig. 7. MPUR policy starts near the Reventlou ferry terminal. No initial speed but in the direction of the target.

5   Discussion

Learning to predict the future states of a MASS environment using an action-conditional forward model poses considerable challenges. Our results indicate that the method we used for training the forward model yields a model capable of predicting the state vector with a degree of precision suitable for collision avoidance tasks. Moreover, the predicted future neighbourhood images encapsulate the waterway's constraints with acceptable accuracy. Implementing the training technique of Henaff et al. [4] for MASS, using the collected AIS data, was met with difficulties due to the model's insensitivity to rare action behaviours within the training dataset. Given the unequal distribution of actions across the environment, the model tends to learn to perform specific actions in specific areas only. In response to this issue, we incorporated the image dropout technique, which significantly enhanced the model's action responsiveness. Unlike the task of navigating dense traffic on a highway, as was the case in Henaff et al.'s study, the task of sailing across the Kiel Fjord is more unconstrained. In the highway scenario, all cars move in the same direction and the steering angles are considerably more limited. In contrast, for MASS, ships can move in various directions, adding to the complexity of predicting the next states.

However, the forward model we developed for MASS failed to produce significant results in predicting other ship movements, largely due to the sparse traffic in the AIS dataset. This sparsity afforded the model too little "active" observational data to learn effectively from. Given the necessity of learning to accurately respond to actions for model predictive policy learning, our focus was primarily on this aspect. The improvement of trajectory predictions remains a subject for further research.

The MPUR policy can effectively guide the agent towards the target, however, it sometimes fails to avoid waterway restrictions and frequently runs aground when land obstructs the path to the target. Nevertheless, these results demonstrate the forward model's capacity to predict states with sufficient accuracy for model-predictive policy learning. The current hyperparameter configuration undervalues the land cost, resulting in the policy's incomplete learning of static obstacle avoidance. The model does not demonstrate an ability to avoid other ships, which is unsurprising given the forward model's insufficient accuracy in predicting the future positions of other vessels.

Potential improvements could be achieved through the expansion of the dataset, although this would require significantly more training time and was not feasible within the scope of this project. Experimenting with different hyperparameters could be conducted to explore the robustness of the approach. An additional area for future work could be the inclusion of the ships' targets, which can also be derived from the AIS data, as an input parameter. Once the model is adequately improved, it would be worthwhile to compare it with other approaches, such as BC or model-free RL.

6   Conclusion

This article aims at learning a path planning and collision avoidance policy for autonomous ship navigation using PPUU. The state space of an agent includes the position, velocity, heading, and image encoding of its neighbourhood. The developed action-conditional forward model faces challenges in predicting ship trajectories and future positions of other ships in the neighbourhood. To improve the model performance, training alternates between the observational dataset and synthetic trajectories. This significantly improves prediction results. Using the trained forward model, the results of the policy learning indicate the ability to avoid running aground, but collision avoidance with dynamic obstacles could not be confirmed. These findings contribute to the overall understanding of the problem and represent the initial steps in learning MASS collision avoidance with PPUU.

References

1. Devi, T.K., Srivatsava, A., Mudgal, K.K., Jayanti, R.R., Karthick, T.: Behaviour cloning for autonomous driving. Webology **17**(2), 694–705 (2020)
2. Felski, A., Jaskólski, K.: The integrity of information received by means of AIS during anti-collision manoeuvring. TransNav: Int. J. Mar. Navig. Saf. Sea Transp. **7**(1), 95–100 (2013)
3. Fisch, D., Jänicke, M., Sick, B., Müller-Schloer, C.: Quantitative emergence-a refined approach based on divergence measures. In: 2010 Fourth IEEE International Conference on Self-Adaptive and Self-Organizing Systems, pp. 94–103. IEEE Computer Society (2010)
4. Henaff, M., Canziani, A., LeCun, Y.: Model-predictive policy learning with uncertainty regularization for driving in dense traffic (2019)
5. Bundesamt für Seeschifffahrt und Hydrographie, B.: German Traffic Regulations for Navigable Maritime Waterways (2022). https://www.bsh.de/DE/PUBLIKATIONEN/Anlagen/Downloads/Nautik_und_Schifffahrt/Seehandbuecher_ueberregional/SeeschStrO_engl.pdf?__blob=publicationFile&v=16. Accessed 3 Oct 2022
6. IMO: Resolution A.1106(29) (2001). https://wwwcdn.imo.org/localresources/en/KnowledgeCentre/IndexofIMOResolutions/AssemblyDocuments/A.917(22).pdf. Accessed 3 Oct 2022
7. IMORULES: SOLAS regulation V/19 (2022). https://www.imorules.com/SOLAS_REGV.A.19.html. Accessed 3 Oct 2022
8. Kebria, P.M., et al.: Autonomous navigation via deep imitation and transfer learning: a comparative study. In: 2020 IEEE International Conference on Systems, Man, and Cybernetics (SMC), pp. 2907–2912. IEEE (2020)
9. Kingma, D.P., Ba, J.: Adam: a method for stochastic optimization (2014). https://doi.org/10.48550/ARXIV.1412.6980. https://arxiv.org/abs/1412.6980
10. Kober, J., Bagnell, J.A., Peters, J.: Reinforcement learning in robotics: a survey. Int. J. Robot. Res. **32**(11), 1238–1274 (2013)
11. Lee, P.T.W., Kwon, O.K., Ruan, X.: Sustainability challenges in maritime transport and logistics industry and its way ahead (2019)

12. Müller-Schloer, C., Tomforde, S.: Organic Computing-Technical Systems for Survival in the Real World. Springer, Cham (2017). https://doi.org/10.1007/978-3-319-68477-2

13. Nguyen, D., Vadaine, R., Hajduch, G., Garello, R., Fablet, R.: A multi-task deep learning architecture for maritime surveillance using AIS data streams. In: 2018 IEEE 5th International Conference on Data Science and Advanced Analytics (DSAA), pp. 331–340. IEEE (2018)

14. Pasha, J., et al.: Holistic tactical-level planning in liner shipping: an exact optimization approach. J. Shipping Trade 5(1), 8 (2020). https://doi.org/10.1186/s41072-020-00060-4

15. Rothblum, A.M.: Human error and marine safety. In: National Safety Council Congress and Expo, Orlando, FL, vol. 7 (2000)

16. Saksena, S.K., Navaneethkrishnan, B., Hegde, S., Raja, P., Vishwanath, R.M.: Towards behavioural cloning for autonomous driving. In: 2019 Third IEEE International Conference on Robotic Computing (IRC), pp. 560–567. IEEE (2019)

17. Sarhadi, P., Naeem, W., Athanasopoulos, N.: A survey of recent machine learning solutions for ship collision avoidance and mission planning (2022)

18. Schaefer, N., Barale, V.: Maritime spatial planning: opportunities & challenges in the framework of the EU integrated maritime policy. J. Coast. Conserv. 15, 237–245 (2011)

19. Schwehr, K.D., McGillivary, P.A.: Marine ship automatic identification system (AIS) for enhanced coastal security capabilities: an oil spill tracking application. In: OCEANS 2007, pp. 1–9. IEEE (2007)

20. Singh, Y., Sharma, S., Sutton, R., Hatton, D., Khan, A.: Efficient optimal path planning of unmanned surface vehicles. In: Navigation and Control of Autonomous Marine Vehicles. Institution of Engineering and Technology (2019)

21. Tomforde, S., et al.: Engineering and mastering interwoven systems. In: ARCS 2014; 2014 Workshop Proceedings on Architecture of Computing Systems, pp. 1–8. VDE (2014)

22. Tomforde, S., Sick, B., Müller-Schloer, C.: Organic computing in the spotlight. arXiv preprint arXiv:1701.08125 (2017)

23. Zhai, P., Zhang, Y., Shaobo, W.: Intelligent ship collision avoidance algorithm based on DDQN with prioritized experience replay under COLREGs. J. Mar. Sci. Eng. 10(5), 585 (2022). https://doi.org/10.3390/jmse10050585. https://www.mdpi.com/2077-1312/10/5/585

24. Zhao, L., Roh, M.I.: COLREGs-compliant multiship collision avoidance based on deep reinforcement learning. Ocean Eng. 191, 106436 (2019)

25. Zhao, L., Roh, M.I., Lee, S.J.: Control method for path following and collision avoidance of autonomous ship based on deep reinforcement learning. J. Mar. Sci. Technol. 27(4), 1 (2019)

26. Zhou, C., Huang, B., Fränti, P.: A review of motion planning algorithms for intelligent robots. J. Intell. Manuf. 1–38 (2021)

Towards Dependable Unmanned Aerial Vehicle Swarms Using Organic Computing

Jonas Diegelmann$^{(\boxtimes)}$, Philipp Homann, Mathias Pacher, and Uwe Brinkschulte

Institut für Informatik, Goethe University Frankfurt, Frankfurt am Main, Germany
{J.Diegelmann,phomann}@em.uni-frankfurt.de, mpacher@uni-frankfurt.de,
brinks@es.cs.uni-frankfurt.de

Abstract. Organic Computing (OC) is a well-known research field aiming to build dependable embedded systems. OC systems often employ self-X properties such as self-configuration, self-healing, etc. These properties are inherent to several biological systems such as the human body and offer a blueprint for technical systems.

The Artificial DNA (ADNA) system was developed in the scope of the OC research. Its basic idea is to build a dependable embedded system from a textual description (the artificial DNA – as a technical counterpart to the DNA in biological cells).

Our contribution in this paper is to use the ADNA system to realize a highly dependable drone swarm providing self-X properties. We describe details of our drone demonstrator which we built for this purpose. In addition, we describe the extensions on the ADNA system to realize functions such as path planning and swarm control. The evaluation considers time delays in the WiFi connection between drones and Ground Control Stations (GCSs) and demonstrates that the real-time requirements of the ADNA system mostly hold despite the delays.

Keywords: Organic Computing · Middleware · Artificial DNA · Dependable drone swarms

1 Introduction

Along with the increasing complexity of distributed computing systems in today's and tomorrow's technical applications such as autonomous cars or Unmanned Aerial Vehicles (UAVs), commonly known as drones, highly dependable and fault-tolerant computing systems are mandatory. An approach to establish dependable systems is proposed in [2]. Its main idea is that most embedded systems are composed of a limited number of (simple) basic blocks such as ALUs, memory cells, counters, etc. The authors define an ADNA as a textual description on (a) which basic blocks are needed to build a specific embedded system and (b) which communication relations these basic blocks have. The ADNA is then spread to all processors/computational nodes in the distributed system. The processors use a task allocation system (i.e. the Artificial Hormone System

© The Author(s), under exclusive license to Springer Nature Switzerland AG 2023
G. Goumas et al. (Eds.): ARCS 2023, LNCS 13949, pp. 311–325, 2023.
https://doi.org/10.1007/978-3-031-42785-5_21

(AHS)) to instantiate the basic blocks. The ADNA system builds the embedded system described in the ADNA in a self-organizing way and is robust to task and processor failures, thus, employing self-X properties [2].

Drone swarms (i.e. autonomous guided vehicles) have a broad application field: They can be used to monitor people, railway lines, and other critical infrastructure. Therefore, it is important that drone swarms are highly dependable and can perform their missions even when some drones are failing.

Thus, our aim is to use the ADNA system for drone swarms. We adopted the ADNA system to run on a GCS as well as on the companion computers on drones thus providing the overall system with the dependability features mentioned above. This scenario is shown in an example in Fig. 1: We have some processors running the ADNA system (the ADNA processors). These processors might be companion computers on the drones or computers in the GCS and communicate by wireless LAN. The ADNA system guarantees high dependability and sends the commands to the flight controllers which are on board of each drone.

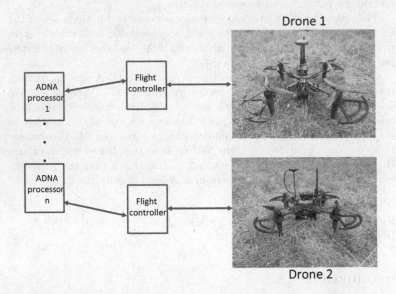

Fig. 1. An ADNA-controlled drone swarm consisting of two drones

Our contributions in this paper are threefold:

- We present complex ADNA building blocks to control a drone or a drone swarm. These new ADNA blocks are necessary for two reasons: (1) They encapsulate specific functions such as a group controller to coordinate the drone swarm or a path planner to compute a drone's trajectory. (2) The purpose of these blocks is so complex that it is not feasible to take the simple basic blocks mentioned above (such as ALUs, multiplexers, and so on) to compose the needed functionality.

- The complex ADNA building blocks need to communicate with each other. While the simple basic blocks just send float messages the complex blocks need to send messages with more information. Therefore, we extended the communication message format for ADNA blocks and present the extensions here.
- We test our ADNA system on a real drone[1] which is connected by WiFi to the GCS. An important factor is the communication latency introduced by this communication method as it affects the dependability of the overall system. Therefore, we evaluated the communication latency between the drone and GCS.

The paper is structured as follows: We describe the related work in Sect. 2. The system architecture of our drones in combination with the ADNA system is explained in Sect. 3. The new complex ADNA building blocks are described in Sect. 4. They need new types of messages which are presented in Sect. 5. The evaluation is provided in Sect. 6. Section 7 concludes the paper.

2   Related Work

The ADNA system's real-world application is an ongoing research topic. The utilization of organic computing principles enables new possibilities for robust system design. The Autonomic Computing project [6], a joint effort by IBM and DARPA, focuses on the self-organization of IT servers within networks. The project postulates several self-X properties, including self-optimization, self-configuration, self-protection, and self-healing.

The integration of new elements into the ADNA system holds significant potential for enhancing the system's performance. In [5] the authors introduce a new ADNA element that extends the basic element library. The presented new ADNA element can be generally used and introduces the functionality of task dependencies. In contrast, the here presented complex ADNA elements fulfill a dedicated role and are specifically designed to match a use case.

A similar approach to the integration of Organic Computing (OC) to a swarm of UAVs is presented in the OCbotics project [7]. The authors use a multi-layer system design and Learning Classifier Systems (LCSs) to achieve swarm-wide objectives, such as cleaning the facades of tall buildings. The presented project focuses on researching different learning algorithms to optimize swarm behavior. Contrary to the here presented approach, this system does not regard self-X properties on a processor level.

In [3] a real-world application of the ADNA system on a self-balancing vehicle is presented. This approach directly applies the ADNA system to control the vehicle hardware. The contribution in our paper aims to apply the ADNA system on a swarm of UAVs to manage superordinate goals, rather than controlling individual drone hardware.

---

[1] Initial tests were performed in a simulation environment for safety reasons.

3 Architecture of the ADNA System for Drones

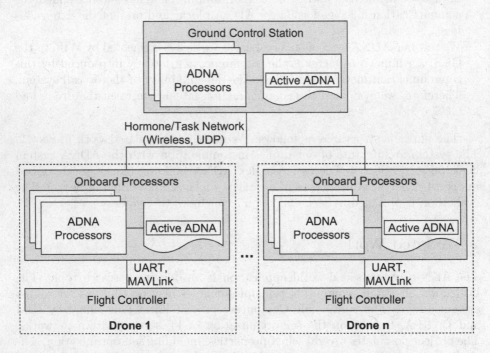

Fig. 2. Architecture of the ADNA system for drones

The integration of the ADNA system has the potential to greatly enhance the resilience of UAV swarms against individual drone failures. The setup in which the ADNA system is applied is depicted in Fig. 2. This system manages the high-level control of a swarm of UAVs, each of which is equipped with at least one onboard processor that can run multiple instances of the ADNA system (referred to as ADNA processors). Additionally, a specialized GCS has been integrated into the system, providing the user with the ability to control individual drones or groups of drones. To facilitate mid-flight communication between individual swarm members and between swarm members and the GCS, ADNA messages need to be transmitted through wireless means. Thus, new challenges such as higher communication latencies and a higher packet loss ratio arise. The onboard computer and the flight controller communicate through a Universal Asynchronous Receiver Transmitter (UART) connection. For the system to interact with a multitude of autopilots without adjustments to the ADNA, the widely adopted MAVLink [8] protocol is used as an interoperability interface. MAVLink is a lightweight communication protocol for controlling and monitoring UAVs and provides an open-source header-only library optimized for resource-constrained systems. MAVLink messages are composed of a very lightweight header, a payload, and a checksum. Additionally, MAVLink 2.0 introduced an optional signature, allowing for message authentication.

MAVLink is supported by several autopilots, such as the open-source autopilots Ardupilot [1] and PX4 [9].

The interface layer between the autopilot and the ADNA system is implemented using two ADNA elements, *MAVLinkSensor* and *MAVLinkActor*. The former handles all incoming MAVLink messages, while the latter handles all outgoing MAVLink messages. Messages received by the *MAVLinkSensor* are evaluated and the relevant data is distributed to the respective ADNA tasks. Complementary to the *MAVLinkSensor*, the *MAVLinkActor* receives messages from other ADNA elements, translates them into MAVLink messages, and sends them to the autopilot. For security reasons, our architecture mandates that the autopilots only accept MAVLink messages transmitted via the UART port. Consequently, both the *MAVLinkSensor* and the *MAVLinkActor* are limited to execution on a processor with direct access to the flight controller.

4   Novel ADNA UAV Elements

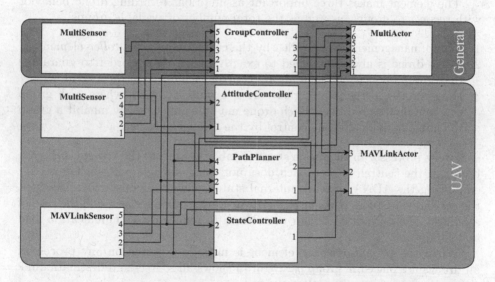

Fig. 3. Block diagram of the ADNA for a setup with a single UAV and a GCS. ADNA elements inside the UAV block (blue) are replicated for each additional drone. (Color figure online)

Controlling swarms of UAVs requires many complex functions, that can not be feasibly built from the available basic blocks. For this reason, the introduction of complex ADNA elements is necessary. Figure 3 shows the ADNA for a setup with a single UAV and a GCS. The ADNA elements inside the blue box are vehicle-specific, while the ADNA elements in the grey box are vehicle-unspecific. As the number of swarm members increases, only the vehicle-specific ADNA elements are replicated. Sensor and actor elements provide interfaces to components outside the ADNA system.

Elements such as *GroupController*, *PathPlanner*, *StateController* and *AttitudeController* manage swarm and/or individual drone behavior. The *StateController* ADNA element works as a state machine that receives the current and target state of the drone and outputs state transitions to the flight controller. The *AttitudeController* ADNA element is able to receive and process drone-specific attitude commands. This includes changing the current yaw. In the following, we will explain the new complex ADNA elements *GroupController* and *PathPlanner* in detail.

4.1   GroupController

Many real-world applications of drone swarms require the division of swarm members into groups so that each group can fulfill a dedicated role. The *GroupController* allows the dynamic grouping of drones during run time and the dynamic positioning of group member drones.

The element makes three important assumptions regarding drone behavior with respect to groups, as well as the total number of available groups:

1. Group management is controlled by the central *GroupController* element.
2. Every drone is always assigned to exactly one group, in order to guarantee that group management can always control each drone in the swarm.
3. For n drones in the swarm there are n groups $g_0...g_{n-1}$, where each group can contain 0 to n drones. Each drone must be able to solely inhabit a group to enable individual drone control by the *GroupController*.

Every processor in the drone swarm is able to execute the *GroupController*, therefore the centralized approach does not cause a single point of failure. By employing the ADNA system's internal state saving mechanism *StateTransfer*, the current state of the *GroupController* instance can be recovered in the case of a failure. The centralized design was chosen to reduce the communication load and complexity.

When the *GroupController* element is initially executed on any processor, all drones are placed in group g_0. Figure 4 shows all source- and destinationlink channels of the *GroupController* element.

The first sourcelink channel receives movement commands for drones or groups. The resulting output is dependent on the type of input command. Drone-specific movement commands will move the affected drone to an empty group and issue the command. Group-specific movement commands will generate output for each group member individually. Since it is not possible for group members to occupy the same position, the original target position of the group is altered, so that the group members position themselves in a circle around the original target position. This process is illustrated in Fig. 5 for groups of three and four drones. This procedure can be extended to any number of drones, as long

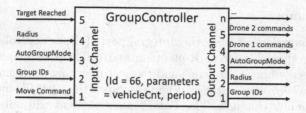

Fig. 4. Visualisation of the GroupController ADNA element and associated sourcelink/destinationlink channels

as there remains enough space between group member drones. The calculated target positions for the individual drones are communicated to the respective *PathPlanner* elements.

Group affiliation of specific drones can be changed through the GroupID sourcelink channel 2. The current group affiliation is then propagated on destinationlink channel 1. This information is mainly used by the GCS for displaying the correct group affiliation.

The remaining sourcelink channels 3 to 5 receive *AutoGroupMode*, radius and target reached information respectively. This information is internally used to dynamically alter swarm positioning, as well as verify that a movement command has been executed. The current radius and *AutoGroupMode* values are saved and output on destinationlink channels 2 and 3, respectively.

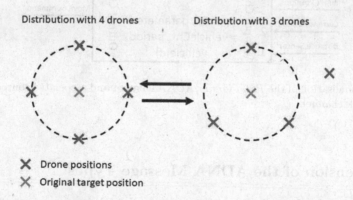

Fig. 5. Visualization of drone group formations and their transition with *AutoGroupMode*

If *AutoGroupMode* is activated, drones that join a group will automatically assume a position in the current circle formation of the group. Likewise, drones that leave a group, will cause the remaining group members to dynamically change their positions in the circle formation. This process is shown in Fig. 5.

4.2 PathPlanner

The *PathPlanner* element is another integral part of drone control in the ADNA system. It is responsible for path planning and collision avoidance. The *Path-Planner* is executed once per drone and receives movement commands from the central *GroupController* instance. Figure 6 shows the *PathPlanner* sourcelink and destinationlink channels. The *PathPlanner* element will only allow drone movement once the distance sensor data (sourcelink channel 1), current position (sourcelink channel 2), current state (sourcelink channel 4), and the other drones' positions (sourcelink channel 5) provide plausible data, to ensure that collision avoidance is feasible.[2]

Movement commands are received on sourcelink channel 3. Once a command has been received, the element will perform sanity checks on the movement command data, concerning format, and acceptable value range. If the command is accepted, the *PathPlanner* proceeds to the movement phase.

Distance sensor data is constantly updated and provides information about obstacles in the vicinity of the drone. To find a collision-free path to the target position the *PathPlanner* element applies a collision avoidance algorithm that utilizes and builds upon ideas expounded in [4].

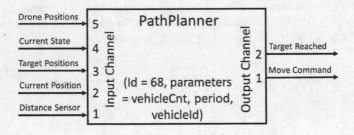

Fig. 6. Visualisation of the *PathPlanner* ADNA element and associated sourcelink/destinationlink channels

5   Extension of the ADNA Message Types

In the original implementation of the system, all ADNA messages employed the basic message type *DNAClassFloatMessage*, which only allows a single `float` value in the message payload. Since communication between basic elements is purposely held very simple, this small message size is sufficient.

In the context of highly heterogeneous communication patterns, the uniformly used ADNA message type *DNAClassFloatMessage* neither provides the required efficiency nor the expected versatility. To match the rising variety in

---

[2] Sourcelink channel 5 only receives data when the drone swarm has two or more members.

communication patterns introduced by complex ADNA elements, new use-case-specific message types are introduced to the system, that allow dynamic allocation of payload memory.

5.1   Prerequisites

ADNA tasks communicate over their source- and destinationlink channels using ADNA messages. The ADNA system is based upon the AHS, a distributed middleware, that handles the inter-processor communication and dynamic task allocation. The AHS uses message-based communication in the form of so-called AHS messages. These messages have a limited size of 256 bytes and apply a 16-byte header, limiting the AHS message payload to 240 bytes. Each message is sent in an individual User Datagram Protocol (UDP) package.

Each ADNA message contains a separate 4-byte header and can subsequently contain up to 236 bytes of payload data. Figure 7a shows the segmentation of a 256-byte AHS message for an ADNA message.

An example of the segmentation of an AHS message can be seen in Fig. 7b. This novel message type is called *DNARotationCommandMessage* and conveys data related to drone rotation commands, resulting in a message payload size of 16 bytes.

(a) ADNA message segmentation

(b) DNARotationCommandMessage segmentation

Fig. 7. (a) Segmentation of a 256-byte AHS message for an ADNA message and (b) Segmentation of an AHS message for a *DNARotationCommandMessage*

5.2   Implementation

The new, use-case-specific message types are defined in a central header file. For each ADNA element exists an explicit mapping between source-/destinationlink channels and corresponding message types. The original message type *DNA-ClassFloatMessage* is part of the header definition and can thus be further used by basic ADNA elements.

Table 1. Mapping between destinationlink channel and message type for the *Group-Controller* ADNA element

Destinationlink Channel	Message Type	Payload Size (bytes)
1	DNAGroupIndicatorMessage	2
2	DNARadiusIndicatorMessage	4
3	DNAAutoGroupMessage	1
4...	DNAClassFloatArray	4 to 236

Table 2. Mapping between destinationlink channel and message type for the *PathPlanner* ADNA element

Destinationlink Channel	Message Type	Payload Size (bytes)
1	DNAClassFloatArray	4 to 236
2	DNATargetReachedMessage	2

Table 1 and 2 show the mapping between the destinationlink channel and message type for the *GroupController* and *PathPlanner* ADNA elements, respectively.

Most of the message types are kept sparse and only use the necessary bytes of memory to convey their payload. An exception to this trend is *DNAClassFloatArray*, which is able to make use of an ADNA message's entire 236-byte payload in the form of 59 `float` values. While the advantages of a dynamically usable message type are manifold, it should be used carefully, since it generates considerable strain on the overall communication load.

5.3   Comparison Between Message Types

With the addition of specific message types to the ADNA-System, ADNA elements gain the ability to communicate complex data. To evaluate the impact of the new message types on communication load, a comparison to the original message type *DNAClassFloatMessage* is necessary. Since the new message types allow sending of other datatypes than `float` (4-byte value), their overall memory usage may lie below the value of the original message type.

Table 3 compares the individual sizes of the ADNA message types. The *DNAClassFloatMessage* message type acts as a benchmark message size value. The direct comparison between message sizes shows that there are message types smaller than *DNAClassFloatMessage*. Message types like *DNAMultirotorStateMessage* are not only more memory efficient than *DNAClassFloatMessage*, but also manage to convey multiple values due to the use of single-byte datatypes.

Table 3 also shows message types that are significantly larger than *DNAClassFloatMessage*. While these message types require more space in an AHS message, they also transmit more values inside a single message. The advantage

Table 3. Comparison of message type sizes (excluding header bytes)

Message Type	Payload Size (bytes)
DNAClassFloatMessage	4
DNAClassFloatArray	4 to 236
DNAAttitudeMessage	13
DNARotationCommandMessage	14
DNAMultirotorStateMessage	2
DNAAutoGroupMessage	1
DNAMultirotorTargetReachedMessage	2
DNARadiusIndicatorMessage	4
DNAMultirotorDistanceSensorMessage	9

of larger ADNA message payloads becomes especially apparent in the direct comparison between *DNAClassFloatMessage* and *DNAClassFloatArray*.

For this comparison, we consider a fully filled *DNAClassFloatArray* is sent between two ADNA elements. The resulting AHS message uses the entirety of the available 256-byte and is conveyed using a single UDP package. The message includes 20 bytes of header data (4-byte ADNA message header and 16-byte AHS message header). The same amount of payload data (59 `float` values) can also be sent with separate *DNAClassFloatMessages*. In this scenario, each message includes header data that account for a 20-byte additional communication load for every message after the first. Additionally, each message is sent using a separate UDP package, which adds an additional 8-byte header.

Generally, the sending of separate *DNACLassFloatMessages* results in a minimum communication overhead of $28 * (n - \lceil \frac{n}{59} \rceil)$ bytes for n float values, over sending a single *DNAClassFloatArray* message. For a fully filled *DNAClassFloatArray* ($n = 59$) this expression accounts for 1624 bytes less communication load and is thus clearly more communication overhead efficient than *DNAClassFloatMessage*.

The same principle can be applied to all message types that are larger than *DNAClassFloatMessage*, like *DNAAttitudeMessage* and *DNARotationCommandMessage*.

6   Evaluation

The basic functionality of the ADNA system for drones was initially tested in a simulation environment. However, the simulation did not incorporate effects such as transmission delays and packet loss, which are inevitable in real-world scenarios using wireless communication mechanisms. Subsequently, the influence of these effects on the AHS needs to be analyzed.

In [10] the authors showed that upper bounds for the real-time behavior of self-configuration and self-healing of the AHS can be guaranteed. These upper bounds are expressed in multiples of the Hormone Loop Period (HLP), which determines the frequency at which hormones are spread in the system. Furthermore, they provide the following constraint on the HLP that must be fulfilled to guarantee correct system behavior:

$$t_C \geq 2t_{DS} + 2t_K$$
$$\text{with } t_{DS} \to 0 : t_C \geq 2t_K, \tag{1}$$

where t_C is the HLP, t_K the maximum communication distance and t_{DS} the time an AHS processor takes for making a decision.

Therefore, it is necessary to evaluate the WiFi latencies in the ADNA system, which determine a lower limit for the HLP.

To measure the communication latencies of hormone telegrams in the ADNA system, we conducted a real test flight. Our test setup consisted of a custom UAV and a GCS. The UAV was carrying a Pixhawk flight controller running Ardupilot. Furthermore, a Raspberry Pi 4 processor was mounted on the drone. Three of its cores were used as ADNA processors. Finally, a Windows PC was used as a GCS running another ADNA processor, resulting in a total of four ADNA processors in the test setup.

The communication between the Raspberry Pi and the GCS was established over a wireless connection (IEEE 802.11n standard in the 2.4 GHz frequency band) using the Raspberry Pi's internal WiFi antenna. On the side of the GCS, a portable router was employed, which was connected to the GCS over ethernet.

The test flight was conducted over a period of 10.5 min on an open field with the drone in direct sight of the router. After takeoff, the drone was moved to a distance of 30 m where it hovered for the remainder of the flight.

Measurements of communication latencies and packet losses were evaluated post-flight, using logs of all four ADNA-processors. It is noteworthy, that due to context changes of the processor, the timestamp in the log file can differ from the actual time of sending and receiving the telegram. This can lead to negative latencies in some cases. However, we believe that this effect is negligible in our study due to the following reasons. Firstly, timestamp inaccuracies impact both the sending and receiving timestamps, thus largely canceling each other out on average. Secondly, we evaluated bidirectional communication between processors, thus nullifying any unilateral effects that might arise due to differences in processor load.

Table 4. Communication delays and packet loss ratio measured during 10.5 min test flight

Communication	Mean (ms)	Median (ms)	Loss Ratio (%)
WiFi	6.87	2	1.32
Inter-Core	0.34	0	0.00

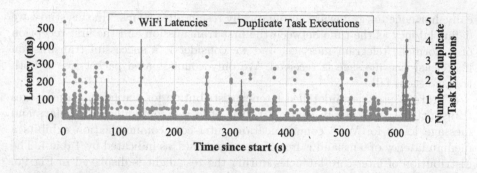

Fig. 8. Measured latencies of WiFi hormone communication during the 10.5 min test flight and resulting duplicate tasks executions

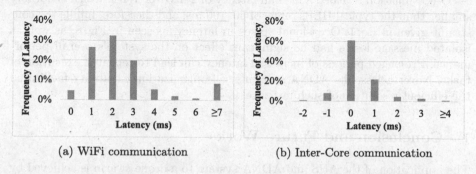

(a) WiFi communication   **(b) Inter-Core communication**

Fig. 9. Comparison of latency distribution for hormone communication for (a) inter-core and (b) WiFi communication

The results of the test flight are presented in Table 4 and Figs. 8, and 9. Figure 8 shows the measured latencies during the test flight for the WiFi communication and the resulting duplicate executions of ADNA tasks. The x-axis of the graph indicates the time at which a measurement was taken, represented as the time that elapsed since the start of the system. The left y-axis of the graph indicates the measured latency for each hormone telegram transmission. Each data point represents the latency of a single hormone telegram message. The right y-axis indicates the number of duplicate task executions. The number of duplicate tasks is calculated by subtracting the number of unique active tasks from the number of total active tasks. Therefore, the value does not distinguish between more than two instances of a single task and multiple tasks that are instantiated twice.

It is evident from Fig. 8 that the majority of measured latencies fall within the lower single-digit millisecond range, which is affirmed by the median latencies of 2 ms for WiFi presented in Table 4. Furthermore, Fig. 8 demonstrates an accumulation of measured latencies in the range of 50 ms for WiFi communication. This pattern can be attributed to the design of the ADNA system, which employs a resend mechanism to mitigate the effect of message losses. Specifically, hormone telegrams are automatically resent after 50 ms.[3] In this study, we define latency as the time between the first transmission and the first reception of a hormone telegram message, and we consider it a successful transmission if at least one message is received. We only count it as a packet loss if both transmissions fail.

Figure 9a provides a detailed latency distribution for the hormone messages transmitted over WiFi. In contrast to the observed communication delays and message losses for WiFi communication, inter-core communication exhibits a median latency of 0 ms and is free of message losses, as indicated by Table 4. The distribution of inter-core latencies during the test flight is displayed in Fig. 9b, which shows that the majority of messages were transmitted without significant delay.

Our evaluation revealed a median latency of 2 ms over WiFi, which is notably smaller than the typical HLPs range of 50–100 ms, and therefore, fulfills the constraint given in Eq. 1. Occasional spikes in latency, as seen in Fig. 8, as well as isolated message losses had no significant effect on the system's overall performance. Prolonged periods of increased latency can lead to repeated execution of tasks. Nevertheless, the ADNA system's self-optimization capability facilitated the efficient resolution of such instances.

7 Conclusion and Future Work

The application of the AHS and ADNA system to a drone swarm is achieved by building a network of distributed processing nodes using companion computers on the individual drones and the GCS. The nodes are interconnected using a WiFi network, which makes real-time critical execution of tasks across vehicles hard. The ADNA drone tasks operate with complex ADNA elements to coordinate individual drones or drone swarms. The flight control of drones is handled by established autopilots such as Ardupilot. To communicate with the autopilot, the dedicated ADNA tasks *MAVLinkActor* and *MAVLinkSensor* provide a UART interface that uses the standardized MAVLink protocol.

Complex swarm objectives such as path planning or handling of drone groups are also performed by dedicated ADNA elements. The elements *GroupController*, *PathPlanner* and *StateController* are integral for drone-swarm control and generate commands for the flight controller software.

Rising complexity in ADNA elements demands the introduction of use case specific ADNA message types. A concept and implementation of novel message types are given and the new message types are compared against the base implementation, regarding their communication load efficiency.

The system is demonstrated on a custom-built drone with an onboard computer that executes the ADNA system. The drone is connected to a GCS that also executes the ADNA system. Results show that the utilized WiFi connection

---

[3] The message repeat delay can be adjusted based on the HLP In this study, we used a repeat delay of 50 ms and a HLP of 100 ms.

is sufficient to support the time requirements of the system. The ADNA system can thus be successfully applied in a drone swarm environment.

The ADNA systems application over a WiFi connection exposes the system to new attack vectors on a hormone- and task-level. Future work will focus on researching these vulnerabilities. Two strategies for protecting ADNA systems will be explored. First, the system can be secured by introducing processor-level message authentication. Allowing only communication with authenticated partners can protect the system against hostile hormone-level attacks. Second, we seek to establish trust mechanisms between processing elements. Subtle, more nuanced attacks against the ADNA system may not be detected through message authentication, either because they are not obviously hostile or because their hostile behavior expresses itself on a semantic level. Inter-processor trust contributes to hardening the system against these attacks.

References

1. Ardupilot Web Page. https://ardupilot.org/
2. Brinkschulte, U.: An artificial DNA for self-descripting and self-building embedded real-time systems. Concurr. Comput. Pract. Exp. **28**(14), 3711–3729 (2015). ISSN 1532-0634
3. Brinkschulte, U.: Prototypic implementation and evaluation of an artificial DNA for self-describing and self-building embedded systems. In: 19th IEEE International Symposium on Real-Time Computing (ISORC 2016), York, UK (2016)
4. Casas Melo, V.F.: Implementable self-organized collision avoidance for UAVs flying alone or in flocks. Dissertation, Technische Universität Ilmenau, 2021. Ph.D. thesis. Ilmenau (2021). https://www.db-thueringen.de/receive/dbt_mods_00048692
5. Homann, P., Pacher, M., Brinkschulte, U.: Evaluation of conditional tasks in an artificial DNA system. In: 2022 IEEE 25th International Symposium on Real-Time Distributed Computing (ISORC), pp. 1–10 (2022). https://doi.org/10.1109/ISORC52572.2022.9812764
6. Kephart, J.O., Chess, D.M.: The vision of autonomic computing. Computer **36**(1), 41–50 (2003). https://doi.org/10.1109/MC.2003.1160055
7. von Mammen, S., et al.: OCbotics: an organic computing approach to collaborative robotic swarms. In: 2014 IEEE Symposium on Swarm Intelligence, pp. 1–8 (2014). https://doi.org/10.1109/SIS.2014.7011781
8. MAVLink Developer Guide. https://mavlink.io/en/
9. PX4 Autopilot Web Page. https://px4.io/
10. von Renteln, A., Brinkschulte, U., Pacher, M.: The artificial hormone system - an organic middleware for self-organising real-time task allocation. In: Müller-Schloer, C., Schmeck, H., Ungerer, T. (eds.) Organic Computing - A Paradigm Shift for Complex Systems, pp. 369–384. Springer, Basel (2011). https://doi.org/10.1007/978-3-0348-0130-0_24

Author Index

G. Goumas et al. (Eds.): ARCS 2023, LNCS 13949, pp. 327–328, 2023.
https://doi.org/10.1007/978-3-031-42785-5

Printed in the United States
by Baker & Taylor Publisher Services